THE FLY-FISHER'S CRAFT

BOOKS BY DARREL MARTIN

Fly-Tying Methods

Micropatterns: Tying and Fishing the Small Fly

*English–Czech and Czech–English Dictionary of Fishing,
With Milan Pohunek*

The Fly-Fisher's Illustrated Dictionary

The Fly-Fisher's Craft

THE FLY-FISHER'S CRAFT

The Art and History

DARREL MARTIN

THE LYONS PRESS
GUILFORD, CONNECTICUT
AN IMPRINT OF THE GLOBE PEQUOT PRESS

The Lyons Press is an imprint of The Globe Pequot Press.

10 8 6 4 2 1 3 5 7 9

Library of Congress Cataloging-in-Publication Data

Martin, Darrel.
  The fly-fisher's craft : the art and history / Darrel Martin.
     p. cm.
  Includes bibliographical references (p.   ) and index.
  ISBN 1-59228-722-0
  1. Fly tying. 2. Flies, Artificial. I. Title.
SH451.M385 2006
688.7'9124—dc22

                                        2005028533

Printed in China

For Michael, Michelle, Ioannis, Nikolaos, Kallista,
and all the Naiads and Hamadryads

CONTENTS

FOREWORD

by
TED LEESON

It has become fashionable these days, particularly among the young, to celebrate a certain lunatic obsessiveness in their fly fishing and pursue the sport with no holds barred and both guns drawn. Big fish, lots of them, all the time has become the contemporary motto. The terms "trout bum" and "extreme angling" have entered the lexicon of the sport, and whether they describe fantasies or facts, affectations or actualities is really beside the point—fly fishing has entered a decidedly post-tweed world. And that's exactly as it should be. Change is inevitable.

Change, however, also cuts both ways, and the contemporary mania for fly fishing tends to reduce the world to the single matter of catching fish—admittedly a reasonable preoccupation if that world must narrow. But the fact is, there's no reason to shrink it, and much is lost in doing so. Fly fishing is as much a space as it is a sport, a small universe within the larger one that is dense with interest of all kinds, many of which are only peripherally related to the pursuit of fish. A great deal, for instance, has been written about the natural worlds that surround a trout stream, about the natural histories of the places we fish. And the pleasure that comes from the angler's intimate contact with nature has been a theme in angling books at least as far back as Izaak Walton.

What Darrel Martin gives us in these pages, however, is a different look at that small universe of fly fishing—not a natural history, but a particular kind of human history. This book opens a window onto the history of fly angling as it is reflected in the making of things, the tools and tackle of fly fishing, what is known in academic circles as the "material culture" of the sport. And the glimpses we get through that window are fascinating.

This is a book for mature audiences, for anglers who, by virtue of their years on the water or a temperamental curiosity, do not regard a basket of trout as all there is to fly fishing. When they pick up an angling book, they are not likely to confuse two questions that on the surface seem similar: "Is it useful?" and "Is it valuable?" Such anglers and readers admire both of these attributes but understand the ways in which they are not necessarily the same thing.

This book is, in some respects, both. The chapter on "Personal Patterns," for instance, presents the type of innovative, practical fly designs that made Darrel Martin's *Micropatterns* an indispensable resource for the fisher of small flies. The chapter on "Fly Design" details the kinds of unusual or lesser-known tying techniques and theories, both historic and modern, that informed the author's fly-tying column for over a decade in *Fly Rod & Reel* magazine and were the foundation of his book *Fly-Tying Methods*. Contributions like these to fly-fishing theory and tying are always welcome.

But the bulk of this book, I would have to say, is not "practical" in this sense. It is distinguished not so much by utility as by the intrinsic interest of its subject, and that is precisely one of its great values. The author's first task here has been to research and recover some of the ways that fly tackle was made by hand—the "craft" of the title—in times when most anglers had little choice but to build their own equipment. But simply recording the words of the older writers is one thing; putting their methods into practice is quite another, and that has been the author's second task—to interpret those words and reconstruct the techniques in order to fashion antique rods, lines, hooks, and flies of his own. And in fact, enough detailed instruction is contained within these pages to enable a reader to reproduce those processes and make, for instance, a loop-rod, a tapered horsehair line, or hook. This kind of hands-on detail is neither an empty exercise in antiquarianism nor a kind of stunt—it is the only way in which a history of manual arts can be truly understood and brought to life.

This is no small job. Reconstructing any type of history solely from the records of the time can be difficult; it is doubly so with fly fishing. Until relatively modern times, the world of fly fishing was small enough that it did not produce a great number of public documents; the footprint it left on the larger culture was light and the trail not always easy to follow. Added to a sketchy record are significant problems of language—the shifting meanings of words over time; archaic idioms and locutions; cryptic expressions and usages; and the enduring fact, then as now, that some authors simply write more clearly than others. Exploring this material, investigating its ambiguities, interpreting the intentions of these older texts, and testing those interpretations is an enormous amount of work. But preserving the past in this way and making it available to modern readers is worth doing for its own sake, valuable apart from any angling "uses" it may serve. Knowing this history does not make an angler fish more knowledgeably, but it does make a more knowledgeable angler.

When I read the older accounts of tackle making in these chapters and the working knowledge of craft they reveal, it all sounds very appealing—knowing the best way to season a piece of rod-building wood, recognizing the precise shade of red that signals the proper temper in a hook wire, knowing how to judge the quality of horsehair. Though such information is no longer necessary, this kind of hands-on quality about the sport is something we still value today.

But most of all, I am struck by how much dedication it took for anglers in centuries past to pursue their small passion in life. And in this era of trout bums and extreme fly fishing, it's worth wondering just what, 400 years ago, a man's neighbors might have thought about his investing so much time, effort, and patience—going to such labor and lengths—for something as unremarkable as catching a fish. Truly, it was the same things that fascinate us today. Certainly fly fishing has grown and evolved over time. But some things never change.

—TED LEESON
Corvallis, Oregon
July 2005

FOREWORD

by
JOHN BETTS

Many anglers have delved into the roots of their sport. And many have found a fascination with the history and tools of early angling. In Darrel Martin's *The Fly-Fisher's Craft*, we meet quite intimately our fishing forefathers and their legacy. We are also introduced to Martin's creative additions, inspired by this past, that form his fly-fishing world.

Martin has written from the twin perspective of historical research and practical craftsmanship. He describes the origins and development of hooks, lines, and rods. One discovers that only moderate skills were needed to convert available materials into functional tools of the sport. His personal narrative of replicating ancient tackle unwraps for us unsuspected and delightful connections between the past and present.

Tackle of times past becomes a reality. Early tackle is seductive in its strength, beauty, and alleged limitations. Darrel and I have both lost and landed fish on our own handmade "antiquated" equipment. Frederick Buller, the respected British angling author and historian observes that, at least in this field, one cannot fully comprehend what is contained in the writing—old or new—unless one has actually made some of what is discussed. For example, making one's own hooks by hand provides insight into a craft where the tools and procedures have remained basically unchanged for thousands of years. Twisted, tapered, and knotted horsehair lines have served for well over two millennia, and may still be in normal use in some parts of the world today. Rods, first made of wood, developed into the elaborate loop-rod of the *Treatyse* of 1496. Martin's journey through historic patterns, hook making, horsehair line, and the loop-rod recall those forgotten skills. Like others, he has tried at every turn to modify and refine his tackle with the goal of making it lighter and stronger. Here, translucent horsehair twists into fly lines, straight-grained wood shaves and shapes into lithe rods, and fine wire bends into barbed hooks: Martin paints a picture of their development with widely varied materials, of various attempts to create better models that would serve with grace and efficiency.

Underlying this panorama is his extensive and rich knowledge of yesterday's English language that so enchants yet, at times, challenges and confounds the reader. Martin's knowledge and scholarship give us a remarkably vital view of the ancient angling crafts.

There are layers of information recounted in this book that require attention and appreciation. I would not try to read it all through in a few sittings. Rather, choose a section and peruse it. Numerous ideas and connections weave through each layer. When the older and odd terms become part of your vocabulary, you will be able to unfold the rich fabric of this book. *The Fly-Fisher's Craft* is not just the detailing of angling history: it is the creation of much of that history in three dimensions. The depth of this creation is a first in our angling literature.

—JOHN BETTS
Denver, Colorado
July 2005

ACKNOWLEDGMENTS

Writing is a notoriously solitary act that invariably requires the help of others. I am especially grateful for the following assistance. Dr. William G. Greenwood, Ph.D., Professor of Physics, Pacific Lutheran University, Tacoma, Washington for his knowledge and time in hook making and metallurgy. Ole Bjerke, Managing Director of Partridge, for his support and interest. The late Harry Ranger of England for his meticulous explication of antique patterns. Dr. Tom Whiting for his feather craft and support of my feather fetish. The Lyons Press for their indulgence of my procrastination: this book required a lifetime. Frank Matarelli, for turning designs into steel. David and Donald Vogel of Anvil Industries for the handsome and efficient Walton's Engine. Mick and Kathy Erholm and the Twin Sisters water. Mr. Richard Broncks of East Lodge for the Itchen memories and the wonderful wine. Mike and Brenda Crate for their friendship and their streamside feasts. Madeleine and Taff Price for their kind companionship on distant waters: we have shared a life of wonders. Ron and Jean Wilton who offered their world with kindness and enthusiasm. My son Michael; may he find his elusive *Astraeus*.

Special recognition: John Betts whose presence permeates the chapters on historic patterns, hook, and rod making. I can only repeat what Frederic Halford wrote of George Marryat, my "deepest gratitude for the unwearying patience and perfect unselfishness" in sharing his knowledge and skill. Ted Leeson for his editorial acumen and invaluable comments: we river rats share a world of words and water.

Once again, I am grateful to Sandra, my wife, for her assistance and support. And for loving this writer and wanderer. Finally, to the early anglers: no one walks the banks alone. That this book lacks some inaccuracies is beyond hope: such errors belong only to the author.

Permission to reprint selections from Fernando Basurto's *Dialogue between a Hunter and a Fisher* (1539) in *Fishers' Craft & Lettered Art* (1997) by Richard C. Hoffmann kindly granted by Richard C. Hoffmann and the University of Toronto Press.

Permission to reprint selections from Juan de Bergara's *El Manuscrito de Astorga* (1624), produced and privately printed in 1984 by Preben Torp Jacobsen, kindly granted by Jacobsen's descendants.

A NOTE ON
THE ILLUSTRATIONS

Line drawings generally present a clearer picture of the tying process than do photographs. It is important, however, to understand the system behind these procedural drawings. The material sequence often indicates the relative position to the hook shank. Although it may appear that the materials mount together (because the thread captures them), such may not be the case. The material mounted first appears closest to the hook shank. The purposely-enlarged tying thread shows placement. Not all thread wraps appear, nor do the drawings always depict the correct diameter or number of fibers. Some drawings lack pattern parts; this permits clear and uncluttered drawings. Miscellaneous and obvious wraps have been omitted for procedural clarity—detailed drawings would only obscure the tying process. The text should clarify all requirements of materials and methods. Unless otherwise noted, all photography and artwork is by the author.

It should be remembered that, during tying, the thread spirals forward (i.e., to the right) of the tying position to secure the material ends. Other drawings, such as the off-side wing, may be shown only in silhouette or omitted completely. Additional detail may appear only in the final illustration. All illustrations demonstrate right-handed tying. A right-handed tyer mounts the hook so that the hook eye points right, and winds the thread *clockwise* facing the eye. Left-handed tyers may find it helpful to reflect complex drawings in a mirror. Historic hand tying (sans vise) has multiple hook holds, including inverted and reversed positions.

AN ANTIQUE DISPOSITION

The number of ways in which flies can be tied is incredible. There are hardly two books which lay down identical methods. . . . And of all the methods in which I have experimented, from Walton downwards, I have never come across one which had nothing to recommend it, and I should be glad to be master of them all.

— G. E. M. Skues, *The Way of a Trout with a Fly* (1921)

*A*fter nearly two millennia, the artificial fly continues to evolve. Nevertheless, despite advances, the artificial fly is still deeply rooted in tradition. W. H. Lawrie, in *A Reference Book of English Trout Flies* (1967), described it best, "The trout fly will not only survive the times, but will assuredly continue its evolution as it has done for nigh on five-hundred years. In all that time, neither trout nor the delicate insects that so largely constitute the trout's diet have changed. Only man and his ideas are changing, and despite all the scientific advances and discoveries of recent years . . . . it is still good to know that the making of a trout fly is something that cannot greatly change, and that the art of such creation is deeply rooted in the past."

The literature of fly tying is rich and enthralling. It has enchanting stories, replete with curious and wonderful theories. Only by reading the ancients can we trace and appreciate this moving drama. I hope this modest work is a glimpse into the old writers and the old methods. John Waller Hills, in *A Summer on the Test*, shared his water with the wraiths of ancient anglers. "Certainly I for one have always been attracted to the old writers, since I first knew them, and the more I have fished the better I seem to understand them. I should be sorry to lose their companionship." The early anglers have much to say in this book. For me, their companionship and conversations are worthy and pleasant.

Few old books actually explain how to tie a pattern. The antique text requires judicious research and reading. Fraught with sins of omission and of commission, these early instructions for making "fly and harness" often offer only fragments and shards. Most list materials, but lack methods. Sometimes our best inquiry is only informed speculation. Early punctuation was often inconsistent and capricious. Words, even those with modern spelling, may have entirely different meanings than they do today. Early tying descriptions are often elusive, cryptic, or ambiguous. They may omit essentials or assume procedures unknown to the modern tyer. Furthermore, an edition can include interpolations done by the editor rather than the author. Some tying procedures will be debated to the final fly pattern. They are, to borrow a phrase from Sir Thomas Browne's *Urn Burial*, "yet wrapped up in a bundle of time, they fall into indistinction."

The clearest evidence of mastery comes from tyers who have thought hard and often about the past, from tyers whose wraps build ingeniously but simply upon it. The excellence of modern tying is its mastery of the tying canon and its continual attempts to expand it. The backcast creates the forecast. So too in tying. The thoughtful tyer pushes his patterns through the past. We wrap the old patterns to understand, not to repeat. G. E. M. Skues proclaimed that traditional tying "is a danger and ceases to be a living art based on up-to-date observations and experiences." Yet, traditional tying, when done to learn and explore, is valuable. In *The Angler and the Loop-Rod* (1885), David Webster notes, "There is no finality in this art, any more than in any other; and even our best imitation is, after all, only the 'cunning't pattern of excelling nature.'"

The Fly-Fisher's Craft examines fly design and tying methods, both historic and modern. Angling is, essentially, a craft—*a making skill*. It was something done with artistry and cunning. If fishing is not mostly about fish, then tying is not mostly about the fly. Tying is essentially about the *why*; the reason behind the design. Among the angler's gear, the fly has perhaps undergone the least change through time. And it is the fly that makes the fly fisher. Can we understand ancient angler more completely by returning to the past? Can we make the line, the hook, and the rod? How essential is the cast, the hook barb, and the running line?

Chapter I, *Antique Tying*, reveals the slow elucidation of tying tactics and theories. It traces the wraps of several early tyers to reveal their craft and cunning. The antique text is our tutor. Only with the original text can a reader test and challenge my reading and my understanding. For this reason, I present the original text unless a translation is required. John Waller Hills, in *A History of Fly Fishing for Trout* (1921), regards *An Older Form of the Treatyse of Fysshynge Wyth an Angle* (printed in 1883 from the Alfred Denison manuscript) as "obviously the purer text" though it lacks some material, including the illustrations. Essentially, this earlier Denison text speaks for the *Treatyse*.

Chapter II, *Fly Design*, presents an overview of pattern anatomy: the tail, the wing, the body, the hackle, and the head. This chapter defines the fly and reveals its architecture. In addition, we look to the past to see how the theories and parts formed patterns.

Chapter III, *Personal Patterns*, shows how a modern tyer takes that past and attempts to extend his understanding. This chapter presents the author's patterns and variations inspired by that past. These exploratory patterns should encourage the true attraction of tying: discovery and lateral thinking.

Next, we return to our angling origins with chapters on constructing antique hooks (Chapter IV), lines (Chapter V), and the spliced loop-rod (Chapter VI)—all simply made with basic tools and knowledge. Even if the reader never makes this tackle, appreciation and understanding increases. The loop-rod chapter includes the construction of an early, simple wood rod based upon the antique text. The furled line, though more recent than horsehair line, offers other modern possibilities. Although I first wrote about furled lines over a decade ago, they were virtually unknown by most American anglers. Furled lines were, however, rather common in Spain and some mid-European countries.

Abundant illustrations and photographs reveal this enthralling journey, told with some surprises along the way. This is a book with an "antique" disposition for the creative and curious. Fly-fishing history has not always been progressive. There are starts and stutters, revivals and revolutions. We return to this past when wrapping a Stewart Spider or shaving woody ringlets for a loop-rod. Though modern rods, patterns, lines, and hooks are marvelous, there is discovery in making the past. I never knew where the loop-rod or horsehair line would take me. Failures were more common than successes. It did not matter: it was a journey shared with ancient anglers. Living within those faded, foxed pages was, in itself, a remarkable delight, and reconstructing the past was pleasurable. Those ancient anglers became thoughtful companions. They willingly, with words and images, shared their world. I can only encourage others to begin the journey.

CHAPTER I

ANTIQUE TYING

THERE IS A MYSTERIOUS AND HAUNTING PLEASURE in tying antique patterns. Moreover, they are as effective as many modern flies. My reading of the historical tying text has been influential in my tying development. Here are the roots of principles and practices that evolved into modern tying. Here also are older and lesser-known methods that can be made modern with contemporary materials. There is history and adventure in early patterns and much to learn from the first masters. These are *artificial* flies in the original sense—"artful," or "skillful." These cunning creations reveal our rich tying past.

Take care, however, when reading any early tying text. It is extremely easy for a reader to superimpose a modern method or meaning to an early text. Early tying descriptions should be read as literally and precisely as possible. Language and meaning change. Thus, diction, punctuation, orthography, and syntax can all obscure a passage. Like modern writers, early writers began with a set of assumptions—how to hold the hook, which feather to use, where to wrap the silk. Before the tying vise, a tyer held the hook, sometimes inverted or reversed, for the application of materials. Sometimes certain words baffle or mislead the reader. Moreover, a text may even defy textual explication. Middle English words may look like modern English words, but they sounded differently and often had entirely different meanings. All of this challenges clarity. Early tying directions will always be contentious and challenged. The fewer the facts, the stronger the opinions. Furthermore, different books often share the same popular engravings. As we shall see, it may be possible to use contemporary and later writers to help us understand a particular passage. Often, though, directions will remain obscure. In the middle of the nineteenth century, James Rennie noted, "Since the time of Cotton, minute directions are given in most of the angling books how to make artificial flies; but the greater part of these are not very intelligible."

The following patterns, selected for their novel approaches and procedures, offer considerable insight to the antique tyer. The following patterns do not create a history of fly tying: they only trace a few tying tactics of some early writers. In most cases, there is scant information about feather selection, hackle wraps, and pattern proportions. Many assumptions (hopefully plausible ones) emerge in order to illustrate a tying maneuver. Though some phrases and passages offer numerous interpretations, only one must be chosen. Remember that the explication of a passage can present several, plausible interpretations. Our only hope in understanding an early text is a cautious, critical, and thoughtful reading.

Orthographic Note: Though later, augmented editions are often used, the author's first edition—as dated in Westwood and Satchell's *Bibliotheca Piscatoria*—creates the following chronology. For the specific source date and text, consult the bibliography. Generally, orthography normalizes only where confusion would occur. The letter "ʃ" (known as the *long-s*) appears as is in the text. The "s" also appears with little or no crossbar, "ʃ." The "Þ" (the "thorn") and "ð" (the "crossed-d or "eth") may normalize to "th." The "Þ" and the "ð" are used arbitrarily for both the voiced and unvoiced "th." Some manuscripts mix them without apparent system. In fifteenth-century handwriting, the thorn (the Þ) was formed much like the y, so that early French printers (who never had the Þ) in England naturally used the y for the Þ. This "open thorn"—always the "th" sound—formed much like a ʊ or y and was extant as late as the nineteenth century. Thus, *yᵉ* and *yᵗ* become *the* and *that*. *Yᵉ Olde* was always *the olde*. Eventually the digraph *th* replaced the "open thorn" *y*. The ʒ (the "yogh"), a modification of the Roman *g*, is a *y* sound in most words, though sometimes a *gh* sound. The term *yogh* [jox]— here in the International Phonetic Alphabet—exemplifies both sound values. Essentially, I have avoided normalization and emendation of the text. Each text has a distinctive voice. Unless normalized, capitalization and orthography appear as in the original text. Definitions of some salient terms appear within the text.

Claudius Aelianus (Aelian)

De Natura Animalium (circa 200 A.D.)

The story of fly tying begins with Claudius Aelianus' *De Natura Animalium*, Book XV, Section 1. Aelianus, known as "the Sophist," was a teacher of rhetoric in Rome during the second century A.D. His surviving work includes *De Natura Animalium*, a copious collection of curiosities of life. Aelianus offers no tying directions. For Aelianus, who had heard the tale, was neither angler nor tyer. The artificial fly was only one of nature's novelties. Fly fishing certainly existed before Aelianus. Martial (Marcus Valerius Martialis), the Roman epigrammatist, mentioned "fraudful flies" in a famous couplet a century and a half before Aelianus. Martial was, however, only a prologue of what would come.

John Waller Hills, in *A History of Fly Fishing for Trout*, quickly dismissed the brief Aelianus entry as "interesting rather than important." To Hills, Aelianus stood detached from fly-fishing history by a thousand-year lacuna. Hills, instead, began the history of fly fishing with *The Treatyse of Fysshynge Wyth an Angle* (1496).

Yet, Aelianus did offer rare insight into early angling. He informed the reader that his information was hearsay—"I have heard and can tell of a way of catching fish in Macedonia, and it is this." Historians have used this as rationale for his presumed vagueness of insect and the imitation. Aelianus' entry is, however, essentially complete, though blurred.

Conrad Voss Bark, in *A History of Flyfishing*, believes that "Aelian flounders when he tries to describe the fly." Actually, the insect description is specific, though scattered. "Now these fish feed upon flies of the country which flit about the river and which are quite unlike flies elsewhere; they do not look like wasps, nor could one fairly describe this creature as comparable in shape with what is called *Anthedomes* (bumble-bee), nor even with actual honey-bees, although they possess a distinctive feature of each of the aforesaid insects. Thus, they have the audacity of the fly; you might say they are the size of the bumble-bee, but their colour imitates that of a wasp, and they buzz like honey-bee. All the natives call them *Hipporus*." This wobbly specificity obscures the passage.

Aelianus, as rhetorician, presented *Hipporus* (or *Hippouros*) according to the three elements of classical definition: the defiens, the genus, and the differentia. The defiens is the word or term to be defined. The genus is the group to which the defiens belongs, and the differentia distinguishes the particular defiens from all other defiens in the same genus. *Hipporus* (defiens) is an insect (genus) with the size and shape of a bumblebee (differentia), the coloration of a wasp (differentia), and the sound of a honeybee (differentia). The similarities and differences define the insect. Though the *Hipporus* does not look like a wasp, bumblebee, or honeybee, it has "distinctive features" of each—it has the size of the bumblebee, the color of the wasp, and the buzz of the honeybee. Moreover, it is, presumably, a "hovering" fly that is either aquatic or frequents the water surface. Depending upon translation, the size varies from "midge" (Lambert and Schwiebert), to hornet (Badham, Westwood, and Satchell), to bumblebee (Scholfield). The ubiquitous "midge" may be any size insect, either terrestrial or aquatic. Frederic M. Halford called the large black drake a Spent Gnat. J. R. Adams, in *Aelian on Fly Fishing*, notes, "The natural is a large fly, and is probably closer to a hornet than a midge in size. According to Radcliffe, the smallest hook in the Greek-Roman collection at the British Museum measures over one-quarter inch at the bend, or about a size 10 or 11."

If the insects were touched, "they lose their natural colour, their wings wither, and they become unfit food for fish." This description seems to suggest a mayfly or other fragile aquatic insect. Tough-bodied terrestrials as well as caddis and stoneflies do not wither readily. The pattern, according to Andrew Herd, does not represent the *Hipporus*. Herd, in *The Fly*, notes the critical conundrum: The insect described (a yellow or yellow and black body) does not match the pattern described (a red body). However, without the specific identity of the insect, we really have no established color. We do not know the color of Aelianus' "wasp." Though historically unprecedented, perhaps this pattern may be more attractor than imitator. Furthermore, some patterns do not necessarily color-match the natural that they imitate. Even the Orange Quill, according to Skues, became the best imitation for the Blue-Winged Olive Spinner. In any case, *if* the Macedonian pattern is an attractor, then we can call it the *Hipporus*.

The Scholfield translation identifies the insect as a species of *Stratiomys*, the aquatic soldier fly. Some aquatic larvae feed upon algae, decaying plants, or aquatic microorganisms. The adult, a moderately large diptera often brightly colored, routinely frequents flowers. Many species are wasplike and brightly colored. In some genera, like the *Ptecticus*, the abdomen is elongated and wasplike. Most are dark with or without lighter markings; some species are yellowish.

The *Hipporus* also has been identified as a mayfly. Latin marginalia to a Greek-Latin Aelianus text notes that the insect is the genus "*Ephemeri Linnaean.*" Additionally, the large *Palingenia longicauda* and *Siphlonurus ssp.* are both candidates. The *Palingenia* has a deep lemon-yellow body with black stripes. The *Siphlonurus croaticus* dun (both sexes) has a light yellow-olive body with dark brown bands. Dr. Ivan Tomka, an authority on European entomology, suggests another nominee, the *Oligoneuriella rhenana*; the female body and egg sack have a distinct pinkish hue, perchance suggesting a crimson body. There is, of course, no definitive identification of the *Hipporus*.

> They fasten red (crimson red) wool around a hook, and fix onto the wool two feathers which grow under a cock's wattles, and which in color are like wax.

Aelianus' Macedonian Pattern (Conjectural)

The body color depends on the translation. The color ranges from purple (Badham), crimson (Lambert), scarlet (Westwood and Satchell), scarlet-red (Scholfield), to "ruby-colored" (Schwiebert). Radcliff favored the Lambert translation. Schwiebert alone wraps the feathers as hackles: "The fisherfolk wrap ruby-colored wool about their hooks, and *wind about this wool* two feathers. . . ."

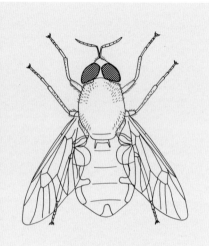

Family Stratiomyidae

1. **Mount thread and attach horsehair to hook shank.**

2. **Wrap body forward.**

3. **Secure wings and whip head.**

A "wind about" is not a "fix onto." It is unclear how the two hackles were mounted. It seems more probable that the *two* hackles were wings, suggesting a diptera. A double-hackle palmer seems less plausible.   The mystery continues.

Though traditionally reserved for bundled wings, the reverse-wing mount, an early winging method, would invariably result in twisted hackle wings. Though the preceding thread-work is traditional, this pattern, like many early ones, may have finished at the shank bend, not the head. It is also possible that a fine wool yarn served as both thread and body. No mention is made of ribbing. Though we know not how the pattern was tied two millennia past, we can make a studied suggestion.

The Treatyse of Fysshynge Wyth an Angle (1496)

Text based on *An Older Form of the Treatyse of Fysshynge Wyth an Angle*, Circa 1450, Printed By W. Satchell & Co., 1883

The *Treatyse*, author undocumented, is a practical textbook. It contains directions for rod, line, and hook making. Lacking reels, the rod was "tight-lined"; a small loop attached the twisted horsehair line to the rod tip. The butt section, hollowed for lightness, stored the other sections. Six hairs bound the rod sections together and ended in a loop to accept the horsehair line. Cork floats and lead weights, all illustrated, determined the drift. Detailed instructions turn needles into barbed hooks, and a dozen fly patterns offer only a trace of tying instructions.

The *Treatyse* lists twelve patterns: the donne flye (March), another donne flye (March), the stone flye (April), the ruddy flye (May), the yelow flye (May), the blacke louper (May), the donne cutte (June), the maure flye (June), the tandy flye (June), the waspe flye (July), the shell flye (July), and the drake flye (August). The *Treatyse* offers few tying directions, notably "Lappid abowte wyth." It lists the materials for the various body parts but little else. It may be advantageous to search later writers—like Barker, Cotton, and Venables—for possible clues. In this regard, John McDonald's *The Origins of Angling* presents a remarkable study of the *Treatyse* patterns based on the later writers. Any *Treatyse* student should consult both *The Origins of Angling* and *The Book of Saint Albans* (Abercrombie & Fitch, 1966) with Joseph Haslewood's literary research. I present here only the possible tying sequence for three representative patterns: the Stonefly, Shell Fly, and Tandy Fly. These patterns generally appear as simple wraps.

The *Treatyse* Stonefly (Conjectural)

> The stone flye. the body of blacke woll: & yelowe onder the wynge. & onder the tayle & the wynges of the drake.

In general form and color, this is still a recognizable pattern. Its legacy continues in such patterns as the Montana Stonefly Nymph.

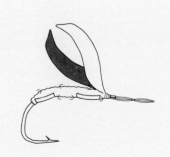

The Stonefly

The Shell Fly

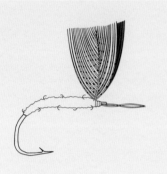

The Tandy Fly

The *Treatyse* Shell Fly (Conjectural)

𝕿𝖍𝖊 𝖘𝖍𝖊𝖑𝖑 𝖋𝖑𝖞𝖊 𝖆𝖙 𝖘𝖆𝖞𝖓𝖙 𝕿𝖍𝖔𝖒𝖆𝖘 𝖉𝖆𝖞𝖊. 𝖙𝖍𝖊 𝖇𝖔𝖉𝖞 𝖔𝖋 𝖌𝖗𝖊𝖓𝖊 𝖜𝖚𝖑𝖑 & 𝖑𝖆𝖕𝖕𝖞𝖉 𝖆𝖇𝖔𝖜𝖙𝖊 𝖜𝖎𝖙𝖍 𝖙𝖍𝖊 𝖍𝖊𝖗𝖑𝖊 𝖔𝖋 𝖙𝖍𝖊 𝖕𝖊𝖈𝖔𝖐𝖘 𝖙𝖆𝖞𝖑𝖊: 𝖜𝖞𝖓𝖌𝖊𝖘 𝖔𝖋 𝖙𝖍𝖊 𝖇𝖔𝖘𝖆𝖗𝖉𝖊.

The Shell Fly may imitate a caddis, the green rock worm larvae (genus *Rhyacophila*). Certainly, the herl suggests the severely segmented abdomen. Perhaps the dark wings indicate an emerging green or olive caddis.

The *Treatyse* Tandy Fly (Conjectural)

𝕿𝖍𝖊 𝖙𝖆𝖓𝖉𝖞 𝖋𝖑𝖞𝖊 𝖆𝖙 𝖘𝖆𝖞𝖓𝖙 𝖂𝖞𝖑𝖑𝖞𝖆𝖒𝖘 𝖉𝖆𝖞𝖊. 𝕿𝖍𝖊 𝖇𝖔𝖉𝖞 𝖔𝖋 𝖙𝖆𝖓𝖉𝖞 𝖜𝖚𝖑𝖑 & 𝖙𝖍𝖊 𝖜𝖞𝖓𝖌𝖊𝖘 𝖈𝖔𝖓𝖙𝖗𝖆𝖗𝖞 𝖊𝖞𝖙𝖍𝖊𝖗 𝖆𝖞𝖊𝖓𝖘𝖙 𝖔𝖙𝖍𝖊𝖗 𝖔𝖋 𝖙𝖍𝖊 𝖜𝖍𝖎𝖙𝖊𝖘 𝖒𝖆𝖞𝖑𝖊 𝖔𝖋 𝖕𝖊 𝖜𝖞𝖑𝖉𝖊 𝖉𝖗𝖆𝖐𝖊.

The Tandy Fly appears down through time as a large drake, a mayfly. Even today, we would recognize this pattern and its natural, such as Green Drake, Yellow Drake, or Gray Drake. Such whole-feather wings were unprecedented in tying history and continue to the present.

Wing posture, body length, and basic proportions of the *Treatyse* patterns are unknown. Reverse winging—a later technique described by Basurto, Barker, Walton, and Venables—creates a moderately erect wing, but there is no indication of the *Treatyse* winging method. Basurto's *Dialogo* (1539), close in time to the *Treatyse*, seems to suggest that the reverse wing may be more common than once recognized. The *Dialogo*, less than half a century after the *Treatyse*, presents explicit directions for mounting reverse wings. Mount the wings "so that the feathers go toward the line" and then fold "the feathers back towards the hook." Even the *Older Form* of the *Treatyse*, also known as the Denison text, is within a century of Basurto. It is reasonably conceivable, then, that the reverse wing—a strong and simple method—could have spanned the time and distance between the *Treatyse* and the *Dialogo*, but we do not know. Though these patterns will always remain controversial, illustrations demand conclusions.

Furthermore, the specific wing feather is unknown. The "𝖜𝖞𝖓𝖌𝖊𝖘 𝖔𝖋 𝖙𝖍𝖊 𝖉𝖗𝖆𝖐𝖊" could either be body (contour) feathers or wing slips. The "𝖜𝖍𝖎𝖙𝖊𝖘 𝖒𝖆𝖞𝖑𝖊 𝖔𝖋 𝖕𝖊 𝖜𝖞𝖑𝖉𝖊 𝖉𝖗𝖆𝖐𝖊" is somewhat more specific. The term "𝖒𝖆𝖞𝖑𝖊" (mayle or mail) is the barred or finely etched breast feather, suggesting chain mail. According to the *Oxford English Dictionary*, the term appears as early as 1486. Thomas Satchell's glossary, in *An Older Form of The Treatyse of Fysshynge Wyth an Angle*, defines 𝖒𝖆𝖞𝖑𝖊: "Speckled feathers; the Latin *macula* became *maille* in Old French." Were complete feathers mounted or only barb panels? Were the panels rolled or flat? Were they reversed or down? Though speculation is rampant, the text is silent.

Fernando Basurto

Dialogo (1539)

R ichard C. Hoffmann's *Fishers' Craft & Lettered Art* (1997) presents facsimiles, translations, and prodigious scholarship on the three oldest European angling tracts: *The Heidelberg Booklet* (Heidelberg, 1493), *The Tergernsee Fishing Advice* (Bavaria, *c.* 1500) and the graphically entitled *Dialogue between a Hunter and Fisher* (Spain, 1539). The *Dialogue* or *Dialogo (Dialogo que agora se hazia. . .)* contains "The Little Treatise on Fishing" ("El Tratadico de la Pesca"), the oldest known Spanish text on angling. The *Dialogo*—translated by Adrian Shubert, Thomas V. Cohen, and Richard C. Hoffmann—includes extensive analysis by Hoffmann. According to Hoffmann, "Basurto lays out the tying process and the way the feathers are presented to the fish more fully and explicitly than is done in other known early texts."

Angling equipment, standard for the late Middle Ages, includes a jointed, wooden rod with a whalebone tip. The fishing line ranges from two hairs for small bait to six strands for the artificial fly. Lead weights or floats (the *vela* or "sail") sink or drift the bait.

A cogent and engaging debate between a Hunter (a young noble) and a Fisher (an aged commoner) forms the social framework of the *Dialogo*. In this text, the artificial fly is merely one tactical technique among several, including angling with algae, yeast, bread, baitfish, figs, grapes, cheese, ants, shrimp, and maggots. "The feather goes on the hook this way" introduces our earliest known tying instructions. Although the *Treatyse* contains phrases like the wynges contrary cyther auenst other (the wings contrary either against other) and lappyd abowte (lapped about), the *Dialogo* offers some intriguing, explicit tying comments.

At the end of the debate, the noble Hunter presents the Fisher with a doubloon for his tutelage and missed sport during the debate. The Hunter asks for more information on angling with the promise of "another greater goodness" for the Fisher. They arrange to meet the next day. As the Fisher parts, he replies: "And with this I go, because night is coming on, and also so that I have enough time to write the little treatise, which I will make so complete that it will be of service to the man, and even draw many to take up this activity." At the end, the Hunter offers the Fisher a strange reward: the Fisher must leave the river and enjoy a comfortable pension. The Fisher, however, demands that he must fish: "Because if I did not fish, death would fish me." The Hunter allows the emendation and the Fisher accepts the Hunter's home and pension.

The "Tratadico de la Pesca" begins with listing various baits and methods for sea and stream. There is even a curious white butterfly with four horns, a bait for barbel and trout, that floats "on the top of the water because the trout catch them flying." At night, a burning candle placed above a black cape harvests the insects for bait. Basurto then turned his attention to the artificial fly.

Basurto described a specific tying method, rather than a list of patterns. He did add, though, dark and light feather variations for different waters. Without proper knowledge of the hook, the feathers, and the proportions, pattern reconstruction is speculative.

The feather of the capon or duck or of another bird called a 'buñal' [unidentified bird] is a very excellent bait for trout in the months of April, May, June, July and August. But note that the feather by itself is worth nothing if it is not tied to the body of some flies made of the same colour of silk, at times yellow, at times brown, and at other times black, because these are the colours of the same flies that the trout eat in the streams evening and morning. And you should know that in different months there run different flies in the streams. And to find out, in those rivers which have trout, you must put yourself by the stream and look at the colour of the fly that flies there and take it alive. If you do it right, you will be able to take all the trout in the stream.

Different insects hatch at different times. Therefore, the angler, following a basic imitative theory, must match both the tying silk and feather to the (live) insect colors (yellow, brown, and black). The angler who matches the hatch takes "all the trout in the stream."

The feather goes on the hook this way. With the line on the hook, white and twisted of only six hairs, and the hook of half a turn well tempered, take some few of the feathers, and from the fastening place of the hook put them so that the feathers go toward the line, and attach them beginning from almost the bend of the hook as far as the spade end. And when the attachment gets that far, turn the feathers back towards the hook in such way that they hide it all the way to the end of the point. Then make the head of the fly of black silk, at the head of the feather next to the

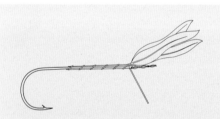

Basurto hackle-wing mount: stripped stems would create a slender underbody, conjectural.

The Basurto pattern with sheathed feathers, conjectural. The body, however, does not "show under the feather." Oddly enough, the word "feather" here is singular.

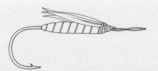

The Basurto pattern with plump body and large head, conjectural. There is no reason to believe that the Basurto pattern was as chubby as the traditional Pallareta. This Spanish pattern has a varnished, straw-yellow silk body with black silk ribbing and steel-gray (*indio acerado*) overhackle which covers the top and the sides of the body.

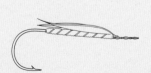

The Basurto pattern with body showing beneath over-wings, conjectural.

The Basurto pattern with cocked wings, conjectural.

spade. And then make the body of black silk. And put on the top yellow silk which is like a little ladder, because the body should show under the feather.

Six twisted hairs create prudent line strength and casting mass for most trout fishing. The white hairs are probably horsehairs and not, as the Fisher claims with burlesque, "the white hairs that Delilah cut from Samson." The hook—"half a turn well tempered"—may indicate that the spear and point lie parallel to the hook shank, rather than a specific bend, such as the semicircular "perfect." Except for "well tempered" strength, the foggy phrase reveals little about the hook design, size, or length. Is this a streamer pattern? Was the hook long? The black and yellow coloration might suggest a stonefly rather than a feathered streamer, but other readings are possible. The *Treatyse* Stonefly has similar coloration: 𝔱𝔥𝔢 𝔟𝔬𝔡𝔲 𝔬𝔣 𝔟𝔩𝔞𝔠𝔨𝔢 𝔴𝔲𝔩𝔩: & 𝔲𝔢𝔩𝔬𝔴𝔢 𝔲𝔫𝔡𝔢𝔯 𝔱𝔥𝔢 𝔴𝔲𝔫𝔤𝔢 & 𝔲𝔫𝔡𝔢𝔯 𝔱𝔥𝔢 𝔱𝔞𝔲𝔩𝔢. The *Treatyse* Stonefly wings may have been mallard quill panels. There is no indication that Basurto's feathers were anything other than full feathers. If the feathers were full hackles, they were probably webby, wide, and triangular, not the modern narrow, stiff, genetic feathers we know. Do the feathers touch or rest on the body or are they above and over the body? The final feather position is enigmatic. This is due to two (apparently) incongruous statements:

1. "turn the feathers back towards the hook in such way that they hide it [the hook] all the way to the end of the point"
2. "the body should show under the feather"

In brief, if the feathers turn back *toward the hook point*, then the body will not show *under* (beneath) the feathers. Moreover, reverse "wings" usually "cock back" above the body; without excessive wraps, it is difficult to "droop" the feathers beneath the body or to flatten the feathers above the body.

The Basurto feathers certainly are not erect wings. Nor do they appear to be feathers drooping beneath the hook shank. If the feathers drooped beneath the shank to the point, then the body would *not* show "under" (below?) the feathers. The feathers may extend *as far back as* the point, rather than *toward* the point. Are these directions for feather length rather than feather position? Should the feathers "hide" the hook (*conceal* the body?) as far back as the hook point? The manuscript word *efcōdā* translates as "hide." The word appears in Modern Spanish as *esconder,* (to) hide. The meaning may be vague. Does this mean to enclose the point or the total hook with "some few feathers"? If the term *esconder* translates *to screen, to mask, to shade,* then the directions might indicate that the feather lies *over* or *above* the body. In this manner, the body would then show beneath or under the feathers as the text indicates.

A close reading merely compounds the questions. We know neither the direction nor the spacing of the ribbing. Furthermore, how many are "some few of the feathers"? Moreover, why the cautionary note concerning the body showing beneath the feather? Would too many feathers conceal the body? If the feathers bend back *before* building the body, do they hug or encircle the body? It is difficult to wrap the body *after* the wings bend back. Reversed wings often stand about 45° to 60° off the body. This would allow body-building space. Are these feathers even wings? If they extend to the hook point, how then do they hide the hook and how then does the body show beneath the feathers? Is the yellow silk "on the top" spiraled ribbing? The text omits crucial details. Selecting materials and determining proportions require choices. Some doubtful choices must be accepted when wrapping this pattern.

> A feather dark in colour is good for very clear water in the mornings. A feather very light in colour is good for somewhat murky water in the evenings and for the mornings, too. With the feather one must fish, as I said, in swift streams without lead and without float but with the feather alone, throwing down the stream and going up the stream with reasonable speed so that the feather goes along the top of the water to the upper part of the stream, for in such a manner the trout eat real flies and so we fool them with artificial ones.

Basurto recommended contrast—dark feathers for clear water and white feathers for murky water. This is more than the downstream, wet-fly swing and retrieve. Here, the fly travels upstream with *reasonable* (?) speed in *swift* flow. The pattern neither emerges slowly nor scrapes along the surface like a skittering caddis. Apparently, this is an active, subsurface draw against a current.

The *Dialogo*, more morality play than tying manual, is a rich puzzle. The brief "Tratadico" presents tying directions for reversed wings, body colors, and possibly even feather proportions. The sum of the directions, however, fails to create a precise portrait. No matter, the "Tratadico" does present a charming, painterly sketch of early tying.

J. D. (John Dennys)

The Secrets of Angling (1613)

Although Walton attributed *The Secrets of Angling* to a John Davors, the authorship is now ascribed to John Dennys. This didactic poem of 150 stanzas reveals important information on early seventeenth-century angling. In the 1620 edition, edited by William Lauson (or Lawson), a famous footnote contains a woodcut of a "water-flie" (apparently the first fly illustration in tying history) and its description.

Lauson's marginalia, which first mentions the whalebone rod tip and fly casting, erroneously asserts that the water fly, a "May flie," is "bred of the cod-bait [caddis]." Lauson's description fails, fundamentally, to match the woodcut.

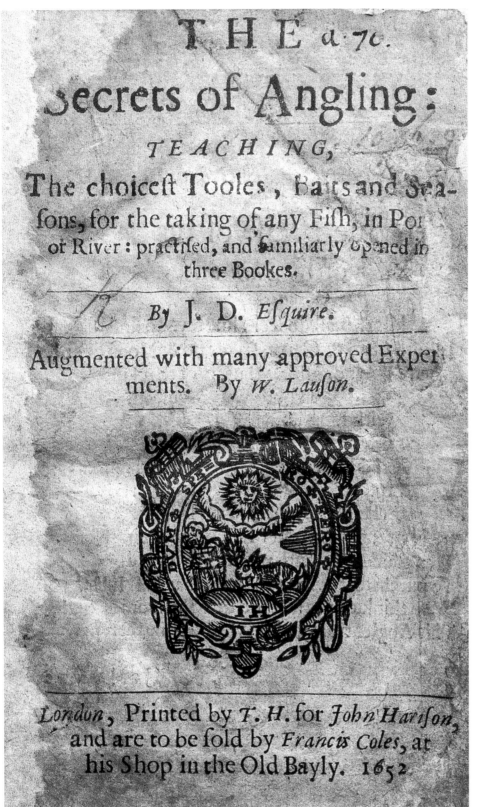

The Secrets of Angling water-flie woodcut

Title page of *The Secrets of Angling*

. . . you must change his colour every moneth, beginning with dark white, and so grow to a yellow, the forme cannot so well be put on a paper, as it may be taught by slight; yet it well be like this forme.

The head is of black silk or haire, the wings of a feather of a mallart, teele, or pickled [speckled] hen-wing. The body of Crewell according to the moneth for colour, and run about with a black haire; all fastened at the taile, with the thread that fastened the hooke you must fish in. . . .

The Water Fly (Highly Conjectural)

"All fastened at the taile" may refer to the terminal whip-finish rather than the initial mounting point of the materials. The black silk or horsehair head is bulky; this might indicate that the pattern finishes forward. Though the description makes no mention of tail material, the woodcut does depict a sparsely branched tail, somewhat like a splayed hackle tip. The "taile," however, may be either an *actual tail*, as depicted in the woodcut, or a specific *shank position*. Black horsehair "runs about" to rib the crewel body. The crewel—a tightly twisted, worsted, wool yarn with long, parallel fibers—was probably spiraled down the shank rather than dubbed on a thread. The soft wing materials—mallard, teal, or speckled-hen barbs—can be rolled and mounted. Harry Ranger, a master English tyer, believed that the wings were barbs from a mallard's mottled, bronze body feather. Although the woodcut depicts a panel (or feather) for wings, the text seems to suggest rolled and bundled barbs: 'the wings [plural] of a feather [singular].' The woodcut shows delta wings and a body extending only as far back as the hook point. Both the woodcut and the text suggest dipterans. Therefore, mount the wings either delta (woodcut) or reversed and divided, approximately body length (woodcut). These *highly conjectural* illustrations borrow from both sources.

1. After attaching the line link and horsehair ribbing, secure crewel above hook point (see woodcut). For a tailed pattern, mount the tail stem first along the shank.

2. Omit the tail (not mentioned in the text) if desired. After attaching the line link and horsehair ribbing, secure the crewel above the hook point. Advance the thread, then spin and spiral crewel forward. Rib with horsehair.

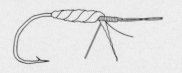

3. Complete the pattern with wings and a full head of black silk or horsehair. Whip and trim excess.

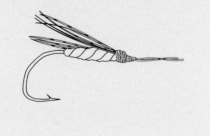

The antennae, the eyes, the undershank wing mount and the tail may be more the artist than the tyer. In the woodcut, the tail resembles a hackle tip with most barbs removed: the stem and splayed barbs forming the tail. Small, stiff body feathers can create a realistic tail in this manner. To a significant extent, either the woodcut or the text defines the pattern. Perhaps our primary authority should be the text rather than the woodcut.

Juan de Bergara

El Manuscrito de Astorga (1624)

The *Astorga* manuscript appeared in 1624, over fifty years before Charles Cotton's fly-fishing contribution to *The Compleat Angler*. A fire allegedly destroyed the original *Astorga* manuscript housed in Generalissimo Francisco Franco's library. The manscript presents a detailed list of forty-seven fly dressings. Although the ascribed author is Juan de Bergara (so indicated on the first manuscript page), Richard C. Hoffmann, in *The American Fly-Fisher* magazine ("The Mysterious Manuscript of Astorga," Fall 1990, Volume 16, Number 3), identifies two manuscript hands.

There are some salient observations on feather color, feather type, and sequential feather mounts. According to a "Spanish expert" in Preben Torp Jacobsen's *El Manuscrito de Astorga* text (modern reprint, 1984), it may also include a possible reference to the spent spinners that "fall as if dead on the water" (Section 23) and the "buzzers" (*Zumbones*, zumbar=to buzz or drone, Section 22). One pattern, the *Salticas*, has a "Body of dark silver silk; orange-yellow side edges; orange colored ribbing and light silk." Apparently, the orange and light silks twist or spin together (again, "the Spanish experts") for "kaleidoscopic" ribbing. Silk and linen fly bodies have stacked or "facing" hackles: "a strong blue dun *negrisco* hackle underneath; over the latter two *pardo* hackles with the blackest fibres and most marbled patterns." (Section 22)   Directions also include hackle orientation: "a blue dun *negrisco* [hackle], the [second] hackle [tied] on the wrong side and the other [hackle] the right side out, as the first [hackle] [should be tied]." (Section 26) This latter detail, even with disputed meanings, is a remarkable entry for an early seventeenth-century tying text.

Though the evidence is inconclusive, there are two references that Erling Kirkegaard believes might suggest that some patterns are dry. First is the salient Section 15 passage:

In March   This month provides great sport for rod-fishing because it is spring-time and the zephyr and (the) "favonio" blow and the waters become warmer.

They have two short-barbed crane-coloured negrisco (hackles), if one can get them. Body of light green linen. As for the ribbing thread, let the angler see to it that it comes from the same linen.

They are deadly in calm weather.

In Section 15, the reference to rod fishing is similar to blow-line dapping or the reel-less *tralla*. The *tralla* or "whip cracker" or "whip-rod," much like the loop-rod, relied upon the light spring winds (the "zephyr and the *favonio*" or "pleasant breeze") for dapping. A footnote on this passage defines the rod as "a very long stick from an ash-tree or a similar tree, with which the bank-owners used to fly-fish." Kirkegaard believes that this passage indicates the emergence of dry-fly fishing—a rod, spring, mild breeze, and warm water.

The second reference to the dry fly, according to Kirkegaard, appears in Section 19 (and elsewhere) with the references to "*dos vueltas de*" (two turns of) hackle. Kirkegaard believes this may imply *radiating hackle* (that is, dry-fly wraps) rather than the traditional, León stacked barbs. Hoffmann, however, does not regard the breezy weather and feather "turns" as dry-fly evidence. Until further research, Hoffmann cautions, "The Astorga manuscript gives (only) patterns for flies, and merely implies an imitative rationale for them."

Thomas Barker's Winged Palmer

The Art of Angling (1651)

As far as we know, Thomas Barker was the first. Although Fernando Basurto's *Dialogo* (1539) offers, in Spanish, the first fly-tying instructions, the first complete English instructions appear in Thomas Barker's *The Art of Angling* (1651), published 155 years after the *Treatyse* and two years before Sir Izaak Walton's *Compleat Angler*. The *Treatyse* lists a dozen fly patterns, their materials and their months when used. However, there are no detailed tying instructions. There are, in fact, no extant tying directions before the *Treatyse*. There are only recipes—the list of ingredients that make the fly. Nearly 350 years ago, a seasoned chef listed ingredients and showed us how to prepare and mix them into a delectable dish.

Thomas Barker was in good company. Barker, a Cromwellian chef at an aristocratic London house in Westminster, went down to the Thames to catch fish for "The Right Honorable Edward Lord Montague, Generall of the Navy, and one of the Lord Commissioners of the Treasury," to whom his book is dedicated. Samuel Pepys, Lord Montague's secretary, mentions angling "with a minikin, a gutt-string varnished over" in the spring of 1667. Silkworm gut was, as Pepys writes, "The secret that I like mightily." This is during the same time when Walton and Cotton fished the Dove. Apparently, Pepys kept the secret well: Cotton made no mention of gut. Surely, the best, though unrecorded, conversations on angling came from Lord Montague's table.

Barker was, as he states with charming modesty, "not a scholar," but his prose is plain and precise. Moreover, his culinary skill reveals itself in his methodical approach to tying. Barker's *Art of Angling* must have been a popular book, as nearly all later writers used his material. The work, only a few leaves long, was later enlarged and reprinted in 1657 under the title, *Barker's Delight*. Certainly a "delight" when it came to succulent recipes—roast a trout stuffed with butter, herbs, and oysters, basted with a claret wine—or how to entertain your guests like the noble Gentleman of Shropshire. "The principal sport to take a Pike is to take a goose. . . take one of the Pike lines. . . tie under the left wing and over the right wing. . . turne the Goose off in a pond where Pikes are, there is no doubt of pleasure betwixt the Goose and the Pike." When the pike snatches the bait, the goose becomes a reluctant, but spirited angler. Barker's slender book contains more recipes than angling, but he does present descriptions that offer a passable portrait of mid-seventeenth-century angling.

Commercial hook making now enters center stage. Although Lauson in 1620 still made his hooks, Dennys apparently bought his hooks as early as 1600. For the best hooks, Barker now recommended a visit to Charles Kirby in Mill Yard. Like today, quality hooks probably encouraged quality tying. For fishing tackle, Barker also encouraged a visit to "Oliver Fletcher at the west end of Paul's, at the sign of the three Trouts." The demand for hooks and rods firmly established the tackle trade by 1650. Even so, parsimonious country anglers probably made much of their own tackle.

Barker, greatly admired by Walton, provided his friend information for the first edition of *The Compleat Angler*, an angling Arcadia published two years after Barker's own first edition. It was not until the fifth edition of *The Compleat Angler* (1676) that Charles Cotton's fly contribution formed Part II.

With sincere modesty, Barker shared his fifty years of experience. "Now to show you how to make flies: learn to make two Flies, and make all." That is, if you learn to make these two fly patterns—the Palmer and the Mayfly—then you learn to make all fly patterns. Thus, the history of English tying begins with the Winged Palmer. The following 1820 text is a reprint of the 1657 edition.

> We will begin to make the Palmer flye. You must arm your line on the in-side your hook,

Arm the blind hook by binding a length of horsehair line to the inside of the hook shank. According to John Waller Hills, silkworm gut was not mentioned until 1724 (in *The Compleat Fisherman* by James Saunder), and was hardly known until the second half of the eighteenth century. Robert Howlett's *Angler's Sure Guide* (1706) recommends "arming" (here meaning "to attach") your hooks with "bowel-strings" or catgut. Catgut usually came from dried and twisted sheep intestine strands. A few wraps of silk around the shank tip (another meaning of "arming") protects the hair from chafing against the hook. Continue overwrapping to secure the hair beneath the shank. Arming both attaches and protects the hair link. Tying vises appear later.

> then take your sizzers and cut so much of the browne of the Mallards feather as in your owne reason shall make the wings, then lay the outermost part of the feather

1. Invert hook to attach line link. Note the shank-tip wraps (the arming) that protect the horsehair line.

2. Mount mallard barb wings.

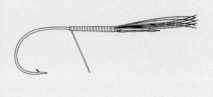

3. Mount the hackle, body, and ribbing.

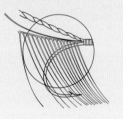

4. Barker's Winged Palmer.

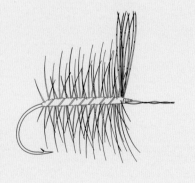

near the hook, and the point of the feather next toward the shank of the hook, so whip it three or four times about the hook with the same silk you armed the hook with, so make your silk fast;

After arming the hook, select and cut the wings. The specific feather (hen or drake) is not identified. It may be bundled barbs (feather fibers), a feather point, or a contour feather from a mallard hen. Bundled barbs appear as the earliest winging method. The brown speckled wing feather and various small wing feathers may have been used. The drake's bronze feather created wings for decades. These finely etched feathers deepen to a rich, chestnut-brown margin. And they are excellent candidates for a barb cluster, as the passage reads "cut so much" of the feather (singular) to make the wings (plural).

The only problem arises from the phrase "outermost part of the feather." This may infer that a single feather tip creates the wing. The phrase may also be a reference to mounting orientation; that is, the top or tip of the feather positioned next to the hook. The "point of the feather" may be, perhaps, the tip section removed from a single feather, that is, the tip or "point" of a feather. We still use the term "point" to describe hackle-point wings. If this were the case, then "the outermost part of the feather" makes sense. A single feather, unlike a barb bundle, has an "outermost part."

We stay with a barb bundle if "the outermost part" is the *feather margin*, "outermost" from the stem. It seems likely that this is the proper reading as the margin of a bronze mallard feather is the deepest and richest color area. Charles Cotton, a contemporary, used the phrase "grew uppermost" to suggest the convex or outer surface of the feather. No matter, variant readings only continue the mystery. Later in the tying directions, you will, with "a needle or pin," "part the wings in two." Surely, this argues a barb bundle, divided and bent back. Therefore, the bronze mallard drake feather appears the likely nominee.

Tightly coil the hook line to open tying space. Select a bronze mallard flank feather (or preferred feather) and clip out the bronze barb section. Align the barb tips by rotating and caressing the barbs into compliance. Stack the barbs to make a wing bundle. Next, mount the wing bundle on top at the front of the shank, tips pointing away from the bend. Early tyers probably quickly discovered that the reverse-wing mount created durable wings that cocked well and resisted casting force. Reverse wings were common in the seventeenth and eighteenth centuries. Though Barker did not give the rationale for the reverse wing, Robert Venables, in *The Experienced Angler* (1662) did: Venables found that soft, flat wings folded around the bend when caught by the current. He argued, "If you set the point of the wings backwards, toward the bending of the hook, the stream, if the feathers be gentle as they ought, will fold the points of the wings in the bending of the hook, as I have often found by experience."

then you must take the hackle of a cock or capon, or a plovers top which is the best; take off the one side of the feather, then take the hackle, silk, or cruell, gold or silver thred, make all fast at the bent of the hook,

After mounting the wings, wrap the silk toward the hook bend. Mount, near the hook bend, "hackle, silk, or cruell, gold or silver thred." Hackle and "cruell" colors, which should match the natural, are not mentioned. "Cruell" (crewel) is merely a common, finely twisted, long-fibered wool yarn. Before mounting the hackle, Barker instructed us to "take off one side of the feather." Strip the barbs by holding the tip and yanking down, a few barbs each time. Barker offered no explanation for stripping. A stripped hackle creates a delicate and sparse palmer.

> then begin to work with the cruell, and silver thred, work it up to the wings, every bout shifting your fingers and making a stop, then the cruell and silver will fall right, then make fast,

It appears that Barker wraps the crewel and the silver thread (body and ribbing) at the same time, changing finger positions to keep them parallel and flat so that the "cruell and silver will fall right." However, this reading does not necessarily preclude wrapping one after the other, that is, the body *then* the ribbing. After all, a *singular* pronoun appears in "work it up to the wings." Perhaps, the "silver thred" is merely a forethought of what comes next. In any case, wrap the body forward and overwrap the ribbing. Make fast at the wing base and trim excess.

> then work up the hackle to the same place, then make the hackle fast;

Then wrap the hackle forward to create a full palmer body. Tie off the hackle at the wing base and trim excess.

> then you must take the hook betwixt your fingers and thumb in the left hand, with a needle or pin part the wings in two, so take the silk you have wrought with all this while, and whip once about the shank that falleth crosse betwixt the wings;

Divide the wings with a needle or pin. And whip about to "falleth crosse betwixt the wings." That is, whip between the wings with figure eights to divide them. Finally,

> than with your thumb you must turn the point of the feather towards the bent of the hook, then whip three or four times about the shank of the hook, so view the proportion.

To erect the wings, press them back toward the hook bend and take three or four wraps of silk and whip off. John Betts, a scholar of ancient tying, believes that such wings were more erect than folded sharply back. Certainly early engravings bear this out, and with only three or four silk wraps it would be difficult to force them back. Nearly all early patterns were finished at the bend or immediately behind the wings; however, the Winged Palmer, like a modern fly, was finished at the head.

Though Barker describes the Mayfly, the Hawthorn Fly, the Oak Fly and others, the Winged Palmer has pride of place, the first English pattern with complete

Modern Winged Palmer on *The Book of Hours,* **fifteenth century.**

tying directions. Remember, too, that this fly is nearly 350 years old. Winged Palmer engravings, perhaps akin to Barker's pattern, appear in the frontispiece (patterns number 7 and 8) of Thomas Best's *A Concise Treatise on The Art of Angling* (first edition, 1787). Pattern 7 (The Great Red Spinner) appears to have a quill wing; pattern 8 (The Wasp Fly), a rolled wing. Though we do not know Barker's original proportions, Best's engravings depict typically portly London ties.

Best's Winged Palmer.

A modern wrap: Barker's Winged Palmer.

Conrad Voss Bark, in *A History of Flyfishing*, suspects that Barker's patterns "would be true wet flies and presented with a sinking line." John Waller Hills, in *A History of Fly Fishing for Trout*, claimed, "Barker specially dressed his flies so that they floated near the top . . . ." Hills found evidence for this is in Barker's poetry:

> Once more, my good brother,
>   Ile speak in thy eare,
> Hogs, red Cows, & Bears wooll,
>   To float best appear,
> And so doth your fur,
>   If rightly it fall . . . .

With a fresh, fully-dressed Palmer and with only a link or two of a short line touching the water, it would be a simple drift "to float best" over a rising trout. Though wet horsehair line is remarkably buoyant, the sparse hackle and wool body would have hastened the sink. Depending upon hook weight, the Winged Palmer might drift just beneath the surface. Tyers and trout, in fact, may find Thomas Barker's feathered cuisine truly savory.

Robert Venables

The Experienced Angler (1662)

Colonel Robert Venables is the curiously forgotten. Though he wrote about fly tying, he did not offer a salient list of fly patterns that would assure his place in history. His life is no less quixotic. In Ireland, he participated in the siege of Drogheda and the resulting Irish slaughter. In 1654, Cromwell fitted out an expeditionary fleet, under the command of Admiral Penn and Colonel Venables, to capture Hispaniola. Through poor planning, disease, and appalling execution, the ill-fated mission to the West Indies failed to take Hispaniola. By sheer chance, they did capture Jamaica. On his return to London, Venables was imprisoned, without trial, in the Tower. On his release, he returned to his homeland of Cheshire, and, during the Restoration, became governor of Cheshire Castle. W. H. Lawrie called Venables an "irascible Cromwellian." Dr. George W. Bethune observed (in Walton's *Compleat Angler*, 1847) that "It would seem that the brave, once most successful, but in the end unfortunate soldier found consolation in angling and writing upon his quiet pleasures." Venables was a proud, petulant, and bitter man who wrote one of the great angling books.

Though Sir Isaac Walton never met Venables, he read and praised the book for its "judicious precepts" and "height of judgment and reason." It was, for Walton, "the epitome of Angling." This is remarkable praise coming from a Royalist. While Charles Cotton, another Royalist, found fame in listing sixty-five trout flies for Part II of Walton's *Compleat Angler*, Venables offered no such list. Curiously enough, the

1676 edition of *The Compleat Angler*—the last edition published during Walton's lifetime—included the Venables text as Part III to make *The Universal Angler*. Venables advocated innovative changes in fly design, fly fishing, and fly tackle.

After an introduction and tackle discussion, Venables opened with the fly. He dismissed the tradition that insects have their individual hatch months: "But I must here beg leave to dissent from the opinion of such who assign a certain fly to each month whereas I am certain, scarce any one sort of fly doth continue its colour and virtue [for] one month." Like Barker, Venables had a "recipe" for pike: "Some use, for more sport, if the Pike be a great one, to tie the same to the foot of a goose, which the Pike, if large, will sometimes pull under the water." It is not certain what the early anglers had against geese and pike, but even here, Venables took the more reasoned leg-line approach: however, not exactly the upstream dry approach.

He noted that fish will "sometimes take the Flie much better at the top of the water, and another time much better a little under the superficies of the water, and in this your own observation must be your constant and daily instructor (for if they will not rise to the top try them under). . . ." There are dry, emerger, and wet patterns. There are even spinners—"of some kinds there are a second sort afterwards." He made the first reference to upstream angling. Trout seldom take flies until the "bush hatch"—"until the flies come to the banks of rivers." To "try the depth of river and pond," he suggested using a "musquet or carbine bullet" on the hook—the first mention of a weighted fly. He also mentioned using a "swivel or turn," and, when trolling for pike, he used a winch or reel and strong cobbler thread for backing. He advised the angler to have three color values for each fly: "a lighter colour, another sadder" and an "exact colour" to match all waters and weathers. Venables had a brilliant, but brief, 145-word description of the bent-shank hook. For discussion of this passage, consult Chapter IV on "The Hook."

He examined trout entrails to "match the hatch." He offered the first description of an "inverted" pattern. However, the pattern inversion is not for a floating fly. The pattern was probably dapped with limited surface line. In addition, if sunk "a little under the superficies of the water," it would not necessarily drift inverted. He even imitated the "cad-bait larva" with a chamois body and black silk head and, in the augmented fourth edition of 1676 (and perhaps in the scarce third edition), offered a curious caddis larva. "You may if you please place a small slender Lead upon the shank of your Hook to sink the Bait where the River is not violently swift, and draw the *Cad Bait* [here, a larval skin] over the Lead, you may make the head of black silk, and the body of yellow wax; this you must often raising from the bottom, and so let it sink again." Explication of this passage varies. Apparently, after extracting the "blue gut," you slide the larval skin over the lead and secure it with a black silk head. It is unclear whether the yellow wax attaches to the lead or forms an underbody for another, lighter pattern. Dressing a hook with a delicate larval skin must have challenged the skill of many anglers. In any case, the angler then jigs the pattern in slow water. Though there is no doubt about the efficacy of this pattern, there is an inkling that it is an untried "paper pattern," created only with ink, perhaps done during his Tower time.

Though reels and running lines were available, he preferred the slender rod and fixed horsehair line for trout. He advocated matching the belly of the fly, "for that colour the fish most observe, as being most in their eye." Venables was a mature, intelligent writer and what he wrote of fly tying is perceptive if not brilliant.

Venables emphasized color, form, and proportion: ". . . . but the angler, as before directed, having found the fly which the fish at present affect, let him make one as like it as possible he can, in colour, shape, proportion; and for his better imitation let him lay the natural fly before him." Venables recommended matching the banded and lateral body colors, head colors, cerci, and antenna colors of the natural. He offered the first thoughtful, scholarly approach to tying. Venables' directions are more a series of tying maneuvers than the creation of a particular pattern.

Venables' Methods

First, I begin to set on my hook, placing the hair on the inside of the shank, with such coloured silk as I conceive most proper for the fly, beginning at the end of the hook, and when I come to that place which I conceived most proportionable for the wings, then I place such coloured feathers there, as I apprehend most resembles the wings of the fly, and set the points of the wings toward the head;

Wrap the tying silk to wing position and mount wings with tips over fly head. As there is no further reference to reversing the wing, this may be the first mention of an *advanced wing*, a wing that extends forward, beyond the hook eye. The wing-mount position is vague: the wings mount either above or beneath the hook shank. For his later inverted pattern, "that place" might be under the hook shank. It is unclear as to whether or not the line link mounts beneath the inverted hook shank.

or else I run the feathers, and these must be stripped from the quill or pen, with part of it still cleaving to the feathers, round the hook, and so make them fast,

Or strip off one side of a feather with part of the quill still attached. With a sharp blade, split the feather by scoring the quill down the center and stripping off one side. Wrap the resulting split-quill hackle as shoulder hackle. Notice that this is not merely stripping the barbs; this is stem-splitting—a method that may accommodate thick-stemmed feathers. The "round the hook" may refer to wrapping the hackle around the hook shank rather than over the body.

if I turn the feathers round the hook; then I clip away those that are upon the back of the hook, that so, if it be possible, the point of the hook may be forced by the feathers left on the inside of the hook, to swim upwards; and by this means I conceive the stream will carry your flies' wings in the posture of one flying; whereas if you set the points of the wings backwards, toward the bending of the hook, the stream, if the feathers be gentle as they ought, will fold the points of the wings in the bending of the hook, as I have often found by experience.

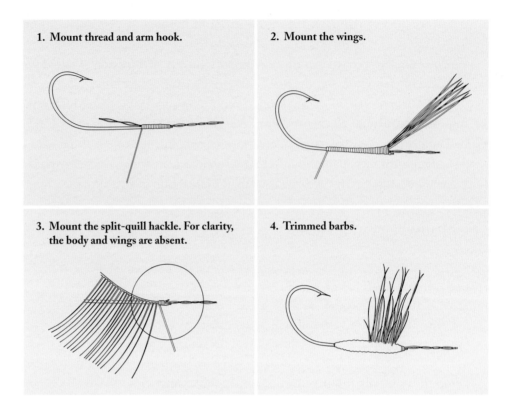

1. Mount thread and arm hook.

2. Mount the wings.

3. Mount the split-quill hackle. For clarity, the body and wings are absent.

4. Trimmed barbs.

Winged pattern with trimmed barbs.

Trim the barbs on the back so that the remaining barbs become wings for an *inverted* pattern. Inverted on the water with line contact on the surface, the extended barbs might suggest flight. Furthermore, if dapped, a vertical fly with advanced wings might also appear "in the posture of one flying." The text describes barbs "inside of the hook." This differs from the brace of plump patterns illustrated (see Chapter VI, "The Experienced Angler," page 250): they have no wings and, *seemingly,* only lateral barbs. It is unclear whether this is a winged or wingless pattern. The hackle barbs may be the wings as suggested by the fly illustrations. The illustrations, however, ultimately fail to illuminate the subtleties of the text.

> After having set on the wing, I go on so far as I judge fit, till I fasten all, and then begin to make the body, and the head last; the body of the fly I make several ways; if the fly be one entire colour, then I take a worsted thread, or moccoda end, or twist wool or fur into a kind of thread, or wax a small slender silk thread, and lay wool, fur, &c. upon it, and then twist, and the material will stick to it, and then go on to make my fly small or large, as I please.

According to John Betts, this may be the first reference to dubbing wax. "Moccoda" (mockado, Italian *Mocaiardo,* "mohair," 1543, *OED*) is a common or inferior fabric (compare fustian) of the sixteenth and seventeenth centuries. Make the body in two ways: with a dubbing "noodle" or with a waxed, dubbing strand. The number of wraps determines the body size, small or large. Notice the modern account of dubbing, laying fibers upon a waxed thread, then twisting and wrapping to create a body. The term *dubbing* refers to any manner of dressing a hook, whether wrapping a body or attaching a line. As far back as 1450, dubbing meant to dress, to array, to adorn, or to invest, apparently in any manner, including *dubbing* a knight. In an early text, dubbing may refer to attaching fibers to a thread, attaching and wrapping a yarn, attaching and folding a yarn along the shank, or attaching the line link to the hook itself. The modern tyer restricts the meaning of dubbing. Early tyers recognized and employed all meanings.

> If the fly, as most are, be of several colours, and those running in circles round the fly, then I either take two of these threads, fastening them first toward the bend of the hook, and so run them round, and fasten all at the wings, and then make the head;

Create contrasting body bands by mounting and wrapping two "threads," the dubbed strands. Mounting at the bend, wrapping toward the wings, and finishing at the head are remarkably modern.

> or else I lay upon the hook, wool, fur of hare, dog, fox, bear, cow, or hog, which, close to their bodies, have a fine fur, and a silk of the other colour bind the same wool or fur down, and then fasten all:

Alternately, I place fine dubbing on the hook shank and overwrap with a contrasting silk thread. Apparently, a silk thread ribs over fine dubbing that mats or entangles the shank. Evidently, no wax shrouds the shank to grip the dubbing.

> or instead of the silk running thus round the fly, you may pluck the feather from one side of those long feathers which grow about a cock or capon's neck or tail, by some called hackle; then run the same round your fly, from head to tail, making both ends fast; but you must be sure to suit the feather answerable to the colour you are to imitate in the fly; and this way you may counterfeit the rough insects, which some call wool beds, because of their wool-like outside and rings of divers colours, though I take them to be palmer worms, which the fish much delight in.

Or mount and wrap a palmer hackle. "From head to tail" is not necessarily the wrap direction. It may merely indicate that the hackle covers the complete body. This, of course, is the palmered Wooly Worm.

> Let me add this only, that some flies have forked tails, and some have horns, both which you must imitate with a slender hair fastened to the head or tail of your fly, when you first set on your hook, and in all things, as length, colour, as like the natural fly as possible you can: the head is made after all the rest of the body, of silk or hair, as being of a more shining glossy colour than the other materials, as usually the head of the fly is more bright than the body, and is usually of a different

The spiraled body bands

The silk lapped dubbing

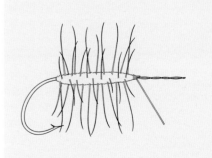

Venables' Palmer

colour from the body. Sometimes I make the body of the fly with a peacock's feather, but that is only one sort of fly, whose colour nothing else I could get would imitate, being the short, sad, golden, green fly I before mentioned, which I make thus: take one strain [compare "strand," a barb or filament, *OED*] of a peacock's feather, or if that be not sufficient, then another, wrap it about the hook, till the body be according to your mind;

Length and color of any antenna or cerci should match the natural. Match the head if it is glossy or contrasting. A peacock barb strand creates an appropriate body for "the short, sad, golden greenfly."

if your fly be of divers colours, and those lying long ways from head to tail, then I take my dubbing, and lay them on the hook long ways, one color by another, as they are mixed in the natural fly, from head to tail, then bind all on, and fasten them with silk of the most predominant colour; and this I conceive is a more artificial [skillful or artful] way than is practiced by many anglers, who use to make such a fly, all of one colour, and bind it on with silk, so that it looks like a fly with round circles, but in nothing at all resembling the fly it is intended for: the head, horns, tail, are made as before.

In viseless tying, it may be easier work "from head to bend." The "dubbing" may or may not be parallel dubbing strands with ribbing. In the original sense, any fiber or yarn is "dubbing." Long-fibered dubbing can be rolled or "noodled," placed along the shank and secured with silk ribbing. The most creative method, though, are *dubbed* strands extending along the hook shank. In both methods, a tyer matches the various *longitudinal* colors of a natural. This is especially appropriate for dorsal, ventral, or lateral color contrast. Although the *Treatyse* records a yellow luste after eyther syde and yellow under the wynge and under the tayle, Venables presented the first extended discussion of "diverse colours." From what had come before him and his own talent, Venables knew how to write about fly tying. One of Venables' contributions to tying is his scrutiny of the insect and his "exact imitation"—his detailing—of an insect's stripes and bands.

Venables' Natural Fly

The lateral body bands

Charles Cotton

The Compleat Angler (Fifth Edition, 1676)

Izaak Walton's *Compleat Angler* first appeared in 1653. According to Kenneth Mansfield, in *The Art of Angling*, the word *Compleat* on the illustrated title page of the first edition is spelled "*Complete* on the pages of the book itself, the *Compleat* being probably a little bit of pedantry on the part of the engraver." It is the fifth edition appearing as *The Universal Angler* (1676) that became the standard text. This edition introduced the world to Part II, Charles Cotton's *Instructions how to angle for a Trout or Grayling in a Clear Stream.* Cotton, a skilled tyer who once hung a portly London fly in his parlor window to laugh at, was a Royalist and poet with modest, yet independent means. Walton wisely relied upon both Venables and Cotton for his fly-fishing additions and emendations.

In Part II and twenty-three years after the first edition of *The Compleat Angler*, Cotton listed sixty-five patterns for trout and grayling. It is impossible to determine how many anglers became tyers by reading his instructions. The sheer number of editions suggests that he taught the world to tie. A footnote in John Hawkins' second edition suggests Cotton's influence: "There needs nothing more be said of these directions than that hundreds have, by means of them alone, become excellent fly-makers." John Waller Hills, so critical of other angling works, regarded Cotton's contribution as perhaps "the best book on fly-fishing ever written." He was, according to Hills, the "spiritual son of Izaak Walton." We can only surmise the influence of Cotton's tying instructions. Cotton notes that "this way of making a flie, which is certainly the best of all other, was taught me by a kinsman of mine Captain Henry Jackson, a near neighbour, an admirable flie angler, by many degrees the best flie-maker, that ever I yet met with."

Cotton's Winged Fly

In making a flie then, which is not a Hackle, or Palmer-flie; (for of thofe, and their feveral kinds we fhall have occafion to fpeak every Month in the Year) you are firft to hold your hook fast betwixt the fore-finger and thumb of your left hand, with the back of the fhank upwards, and the point towards your finger's end; then take a ftrong fmall filk of the colour of the flie you intend to make, wax it well with wax of the fame colour, to which end you are always, by the way, to have wax of all colours about you, and draw it betwixt your finger and thumb, to the head of the fhank, and then whip it twice or thrice about the bare hook, which you muft know is done, both to prevent flipping, and alfo that the fhank of the hook may not cut the hairs of your towght [the line link], which fometimes it will otherwife do;

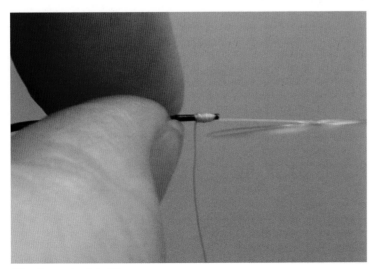

The Cotton hook hold

The Cotton hook hold presents some problems. If held by the bend, the hook point cannot "point towards your finger's end." In *Izaak Waltons & Charles Cotton Flugor* (1992), Gunnar Johnson and Anders Forsling depict Cotton's tying sequence with the shank tips pointing to the left. If held by the shank tip in this manner, it would be impossible to wrap the tip with silk. However, if you hold the hook *within the left palm cup* and the fingers directly behind the tip wraps, then the point is toward the fingertips. This position tallies with Cotton's text and permits significant pressure when wrapping the tip. For this reason, the following hook drawings point to the right.

> which being done, take your line and draw it likewiſe betwixt your finger and thumb, holding the hook ſo faſt, as only to ſuffer it to paſſ by, until you have the knot of your towght almoſt to the middle of the ſhank of your hook, on the inſide of it; then whip your ſilk twice or thrice about both hook and line, as hard as the ſtrength of the ſilk will permit; which being done, ſtrip the feather for the wings proportionable to the bigneſs of your flie, placing that ſide downwards, which grew uppermoſt [the convex or outer surface] before, upon the back of the hook, leaving ſo much only as to ſerve for the length of the wing of the point of the plume, lying reverſed from the end of the ſhank upwards; then whip your ſilk twice or thrice about the root-end of the feather, hook, and towght; which being done, clip off the root end of the feather cloſe by the arming, and then whip the ſilk fast and firm about the hook, and towght until you come to the bend of the hook; but not fur-ther, as you do at London; and ſo make a very unhandſome, and, in plain Engliſh, a very unnatural and ſhapeleſs flie; which being done, cut away the end of the towght, and fasten it, and then take your dubbing, which is to make the body of your flie, as much as you think convenient, and holding it lightly with your hook betwixt the finger and thumb of your left-hand, take your silk with the right, and twisting it betwixt the finger and thumb of that hand, the dubbing will spin itself about the silk,

Rather than a chopped dubbing mix, the body could have been a wispy "noo-dle" spun around the silk. For a tight noodle, trap one end on the shank before twisting it together with the thread.

> which when it has done, whip it about the armed hook backward, till you come to the ſetting on of the wings; and then take the feather for the wings, and divide it equally into two parts, and turn them back towards the bend of the hook, the one on the one ſide, and the other on the other of the ſhank, holding them faſt in that poſture betwixt the fore-finger and thumb of your left-hand; which done, warp them ſo down as to ſtand, and ſlope towards the bend of the hook: and having warped up to the end of the ſhank, hold the flie faſt betwixt the finger and thumb of your left-hand, and then take the ſilk betwixt the finger and thumb of your right-hand, and where the warping ends, pinch or nip it with your thumb-nail againſt your finger, and ſtrip away the remainder of your dubbing from the ſilk, and then with the bare ſilk, whip it once or twice about, make the wings to ſtand in due order, faſten, and cut it off after which with the point of a needle raiſe up the dubbing gen-

tly from the warp, twitch off the ſuperfluous hairs of your dubbing, leave the wings
of an equal length, your fly will never elſe ſwim true, and the work is done.

The extent of fluffing is unknown. Later, fluffing patterns improve floatation.
These prototypical tying directions create erect, divided wings with a rearward
cant. There is no mention of dubbing bracing the wing in front. Such wings dominated centuries of tying. There appeared in 1747, according to the Bodleian
Library entry, Richard Bowlker's *Art of Angling*. The second (1774) and later editions were claimed by Charles Bowlker, his son. *The Art of Angling* is modern in
attitude and approach. It rejects many patterns presented by the *Treatyse* and Cotton as ineffective, and then offers a list of twenty-nine useful patterns, some in use
today. Bowlker noted that "Even the preparation of the Materials for the Artificial

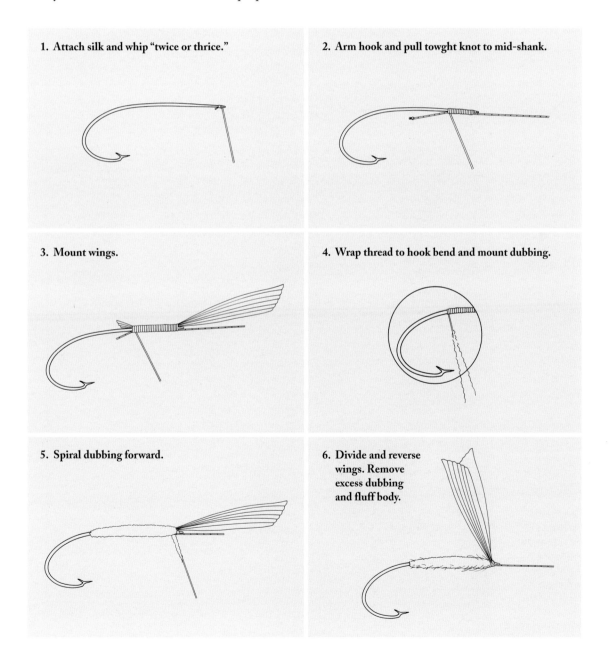

1. Attach silk and whip "twice or thrice."

2. Arm hook and pull towght knot to mid-shank.

3. Mount wings.

4. Wrap thread to hook bend and mount dubbing.

5. Spiral dubbing forward.

6. Divide and reverse wings. Remove excess dubbing and fluff body.

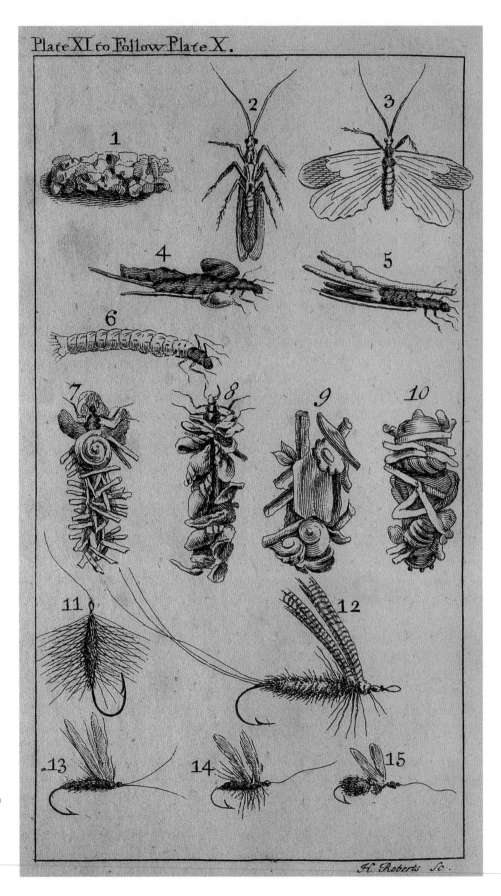

The John Hawkins plate for the 1766 edition of *The Compleat Angler*. This plate, first appearing in 1760, presents several informative patterns. Numbers 12 and 13 may be similar to Cotton's Winged Fly. Perhaps the long fibers of pattern 12 result from fluffing.

Fly, and the skill and contrivance in making them, and comparing them with the natural, is a very pleasing amusement." His upstream strategy, entomological knowledge, and tying theory excel all others. And his directions for making a winged fly are clear and economical. "To make a winged fly, the same method may be observed in tying on the hook; then take the feather which is to form the wings, and place it even on the upper side of the shank, with the roots pointed towards the bend of the hook; after fastening the feather by winding the silk over it, cut the root ends close with a pair of scissors, and divide the wings as equally as possible with a needle, passing the silk twice or thrice between them, which will make them stand in a proper position; then carry the silk from the wings down the shank of the hook, about the proposed length of the body, and, after fastening, apply the dubbing to the silk, and form the body by warping [twisting or bending] towards the wings; when within a turn or two of the wings, fasten in the hackle for legs, and wind it neatly under the wings so as to hide the ends of the cut fibres; fasten above the wings." His delicate, reversed-wing patterns have dominated tying for well over a century and a half. We expect nothing less from the finest fly fisher of his century and the most erudite tying book to date.

John Younger

River Angling for Salmon and Trout (1840)

John Younger, the cobbler of St. Boswells, was a poor man, rich in friends and reputation. At his death in 1860, the *Scotsman* described him as a "genial writer" of prose and verse, "a man of high conversational powers, and clear common sense," who left behind him "no enemies, and the memory of a guileless, unblameable, honest life."

River Angling for Salmon and Trout, published in 1840, earned £30, for him, a princely fortune. Written in the best style that he could afford "from thirty shillings' worth of scholastic education" the work contains remarkable insight. His contribution to angling is his astute and original observations.

Younger grappled with poverty all of his life. The "Sketch of the Author's Life," in the 1864 edition of *River Angling for Salmon and Trout,* describes an incident of youth. Sent to seek credit at the local corn mill, he gathered what meal he could.

> When he had procured a supply he set off at full speed (for he knew the household was at the starving point), running over the dreary fields with the pock under his arm. Temptation would assail him, and he would untwist the neck of the bag, and gulp down with hungry hurry the dry meal, and then, lest he should be tempted again, he would twirl up the neck beyond ready reach, and run with additional speed.

Younger was an astute observer of nature, his watercraft teeming with keen observations and pleasure.

Not a more delectable half-hour's amusement have I ever had in my long life (except in sweethearting when young), than in lifting one of these aurelia from the stream, and sitting down with it on the palm of my hand in the sun, till it put out its feelers, and drew itself by degrees from its envelopment. Then its wings sprang erect, showing it off as tenderly-pure as a vision of thought; and when dried, it mounted in its new element, to delight its hour or its day in the pleasures of a new state of joyous existence.

Some observations were advanced—recognizing, for example, that on salmon flies "the hackle is laid close in to the wake of the tinsel" to guard the hackle, and that the term "striking" was faulty. Strike is a "retentive hold," and not a brisk tug. Little wonder that other anglers always sought his counsel and conversation.

Younger described, apparently, swamped, spent spinners. "As these flies are tender, you may perceive them in breezy weather all dishevelled [a favorite term] by being blown in from the ruffled surface to the sheltered eddies—their wings being dashed asunder, and spread on the water like shivered oars. In this state the trouts devour them. . . ." This surface density seems to suggest spinners rather than drowned duns.

Though Younger used his Pale Yellow Dun, he conceded that a spider was a good imitation of this fly. It wore "the body feather of a grouse, a lightish fine freckle, stripped off the right side" rolled around as hackle. "This imitates the dishevelled wings of the natural fly, and is technically called a spider fly." He also recognized the imitative value of rough-and-tumble patterns.

In addition, Younger described what would become the modern emerger: "they float for some time enclosed in a second tough film, within which their wings lie in one single fold, and from which they creep out by degrees, leaving their last vestment a floating wreck. So soon as extricated, their wings spring erect, shewing them off the finished, lovely gentle denizens of air." Though he called it a "maggot," his description was essentially accurate. So too was his angling technique.

When the flies come up thickly to the surface . . . and no trout takes them; for a trial of skill mutilate the wings of your flies by picking them off about half-middle (not cutting them); or rather by tying down the top of the wings to near the tail of the fly, which makes its appearance something like the maggot released from its first case on the bottom stone, and on its ascent to the surface. Then, as much as you can, let them sink low in the water, altogether below those flies on the surface, and you will most likely succeed in getting a few trouts, as then they take them for the grub newly come out of its case on the ground stone, and not yet quit of the silk-like film in which it is bound up—with its wings laid up in one fold, like a man with his wrists tied to his arms below his oxter [armpit], with the arm-pit joints having free motion. These pellicles, or second skins, which the flies cast off, you may see lying like chaff, covering the water edge, as drifted into coves and eddies. . . .

To mutilate the wings, use the fingernail to rip the wings off at "half-middle"—leaving a truncated wing. The tautological "half-middle" apparently means at the middle. This colloquialism is unclear. A half-wing might suggest an emerger, and a quarter-wing, a nymph. Although some anglers might find the half-wing excessive, it can suggest the developing wing-buds of an emerger. In any case, it is little wonder that Skues, the nymph master, owned and studied a copy of Younger's book. Although he did not develop imitations of nymphs and emergers, Younger "modified and mutilated" to match them.

"Mutilate the wings."

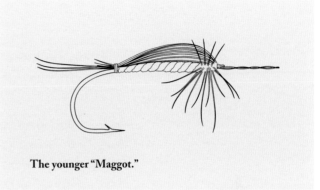

The younger "Maggot."

Younger usually fished "aslant upstream or straight across" rather than downstream. The fly then drifted downstream with tension. Despite this, John Waller Hills believed that region might have determined the chosen drift: Scotland and South England fished downstream, while North England fished upstream. For anglers residing near water, Younger recommended a fourteen to sixteen foot, ringed trout rod with wood-glued and lint-thread wrapped and varnished joints. His casting line, nearly as thick as his wheel-line, was eight to fifteen horsehairs, tapering downwards by two or three hairs in each link to five or six feet, ending in four or five links of gut.

He tied trout patterns in a "twinkling" by attaching the gut at the tail, lapping the thread toward the head and then mounting the wings. After adjusting the wings with cross-wraps, he rolled fur dubbing around for body. Younger, who had knowledge of thread-work as a cobbler, described the mechanics of the soft-loop.

> To dress trout flies in a superior style:—When the hook is tied to the gut and ready for the wings, cut with a pen-knife two close from the rib of the feather, lay the one piece upon your left fore-finger, and the other exactly upon it, with the two insides together, then close your thumb upon them, and place the hook below, pressing it up close to the wings; and while in this position, lay the tying thread round over it, press the point of your finger closely on the tying thread, and while in the act of drawing tight, also cause it to draw the wings straight down together on the hook so as to prevent it ruffling or twisting them to one side; then lap the thread once or twice more around on the same place to secure the wings, and letting the wings escape from your fingers, divide them asunder, and cross them round between with the tying thread, and they will stand up unruffled in the texture, a beautiful model of the living water fly.

No modern tyer requires an illustration for the soft-loop. Younger wraps are simple and precise. He did suggest, "One may even go the length of cutting the two wings from two corresponding feathers of the pair of wings from the same bird, but this is extreme nicety, which may be resorted to as a trial of skill." Our "Tweedside Gnostic" denounced patterns with too much "variety" and "tinsel-glitter," preferring instead, the simple, natural muted tones. Younger gave us sparkling comments and common sense.

William Blacker

The Art of Fly-Making, &c, Comprising Angling & Dyeing of Colours (1842)

Blacker's *Art of Fly-Making*—some two centuries after Barker, Venables, and Cotton—is a handsome book stuffed with delicate engravings, knowledgeable tying instructions and a few oddities. The illustrations that follow appeared in the greatly augmented, and admired, 1855 edition. The meticulous illustrations alone can teach the tyer. Westwood and Satchell described the work as "a strange medley of practical usefulness and rhapsodical extravagance. The instructions for fly-making are peculiarly precise and clear." This "rhapsodical extravagance" probably referred to some of Blacker's tying descriptions. For example, Blacker made a fly body with a length of very flat gut, soaked in hot water until soft and tied in at the tail. After a tapered straw formed an underbody, you then "roll some white floss silk over it at intervals, roll the soft gut closely over it to the head and tie fast; then put a small partridge hackle round the throat, and wing it. . . . Before you lay on the straw, cut it taper to suit the size of hook you are using, gold-beater's skin rolled over flat gold tinsel is also good." Blacker, with studied skill, clearly was a gifted tyer.

His "Catechism of Fly-Making" and the sequential illustrations are clear and charmingly quaint.

The rarest pattern, however, was his "winged larva." Without reticence, he asserted that "There is nothing can exceed the beauty of these flies." The shank body was brown mohair and the wings were barbs from the hen pheasant tail and the woodcock wing. A piece of "shriveled larva" (the silk capsule) at the end of a salmon gut made the detached body. This body was firmly mounted at the shoulder. Two golden pheasant neck fibers, whipped and varnished to the fine end of the larva, formed the tail. "Tie the larva at the side, so as it may appear like a double body to the fish in the water." Two wraps of a woodcock feather from outside the base of the wings became the best legs. A brown peacock herl covered the wing root. Blacker concluded: "The great nicety in making this fly to look well is, in tying on the two fibres of the golden pheasant feathers at the tail with fine silk, and tying on of the larva itself at the shoulder of the fly, and then covering the silk that appeared bare with a little mohair twisted round the tying silk, and then rolled over it; it is over this bit of mohair the hackle should be rolled, and secured with two knots." None can doubt the dexterity required to whip two barbs to shriveled gut.

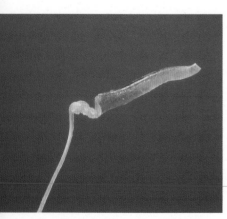

The capsule or nodule on silk gut.

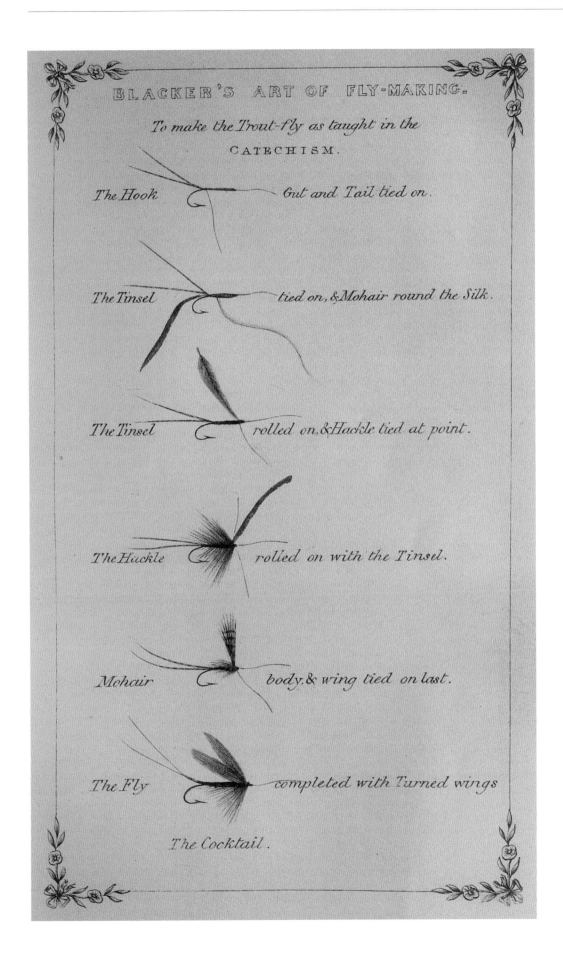

BLACKER'S ART OF FLY-MAKING.

To make the Trout-fly as taught in the
CATECHISM.

The Hook   Gut and Tail tied on.

The Tinsel   tied on, & Mohair round the Silk.

The Tinsel   rolled on, & Hackle tied at point.

The Hackle   rolled on with the Tinsel.

Mohair   body, & wing tied on last.

The Fly   completed with Turned wings

The Cocktail.

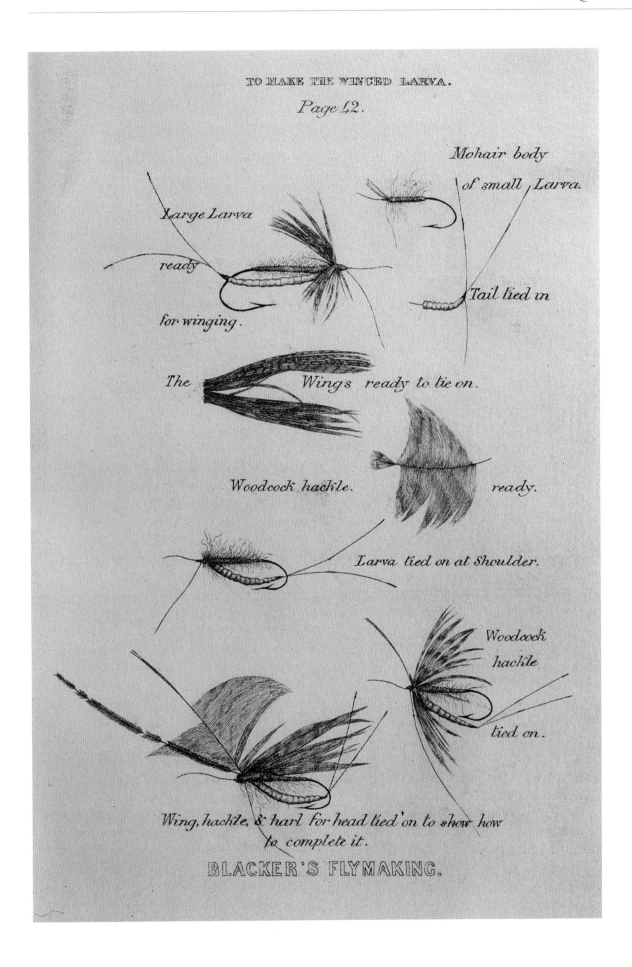

TO MAKE THE WINGED LARVA.

Page 42.

Large Larva ready for winging.

Mohair body of small Larva.

Tail tied in

The Wings ready to tie on.

Woodcock hackle. ready.

Larva tied on at Shoulder.

Woodcock hackle tied on.

Wing, hackle, & harl for head tied on to show how to complete it.

BLACKER'S FLYMAKING.

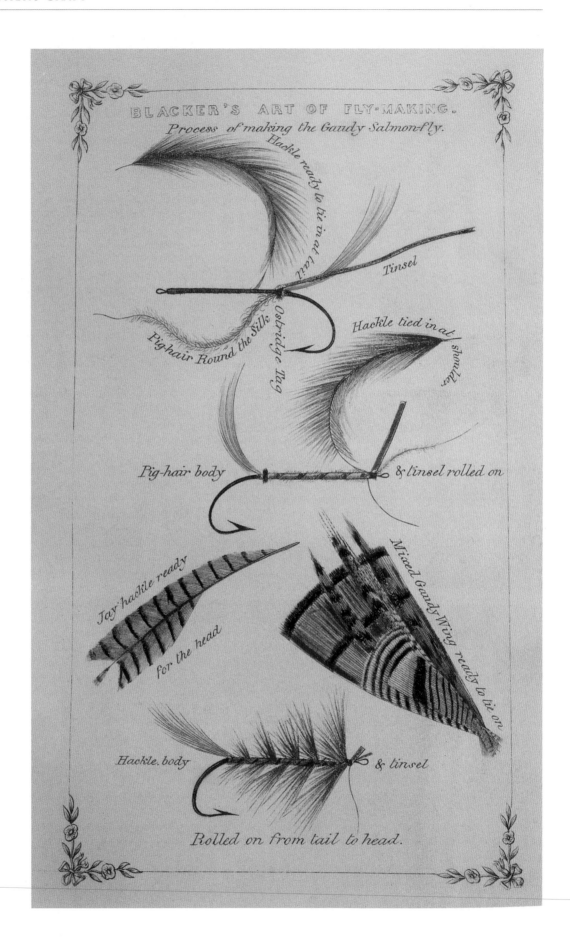

Although most of his methods were traditional, his instructions and engravings had more detail and precision than any earlier tying book. His two major contributions were the detached body and the matched panel wings. "You strip off two pieces from the woodcock or starling wing, and lay them together evenly at the points, that the wings may be double when tied on. . . ." The engravings depict these matched quills. There were two ways of assembling and two ways of mounting upright wings. They could be a single piece (sometimes rolled) or they could be two quill panels. They could be mounted, slanting aft, or sloping forward and then reversed. The reversed, single-bundle method was older and stronger.

Duplicating earlier writers, Blacker presented this traditional method as "An easy method to make the trout fly," by mounting the wings before making the body or attaching the hackle, then "turn the wings up in their place with the thumb nail of the right [hand], and divide them in equal parts with a needle."

Blacker was specific and selective about his hackles. Historically, Cotton apparently did not hackle his winged flies; his dubbed bodies, though, could be teased out for improved floatation. Barker hackled with one side stripped, while Venables apparently hackled patterns capriciously. To make a double-hackle fly (the Palmer), Blacker tied two hackles together.

Blacker's feather plate (page 46) showed "Two Hackles for the Palmer Fly" and, to the right, "Hackle prepared." John Betts believes the "Hackle prepared" illustrates *two* hackles, one over the other, revealing the muted transparency of the feather beneath. The top feather had a section cut away to reveal part of the under feather. The "Hackle prepared" (singular) is then actually *two hackles* prepared as a single hackle. Blacker's description apparently supports this: "as you may see in the plate of Feathers, two hackles tied together at the roots ["Two Hackles for the Palmer Fly"], which keeps them on their sides evenly while rolling them on; you hold the hook by the shank in your left hand, tie in the hackles, the inside downwards, that when tied on and finished, the outside of the feathers appears to the eye…." If true, the engraving of these "stacked" hackles, showing a lighter feather *beneath* a darker feather, is unique in an early tying text. To his credit, Blacker "stood at the elbow of the artist" to bring the fly engravings to "the greatest perfection" just like his patterns. At forty-three years old, Blacker died of certified consumption on March 19, 1856. Though dying relatively young, Blacker, nevertheless, showed us some of his extraordinary talent.

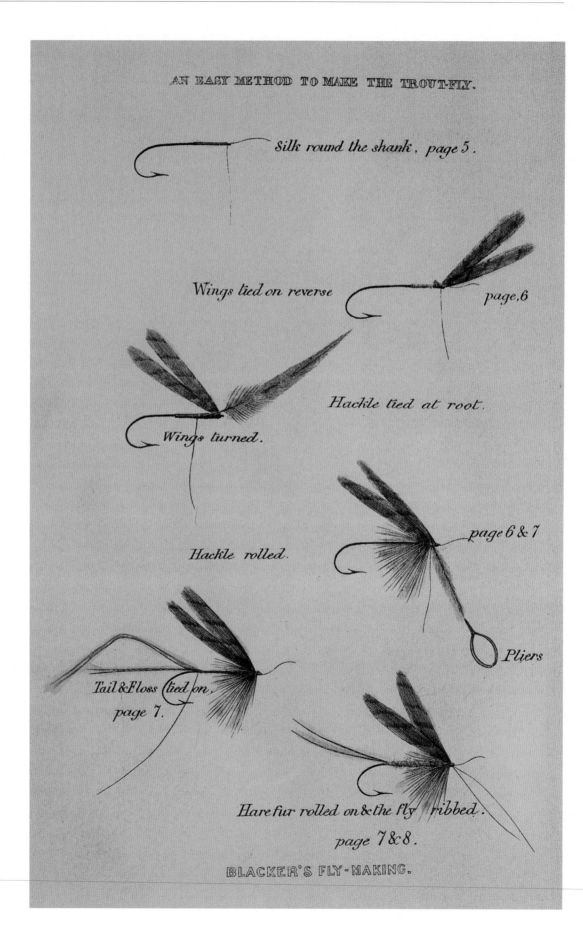

AN EASY METHOD TO MAKE THE TROUT-FLY.

Silk round the shank, page 5.

Wings tied on reverse   page, 6

Hackle tied at root.

Wings turned.

Hackle rolled.   page 6 & 7

                                         Pliers

Tail & Floss tied on,
page 7.

Hare fur rolled on & the fly ribbed.

page 7 & 8.

BLACKER'S FLY-MAKING.

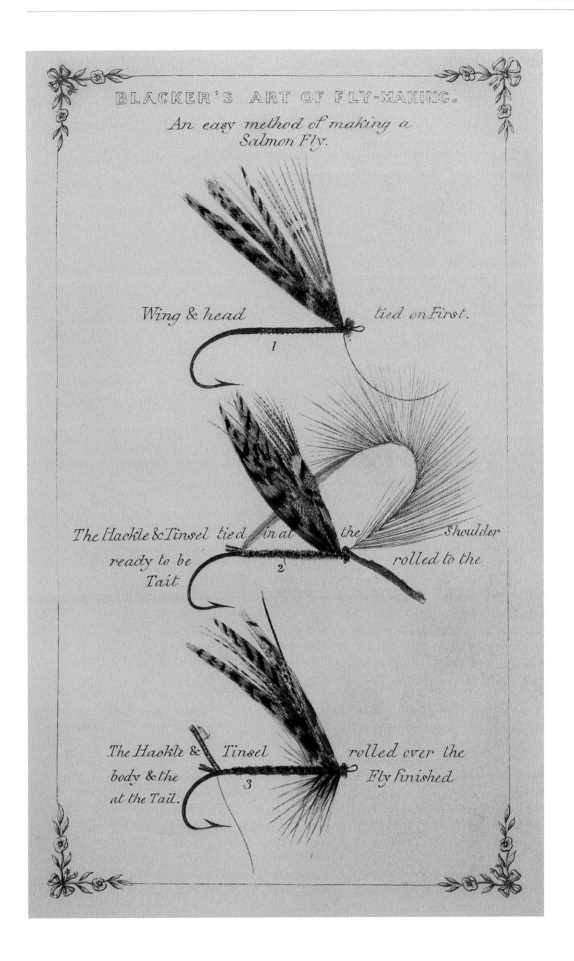

BLACKER'S ART OF FLY-MAKING.

Grouse Hackle prepared

Golden Pheasant topping

Trout Fly Wing

Bunch of Hackles prepared for dyeing

Woodcock Wing Feather

Two Hackles for the Palmer Fly

Hackle prepared

Hackle cut at point

Irish Gaudy Wing prepared

Mallard Wing prepared for Scotch Fly

Turkey Wing prepared

Sprake Sc.

W. C. Stewart

The Practical Angler (1857) Stewart's Spider

Stewart's spider trinity—the black spider (brown silk body and cock starling hackle), the red spider (landrail shoulder hackle and yellow silk body) and the dun spider (ash or dun hackle from dotterel or dun hackle from inside wing of starling)—is sacred, but not eternal. When aggressive trout shredded spiders, Stewart then switched to three-winged wets. Most wings came from corn bunting, lark, chaffinch, woodcock, and landrail, while hare-ear dubbing (from dingy white to solid black) formed the bodies. His three, unnamed winged flies, were:

1. Woodcock and Yellow

   A woodcock wing with a single turn of red hackle, or landrail feather, dressed with yellow silk, freely exposed on the body

2. Corn bunting and Hare's ear

   A hare-lug body, with a corn bunting or chaffinch wing.

3. Corn bunting and Black hackle

   The same wing as the last fly, with a single turn of a soft black hen-hackle, or small feather taken from the shoulder of a starling, dressed with dark-coloured silk.

Other minor permutations appeared in these three patterns. For Stewart, there are flies and there are spiders.

> The artificial flies in common use may be divided into two classes. There is first the winged fly, which alone, properly speaking, merits the appellation; and there is the palmer hackle or spider, by which last name we mean to call it, believing that if it resembles anything in the insect tribe, it is a spider.

The term *resembles*, rather than *imitates*, is important. Stewart's spider, more akin to the palmer hackle as he noted, lacks the *sparse* hackling of North Country spiders. He also emphasized "the *necessity of avoiding bulky flies*." This may refer more to the body than the hackle. The North Country spiders, some with only a single wrap of soft hackle, were fished upstream with line held high. Stewart fished his flies, cast upstream, either on the surface or slightly below.

> The moment the flies alight—being the only one in which the trout take the artificial fly for a live one—is the most deadly in the whole cast, and consequently it is of immense importance to make the flies light in a soft and natural manner.

After all,

> . . . there is no occasion for keeping them on the surface, they will be quite as attractive a few inches under the water.
>
> Dressing a spider is a much simpler operation than dressing a fly, and therefore it is better to begin with it. Having selected a thread of gut and a hook, the next thing is to choose a feather, which, to make a neat spider, must be so proportioned to the size of the hook that the legs of the spider, when dressed, will be about the length of the hook. Before commencing, bite the end of the gut between your teeth; this flattens and makes it broader in the point, which prevents it slipping, a thing very liable to occur with small flies.
>
> Next take the hook firmly between the forefinger and thumb of your left hand, lay the gut along its shank, and with well-waxed silk thread, commencing about the centre of the hook, whip it and the gut firmly together, till you come near the end of the shank, where form the head with a few turns of the thread.
>
> This done, take the feather, and laying it on with the root end toward the bend of the hook, wrap the silk three or four times round it, and then cut off the root end.
>
> What remains to be done is the most critical part of the whole operation: still holding the hook between the forefinger and thumb of your left hand, take the thread, lay it along the centre of the inside of the feather, and with the forefinger and thumb of your right hand twirl them round together till the feather is rolled around the thread;

The twirled thread and hackle create insectile and "spidery" patterns, much like a drowned or swamped natural.

> and in this state wrap it around the hook, taking care that a sufficient number of fibres stick out to represent the legs; to effect this it will sometimes be necessary to raise the fibres with a needle during the operation. Having carried the thread and feather down to where you commenced, wrap the silk three or four times round the end of the feather, and if there is any left cut it off, and finish with a succession of hitch-knots, or the common whip-fastening. If the legs of the spider are too long, there is no remedy for it; cutting injures rather than improves them. This is a very rough and simple mode of dressing a spider, and does not make it so neat as if the feather were put on by a pair of nippers, but, it is more natural-looking, and much more durable as the feather is fastened on by the thread the whole way down.

Feather selection is the keystone. The feather stem should be fine and flexible. The barb length should equal total hook length. Modern, genetic hen hackles offer excellent feathers for this pattern. Though tied sans-vice, the spidery appearance and spun-stem method creates an attractive and durable pattern. Though Hills called Stewart's three spiders, "fancy flies" (imitating neither species nor genus), different hackle colors can suggest a variety of insects. Wrap proportion, the barb length, into the pattern: never trim the barbs to length.

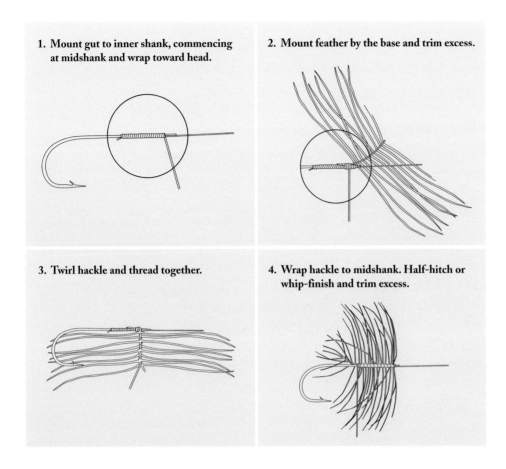

1. Mount gut to inner shank, commencing at midshank and wrap toward head.

2. Mount feather by the base and trim excess.

3. Twirl hackle and thread together.

4. Wrap hackle to midshank. Half-hitch or whip-finish and trim excess.

The pattern looked more like a truncated palmer than a soft-hackle pattern. Stewart offered a rationale for the thick wraps. "The spider is made rather more bushy than is advisable at first, as the trout's teeth would otherwise tear it away too fast. After capturing a dozen trout it will be spare enough." Trout *eventually* create the proper proportions of these spiders.

Harry Cholmondeley-Pennell

Fly-Fishing and Worm Fishing for Salmon, Trout and Grayling (1876)

Pennell's Typical Fly (Green, Brown, and Yellow)

Pennell, a knowledgeable and eclectic all-rounder, was a remarkable combination of new and old. He favored the traditional long, double-handed trout rod fished downstream. William C. Stewart, who regarded downstream as the great fly-fishing error, advocated a shorter, somewhat stiffer, single-handed trout rod fished upstream. The upstream clan eventually dominated. Pennell's generic "Typical Fly" had modernity and simplicity. This pattern consisted of a hook, sewing silk, and hackle. He believed that trout could only distinguish "general shape, general colour, and size." To imitate various insects, silk color and hook size changed. He also curiously encouraged a large head (trying "to exaggerate [rather] than to

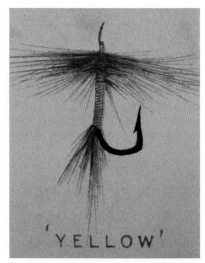

A frontispiece's yellow pattern

diminish in the artificial imitation all the prominent features of the natural insect") and "larger whisks" ("the larger the whisks the better and straighter the fly will swim"). The extent of these exaggerations is vague. Note that the tying directions refer to "up" as toward the bend and "down" as toward the eye or shank tip. The trout patterns illustrated in the frontispiece appear to have the gut mounted on top of the shank: this, I assume, is an error.

> A strand of common coloured sewing silk (not floss), of the required thickness having been waxed in a manner presently described, take two or three turns over the end of the hook-shank and gut;

Prior to mounting, wax the silk thread with a colorless wax. Standard "chippy" cobbler's wax discolored the tying silk, especially the yellows and greens, and unwaxed silk failed to hold the gut. Pennell solved the problem by creating a colorless wax from Burgundy pitch, white resin, and tallow. He even drew the freshly waxed silk between his fingers to produce a blotched or mottled yellow-brown body to match the March brown, stonefly, and other insects. Silk color should imitate one of the basic insect colors: green, brown, or yellow.

> lay the hackle on the back of the hook, hollow side upwards, with the large end towards the hook bend; lap over it with three or four turns of the silk;

The hollow side (the concave side) faces up. The hackle overlap beyond the shank tip becomes the shoulder hackle. Barb length in the overlap should be appropriate for the pattern.

> spin the hackle on over these turns (the same way round as the silk), leaving some of the hackle over, then fasten the hackle off with the silk,

Create the shoulder hackle by wrapping the overlap hackle back toward the bend and secure with a half-hitch or whip.

> continuing to work upwards towards the bend of the hook, and lapping over the hackle until the body is of sufficient length; then fasten off the silk and cut the stem (only) of the hackle almost close to the end of the lapping, so as to leave the fibres in a V-shaped form to represent the whisks.

Create the body by wrapping the silk toward the bend ("upwards"). At the proper body length, secure the silk. Trim the stem, leaving a few lateral barbs as tail whisks. Wrap firmly as the silk also secures the gut to the hook shank.

By leaving and lapping over the stem of the hackle and the end of the silk, or by "stripping" the former and cutting the latter off close, the body can be made thick or thin as desired.

An alternate method creates a thin body; before overwrapping the body, strip the body barbs, leaving only the tail barbs.

It will thus be seen that the body of the fly is made of the same strand of silk with which the gut is tied on, and that the "whisk" is made from the same feather that forms the legs, or hackle.

Here is the first single-feather fly. There is no doubt that the fly is effective and, with simple changes of silk and hackle color, quick and imitative.

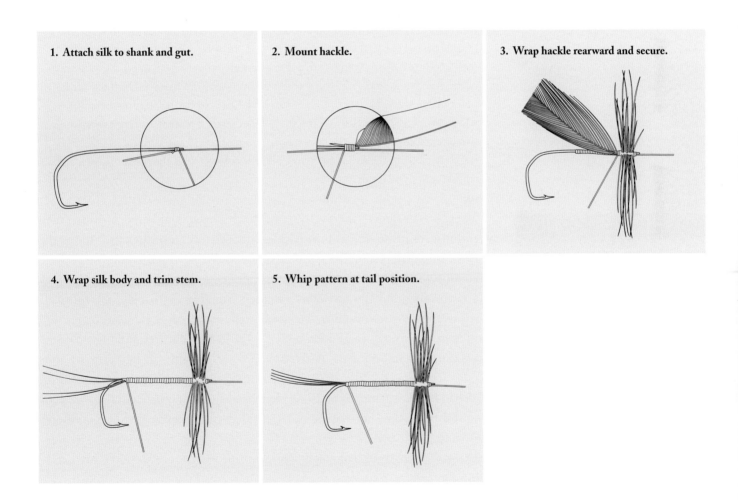

1. Attach silk to shank and gut.

2. Mount hackle.

3. Wrap hackle rearward and secure.

4. Wrap silk body and trim stem.

5. Whip pattern at tail position.

James Ogden

Ogden on Fly Tying (1879)

Ogden on Fly Tying is a slender book of thick importance. John Waller Hills, in *A History of Fly Fishing for Trout*, wrote that we can see what the Ogden floating flies look like from the two original mayflies tied by him in Aldam's *A Quaint Treatise on Flees and the Art of Artyfichiall Flee Making* (1876). According to Hills, the Ogden mayflies may be the oldest example of floating flies extant. Some of the hooks, both identified and doubted as Bartleet Limericks—had a vertical-eye formed on the hook-bend plane. Hills also believed that Ogden was the first writer to offer comprehensive tying directions for the floating dun. His directions were modern for the first time. Although tyers wrapped hackles edge-on, Ogden was the first to describe keeping the hackle "well on the edge" while wrapping:

> Strip the fluff off the hackle, and take it in the right hand, root downwards, the outside part of the hackle to the right; tie it in sideways, close up behind the wings, with two turns of silk, taking care not to disarrange the wings. Cut off the quill end of the hackle, not too close, or it will pull out. With the tweezers lay hold of the point of hackle, keep it well on the edge, and put two or three turns behind the wings, bringing the hackle well forward underneath. Secure it with one wrap and two hitches before taking the tweezers off; cut off the silk and point of hackle; press it well back from the head; open and adjust the wings with the scissor points, and cut out any straw fibres.

Thus, he concluded, the fly "will last much longer, and is much neater, than when finished at the head." This hackle, wrapped "well on the edge," forms the modern, supporting shoulder hackle. Although two or three hackle wraps were behind the wing, no hackle wraps, if any, appeared in front of the wing. This may be a misreading, but the text blurs whether "bringing the hackle well forward" means wrapping or positioning the hackle well forward. A significant regret, and a common one among early tying books, is the lack of illustrations. Ogden noted that during his father's day, "A fly vise was not thought of; but they are now become very general." The 1879 comment suggests that the tying vise, scarce in 1850, had become common by 1880. Ogden, ever the tradesman, did illustrate his improved tying vise, but the captured, divided-wing mayfly reveals few, if any, front wraps.

David Foster's sons compiled *The Scientific Angler* (1882) after his death, within three years of Ogden's work. Foster instructed the tyer to place the hackle wraps directly beneath: "The hackle, with which it is intended to form the legs, is then turned or wrapped into position *underneath the wings*, the whole being well supported by a few well-planted turns of tying silk, which done, all that remains is for the silk to be knotted or looped off in the usual way, and your up-wing fly is complete." To place barbs beneath the wings, hackle wraps must appear on one or both sides of the wings. Like many period patterns, the Foster illustrations

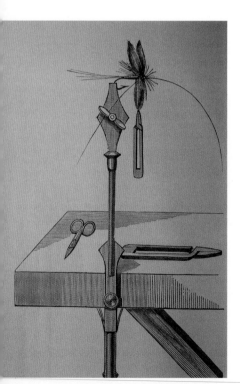

Ogden's improved fly vise

often showed more hackle behind than in front of the wing. His "Favorite," nonetheless, showed remarkably long and soft hackle in front. Foster concluded that "The hackle, with which it is intended to form the legs, is then turned or wrapped into position *underneath the wings* [Foster's italics], the whole being well supported by a few well-planted turns of tying silk. . . ."

Ogden, an angling companion of Alfred Ronalds, was a fly dresser and purveyor of angling goods. He was, apparently, one of the first dealers to market floating flies. His little book, written to give "a lesson on fly dressing," is replete with advertisements of his wares, such as his popular *Multum in Parvo*, "much in little," fly rods originally made of greenheart in lengths from eight (!) to twelve feet, "in two joints, spliced and handled in leather." He also included clever folding landing-nets, seat baskets, and strutting tales of his angling exploits.

Foster's "favourite" Floating May.

His book contains the celebrated tale of his introduction of the floating fly on the Derbyshire Wye, June 5, 1865. Ogden most likely did not invent the dry fly. Andrew Herd recorded that "it is probably safe to assume the dry fly saw use in the 1850's" and "Francis Francis said that the first use was on the Itchen in 1857." Nevertheless, Ogden certainly increased the artificial hatch by encouraging the dry fly. His success with the artificial caused the keeper to prohibit the use of naturals.

Ogden tied on an artificial drake—a straw body ribbed with red silk, three tail fibers from a hen pheasant, a pale buff hackle with brown center, and cocked wood-duck wings. He waded in and cast to a rise. The fly touched the water and the trout took. A Mr. Hobson, observing from the bridge, shouted, "That was a live fly you used." Ogden told him to come and see for himself. Hobson replied, "If it is not so, I am convinced you will kill fish, for it alighted like the natural fly." Soon Ogden had nine trout. He then made a long cast that hooked a good fish. But Ogden found himself caught, stuck in the mud. While struggling to extricate his right leg, he lost his balance and fell in. He finally worked the plump "two-pounder plus" downstream where the river keeper netted it. A voice from the bridge wailed. "If he hadn't fell in, he'd a killed every fish in the water." Ogden returned to the inn to dry. The following day, he met the keeper and the regulars reacted. "We met several anglers on the bridge, who insulted me as being the cause of stopping the use of the natural fly. I found it would not do to fish there again...." The keeper, who apparently favored the artificial, consoled Ogden. "Never mind, Ogden; you have carried out my wishes, and from this morning I have prohibited all natural fly fishing. If they cannot kill with the artificial, they shall not with the live fly." We may never know why the keeper favored the artificial. We only know that Ogden received a week's ticket on the river Lathkill, the duke's private water. He had a pleasant week.

Ogden, a professional tyer, had a comprehensive tying credo. He regarded color combined with size as the "great secret" of imitation, he blended dubbing to avoid single-color dominance, and matched thread color to the natural fly. Wings were, for Ogden, "the most essential point in the dry fly." For dry flies, he advocated the oily Egyptian goose breast feathers for wings as they were "whipped dry much quicker" than summer or wood duck. For shorter hooks, he merely snapped off the blind-eye shank to length. He aligned wing barbs for flush tips and wrapped hackle, as we do, on its edge. An interesting angling trinket was Ogden's buffer knot. After knotting two lengths of gut together with a jam knot, he wrapped silk between the knots, creating a silk cushion to soften the shock.

Ogden, like many early tyers, mounted the hackle after the wings. This process, considered at the time as often troublesome, erects or "cocks" the wings with the bracing hackle. Ogden's directions also included the modern soft-loop, minimal wraps, and the alignment of wing barbs for a flush edge. "I commence dressing my flies with up-right wings, as follows: Make the body first, next set the wings on upright, and then the hackle close up behind the wings, finishing off close up *behind* [italics mine]the hackle; but for a sunk fly the wings should be set on last." Ogden offered practical but fragmentary directions. The following illustrations of a dubbed-body pattern reflect the proportions and tying of the frontispiece fly in Ogden's vise.

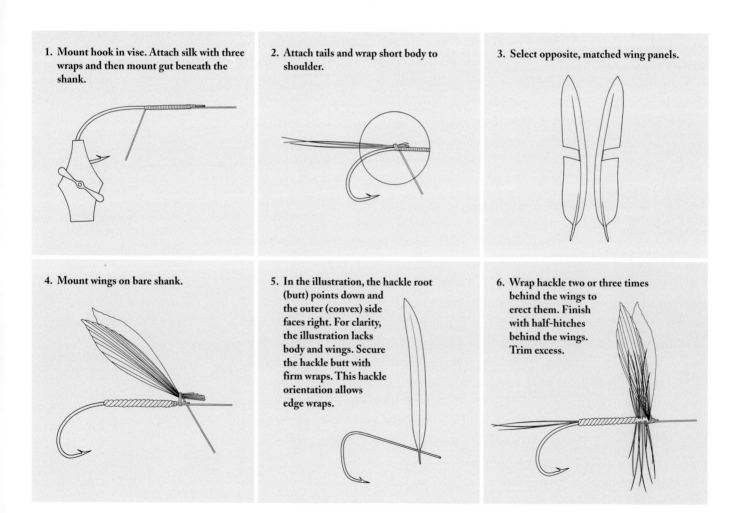

1. Mount hook in vise. Attach silk with three wraps and then mount gut beneath the shank.

2. Attach tails and wrap short body to shoulder.

3. Select opposite, matched wing panels.

4. Mount wings on bare shank.

5. In the illustration, the hackle root (butt) points down and the outer (convex) side faces right. For clarity, the illustration lacks body and wings. Secure the hackle butt with firm wraps. This hackle orientation allows edge wraps.

6. Wrap hackle two or three times behind the wings to erect them. Finish with half-hitches behind the wings. Trim excess.

Ogden's Methods

To commence, fix your hook firm in the jaws of the vise, leaving sufficient of the shank out to the right to form the body of the fly. Put three turns of waxed silk around the shank of the hook, leaving less than the eighth of an inch bare hook to wing and head upon. Take a length of gut . . . lay it underneath the hook, and wrap down with the waxed silk close and even, not one wrap on another, neither allow the silk to slack. The smoother the foundation, the better the fly will look.

Mounting the wings on a bare shank (void of foundation wraps) requires consummate skill. Mounting on a "bare shank," a repeated edict, must have been important to Ogden. Perhaps this was an attempt to minimize bulk created by thick, heavily-waxed tying silk.

Avoid making the body too long. I would rather see them a little too short than otherwise. If the fly you wish to copy has tails, take three strands of a large cock's hackle, either duns or reds; secure them with two wraps of silk, cut off the waste ends, give the silk a twist and wrap close back up to the shoulder, still leaving the bare hook to wing and head upon. This is a plain silk body which I prefer.

Ogden favored a short silk body and minimal tails. Incredibly, only two wraps secured the tail; there is no mention of foundation wraps. Ogden used two wraps to secure most materials. These may be "print tying," rather than actual tying tactics. Unlike a flat silk body, Ogden's *twisted* silk body could be corded or segmented.

Now for setting on the wings, which is the most difficult part in making a midge fly. We will commence with staring [starling] wing, which should be smooth and clean. Take a right and left wing. Get a centre feather from each wing; strip off the fag end, and with the right finger and thumb divide as broad a piece as you wish one side of the wing to be. Draw the tips carefully down, till quite even, without separating the fibres; at the same time holding the quill and roots firm with the left finger and thumb, easing them occasionally to let the wing lay even and smooth coaxing the fibers gently together. (Practice alone will accomplish this satisfactorily.) This being done, with the left finger and thumb hold the quill and roots of the wing firm, while with the right finger and thumb press very tight, keeping the wing flat, and with a sharp twitch separate the wing from the quill, taking care not to slack your hold or disarrange the fibres. Lay it carefully down on the work table, the outside part of the feathers uppermost. In precisely the same manner take a wing from the other feather exactly the size as the one just take off.

Ogden regarded the wings as essential for dry flies. For matched curvature, he selected wing slips from paired, opposite feathers. He carefully aligned the barb tips and stripped the quill slips off the stem. To avoid wing splits during the cast, early tyers often mounted quill wings so that the natural fiber curve pointed aft. Ogden gave no indication, in either text or figure, of the mounted, natural wing curve. Modern tyers follow Halford's method of mounting the "natural curve" forward, less durable but more realistic as previously mentioned. John Younger, unlike Ogden, considered paired wings from corresponding feathers as an "extreme nicety" in *River Angling for Salmon and Trout* (1840). Ogden approved this "extreme nicety."

> When done, place it carefully on the inside of the forefinger of the left hand, the inside [the underside] of feather uppermost, and the roots of wing pointing to tip of finger. Pick up the other half of wing (which I do by moistening the tip of my forefinger of right hand), and put it to the other half of wing. Lay the tips very evenly together, and (inside of feathers facing) press them together, keeping them flat, and, without altering their position, place them on top of the bare hook. For length they should reach to the bend of the hook, but no longer. Take the tying silk in the right hand, open the left finger and thumb slightly at the tips, to allow the silk to pass up and down, then close and press tight, at the same time drawing the silk very carefully down (or it will break) on the roots of the wing [hence the soft-loop of modern tying]. Take two more turns of silk in the same manner, keeping all the time a gentle strain on the silk or the wings will twist round. Pass the silk securely round the screw of the vice, and release the left finger and thumb to see that the wings set properly. If so, draw your gut carefully on one side, avoiding the shank end of hook, as it will sometimes fray it.

Match and mount wings with the "inside" or *underside* of the feathers facing. Mount the wings with the natural tips toward the hook bend. When mounted, wings should extend only to hook bend. Wing length is slightly short of shank length. A couple of wraps with the soft-loop anchors the wings on the shank. The vise screw becomes a thread holder. "Draw your gut carefully on one side" is a problematic phrase. It may be that when the silk tightens over the wing butts, the *bare shank*, and the gut, then the gut twists or pulls to one side and, consequently, must be realigned beneath the shank. The phrasing seems awkward at best.

> Trim off the roots of the wing neatly with a sharp pair of fly-dressing scissors; then take two turns of silk on the head, holding the wings as before, not allowing the silk to slack or the wings will draw out. (I always try the wings to see if they are firm.)

Although there were already "two or more turns of silk" on the wing base, Ogden then formed a small head with two, tight wraps.

> Pass the silk behind the wings ready to tie the hackle in, which should be proportioned to size of hook and tapering. Strip the fluff off the hackle, and take it in the right hand, root downwards, the outside part of the hackle to the right; tie it in sideways, close up behind the wings, with two turns of silk, taking care not

to disarrange the wings. Cut off the quill end of hackle, not too close, or it will pull out.

Now, pass the silk behind the wings and mount hackle. The term *sideways* can mean two different positions: a hackle side or the hackle edge against the shank. If the hackle *side* mounts parallel to the shank then "the outside part of the hackle" faces the tyer. If a *vertical* hackle *edge* mounts against the shank, then the "root" is down and the "outside part" faces to the right. This mount matches the text better. No matter which mount is used, something fails to correspond with his directions. In any case, holding the hackle in the right hand and securing the hackle is awkward, if not impossible. The illustration shows a side-mounted, vertical hackle with butt down and the "outside part" (the bright or convex side) facing to the right. The hackle face depicted is at a *right angle* to the hook shank. In this posture, the hackle stem aligns with the wrapping direction, hence a short stem might "pull out." Other mounts are possible and may even be correct. Again, Ogden used only two wraps.

> With tweezers lay hold of the point of hackle, keep it well on the edge, and put two or three turns behind the wings, bringing the hackle well forward underneath. Secure it with one wrap and two hitches before taking the tweezers off; cut off the silk and point of hackle; press it well back from the head; open and adjust the wings with scissor points, and cut out any stray fibres. The fly is now finished; and made this way will last much longer, and is much neater, than when finished at the head.

Wrap the hackle, two or three times, on its edge behind the wings. Bring the hackle "well forward underneath" the wings to force them up and secure with one wrap or two half-hitches before trimming excess. The finishing hitches occur behind the wings: there are no hackle wraps in front of the wings.

> I know from experience it is not possible to set the wings well upright, like the natural fly, if they are put on last. It may do for a sunk fly, but not for a floater. As a rule I made all bodies of flies first. For a dubbing or wool body I twist it sparingly on the waxed silk, and wrap up from the tail to the shoulder, tapering the body and setting the wings on as described before.
>
> In dressing buzz or hackle flies I make the body first and form the head with two or three turns of tying silk. I then tie the hackle in at the proper distance from the head, and either take two or three turns with the hackle close together, or carry it half way down the body, according to fancy. But in no case should it be finished off at the head, as the fly will wear so much better finished off behind the hackle.

Although the fly depicted in Ogden's vise has "wings well upright," sparse hackle wraps usually will not fully erect such wings. Wings usually slant back about 60 degrees. For a buzz or palmer pattern, complete the body and mount hackle behind head. Wrap palmer back (toward the bend) and secure "behind the hackle" at the proper body position.

Frederic M. Halford

Floating Flies and How to Dress Them (1886)

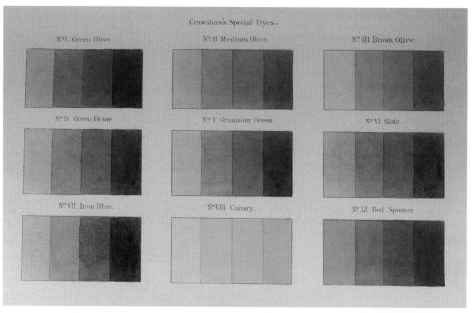

The Halford tying vise

Fredric Halford published in 1886 one of the great angling books, *Floating Flies and How to Dress Them*. No writer is so esteemed or so censured. Halford is the dry-fly historian (Waller Hills), the high priest (Overfield and Herd), the *eminence grise* (Bark), and prophet (Schwiebert). None of these titles, however, comes without reservation. The various controversies that engulfed Halford, often viewed as the apostolic authority on the dry fly, diminished when he concluded that each angling method, whether wet or dry, "is beyond doubt effective in its own particular streams and under circumstances favouring its use, and a considerable degree of science is attained by the earnest follower of both." Halford was more than a scribe for George Marryat's tying techniques. He drew from many sources (from people and from print) for his tying, including Alfred Ronalds, Henry Hall, G. Holland, and various professionals. Halford advocated the use of the tying vise; his improved vise had a table mount and a silk hook for twisting and waxing doubled silk for larger flies.

Halford was passionate about imitating the exact color of a natural. The Halford dyes, made by Messrs. E. Crawshaw of London, allowed any tyer to duplicate the precise colors of his patterns. Color plates of these dyes appear in his first work, *Floating Flies and How to Dress Them* (1886). His explicit *raison d'être* of a *Modern Development of the Dry Fly* (1910) was "an attempt to reproduce in the artificial flies the exact shades and tones of colour of the natural insects they are intended to counterfeit." In this work, Halford included eighteen color plates from the Société Française des Chrysanthémistes as a tying standard for his patterns.

Hand-colored block plate in *Floating Flies*. These dyes—developed by Halford and produced by Messrs. E. Crawshaw and Company, London—produced, when blended, "any of the shades given" for his patterns.

Floating Flies set a new standard in tying directions. Halford, according to the preface, worked closely with the printers and engravers to "convey accurately" his ideas. The engravings depict a *reversed* thread wrap; that is, they lap *over* the shank *toward* the tyer. This is not an error on the part of the engraver. "It may be noticed that in the diagrams of fly-dressing, the tying silk is lapped in the opposite (or what some might call the *left-handed*) direction. . . ." Halford concluded, "By proceeding in this way there is a natural inclination to pause and draw the silk down tightly when the hand is below the hook, and this is less likely to obscure the view of the work than with the more usual plan of winding the silk away from the operator." This direction also pulls any mistakes toward the tyer. The common wrapping direction conceals mistakes on the hidden, far side of the hook. The fly-tying engravings also deliberately exaggerated the size of the tying silk. "All the diagrams of fly-making are magnified, and in these magnified diagrams the relative thickness of the tying-silk is purposely exaggerated in order to give a clearer idea of the method, and the exact number of turns used."

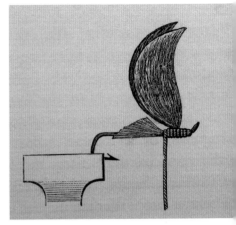

A *Floating Flies* engraving of the improved winging method.

Halford's Improved Method of Winging Upright Duns

Halford's exceptional talent is apparent in the design and range of his smaller mayflies, true flat-wing spinners and duns with stiff, supporting hackles and tails. According to Andrew Herd, Halford, who invented neither the dry fly nor the dry method, devised "a brilliant series of patterns which allowed his peers to fish imitative small dry flies right through the season." For these small patterns, Halford (perhaps with Marryat) presented a remarkable dun-wing method. This simple, practical method created a compact wing base while eliminating wing-barb separation. It remains as the best method for mounting vertical, symmetrical quill wings. This "efficacious mode" of winging makes the wings "float" above the hackle. The following drawings, based on the original engravings, change the thread direction to standard (right-handed) tying. The drawings depict single, rather than double wings. Double wings, usually tied for durability, have two quill panels on each side, creating four total wings.

> This is considered to be the latest improvement, and the most efficacious mode of setting on upright wings, whether double or single.
>
> Strip off entirely and discard the shorter plume of a pair of starling wing feathers, one right and one left. Pare the central quill running down the feathers as thin as possible with a pair of curved scissors such as are used by oculists. Cut through the quill of each feather at regular intervals, each being of the width required for a wing. . . .

First, carefully *split the stem* and remove the individual wing panels. For a foundation, I overwrap the forward third of the shank. Then select two matching wing panels. Cut them to width with *the stem sections attached*. The attached stems lock the barbs together during mounting.

Having worked the silk on close to the eye of the hook, detach one if single, and two if double wings from each feather; lay them with their points evenly one on the other, with the darker side outwards. Holding the wings, and, proceeding as usual, secure them at once in their proper position close to the neck of the eye, and take one turn behind the wings, and over the wire of the hook. . . .

Mount the matched wings with the base pointing forward and the front edge pointing up. Wing length should equal shank length. Pass two thread wraps over the wings to compress the barbs directly down on top of the shank. Although not so depicted in the engravings, I stack the wraps to create a *single* rotation point. Wide thread wraps create an awkward wing base. A single rotation point forms a miniature "base basket" that consolidates the wings. Then take one wrap *behind* the wings.

Set the stumps of the wings horizontally at right angles to the length of the hook, each stump or pair of stumps (according to whether the wings are single or double) on their proper side, and pull the tying-silk forward between them and under the hook-shank . . . .

Note that "forward" here—forward toward the fingers—means toward the hook bend.

Press the stumps tightly back, and bind them firmly behind the wings. . . .

Then fold the wing stumps (the stemmed bases) back on their respective sides and rotate the wing up. Rotate the wings forward to allow overwrapping the rear wing base.

Wrap the thread immediately against the wing base while erecting them. The wings now grow out of a "basket." Keep the basket base as small as possible. If a barb does separate, merely stroke it into position. For permanent wing formation, smear a *fine* strip of cement along the natural tip. Skues—in a 1944 letter appearing in *The Essential G. E. M. Skues* (1998)—refused to recommend varnishing the wing tips of split-winged floaters because "after a little while the wings tend to split up and to shred in a number of streamy fibres right and left."

Cut the stumps away diagonally to taper the body. . . . The remaining operations being then carried out precisely as described for the upright reverse-winged duns, complete the fly as before. . .

Finally, for a smoothly tapered underbody, trim both wing stumps diagonally and overwrap with flat thread. After mounting the wings, complete the pattern as desired.

1. Mount wings on hook shank.

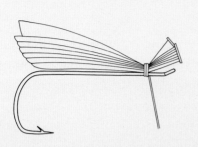

2. Fold wing bases aft and erect wings.

3. Wrap wing base immediately behind wings.

4. The completed dun wings

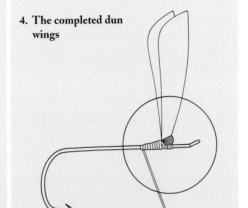

The Halford wing revisited

Charles Edward Walker

Old Flies in New Dresses (1898)

C. E. Walker's book explores wing position and he presented that first method of wrapping flat or horizontal wings. "What I have tried to do," he stated, "is to work out and bring down to a definite rule the position in which the wings of the imitations of the various kinds of flies should be placed." It is neither pattern nor the color that is wrong: it is the shape. "The wings of a fly undoubtedly play a most important part in forming the outline, and consequently the general appearance of the fly. Therefore, if they are not put on in the natural position, the whole contour of the imitation must be entirely different from that of the natural fly." Historically, Walker found that all patterns were treated like standing-wing mayflies. David Foster, in *The Scientific Angler* (1882), avoided the problem with a palmer: "The first thing to note when a strange natural is taken in hand to copy, is the position of the wings; as if it be 'flat-winged,' it may be dressed hackle, or palmer-wise, instead of being winged." Winging caddis and alder patterns was, according to Walker, the most difficult operation of all. The tying vise was common in the late nineteenth century. Walker conceded that the vise created the neater pattern, but hand tying allowed him to create flies anywhere at any time. What he needed was a hand method for mounting flat wings. He offered the reader a new method for mounting these wings.

After the wings are matched and stacked "delta" fashion, "The hook should then be taken in the left hand, and held by the bend between the first and second fingers, with the head pointing towards the right. The wings are then laid flat on the body with the right hand, and held there firmly with the left thumb. The wings are now tied in, the quill and the part of the fibres attached cut off close, and the head finished off."

When the left thumb and index finger holds the hook, there is no way to mount flat wings. Walker created an original solution. The traditional hold, between the thumb and index finger, does not permit mounting wings. He acknowledged that the vise creates a neater pattern. In fact, the Walker hold works well with a vise. With the left palm up, he secured the hook bend between the index and middle fingers, near the tips. His method works if you begin with palm up and use part of the index finger beneath the body to support the pattern during whip-finishing.

If Aelian's Macedonian pattern wore flat wings then we have come, in this small aspect, full circle. Now, however, the circle is larger and more enriched. It is odd that early observations of insects did not inspire imitations that were more accurate. The trout, evidently, did not demand it. At the *fin d'siecle*, Walker found an essential error in our tying. He hoped the reader would discover "a definite theory which is sufficiently plausible to interest him, at least for the moment." No writer can hope for more.

Delta stacked wing panels

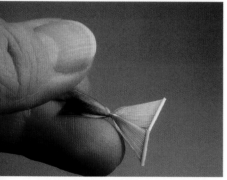

The Walker flat-wing hand position. The thumb presses down on the wings to position them.

C. E. Walker's artificial flies (detail)

George Edward Mackensie Skues

The Way of a Trout with a Fly (1921)

Long ago, I fished England's Highbridge waters of the Itchen with the late John French. What impressed me on that visit was not the trout that rose to the dry, rather that French had in his possession, though only briefly, Skues' slouched, cotton fishing bag captured in so many photographs. The past was closer than I thought. Skues was deeply indebted to Clyde and Tweed patterns and Stewart's tying methods. His patterns were not a challenge to the floating fly; they only added to the angler's arsenal.

Skues, steeped in tying scholarship, used the past to turn the wet fly into the nymph and, though not designated as such, the emerger. In *Side-Lines, Side-Lights and Reflections* (1932), he described the "untidy struggle" of eclosion (adult emergence) and its angling importance. "The up-winged dun, when it is once hatched out, is such a lovely, delicate, clean-cut little creature that one is apt to forget that at the moment of eclosion from the envelope which clad its nymphal form, it passes through a stage of untidy struggle. . . ." Skues compared this struggle to a golfer or footballer "extricating himself from a tight-fitting pullover." This is a very important stage for trout and angler. "Sometimes, indeed frequently, the operation of emergence is performed with neatness and dispatch. Often, however, it is an awkward and fumbling occasion, affording the fish a much longer and better chance than is given the dun which hatches neatly and quickly. At this stage the dun is something like the earth in the early stage of its creation, 'without form' if not 'void.'" This may be the reason why, he argued, trout take the Hare's Ear during an olive dun hatch; it imitates the struggling, crumpled-wing subimago. His best rationale, though, appeared with the sparsely dressed Yorkshire and North Country patterns. "Yet the contents of a trout's stomach floated in a white saucer will show the wings of duns reduced to mere dark shreds, which are strikingly like thin clotted strands of soft hackle." Skues concluded, "Nothing in nature occurs without good reason, and it may well be believed that the taking of nymphs at the fumbling stage of the hatch affords the true explanation for the taking of otherwise unnatural-looking soft hackled flies. It would be interesting to know whether in the early days of fly dressing any deliberate efforts were made to represent the natural fly at this stage of partial emergence. . . ." Skues' "fumblers" would become our emergers.

Transparency was another major topic for Skues. White sunlight penetrates or transforms the transparent and opaque parts of a floating insect. The resulting coloration, Skues believed, was a critical factor for tyer and angler. Skues achieved translucency by carefully selecting dubbing and silk colors. The importance of the base silk appears in *Minor Tactics of the Chalk Stream* (1910). His Yellow Dun, dubbed with primrose wool, only revealed its character beneath the surface. When dry, the tying silk hid, but when looking at the fly under the water, every silk turn was distinct and the dubbing, though scarcely noticeable, harmonized perfectly. Since Charles Cotton stepped into the threshold sunlight to reveal the covert color of dubbing, translucency has fascinated tyers. Ignited by the sun, Cotton's black dubbing burst into "shining red." Skues, who had read J. W. Dunne's *Sunshine and the Dry Fly*, recognized both the value and limits of translucency. In *Side-Lines, Side-Lights and Reflections* (1932), he concluded that "The argument in favor of translucency is in truth a counsel of almost unobtainable perfection. If it were obtainable it would, I agree, be desirable, but in practice it is not obtained very often."

Skues offered "another method for dressing nymphs" in Plate III. This method overcame the difficulty of estimating proper leg length. It also splayed the legs forward. "The variation has the added merit of making the legs stand out on each side in the most satisfactory way. Its defect is that it does not lend itself to nymphs tied with a gold or silver ribbing, as it has to be finished with an invisible whip finish in the middle of the body, just behind the wing cases." Having the legs stand out was important to Skues. In *The Way of a Trout with a Fly* (1921), he explained why he tied off *behind* the hackle. "The turns of silk behind the hackle make each fibre sit up and stand out, the fly has kick, and it will improve rather than deteriorate with use. Hackles with good natural resilience are, of course, essential." The pattern "is alive and struggling" and "has a fascination for the trout which no dead thing has." And good hackle, according to Skues, is tied in by the butt or stalk.

Method of Dressing Nymphs

Placing your hook—say, a Limerick No. 16—in your vice, begin whipping near the eye, and whip nearly half-way down the shank.

Tie in here, with point towards head of hook, a bunch of six or eight fibres of feather of suitable colour, regulating the length so that when the fibre is bent over to the eye of the hook and tied down there will be enough of the points left to be pressed out on either side to represent the legs.

Then pass the silk under the ends of the fibres of feather on the side of the bend of the hook, and whip on the bare hook to the tail; tie in two short, stout, soft whisks of suitable colour, tie in gold or silver wire, twirl on dubbing thinly, and wind to the place where the fibre is tied in; wind on the wire in regular spacing to the same point, and secure on the head side of the place where the fibre is tied in; thicken the dubbing, and wind over roots of feather fibre to head.

Then divide the points equally, and press backward from the eye; bring over the feather fibre to the head, tie it down with two turns, including a half-hitch, cut off the waste ends, and finish with a whip finish on the eye. Thus the legs are forced to stand out at right angles, or rather more backward, from the eye, and below the level of the hook shank, and the effect of wing cases is produced.

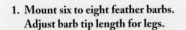

1. **Mount six to eight feather barbs. Adjust barb tip length for legs.**

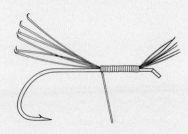

2. **Wrap thread to tail position. Mount tail, gold, or silver wire and sparse dubbing.**

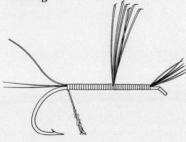

3. **Wrap dubbing forward to wing case and overwrap with wire. Secure dubbing and wire in front of wing case. Increase thoracic dubbing and wrap to head.**

4. **Divide and press the leg fibers down and back.**

5. **Fold wing case forward and overwrap twice, including one half-hitch. Trim excess and whip the head. Legs droop rearward beneath shank.**

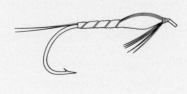

Another Method of Dressing Nymphs

Placing your hook in the vice, take two turns near the eye, tie down your bunch of fibres, which are to represent legs and wing cases, with the points toward the tail, with one firm turn, then bring the silk under the points close up against the last turn and pull taut.

Now press back the points firmly. They can be divided a little later.

For convenience, divide and separate leg barbs now.

Spin your seal's furs dubbing on the silk in just sufficient quantity to represent the thorax, and wind it on.

Then bring over the waste ends, which were pointing over the head, so that they point over the tail, dividing the points, which are to represent the legs, in equal portions to right and left. Tie down the fibres with two turns, and break them off, either singly or in groups.

Although Skues divides the legs now, most tyers will have divided them during the initial mounting of the thoracic barbs. Wrap silk to bend, secure required tails and mount dubbing.

Whip to the tail, tie in the whisks as before, roll on more dubbing, . . . whip to the wing case, clear the silk, and finish close up to the wing cases with a close, hard whip finish, into which a drop of celluloid varnish has been introduced, by placing it on the loop of the tying silk as it is being drawn taut.

After applying a bead of varnish to the *silk*, firmly whip-finish immediately behind the wing case. The bead of cement on the thread prior to whipping is remarkably modern and avoids a clogged hook eye.

With Skues we have a profound understanding of the insect and its imitation. And we have discovered a prevailing trend in tying history toward instructional clarity and specificity. The ancient audience of the *Treatyse* was limited and local—tyers had to make their methods and find their feathers. However, as the audience increased in size and distance, greater instructional detail and lucidity were required. As tyers grew, so did tying itself. Wisely, the early writers drew upon each other to increase knowledge and to complete the pursuit. Apart from the technical advances, there is little new in the modern tying text. The early tyer was as perceptive and creative as the modern tyer. Our clever patterns take fish, but there is always a clever fish. To our agony, trout eventually confound every tying theory and technique. The early tyers understood this and found a supreme pleasure in the search for solutions.

Skues also gives us the best conclusion, in *Silk, Fur and Feather*, to this historic tying chapter. He invited us to read freely, but do so with "wisdom and judgment." We should read to master the early methods and adapt them to our own creations. This glance at tying history reminds us, most of all, that the early artificial fly was always artful.

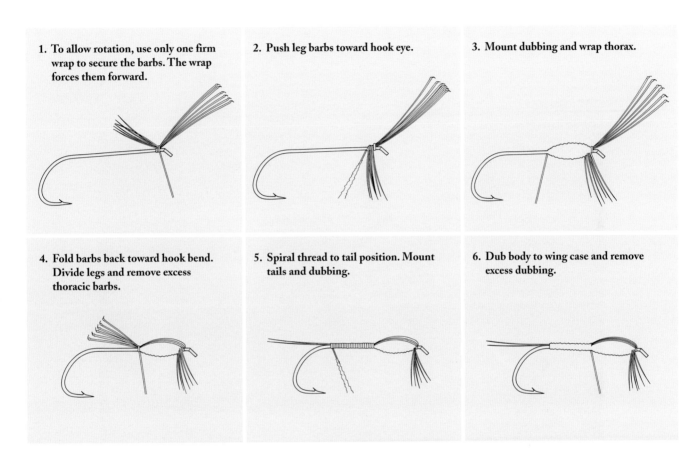

1. **To allow rotation, use only one firm wrap to secure the barbs. The wrap forces them forward.**

2. **Push leg barbs toward hook eye.**

3. **Mount dubbing and wrap thorax.**

4. **Fold barbs back toward hook bend. Divide legs and remove excess thoracic barbs.**

5. **Spiral thread to tail position. Mount tails and dubbing.**

6. **Dub body to wing case and remove excess dubbing.**

CHAPTER II

FLY DESIGN

The secret of optimum representation has still to be discovered.

—W. H. Lawrie, *A Reference Book of English Trout Flies* (1967)

FLY TYING IS A CREATIVE PROCESS WHERE EVEN FRAGMENTS of materials and ideas have value. The abundant materials, the profuse publications, the shelves of videos and books, the cadre of tying teachers and the World Wide Web make this the golden age of tying. Never has so much been available to so many. The modern tyer, often wrapping art as well as imitations, is remarkably skilled and informed.

The various parts of a pattern—such as tail, wing, body, and hackle—give form and function to a pattern. The perfection of a fly comes not from labored ritual but from harmony and subtle refinement. For example, if ribbing is perfectly uniform or tail fibers are abruptly flush, a pattern may appear flat or dead to the eye. Perhaps a pattern should present, as nature usually does, a balance of parts with casual, natural art.

I have never tied a perfect pattern. Every fly has an antic disposition, an errant fiber, or faulty wrap. I understand the frustration when tying faults "multiply like villainy." Yet there are things that bring perfection closer. A tyer should recognize that failure is part of apprenticeship. Recognize the faults, but do not tolerate them. If possible, unwrap the faults as they appear. Tying faults can sometimes lead to better solutions. Some methods are simple; some, complex. Collect tying methods as you would tying materials. Though there may be no single tying method for a particular pattern, there may be an appropriate tying sequence. When tying, always seek the simple and the strong. For accurate proportions, use thread wraps to mark the body sections on the shank. For example, mount the thread two eye lengths behind the hook eye: reserve this space for the forward hackle and the head.

A light, tentative hand often allows tying material to express itself. Some materials mulishly defy tying. Experienced tyers select materials that can be controlled, rejecting those that resist. Inexperienced tyers often select churlish materials and use gentle force. The experienced tyer has small secrets that control and master material. He may twist tighter and compress harder to subdue. He does not permit the material to assert its character. The tyer, not the material, is master. Be honest about your tying. You are the best critic. Some of my early patterns were miserable miscreants, matching nothing in nature or mind. And no matter how experienced, a tyer can always create a beast now and then.

Tying is both a craft and an art, depending upon whether the tyer is a craftsman or an artist. To a few, tying may be a fine art. Their wrapped artistry ends up on the wall rather than in the water. These tyers are sensitive to the vagaries of form, texture, and color. Their patterns meld sundry furs and fibers into an attractive whole. Other tyers may be satisfied with Woolly Worms and Griffith Gnats. Some tyers just think more than others think and enjoy the science and poetry of tying more. Yet these thinking tyers are seldom satisfied with their creations.

The clearest evidence of mastery comes from tyers who have thought hard and often about the past and whose work builds ingeniously but simply upon it. The excellence of a modern tyer is the mastery of the tying canon and the continual attempts to extend it. The tyer reads the rise triggers, the hook colors, the starburst of insect feet, the trout's window, and other theories that have tumbled down the stream.

Deformed and bizarre patterns catch fish, sometimes more often than skillful patterns. Trout apparently find beauty in the beast, and that is the classical tying conundrum. There may be a coarse beauty in some rough patterns; rough and buggy is not an error. John Younger, in *River Angling for Salmon and Trout* (1840), encouraged tyers to "mutilate the wings of your flies." This creates an effective spidery shape. Essential tying faults, however, should be scraped off. Don't tolerate mediocrity. We might argue that a homely pattern is more fascinating or that a tying fault, like the blemish of the beauty spot, only intensifies the pattern's charm. No matter.

Though you can tie a pattern any way you want, most tyers seek some approval of their creations. They want attractive and effective patterns, patterns that recognize the past, yet go beyond it. The following principles of tying are not dogma. Ignore them if you want, but recognize them. There are, obviously, exceptions to these principles. In most cases, however, there should be a rationale for the exception.

The Principles of Tying

The Tidy Head

Any exposed thread, such as head wraps, should be tidy and precise. Some tyers judge the head as a visual clue to the quality of thread-work buried beneath. Though the head may assume different shapes (such as the traditional taper, the saltwater bulb, or the truncated Catskill), all wraps should be precise.

The Proper Proportions

Although not absolute, tying proportions (the bulk and length of pattern parts) can breed a consistency in tying. There may be a reason why one proportion is better than another proportion. In any case, an experienced tyer selects a particular proportion and maintains it. Proportion is tied into the pattern as each part is added. If a mistake occurs, make corrections before continuing.

Proportion may embrace material placement—the placement of pattern parts on the hook. The inexperienced tyer often advances the pattern parts on the shank, producing a stunted body and a cramped head. He fails to anticipate the space required for the completion of the pattern. This is the placement—the start and finish of materials on the hook. The improper beginning and end (the "alpha and omega" error) creates awkward patterns. Perhaps the best solution is to constantly calculate the space left for the pattern parts. A soft-hackle fly may require only half a head space for hackle: a Humpy, half a shank length. Some tyers mark tying limits with thread wraps. For example, tying thread may mark and delineate the head space. This encourages the tyer to mount wings, body, and hackle behind the space required for the head. If a pattern has a particular mounting point (such as a nymph wing case at half-shank), a thread wrap can mark it. Experience finally solves this problem.

In addition, proportion includes the quantity, the bulk of material mounted. The amount is often based upon the particular pattern or tying preference. Experienced tyers usually err (if they must) on the side of sparsity. Sparsity, Sparsity, Sparsity. How many tail fibers does a dry fly require? Just enough to float the pattern and no more. A natural mayfly has only two or three tails. The fewer fibers used, the more delicate and realistic the pattern, but the less functional, in terms of floatation. The tyer must decide.

The Symmetry of Parts

This includes the balance and stance of such elements as the wing, tail, and hackle. For example, the cant or attitude of paired wings or outrigger tails should match. They should be mirror images. Hackle barbs might tilt forward at the same angle. Symmetry creates an appealing form.

The Materials Match the Method

Particular materials respond to particular methods in particular ways. An experienced tyer usually knows what methods match what materials. For example, different effects result when dubbing fibers are parallel or cross the thread. Experiment to determine what can and cannot be done with various materials and methods.

The Materials Match the Pattern

Know what is available and select the most appropriate material for a particular pattern. In the simplest terms, absorbent or heavy materials produce wet patterns. More subtle matches include transparency, buoyancy, texture, and iridescence. Material matching also includes selecting the most appropriate hook size, weight, and design. These previous two principles, four and five, will match the method to the pattern.

The Model or Paradigm

Some patterns re-create a particular historic tradition. There is pleasure in accurately replicating antique patterns. Years ago, Ted Niemeyer wrote a brief article on untying. Niemeyer wanted to know how certain historic patterns were constructed, so he slowly unraveled several flies tied by the masters. The untying exposed each lap and bind in the tyer's process. It revealed the skillful economy and placement of the thread's journey. Every fiber selected, every thread wrap had value calculated for an end. A master tyer seeks economy and simplicity in wrapping. Later, Niemeyer carefully retied each pattern. Though I would not recommend eviscerating an original Quill Gordon or Hewitt Spider, untying can teach. Fortunately, some early tying methods are extant and explained in print.

The Restricted Wraps

Each thread wrap should fuse and form the pattern. Delicate patterns come from few wraps and effective thread-work.

The Color and Color Harmony

Color is often based on caprice, tradition, or the natural. Although "the proper color" is often disputed, some colors add a subtle beauty. "The grand point," as H. C. Cutcliffe recorded in *Trout Fishing on Rapid Streams* (1863),

> in making flies is to have every part of the correct shade; it is not that all the fly, the body and the hackle, should be precisely the same colour, but there must be an harmonious blending of tints, and shading of colour; and in choice of our feathers we strive to heighten the tones of shading above the fur of the body as much as possible, keeping within the limits of general harmony, and carefully avoiding anything approaching a contrast of colours; there should be a richness, brilliancy, and variation in the aspect of our fly, so that when immersed in water, vivid shades may spangle amongst duller hues."

Subtle variations meld the separate parts into an attractive whole.

Fly colors are often examined when wet in natural, back-lit light. Color is, however, a paradoxical part of tying. Dr. Thomas Whiting, of Whiting Farms, notes "The visible range of colors humans see is comparatively unimportant to fish. The spectrum of colors we sense and appreciate is beautiful, in a gaseous atmosphere, but they do not transmit well through water, making the aquatic inhabitants understandingly insensitive to them. Under water the ultraviolet wave lengths of light transmit more effectively and so are more important to fish vision." He contends that "if fly tyers were expressly interested in creating flies whose *colors* attract fish, they'd be researching the ultraviolet image of the food insects fish eat, and with the aid of black lights trying to match their materials and designs to imitate the ultraviolet signature these insects present to fish." To illustrate the point, Dr. Whiting points out that a brown hackle—any shade, dyed or natural—turns black under ultraviolet light. Perhaps this suggests that hue (the color itself) is less important than value (the light-dark range of a color). Evidence indicates that trout perceive color and select food based on it. W. B. Willers, in *Trout Biology* (1981), indicates that certain color combinations, in natural light against a green-blue background, stimulate high consumption by trout: yellow-black, yellow-blue, and red-orange. In reduced light, the colors, in order of preference, were different: yellow, red, blue, and black. Frederick Gardner Johnson, in *Trout* magazine (1991), reports that "Trouts and other freshwater fishes generally have three cone pigments, as do humans" and that "Brown trout and rainbow trout also have a fourth type of cone that absorbs ultraviolet wavelengths . . . from which we infer that they see light wavelengths that are completely invisible to us." Research seems to indicate that trout see our colors as well as colors unseen by us. Color is important to fish under certain conditions and important to most tyers under all conditions.

The Quality Materials

Use the best quality materials possible. Quality materials and quality tying make a quality pattern. Although an experienced tyer is best able to create beauty from beastly materials, quality materials make quality patterns.

The Tying Tension

Material wraps—whether herl or hackle, flue or floss—should be tight and tidy. Tie with continuous tension. Materials should remain where mounted. Material creep—when materials move and migrate on the hook shank—can be solved with tight tying. Wrap near the breaking strength of the thread and learn when to flatten and when to "cord" the thread.

The Sequencing

Experienced tyers conceive spatially; they easily envision the tying sequence, the order of mounting and wrapping pattern parts. Proper sequencing makes complex patterns simple. Some winging methods, for example, may require that they are mounted first; other methods may require that the wings are mounted after the body.

The Thread

Thread material, color, twist, size or denier, and surface all influence the final pattern. Unless desired, thread wraps are hidden. There are two traditional exceptions: the head and dubbing. Thread colors may meld with *sparse* dubbing to create new colors. To obscure the thread, some tyers match the thread color to the dubbing or the wings when posting. There are, of course, some legitimate reasons for exposing the thread.

Most modern patterns have some traditional touch such as material proportions or placement. However, not all patterns have an historic exemplar. It may be a mental model or a specific insect that the tyer attempts to match. Most tyers eventually want to create their own patterns as well as their own methods. Often it is the thought behind the tying tactic that becomes as important as the pattern itself. Though a tyer may regard a specific insect as the object imitated, imitations always fall short. Every insect loses truth when converted to feather and steel. Sometimes an exaggerated element encourages the take. The four classical causes of any art object—the material cause (the materials used), the formal cause (the object imitated), the efficient cause (the artist or maker), and the telic cause (the purpose of the object)—modify the object made. The selection of materials, the insect imitated, the tyer's skill, and the pattern's purpose all inform and imprint a pattern. In the mid-nineteenth century, G. P. R. Pulman noted that it is impossible to dress a pattern delicately enough to match nature. It may be "necessary to exaggerate some part, so as to produce harmony and proportion in the general form." A single element then may override any principles of size, form, or color.

Testing the truth or effectiveness of a pattern is impossible. One pattern cannot take all fish under all conditions. We cannot cast the *same* pattern to the *same* trout at the *same* time under the *same* conditions. Every cast is a different test. Most angling writers list the various elements of imitation—size, presentation, color, and form. Yet, even here, the variables multiply like villainy. Anglers have always debated the importance and the order of the imitative elements. Although there is no definitive ranking, anglers usually accept the following, with minor changes:

The Floating Fly

1. Size
2. Presentation

   Sometimes presentation appears first. Color also sometimes ranks in the top three.
3. Form (Silhouette)
4. Buoyancy
5. Transparency
6. Color

The Submerged Fly

1. Size
2. Form (Silhouette)
3. Presentation (Movement)
4. Color

   Color may rank higher with the submerged fly than with the floating fly.
5. Transparency

Hatching flies have various "forms," even various "colors" as the hatch wanes. Furthermore, male and female ephemerids are usually different sizes. Presentation should include time, trout disposition (hunger, curiosity, or envy) and angling conditions. There is the hackle stance, the footprint (the imprint of the pattern on the water), and visibility (unseen is unsought) and, the opposite, camouflage (such as cloaking the spear and bend). Other elements might include buoyancy, transparency, weather, and water. In terms of buoyancy, a floating fly should float well and dry quickly. In terms of form, we may imitate the various stages of the hatch or the particular sex of the insect. There are variables within variables. Consider color: The position and quality of the sun influences color at any given time. Because color changes under varying light condition, it becomes a minor ingredient. Reflective surface light, reflective under-light and background color all influence the hue (the color) and value (the light-dark degree). But when fish key on small dark duns, color may become a major ingredient. For the meticulous feather artisan, such is the complexity of tying.

After the glance to the past, here then are the parts of the whole, the anatomy of a pattern. As we have seen, the early tyers defined and debated those pattern parts. Their theories and thoughtful wraps began this long journey. Tying continues to evolve and expand with greater understanding, new materials, and creative methods. When we dissect the fly, the parts seem greater than the whole. Each part demands understanding and a craft. The following illustrations may depict only a *specific part and method* and not a completed pattern. These theories and methods define, fundamentally, the fly.

The Tail

"Fly dressers have never really profited from the enormous mechanical advantages to be gained by a proper arrangement of tail fibers."

—Vincent C. Marinaro,
A Modern Dry-Fly Code (1950)

Like a vanishing Cheshire cat, we begin at the tail. There is more to tailing a dry fly than merely mounting fibers. The proper selection and mounting of tail fibers creates an attractive and functional fly. The tail, often the first thing mounted, defines the pattern—dun or spinner, dry or wet.

Selecting and mounting a tail, though fundamentally simple, requires some knowledge. A glance through tying history reveals that tails, usually called "whisks" or "wisps" by early tyers, come from a variety of materials. Stiff hackle barbs, wing covert feather barbs, rabbit whiskers, "hair from under the jams of a brown horse," have all served as tailing. Roger Woolley, a once-popular tying writer, noted that nothing imitates the tail of a natural like "the fibres from a good stiff cock's hackle, unless it be human hair."

In *Modern Development of the Dry Fly* (1923), Frederic Halford proclaimed, like G. S. Marryat before him, that the "gallina" (a term for domestic poultry and other birds, including pheasants, partridge, etc.) offers "the only feather fit" for mayfly tails. The tough barb is "in substance and appearance so similar to the setae for the natural insect." John Veniard's *Fly Dresser's Guide* (1952) praises the smoky-blue and white barbs from the guinea fowl's feather for tailing nymphs. In fact, neck, throat, breast, flank, and wing feathers all offer tailing barbs. Skues, in *The Way of a Trout with a Fly*, recommended the spade feather for drys. "A soft feather has advantages for a sunk fly intended to represent a nymph. But a bright, sharp, stiff feather undoubtedly assists floatation, and far better for the purpose than the saddle hackle so often used is the spade-shaped shoulder hackle of a cock of suitable colour in its finest fettle, especially for spinners."

H. G. McClelland, in *The Trout Fly Dresser's Cabinet of Devices* (1931), offers tails or whisks made from rat and rabbit whiskers. He also suggested that wing coverts, perhaps, produce the best fibers for dry tails. The finest tails that I have encountered have been the covert feathers of Elsie Darbie and the coq de Leon spade feathers from Spain. Only a few feather merchants market feathers especially for tailing. Long, stiff, barbed tailing feathers, in various colors, are available. Most companies point out that you will find all the tailing materials required from long cape hackles. Tailing comes from two places on a dry cape—the longer center hackles, and from the stiff side hackles. Side hackles often offer the best tailing barbs.

Some of the finest tailing barbs come from the coq de Leon rooster shoulder pelt (the humoral tract). These are long, stiff, straight, and substantial barbs. The translucency is especially evident by rotating the feather in the sunlight. The barbs reflect all the gathered light until they burst into subtle and rich shades. Due to their gloss and rigidity, coq de Leon barbs make exceptional tails. Many coq de Leon barbs have unique and dramatic markings, usually specks, flecks, spots, or blotches. The important reddish-brown *Pardos* are the *corzuno* (roebuck), the *sarrioso* (chamois), the *langareto* (meaning "long," possible reference to a natural fly or the long pale Naples yellow markings), the *aconchado* (conch shell) and the *flor de escorba* (broom bush). The *Indio* feathers range from chalk white to glossy black. The most interesting *Indios* are *negrisco* (gray to deep black), the *acerado* (steel or ash gray), the *avellanado* (hazelnut), the *perla* (pearl), and the *rubion* (ginger to reddish golden yellow). Developed over a hundred years ago, the coq de Leon is actually the oldest genetic feather produced for fly tying.

Today, tail materials usually include various body and tail hairs, guard hairs, feather barbs, and synthetic strands. Various materials may be used: lateral hackle barbs, long hackle barbs, wing covert barbs, coq de Leon spade barbs, stripped CDC (cul de canard) stems (for stonefly nymphs), stripped hackle stems (also for stonefly nymphs), calf tail hairs, calf body hairs, polar bear guard hairs, rabbit whiskers, moose mane, and moose hock. Other unusual fibers include nutria and mongoose guard hairs. The most popular synthetic tail fibers are Microfibetts, tapered watercolor brush bristles. Due to the slick surface of Microfibetts, some tyers lock the butts down by bending them back and securing them with overwraps of flat thread. To reduce bulk, fold the butts along the sides of the mounted stems. The "kink lock"—with wraps that abruptly kink or bend the fiber—traps synthetic and natural fibers with minimal bulk. Microfibetts, available in two diameters and various solids and barred colors, create excellent dun and spinner tails.

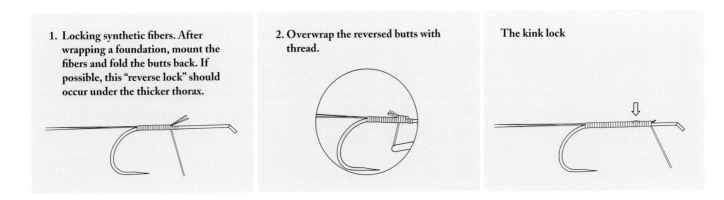

1. Locking synthetic fibers. After wrapping a foundation, mount the fibers and fold the butts back. If possible, this "reverse lock" should occur under the thicker thorax.

2. Overwrap the reversed butts with thread.

The kink lock

The Natural Tail

Most aquatic insects possess segmented, tail-like structures at the end of the abdomen, and although called by various academic names—cerci (singular, circus), caudal lamellae, caudal gills—they are all called "tails" by modern tyers. Insect tails have some unique and special functions. Some even function as gills.

Mayfly tails are usually long and slender. In some species there are two and in others, three. In most cases, the tails of a freshly hatched dun are short, but rapidly lengthen with age. Spinner tails are often conspicuously long. Spinner tails on naturals range from $1\frac{1}{4}$ to approximately $1\frac{1}{2}$ times the body length (including head). A few are short and a few are remarkably long. For traditional tying, spinner tails should be about $1\frac{1}{2}$ to 2 times the body length. In any case, tails probably should not exceed 3 times the body length. Longer tails—especially longer, stiff tails—may interfere with the take.

Insect tails may be boldly segmented and vary in color. Stonefly nymphs have two whiplike tails, often rapidly tapered or truncated. The stonefly nymph tails, which may vary significantly in length according to the species, often display distinct bands or rings.

The Function of the Dry-Fly Tail

A tail has four distinct functions. It aids floatation. It may attract fish through flash, color, or contrast. It imitates the cerci of the natural and, especially when splayed, it slows the descent of the pattern. The basic function, of course, is to support the pattern and imitate (in a general manner) the cerci of the insect. Tails may be added to patterns that imitate tailless naturals, such as adult caddis, to increase buoyancy.

Colonel E. W. Harding, in *The Flyfisher & the Trout's Point of View* (1931), clarified the function of the tail. "It is the whisks [tails] which balance and support the artificial fly on the water, so that the finest possible quality of fibre is required to form them and, in dressing of the fly, care must be taken that the whisks diverge symmetrically from the top of the shank." Colonel Harding's term "balance" embraces two meanings—aesthetic and mechanical. A tail should successfully integrate all pattern parts into a whole and successfully support the pattern upon the water. When Al Caucci and Bob Nastasi, in *Hatches* (1975), addressed tying their Comparadun patterns, they recognized the "balance and support" mechanics of the tail. "A very important factor in the creation of a good Comparadun is that the tailing fibers be of excellent quality. We generally use good dry-fly necks or saddle hackle for medium or small sized flies. However, the long fiber required for a #10 hook or larger is best acquired from the guard hairs of animal tails. Mink, woodchuck and badger are just a few of the animal tails we use."

The stiff outrigger tails, that cover more surface area and ensure a "cocked landing," are essential to the Comparadun patterns. A tiny fur ball divides the widely spread, outrigger tail fibers. A fiber that parallels the water has a greater surface area and, consequently, greater floatation force. For the same reason, the parachute hackle mount, using the same number of wraps, will float a pattern better than the traditional hackle mount. If you wish to improve floatation of a dry hackle, increase the barb length rather than the number of wraps. The greater length and flex of a longer barb pushes against more surface area. In addition, if you wish to improve floatation of the tail, merely spread and lengthen the tail fibers. Bundled tail fibers have a contradictory character—the tail bundle traps air for increased floatation while the bundle encourages the penetration of water through capillary action. In *Fly-Tying* (1940), William Sturgis advocated curling the tails upward by scraping "them gently on the top side with the thumbnail, or the back of a knife blade. In the same manner, they can be caused to diverge, which is preferable to having them in a compact bunch." Sturgis considered that only five or six barbs, if sufficiently long and stiff, are required for a tail. The total fiber area pressed against the surface may be as important to floatation as the number and specific gravity of the fibers.

The Tail Mass

Barb diameters vary from hackle to hackle. Thus, when mounting a stacked tail bundle, you should adjust the number of barbs according to the diameter of the feather barb and the size of the hook. Mount just enough tail to support the pattern and no more. When in doubt, leave some out. This produces a sparse, delicate tail more in keeping with the natural. Even early angling writers, such as Francis Francis and H. G. McClelland, recommended only two or three fibers. Two or three fibers could support a pattern on a dallying English chalk stream.

Perhaps the water determines the tail. Rough, heavy western waters may demand denser tails. Spring creek tails are often fine and few. W. H. Lawrie, in *All-Fur Flies & How to Dress Them* (1967), contended that the tails for floating artificials are important and deserve the same attention in selection and mounting as the hackle itself. Furthermore, he asserted that "It is very desirable—indeed essential that the rear-end of the dry fly be adequately supported above the surface, and to this end it is necessary to use fur-fibers of stiff, but not too stiff a quality, and to judge correctly their length and manner of tying on the hook shank. Obviously, too short a whisk will not serve, while too long a tail is unnecessary." In the proper mounting, the "fibers project straight out from the end of the hook shank—i.e., in no way 'cocked' upwards—and are spread fanwise as are the tails of natural insects." He believed that three fur fibers (guard hairs), the preferable whisks for "coloration and courage," properly mounted and spread offer sufficient support. To give complete and meticulous attention to the tails, he also advocated mounting and varnishing the tails as the first act of fly dressing.

For Lawrie, there was "no need for attachments of the 'shaving-brush' variety." He rejected the excessive use of material, especially the American practice of using "anything up to half a dozen whisks." Moreover, Lawrie failed to recognize the tail bundle as a possible suggestion of the dun shuck. Fast, steep waters usually require more tail fibers.

According to Vincent Marinaro, "Four fibres only, spread widely and maintained in that position, will support a size 14 to 20 fly better than a dozen fibres bunched together. The bunched fibres are all wrong, not only in practice, but in principle also. They cause capillarity, which makes them sodden and difficult to dry." Marinaro fished the Pennsylvania limestone streams, such as the Letort at Carlisle. A sparse tail was all that was required when "fishing the dry fly on quiet waters." On most waters, we can usually increase our rises by reducing the number of tail fibers. Furthermore, by keeping the tail bundle to a minimum, we suggestively shorten the pattern. A thick tail merely continues the body mass and may suggest a larger insect.

The Tail Length

According W. B. Sturgis and Eric Taverner, in *New Lines for Fly-Fishers* (1946), tail length is a critical component. Function and aesthetics determine tail length. "The tail extends beyond the wing but should not, except in dry fly patterns, exceed a total length of more than twice the gape of the hook, and preferably not more than one and a half. If these proportions are followed, the fly will have a neat, well-balanced appearance." Twice hook gap approximately equals the shank length on a Mustad 94840, a standard dry-fly hook. Most tyers accept the practice that both the wing and tail lengths equal shank length. A few early tying books equate wing length with hook length, rather than with shank length. H. Cholmondeley Pennell, in *Fly-Fishing and Worm Fishing for Salmon, Trout and*

Grayling (1876), sought to exaggerate rather than to diminish "all the prominent features of the natural insect, so that on a quick glimpse the resemblance may be unmistakable." He concluded that "This last observation applies also to the 'whisks' or tails, in exaggerating which there is an additional advantage, inasmuch as the larger the whisk the better and straighter will the fly swim." Surely there must be a point when the exaggeration destroys the imitation. In any case, here are a few traditional and creative options for tail lengths.

Dry-Fly Tail Length

Hackle-barb tail equals 2$\frac{1}{2}$ times the hook gap or equals shank length. To me, a slender tail "slightly proud" of the shank length carries and completes the form. Some drys seem to function better if the tail length falls somewhere between the shank and hook length or if the tail length equals the *hook* length. All tyers have their petty prejudices: that added smidgen of length appeals to my sense of proportion.

Wet-Fly Tail Length

The wet-fly tail equals $\frac{1}{2}$ shank length or the wet-fly tail extends to the rear extremity of the overwing, which is slightly beyond or proud of the hook bend.

The Nymph Tail Length

The nymph tail equals $\frac{1}{2}$ the shank length (stonefly and mayfly) or, for some patterns, $\frac{1}{3}$ the shank length.

Hair-Wing, Dry-Fly Tail Length

Hair tail equals 2 times the hook gap or $\frac{1}{2}$ to $\frac{3}{4}$ of the hook shank. The plumper hair tail intercepts the float line sooner, thus the hair tail is usually shorter than a standard dry tail.

The Streamer Tail Length

The streamer tail, if present, usually is either $\frac{1}{3}$ or $\frac{1}{2}$ to 2 times the shank length. In most cases, it should not exceed 3 times the shank length.

The Mayfly Spinner

The mayfly spinner tail generally ranges from 1$\frac{1}{2}$ to 2 times the shank length. In most cases, it should not exceed 3 times the shank length.

Tail length is not absolute. Tradition, the natural insect, or capricious decree may determine tail length. It is important to recognize that we need not duplicate the number or the length of an insect's tail to produce an effective fly. Some duns have extremely short tails; some spinners, extremely long tails. For example, the *Epeorus longimanus* spinner may have extremely long tails. And the *Tricory-thodes* spinner can have tails 4 times the body length or more. Even extended shucks function like a tail. Perhaps shucks should be about ¾ the shank length. This assumes that the insect (the shank length) is still partially cased within the shuck.

Aligning and Stripping the Tail Barbs

The novice tyer may have problems aligning and stripping the barbs from a hackle. When stripping tail barbs from a hackle, select a section of barbs that have negligible webbing at the base. The best tail barbs are those void of webbing when trimmed to length. Caress the barbs down toward the feather base to align the tips. With the tips aligned at a right angle to the stem, gather sufficient barbs between the thumb and index finger. Pull sharply to tear the barbs from the hackle stem. With practice, only minor adjustment—such as finger stacking—may be required before mounting the barb bundle.

Stacking the Tail Bundle

Most tyers stack the tail bundle to achieve a perfectly flush tail match. Sometimes, however, perfectly stacked tail tips may appear unduly abrupt, as though they were cut to length. This is especially true of tail fibers that have little or no taper. Always reject broken tail fibers.

Some hair stackers have a moderately concaved interior base that gently cups the tail tips for a more natural or aesthetic stop. When stacking, avoid any fibers that have fine terminal threads. These fine terminal ends may bend, misaligning the fibers. Such fibers—usually deer or moose body hairs—will not stack evenly. When aligning tail fibers in a stacker, use vertical taps to separate the fibers and 45° taps to gather them. Sharp, strong taps may even bounce the fibers into misalignment. Hairs with a significant crinkle, like calf-tail hairs, may require a large-bore stacker as well as some finger stacking to eliminate the overly long and short fibers.

The Hard and Soft Thread Mount

For a smooth underbody, the tail bundle may extend to the rear of the wing base. For patterns without wings, the tail may extend full shank, excluding the head space. When mounting soft, chambered fibers (such as deer hair), the first few mid-shank wraps should be tight and secure. This locks the fibers down. As the thread spirals back, the wraps should be less firm. The softer butt wraps gather the fibers without creating flare. The butt wraps must *form* without *deforming* the fibers.

Mount tail fibers either on top or on the side (especially for outrigger style) of the hook shank. Often a thread foundation on the hook shank assists in positioning the tails. Use soft-loops and pinch holds to prevent the tail fibers from

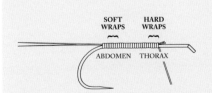

Soft and hard wraps. Place hard, firm wraps on the tail butts and soft wraps at shank end to consolidate the tail fibers.

rotating on the shank. Care should be taken when mounting or after mounting the tail that all subsequent wraps fall only on the tail supported by the shank. If the wraps fall on an unsupported tail, then the tail cocks down. J. Edson Leonard, in *Flies* (1960), actually advocates a downward tail. He recommends that the tail fibers should be "either parallel or bent slightly downward in dry flies." The slightly "drooping" tail posture possibly creates a spring or lever that supports the pattern; however, an excessive downward stance may, in fact twirl the pattern on its side.

The Underthread

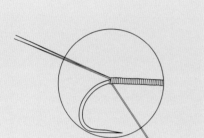

The raised tail float stance. A single underthread cocks the tails.

Sir Gerald Burrard, in *Fly-Tying: Principles & Practice* (1942), recommended that the tyer finish the wrapping with "one turn *under* the whisks—that is between the tail fibers and the hook. This will cock them up and make them look "jaunty." This jaunty profile, though, adds nothing to conventional floatation. It would be better, surely, if the tails extend *in line* with the hook shank. The tail would then bestow better support for the hook. This jaunty profile may be an attempt to force the butt down in imitation of the attitude or stance of particular mayflies or emergers. A jaunty or raised tail posture may prevent the tail from wrapping around the bend; however, "tail wrap" is usually the result of mounting extremely soft tail fibers or positioning the tail too far forward.

More recently the underthread is sometimes used to splay the tail fibers. Walter Dette, the famous Catskill-style tyer, occasionally took a turn of thread under the tail to create a slight spread for better floatation. Burrard also noted, and correctly, the "classic" cardinal sin of tying tails: "The chief point to make sure of is that there is no hiatus between the whisk and tail end of the body and the individual turns of the body." In short, the tail should extend from the body without gaps or exposed thread.

The Tail-Loop Method for Divided Tails

Various tying methods split and divide spinner tails. Doug Swisher and Carl Richards, in *Selective Trout* (1971), recommended a dubbing tuft to separate the split tails of female spinners. For durabililty and buoyancy, they used two barbs on each side. They also advised, for improved floatation, that the tails spread a full 45° to the hook shank. According to Vincent Marinaro's *A Modern Dry-Fly Code* (1950), figure eights of thread should split and lock the tails. A drop of cement at the base secures the forked position. Marinaro believed that even thoracic patterns, where "the tail fibers seldom touch the water," require outrigger or split tails "to act as governors," ensuring the proper stance upon the water.

The tail-loop method, which most tyers find niggling, also symmetrically splits and splays tails for duns and spinners. After mounting the tails directly on top of the hook shank, loop a length of fine tying thread under the hook bend. With a

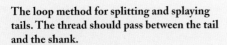

The loop method for splitting and splaying tails. The thread should pass between the tail and the shank.

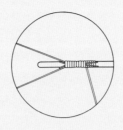

Top view: Fold thread ends forward and capture with working thread.

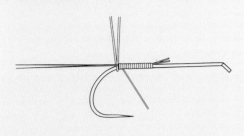

dubbing needle or the thread loop itself, divide the tails and pull the loop up *between* the tail fibers. Fold the looped thread forward, separating the tail fibers. Capture the looped thread (on the top of the hook shank) with three *flat* wraps of the tying thread. Make further tail adjustments by pulling either thread strand or by pulling the double strands of the thread loop. Trim the thread loop closely. Remember to overwrap the loop only three times with a flat thread (a counter-spun thread) to avoid bulk.

Some tyers fold a single thread (mounted on top of the hook shank) between the tails to spread them. When lightly dubbed, the tails spread. Try dubbing an egg sack that will splay the tails. In this method, carefully calculate the tail butts and thread mount points to achieve symmetry.

Marrying Tails

When mounting divided barb tails, a single barb on each side may be too sparse. When two or three barbs are mounted on each side, seldom will all the fibers be in alignment. One method that I have found produces "married" tails. First, mount two or three barbs as outrigger tails on each side of the hook. Then touch each tail with a smear of flexible cement. Press the barbs together and spread the cement slowly along each tail section forming a single, fused tail. Each tail section becomes stiffer and thicker, while retaining its outrigger stance. Cement does add a modicum of weight. Other tyers fuse each tail section with a smear of high-tack wax. The wax, although not as durable as cement, does improve floatation.

So ends the tale of a tail. Though often casually dismissed, the tail is important. Not only does it imitate a significant part of some insects, but it also may serve a function. The proper selection and mounting of tail fibers creates an attractive and functional fly. The pattern becomes a nymph or an emerger, a dun or a spinner, a dry or a wet. All depends upon the tail. Like the Cheshire cat, if the tail is properly finished, there is only a grin left.

The Wings

> The Wings of a fly undoubtedly play a most important part in forming
> the outline, and consequently the general appearance of the fly.
>
> —Charles Edward Walker, *Old Flies in New Dresses* (1898)

Wings—delicate and seductive wings—may be the only reason why some trout rise. There are complete books devoted to wings and winging. Charles Walker's *Old Flies in New Dresses* (1898) focused on mounting wings in the natural position. His explicit thesis was "to work out and bring down to a definite rule" the wing positions of the various imitations. For Walker, "if they are not put in the natural position, the whole contour of the imitation must be entirely different from that of the natural fly." He failed to acknowledge stillborn duns with emergent or trapped wings—the "captives and cripples" of Doug Swisher and Carl Richards in *Selective Trout* (1971). Walker then cataloged the various wing positions of the naturals and the various winging methods. To him, the winged profile was far more important than pattern color.

Antique fly patterns, imitating the natural, often wore wings. Though wings are not always required, they do somehow seem to complete many patterns. Usually, wing length equals shank length on duns. Caddis and grasshopper wings extend beyond the hook. Immature wings, such as those on nymphs and emergers, are shorter. David Foster, in *The Scientific Angler* (1882), claimed that the wings "should be about the length of the hook, thus a little longer than the body. . . ." Some patterns do seem better balanced and more realistic with wings slightly proud of the shank or body length. Colonel E. W. Harding, in *The Flyfisher & the Trout's Point of View* (1931), would readily replace the traditional quill wing with a wrapped hackle. There was, according to Harding, "a large and successful school of fly fishers who question the necessity for winging a fly at all." Moreover, a hackle could become wings: "A hackle of a colour and density which represents the combined effects of the legs and wings of the natural fly is considered to represent the fly more accurately on the water and makes the fly lighter in weight and easier to fish." Nonetheless, he reluctantly added, "but it seems to me that there are occasions when the general silhouette and colour effect of the wings can be obtained in no other way except by direct representation of wings in the conventional manner." Today, the conventional manner includes methods beyond the quill panel. Like most tyers, I would rather wrap hackle than mount matched wings. However, some wing methods are attractive and functional. Moreover, some methods make winging as simple as wrapping.

Colonel Harding noted the critical problem in spinner imitation: "The suggestion of outspread wings is essential for a spent spinner pattern and how to obtain it is one of the most difficult problems in fly dressing." He rejected hackle-tip wings: they fold beneath the bend and, when wet, become useless for support. Despite Colonel Harding's censure, hackle-tip wings—when properly selected

The Wings

1. The double-hackle dun mount. For a low-floating pattern, select short "leg" barbs.

2. The Double-Hackle Dun

3. The Double-Hackle Spinner

and mounted—neither wrap around the hook bend nor sink readily. In any case, for transparent spinner wings, Harding wrapped double hackles. "In using two hackles, the first is wound and adjusted to simulate wings, the under fibers being cut away and not more than three turns of the second hackle." This method may have variations for both dun and spinner.

First, mount the "leg" hackle (barb length equals ¾ shank length). Then mount the "wing" hackle (barb length equals shank length). Wrap a dense "wing" hackle, secure, and trim excess. Next, carefully clip all underbarbs. Finally, wrap the "leg" hackle through the wing barbs, secure, and trim excess. With standard hackles, the darker underbarbs melt into the paler wings. Any wing-leg color contrast can be used. When wrapping hackle through hackle, do not avoid barbs by *weaving* through them. Merely match the barb stance of the wing hackle with the leg hackle and then ignore the barbs as you wrap the leg hackle forward. Trapped or bent barbs usually snap back into place. Wrapping two different colored hackles creates a soft and subtle blend that appeals to both tyer and trout.

With modern microhackles, this method also creates the swollen thorax of small spinners and duns. For double-hackle spinners, trim both top and bottom of the wing hackle and then wrap a short-barbed hackle to suggest the legs and thicker thorax. Hackles with a dark center list, such as a badger or furnace, create the illusion of a larger thorax. The thorax-leg hackle also increases buoyancy and visibility.

The Fan Wing

Usually regarded as annoying and niggling, mounting fan wings challenges many tyers. Furthermore, finding quality fan feathers may also pose a problem. The small, white breast feathers (the pale contour feathers) of the wood duck and Mandarin duck are traditional, as are the small, mottled breast feathers of the mallard. Try this method for mounting fan wings for various patterns.

The Fan Wing

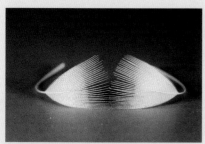

1. Wrap a thread foundation for the wings. No matter what the pattern, mount the wings first. Select two breast feathers that have a modest stem curvature. Reject those that have twisted or splayed barbs. The feathers should match in curvature, width, and length. Feathers that grow in close proximity on the bird match best. Strip surplus barbs so that the wing length matches shank length. Fan-wing width, at the widest point, is approximately the hook-gap span. Leave stems long for mounting. Sometimes it may be necessary to flatten thick stems prior to mounting. Merely flatten thick stems with small pliers.

2. Stem curve (often an extravagant curve) prohibits gluing the stems together. After sizing and matching the feathers, place a *small* dot of cyanoacrylate *gel*, such as superglue gel, at the base of feather as illustrated. Apply the gel "micro" dot with a fine needle. Avoid the thinner, "wicking" cyanoacrylate glues: thin cyanoacrylate glues, through capillary action, will invade the wing barbs.

3. Next, carefully join the two wing feathers—convex side to convex side—and set them aside to dry. The flat barb base keeps the wings aligned and parallel.

4. When dry, "saddle" the wings on the hook shank: straddle a stem on each side. Mount the wings with figure-eight wraps (fore and aft) over the stems. Each wrap should capture both stems on their respective sides.

5. After securing the wings, trim the stems to about ⅛" and fold them back. Lock the wings with several tight wraps over the stems.

6. Finally complete the pattern with tail, body, and hackle. The following pattern is a fan-wing quill. Though fan wings are not as popular as they once were, they are attractive and, with this method, charmingly simple.

The Rolled and Divided Wing

The rolled and divided wing is antique. Rolled wings, also known as bunched wings, are merely barb fibers or hairs matched, bundled, and mounted. Rolled wings are often mounted as a single wing on smaller patterns or divided, paired wings on larger patterns. Match or stack the natural tips to display a sharp wing profile. J. Edson Leonard, in *Flies* (1960), advocated rolling soft breast feather barbs back and forth between the fingers to quash their natural lay. Roll *gently*, however, to avoid twisting or bending the barbs.

The Rolled and Divided Wing

Long, soft barbs—such as wood-duck breast feathers—do not stack well. The best method for aligning the natural tips is to remove a few barb "panels" at a time. Then carefully align the natural tips by gently rocking or pulling the panel with the fingers. Finger-stack several tip-aligned panels for mounting.

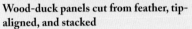

Wood-duck panels cut from feather, tip-aligned, and stacked

A winged wood-duck quill pattern

Reverse-mount the bundled wing, i.e., butts face aft and natural tip over the hook eye. Wing length should equal shank length. Securely mount the wing butts, and erect the wings with "fore-wraps" pressed against the wing base. Then divide the wings with figure eights. Finally, complete the pattern with tail, body, and hackle.

The Hackle-Tip Wing

Mounting hackle-tip wings for the ubiquitous Adams and its relatives requires a modified method. Select grizzly hackles that are rectangular with contrasting bands. The softer hen hackles are easily mounted and often have full width at their tips. This makes an attractive wing, unlike the more common pointed and tapered cock hackles.

If proper wide-tip hackles are not available, wings may be burnt from soft hen or cock capes. Hen grizzly hackle, especially the larger hackle, usually lacks the narrow, close bands or bars common in the smaller cock hackle. Whenever possible, always select those hackles that have narrow, contrasting bars and straight stems. For a shaped wing, merely position the hackle within the wing burner and, with a propane lighter, remove the excess. When burning grizzly hackle, I usually position the hackle to create a black band at the tip. This gives a natural "terminal" to the tip. This arbitrary bias perhaps comes from the standard feather. *British Poultry Standards* defines the Plymouth Rock male hackle: "barring practically straight across feather, sound contrast in black and blue-white, barring and ground colour in equal widths, and barring carried down underfluff to skin. Tip of feather must be black." In any case, if one wing tip is black and the other white, the wings appear awry. So much for foolish consistencies. Mount the shaped wing in the same manner as a natural hackle wing.

Hackle-tip wings may be mounted spinner style. J. Edson Leonard advocated a *vibrator* mount: "Hackle tips cocked so far forward they are nearly parallel with the shank, thus vibrating when the fly is set in motion by either the current or the retrieve." A secure spinner mount comes from Major Sir Gerald Burrard's *Fly Tying: Principles & Practice* (1945). The wing stems cross the shank. Figure-eight wraps hold the wings in place. Cement the crossing and, when dry, fold the stems

The Hackle Tip Wing

1. First, select matching (length and width) hackles. Remove those barbs not required for wing length and width. For most patterns, wing length equals hook-shank length.

2. Place a drop of cyanoacrylate *gel* at the *barb base and stem*. Quality cape hackles are usually flat, thus the stems may be cemented together. The gel should just enter, rather than invade, the barb base. Set the wing assembly aside to dry. When dry, place the doubled stem on top of the hook shank at the wing position. Note that the double stems form a shallow furrow that positions the wings on the hook shank. When mounting the wings, position the natural tips to the right (over the hook eye) and firmly overwrap.

3. Finally, fold the wings back to erect them and place three or four wraps in front to retain stance. Complete the pattern.

forward and secure. It may be best, however, to flatten the stems before mounting and, after mounting, fold them *back* to become the underbody of the thorax.

The Wing Burner

A wing burner is a metal template that holds feathers or fabrics so that a flame, usually from a butane lighter, burns the surplus, thereby forming a shaped wing for fly tying. Wing burners come in a variety of shapes for mayfly, dragonfly, damselfly, stonefly, and caddis wings. Some burners create sized and shaped wings for nymphs as well as adult patterns. Wing *burners* offer several advantages: (1) a wide variety of sizes, (2) realistic shapes, and (3) no blades to dull. In contrast, wing *cutter* blades eventually dull and deform the feather.

For some patterns, commercial wing burners are either the wrong shape or the wrong size. To solve this, I often make wing burners by modifying commercial burners or by shaping brass strips. Depending upon the template size required, brass strips, in various lengths and thicknesses, are available from most hobby or hardware stores and catalogs. Brass strips—½" or ¼" wide and .032" thick—make excellent burners for wings, legs, and other pattern parts. Thinner strips, such as .016" thick, form more easily, but bend or deform readily. Shape the burners with metal shears, files, and grinders. **Note:** Remember to use protective eyewear and dust mask when shaping metal.

The Wing Burner

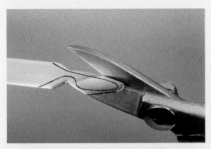

1. First, draw the desired wing shape on one end of the brass strip and then rough-shape the template with metal shears.

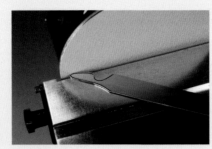

Cutting disks also quickly shape the template.

2. With files and grinders, take the metal down to within a couple of millimeters of the final desired shape. A small Minimite Dremel tool, mounted with ¼", ⅜", and ½" cap or drum sander/grinder works well in this close shaping. Select fine or extrafine grit grinders.

3. Finally, bring the template down to final form with the Dremel and disk grinder. Polish when done. Grinders may heat the metal. If required, cool the metal by water immersion. Make certain that both template ends accurately match. Sometimes I inscribe a stem-line on both sides of the burner for wing replication.

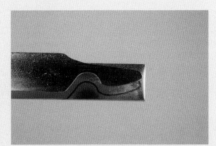

4. Once the template is close-shaped, fold and match both ends together. I generally fold the strip so that the burner is approximately 4" or 5" long. Short wing burners index or match better than long ones. Now, firmly tape the folded strip to match the ends for final shaping. Then, trim and rough-cut the matching end.

5. Wing burning

For the Adams' wing, I make a rather narrow wing shape with a slightly advanced wing tip. A narrow wing resembles a hackle-tip wing (rather than a natural wing shape) that reduces casting flutter and drag. A single wing burner may accommodate two or more hook sizes. I also use burners to make delicate, wispy CDC wings. These wings float well and neither spin nor plane during the cast.

An excellent CDC spinner wears a stripped-quill body and CDC wings formed with a wing burner. Though not as durable as some spinners, the stiff stem and splayed barbs do float the pattern well. After mounting the wings, merely insert CDC barbs in a split-thread loop, spin, and figure-eight for hackle. This creates a gauzy and graceful spinner. Like some natural spinner wings, the CDC barbs imprint the surface with minute bubbles and sparkles.

For wing burning, select patterned hen feathers that have the barbs at right angles or nearly so. Acutely angled barbs may burn through at the base, resulting in a truncated or angular wing. Match the wing-burner base with the barb angle.

This creates an off-center wing stem and avoids a truncated wing base. When making or selecting a burner consider these following features:

1. An appropriate wing size and shape
2. A well-matched template edge for clean, sharp wings
3. A proper metal thickness to prevent warped or fuzzed wing edges
4. An adequate length for cool handling
5. A secure clamping of the feather
6. A template design that allows for various stem angles for dun, thoracic dun, and spinner wings.

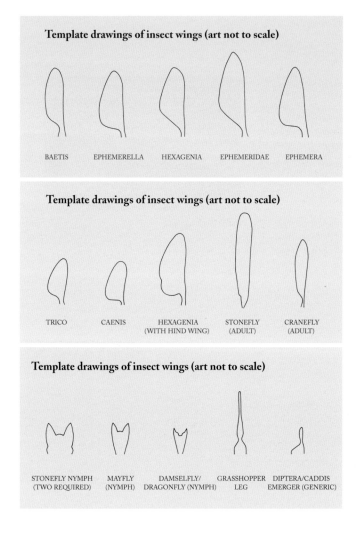

Template drawings of insect wings (art not to scale)

BAETIS   EPHEMERELLA   HEXAGENIA   EPHEMERIDAE   EPHEMERA

Template drawings of insect wings (art not to scale)

TRICO   CAENIS   HEXAGENIA (WITH HIND WING)   STONEFLY (ADULT)   CRANEFLY (ADULT)

Template drawings of insect wings (art not to scale)

STONEFLY NYMPH (TWO REQUIRED)   MAYFLY (NYMPH)   DAMSELFLY/ DRAGONFLY (NYMPH)   GRASSHOPPER LEG   DIPTERA/CADDIS EMERGER (GENERIC)

Some completed wing burners. From left to right: shaped mayfly wing, dragonfly nymph wing pod, hackle-tip wing, grasshopper hind leg, caddis pupa wing, and crane fly wing.

Burnt CDC Spinner wing

A Burnt-Wing Quill

Imitating the precise wing shape is seldom, if ever, required. Wings, however, can distinguish (by size and shape) one insect from another. In that regard, wings may be critical. Insect families often have distinctive wing shapes: the small circle wing (*Caenidae*); the small, elongated oval wing (*Baetidae*); the medium, elongated oval wing (*Ephemerellidae* and *Leptophlebiidae*); the medium triangle wing (*Heptageniidae*); the large triangle wing (*Ephemeridae* and *Potomanthidae*), and so on. Some insects, such as the *Ephemeridae*, have a large hind wing that is best incorporated into the forewing shape. Though most tyers use a generic wing shape, specific burners create specific wing shapes. Size, however, is generally considered more important than the specific wing profile. The shapes opposite replicate some standard insect wings.

Grasshopper Legs

In addition, brass burners can create other body parts. The most realistic grasshopper legs are burnt yellow grizzly hackles. The grizzly banding creates a realistic leg. Insect legs, such as those of the grasshopper, are easily burnt. Some judicious trimming may be required to slim and match the legs. Once shaped, bend the legs as illustrated.

Dubbing Teaser

A brass dubbing teaser, merely a brass handle with a narrow extension and a Velcro™ hook patch, combs and shapes dubbed patterns. First, shape the dubbing teaser the same way as a wing burner. After polishing the handle, apply the adhesive Velcro™ hook patch to the narrow extension. Trim the excess Velcro™ to create the teaser. To fluff a pattern, merely pet or caress the dubbing with the Velcro™ hooks. Use the opposite side of the dubbing teaser to apply the proper amount of wax to a thread or dubbing loop. A broad blade controls the amount of wax applied far better than a wax tube. Clean the wax blade after use.

Sometimes, wings can be a trigger to a rise. Brian Clarke and John Goddard, in *The Trout and the Fly* (1980), identified "the star-bursts of light created by the indentations of the feet of the dun floating in the surface" as the first trigger to

A burnt-leg grasshopper

The wax blade and dubbing teaser

the rise. "There is a second trip-mechanism: the *wings* [*sic*] of the fly." The "flaring of the wings over the edge of the window" may encourage a trout to rise. "It is largely because of this flaring effect that we believe that wings in floating flies . . . can be helpful when addressing sophisticated trout." Moreover, wings often complete a pattern. Michael, my son, recently recalled a recurring dream:

> As we drove through the desert, Dad lectured on the advantages of winged patterns, but I was more intent upon visions of rising trout. After hours of highway, we turned onto a dry track. Heavy dust swirled and floated behind us. Soon, Dad pulled off the track and parked, waiting for the dust to settle. Quickly armed with rod and vest, he said there was no need for waders. We made our way through scrub and channeled scabland down to a dry, ancient riverbed, scattered with rocks white in the sun. Dad tied on a winged Dust Devil and made a cast. The fly settled lightly on a rock. He slowly pulled it off onto the sand. Suddenly, dust and rocks exploded as a fish—half grayling and half mudskipper—struck the fly. Dad quickly landed the fish. Grinning, with fish in hand, he turned and said, "Now it's your turn."

Perhaps delicate, seductive wings can even make a fish rise through dust and rock in an ancient streambed. Dreams are part of fishing, and daydreams surely are part of fly tying.

The Body

> In making Dub-flies, chiefly observe and imitate the Belly of the Fly,
> for that colour Fish most take notice of, as being most in their Eye. . . .
>
> —James Chetham, *Angler's Vade Mecum* (1700)

Body material and body methods offer the greatest creative scope in fly tying. There are more materials and methods for tying bodies than for wings, tails, and hackles combined. The curious and creative tyer will experiment with various body materials and methods. Though the insect body consists of the head, thorax, and abdomen, it is the latter, often dramatically segmented and distinctly colored, that is the most conspicuous to tyer and trout. For the tyer, the abdomen is the body. Surely, it deserves close and careful imitation.

The Insect Body

An insect body, typically the longest of the three parts, consists of dorsal plates (tergites) and ventral plates (sternites) bounded or connected by membranous channels (sutures). The abdomen, often dark on top with a pale underbelly consists of eight to eleven body segments separated by the sutures.

Some patterns duplicate only the paler underbelly of the insect. The darker top, being less visible to the trout, is often ignored. Many modern patterns also ignore the color variance of the thorax. Saltwater and streamer patterns may have head colors that imitate the naturals. Some insects have prominent and colorful eyes. A few early tyers advocated that the thread color match the eye color. Depending upon the materials and methods, most bodies are tied with a slight taper increase. For a smooth, neat body, the base materials, such as ribbing tags or tail butts, should extend the complete length of the shank. This avoids cracks and knobs in the overbody. Tinsel, herl, hackle, and thread all make attractive and effective bodies. Ribbing roughly imitates the suture, though ribbing spirals forward with fewer bands than the natural. In the insect world, all legs are located on the thorax. If we were tying "truth," only six hackle barbs would form the legs and eight or nine, nonspiraling ribbing bands would duplicate the sutures. But tying is not truth; it is impressionism.

The imitation of an insect body includes several factors: buoyancy, transparency, color, color contrast, durability, weight, texture, and simplicity of construction. Early tyers used a variety of materials, such as cork, balsam, quill, raffia, mohair, gut, feather barbs, clipped hackle, hackle stems, stripped or flued peacock herl, horsehair, India rubber, silk, wool, chenille, fur, and hair. Many of these materials are still used by the modern tyer. Though the body is seldom regarded as critical for floatation, it may offer, in fact, as much buoyancy as the hackle. Judiciously select body materials for drys: proper material turns a brief drift into an extended one.

Perhaps the most unusual bodies appear in William Blacker's rare and beautiful *The Art of Fly-Making, &c, Comprising Angling & Dyeing of Colours* (first edition, 1843). "Gold-beater's skin rolled over flat tinsel" sheathes one body. His "winged larva" body is made from the shriveled sack found at the end of raw silk gut. Golden pheasant tippet barbs whipped to the sack create tails. The "larva" is mounted, detached fashion, immediately behind the hackle. Blacker noted that "There is nothing can exceed the beauty of these flies . . . ." This curious, attractive pattern, however, must have been a challenge to tie and rather fragile. Consult Chapter I for an illustration of Blacker's Winged Larva.

David Foster, in *The Scientific Angler* (1882) offered one of the earliest and most comprehensive analyses of the fly body. "To distinguish the correct colour of a fly as presented to the fish, we know of no better method than to place it in a clear glass of water, and hold it between the eye and the light in such a position as to be able to see underneath the insect." Seen from the trout's point of view, the precise body color and translucency are apparent. But the dead opacity of some body materials defeats any attempts at proper color translucency. After Foster, the quest for the perfect body expanded. Even the so-called imitationists, such as Halford, wished, within the confines of his chosen materials and methods, to imitate only two features of the insect's body—color and size. And for Halford, wing and body color was supreme.

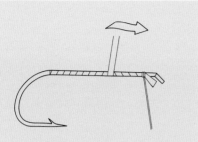

The tinsel body: Slide tinsel toward the eye until it clicks into place.

The Tinsel Body

Often an unsightly lump occurs when tinsel is tied in at the rear and then wrapped forward. To avoid this, first mount the thread at the shoulder. Do not lay down a thread foundation. With three thread laps anchor the end of the tinsel and—with smooth, taut turns—wrap the tinsel to the tail. Then reverse the tinsel and advance back to the shoulder, near the mounting point. When wrapping, slightly overlap each turn and then, with added tension, force the tinsel to slip over the edge of the previous wrap and "click" into place. You will actually hear the tinsel snap into place. This produces tight, touching wraps. After wrapping forward, hold the tinsel end and carefully undo the initial three thread wraps. Next, capturing both tinsel ends with the thread, rewrap three times over both ends. This creates a remarkably smooth, slender, taut tinsel body held with only three wraps.

For fine control, select narrower tinsel than recommended for the pattern. Narrow Mylar tinsel is more elastic and more maneuverable than wide tinsel. Narrow tinsel makes neater patterns and cleaner turns, especially when reversing the wraps or when wrapping into hook bends.

The Stripped Peacock Herl Body

First, check to see that the selected herl has a contrasting dark edge. These are found within the eye of the peacock tail. The eyed herls show a larger proportion of the pale ground and a finer, darker edge strip. Peacock eyes may be checked by turning the eye over and pressing the eye herls flat against a surface. The paler the herls, the darker the edges. There are various methods for removing the "metallic" flue, from hot wax baths to eraser scrubbing. The best method, however, is simple and swift. First, select a soft, high-tack tying wax. Then lay the tip of the herl across the wax and draw the herl, from tip to base (opposite flue growth direction), along the wax. Do this two or three times; then, with the fingernail moving the same direction, scrape the flue off. The modern high-tack waxes make this possible. The result is a clean, waxed stripped herl. Label and set aside a super-soft, high-tack wax, such as Loon Tackle Swax or Wapsi Premium Dubbing Wax, expressly for this purpose.

To wrap a stripped herl body, snap off the tender herl tip. Pulling, rather than cutting, breaks the tip at the naturally weak point. Then lay the herl along the shank, extending about to the shoulder. With fine, flat thread, mount the slender tip first to take advantage of the herl's natural taper. As the flat herl wraps forward, the herl becomes wider and fuller. When wrapping the herl forward, the dark stem-edge should face aft, creating a finished body edge. To strengthen a stripped herl body, lacquer or counterwrap with fine wire.

The Clipped-Hackle Body

In *Fly-Tying: Principles & Practice* (1945), Sir Gerald Burrard advocated the clipped-hackle body for dry flies. First select a hackle of the proper length. Stroke the barbs toward the base to erect them; then, with long, sharp scissors, trim the

The clipped-hackle body dun   The hackle-stem body

barbs, leaving only short stubble on both sides. Mount the hackle by the point and wrap on as body. Despite the conventional wisdom that clipped barbs absorb water, the resulting barb stubble, when saturated with floatant, repels water. Burrard tenuously asserted that the clipped hackle is not appropriate for small flies. Perhaps he thought that the short stubble would not support a small pattern. However, the dense barb stubble, which traps floatant, effectively supports small and large patterns. Fine ribbing will increase durabililty. Multicolored hackles, such as Cree and grizzly, create mottled translucent effects. Clipped-hackle bodies are attractive on shaggy sedges and rough nymphs. The singular advantage of the clipped hackle is that larger hackles may be used for smaller applications. The modern, ultranarrow saddle hackles, however, might depose the clipped-hackle body.

The Hackle-Stem Body

Stripped-hackle stems are more durable and often more colorful than stripped herls. The natural taper produces a shaped body. A famous hackle-stem pattern is Lunn's Particular of 1917. The body is the stripped stem from a Rhode Island Red hackle. Multicolored hackles, such as grizzly, produce a mottled body. When removing the barbs from the stem, pull the barbs toward the base. Mount the stem by the tip and overwrap the shank with fine, flat thread. Then, spiral the stem forward with touching wraps. Some tyers flatten the stem with pliers prior to mounting. A protective coat of lacquer over the body creates an attractive gloss, and permanent markers create desired colors. Although the abrupt taper of a cape stem creates wider abdominal segments, a long, fine saddle stem wraps willingly.

The Married-Thread Body

Tying thread alone often makes small bodies. Waxed tying thread comes in various diameters and colors. Bodies are simply wrapped as well as shaped with a single thread. If a change of color is required, then another colored thread may be added. Permanent markers make white tying thread any color at any time when required. The swell of a Trico's thorax, for example, is easily built and color-matched with thread.

Another technique, not much seen today, is the married-thread body. Various colored waxed threads "marry" to produce a single, flat "ribbon" thread. Traditionally, the choice strands are the ultrafine flosses or Pearsall's Gossamer silks. Leonard West, however, entirely rejected silk for dry flies. He ardently rejected silk's color change when wet.

On small patterns, 3/0 tying thread may be used. When wrapped, the married threads create a vibrant, multicolored body. Normally the threads are kept flat so they do not entwine. Spun married threads create swirled dazzle bodies, often kaleidoscopic. Different degrees of spin create different body patterns.

To make traditional married threads, apply a smooth coat of clear high-tack wax to two or three contrasting colored threads. The wax waterproofs and, more importantly, fuses the thread strands. Mount and wrap the married threads as a single body strand. To preserve the color intensity, spin unwaxed threads. Attractive multicolored bodies, such as those for mosquitoes and some duns, may be fashioned in this manner. These spun bodies can also mimic specific hackle colors: stack and spin red (ginger), black (gray), and cream (white) threads for a Cree body. Furthermore, spun bodies may suggest the iridescence or opalescence observed in some insects.

The married-thread body

J. C. Mottram, in *Fly-Fishing: Some New Arts and Mysteries* (1915), had a brilliant but absurd theory for creating a transparent body. "To my mind, one of the best ways of indicating transparency is to omit the transparent parts altogether." Mottram's Transparent Jenny Spinner has wraps of red-brown floss at the tail and at the thorax. The body between is vacant. Unfortunately, the hook shank is still visible. Perhaps Mottram believed that the slender shank, especially when backlit against the sky, was less visible than a wrapped body. But even if he ignored the body, he could never actually eliminate the shank. Mottram, prudently, did not mention the pattern's effectiveness. His sketches of the transparent natural and the pattern best suggest the answer. Modern tyers, however, are quite willing to accept fly bodies and the myriad body materials.

Although it is impossible in any text to explore and appraise all body materials, here are some thoughts on the body beautiful. Even a brief listing suggests the mosaic of available materials: synthetic and natural dubbing (Antron to angora), dubbing brushes, biot barbs, vinyl lace, Flashabou and Krystal Flash, mohair, yarns, and chenilles (polypropylene, fluorescent, sparkle, glitter, variegated, tinseled, crystal, Ice, Estax, and Vernille), laces (Swannundaze, larva lace, vinyl-rib), tinsels (flat Mylar, holographic, oval), Mylars (Krystal Flash, Flashabou, and holographic Flashabou), braided piping (Corsair, pearl, and holographic tubing), feathers (from cul de canard to hybrid hackles), natural hairs (body hair, arctic fox tails, squirrel tails, zonker strips), synthetic hairs (Super Hair, Ultra Hair, Fishair, Furabou), foam, epoxy, and molded or preformed synthetic bodies. Any material that can be wrapped or attached to a hook probably has been used for body material.

The Return of the Native

History offers some unusual body materials. The pages are brittle and brown and I paid too much for it, but it is a treasure of tying tidbits. *Favorite Flies and Their Histories* (1892) is a large, attractive book by Mary Orvis Marbury, the daughter of Charles Orvis and head of tying operations. After an overview of angling entomology and the "History of the Red Hackle," Marbury's historic record of a fly pattern, the text settles down in Part II with more than 450 pages of letters, requested by Charles Orvis and gleaned throughout America, on "favorite flies and their histories."

Marbury's book contains 32 chromolithographs of flies—flies that Paul Schullery calls "Victorian glories," colorful patterns tied at the end of the century. Marbury herself considered them "fancy flies," apparently due to "certain combinations of colors." Hidden among those glorious gaudies, however, is a casual description of a strange and subtle body. J. H. Stewart, of Mississippi, sent a letter dated 1887 that described two Native American patterns: "The two specimen flies which I enclose you will see are reversed hackles, made by cutting narrow strips of deerskin with the hair left on, wrapped around the hook a few times, and well tied at each end. The North Carolina Indians tie them to perfection, using some sort of cement or waterproof varnish over the thread, and for the bodies the various colors and lengths of hair from different skins, but usually rather stiff hair, preferring it from the deer's leg."

The "North Carolina Indians" are usually identified as the Eastern Cherokee. In 1838, after the state of Georgia claimed Indian lands, the U.S. Army set out to gather the entire population and move them West. A small band, however, refused to leave; they hid in the hills of North Carolina and Tennessee. The Civil War eventually distracted the government from this isolated band.

Apparently, the Eastern Cherokee had a tradition of fly making. In a footnote, Marbury stated that the patterns "were tied in exactly the method of the recently patented 'flutter fly,' and it is claimed that these flies have been used by the North Carolina Indians for generations." Unfortunately, there is no Native American treatise on "fishing with an angle." Sequoya, born in Eastern Tennessee (1760?–1843) created a Cherokee alphabet, completed in 1821, and within months the majority could read and write their own language. Evidently, their *Compleat Angler* was an oral tradition.

Though the description seems simple, tying the pattern is not, especially if we wish historical accuracy. There is neither illustration nor tying directions, and there is no indication of hair length, taper, or "hackle" density. If the fly were tied in touching turns like a hairy "palmer," it would not twist and turn in moving water or when rapidly retrieved. Clearly, the pattern was made to dance and struggle in the current.

J. H. Stewart wrote, "The effect of this reverse method, *i.e.* tying the hair to point [away] from instead of towards the bend of the hook, is very perceptible in swift water. Every little move in drawing back, as the fly floats down, gives them the appearance of a live worm trying to get out of the water."

"In addition to the forms I send to you, they sometimes use three or more stiff hairs, running down over the curve of the hook half an inch or more, to represent the feelers on the caterpillar's head. The advantage of twisting the skin around the hook is to give it a sort of whirling motion in the water as the current strikes it." To increase this action, the fly should have open, spiraling wraps of stiff deer hair. Short hock hair might not react in a current. I assume that the thread wraps are discernable, especially if the feelers are mounted half an inch or more down the hook bend.

Creating the long fine strips from deer hair can be done in several ways. Select a tanned deer hair leg patch. Working from the hide side, draw two parallel lines about two millimeters apart. Then with a razor blade, carefully cut a narrow strip. Take care that the blade does not extend beyond the hide and cut the hair. A better method is to make a simple Stripper for cutting fur strips. This practical tool can be used on various furred hides, including squirrel, rabbit, and deer. For stripping, always select *thin, tanned hides*.

Marbury gives no indication of hook size or fish species. A blind hook with gut loop is more in keeping with the illustrations. The hook should have an adequate gap and extended shank. When cutting the strip, stretch the hide. Place nothing behind or beneath the hair side when cutting. And cut the strip in such as manner that *the hair stands at a right angle to the skin strip*.

The Stripper

Select a ¼" solid hardwood panel. Use safety glasses and all safety precautions when operating power tools. First, with a router and the proper bit, rabbet the top and bottom of one edge of the panel to create a lip. The width of the lip determines the distance between the cutters, two mounted single-edged razor blades. Although lip width may differ for various patterns, a two-millimeter lip works well for the Cherokee fly. Next, carefully scroll-cut the Stripper. The lip length should match the razor blade length. Note that the shoulders on the handle prevent blade movement. The distance (the depth) that the lip penetrates between

The Stripper

The Cherokee tied on an antique Allcock Limerick, Number 5874, Size 1

the blades controls how deeply the blade cuts. To minimize cutting hairs, the blade should extend only about 3 or 4 millimeters beyond the lip. Once the tool is cut out, drilled, and sanded, a small bolt, washers and nut capture the blades. Be careful: this tool is very sharp. Store the Stripper in a heavy leather holster or protective, plastic box.

Soak the hair strip prior to wrapping to create a slight stretch and firm spiral. Remember to wrap the strip "around the hook a few times." "Few" is the key. For mounting, taper both ends of the strip. Give the strip—even on a size 1, extended shank hook—only four or five turns. The fewer the wraps, the more dramatic the fly action. Due to the taper and angle of the hairs, it may be necessary to wrap the strip on in reverse, i.e., mount the long-haired end at the head and spiral the strip toward the bend. This may also necessitate wrapping the strip under-and-over rather than the traditional (right-handed) over-and-under. In any case, mount and wrap the strip so that the hairs cup toward the head, with the shortest hairs at the bend. Such a pattern is still effective for fish attracted by sound or motion. Though apparently a wet pattern, it may have been worked just beneath the surface in swift water, tugged sporadically in still water, or scraped along the surface. Each hair spiral creates a disturbance as the fly tosses, twists, and turns. This Native "Whirling Woolly Worm" dances with fish.

Other Body Materials

Most body materials have specific properties that serve the pattern. Chenille, for example, has a wide size-range, rapidly builds bodies and, when saturated, sinks quickly. The newer sparkle chenilles, those mixed with tinsels or flash, increase visibility. Vernille, denser and stronger than chenille, is often used for San Juan Worms, bonefish, and woven patterns. Preformed foam bodies quickly create beetles, spiders, and ants.

Let us examine now, in greater detail, four materials with a long history: peacock herl, dubbing, silk, and preformed bodies. It is, in fact, their long history that continues to make them and their methods important to modern tyers.

Peacock herl, one of the first body materials, remains popular. It is inexpensive and iridescent. Although both herl edges have flue, the upper edge (on the base herls, the edge toward the peacock eye) has longer, denser flue. Thus, mount and wrap the herl so that the plump flue extends outward. Stripped peacock herl, used for decades, produces a banded, realistic body, but is rather fragile without fine-wire ribbing or a thin lacquered cover. Early tyers often spun the plump or flued herl with the tying thread. After they attached the herl tip to the hook shank, the herl hung alongside the dangling thread. Heavy hackle pliers spun both the herl and the thread together. Once spun, the herl was then wrapped forward as body. Though not as neat, perhaps, as a ribbed herl body, the thread core strengthened the herl.

Dubbing is perhaps the most common and most versatile material today. Natural and synthetic dubbings have countless characteristics—coarse, fine, stiff, supple, straight, crinkled, short, long, absorbent, hydrophobic, reflective, and fluorescent. In 1886, Frederic Halford prophesied "Probably at some future date a means of thoroughly waterproofing dubbing may be invented and if so, I venture to predict that the dubbing body will entirely supersede the quill, as being so much more transparent and watery in appearance. . . ." Not only do we have waterproof dubbing, we also have dubbings with a specific gravity lighter than water. When applied properly, dubbing is remarkably transparent and when blended, infinite colors are possible. And there are more methods for applying dubbing than there are guard hairs on an otter. Every year new fibers and new blends appear.

The Spinning Block

Although not as popular as it once was, the spinning block allows tuning or tweaking of the dubbing loop for special applications. According to Thomas Carlyle, man is a tool-using animal. Some fly tyers are tool *makers* as well. Though tools can get in the way of good tying, there are some tools that just have to be tried; and the spinning block—a product of Yankee ingenuity—is one of them. The method harkens back to Frederic M. Halford's dubbing loop. The first illustration of a dubbing loop appeared in Halford's *Floating Flies and How to Dress Them* (1886). Curiously enough, Halford uses this method to create "fibre-hackles," rather than bodies.

Halford waxed a length of tying silk and looped it over a dubbing needle stuck in the edge of a table. He then laid dubbing fibers "horizontally" between the two strands and tightly spun the ends of the silk between his thumb and forefinger to create a hackle. The spun silk is the quill; the fur, the hackle barbs. Halford also creates spun loops with hackle barbs. The "dresser can, by detaching the separate [barb] strands, laying them horizontally across a length of thoroughly waxed doubled tying-silk, and, twisting them up. . . . produce an imitation hackle with fibres only half the length of the natural ones from which they are taken." The modern spinning block creates such "hackles" faster and easier than Halford's finger-spun dangling silk.

The spinning block, also known as a dubbing block, first appeared in James E. Leisenring's *The Art of Tying the Wet Fly* (first edition, 1941). Leisenring twisted

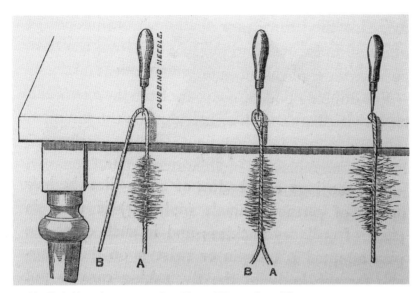

Gold Ribbed Hare's Ear with dubbing hackle and Halford "basket" wings

Halford's dubbing loop in *Floating Flies and How to Dress Them*

his dubbing loops by rolling them along his pant leg. Dick Clark, a friend and associate of Leisenring, invented the spinning block to avoid "the use of sophisticated fingering and an untidy trouser leg." The description for construction and directions for use of Clark's original block were simple: "The waxed thread is looped over the headless brads and secured in knife-cuts in the close-grained hardwood block leaving both hands free to arrange the dubbing. Then the right-hand thread is laid over the dubbing along the shallow groove, and all are twisted to make a fly body. Block shape and dimensions are not critical but everything, particularly the cut-off brads, must be sandpapered glass-smooth."

The dubbing block has several distinct advantages. First and foremost, both hands are free to arrange the dubbing. One can place material at right angles to the dubbing loop, creating a chenilled strand. Both double- and single-thread methods are possible. Materials are easy to blend or position to create a color gradient, and chopped sections of fine flash material add sparkle. After spinning, each strand may be mounted on a card. Thus, various bodies and hackles may be made, stored and used when needed. There are also a few disadvantages: the dubbing block demands time and exacting care. Some tyers may find it fussy and fastidious. Although not as consistent, nearly all dubbing-block methods can be done with a draped dubbing loop.

A modern French dubbing block variation, the Dubspeed, has a shelf or channel (the *goulotte*) mounted atop a cradle arm attached to the vise stem. The adjustable shelf, a small dubbing block, rotates against the hook shank. The thread, attached to the hook, forms a loop and hangs over the shelf. After inserting dubbing within the loop, a hook spinner (the *crochet*) closes the loop. Before spinning, the shelf rotates away from the vise. The dubbing loop is then spun and wrapped as body or hackle on the hook. The singular (and significant) advantage is that the thread loop mounts directly to the hook shank. The Dubspeed is merely a "dubbing block" that rotates against the hook for loading and then rotates away when spinning the loop. The dubbing loop remains attached to the hook shank.

The following directions produce a modified spinning block and include some creative ways for using it. You will need a fine-grained hardwood block, a router and bits, sandpaper, steel wool, two brass brads, side-cut pliers, one brass screw, one O-ring, one plastic washer, and a clear wood finish such as H. Behlen Master-Gel.

Select a straight and tightly grained hardwood block approximately 3" wide, 6" long and ¾" high. Select straight-grained wood: center-cut, curved-grained wood may warp. To readily see the dubbing, I select a light-color wood, such as cherry, white oak, ash, or hickory. When spinning light-color materials, merely slip a dark background card beneath the dubbing loop for better visibility. The original block had a knife-edge thread line and a small V-groove near the end that held the underthread. The overthread was held by a fine slice on the right edge. Though a finely scribed knife line can hold the thread, I prefer a shallow, routered bed and fine groove for the thread channel.

After sizing, squaring, and sanding the block, pass it over a *shallow-cutting* 1"-radius end-cove router bit. Make only a *slight* impression. Then, for the fine thread line, pass the block over a shallow-cutting ¹⁄₁₆" straight bit. Make both passes ¹⁄₁₆" deep or *less*.

Smooth the block with fine—400- or 600-grit—sandpaper. Do your final finish with ultrafine 4/0 steel wool. Follow the grain when smoothing with the steel wool, and wipe off any dust residue.

Apply a fine coat of clear finish. If using Master-Gel, which fills and smoothes the wood grain, make certain you follow all directions carefully. Use a lint-free cloth to apply the gel along the grain direction. Wipe off any excess, especially along the edges. When the block is completely dry, smooth with 4/0 steel wool and apply another light coat of Master-Gel. Three coats, and polishing with 4/0 steel wool, will create a glass-smooth surface.

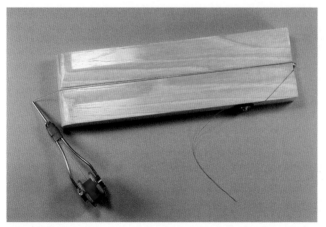

The dubbing block

Rear of dubbing block, detail

I use two headless brass brads, sanded smooth, to cradle the thread at the front. The loop is held at the back side by a brass wood screw, one O-ring and a plastic washer. If the thread groove continues down the front of the block, there is no need for two brass pins; the router groove will hold the spinning thread in position. The rear wood screw that holds the tying thread should have a smooth extension before the threads; sharp screw threads can readily cut tying thread. Mount the brass screw, O-ring(s), and washer. Because of the dense, hardwood block, predrill the hole for the screw.

To attach a dubbing loop, catch the thread ends between the O-ring and the plastic washer. The underthread drapes between the two brads and the overthread merely hangs off either side until placed on top for spinning. Position the block so that the dubbing hook or Dubbing Whirl hangs over the edge of the table. Years ago, I needed a spinner for dubbing loops. It had to have weight (to lock in materials), centrifugal force (based on a spinning top), a narrow hold or handle (for rapid spinning), and compact size (to dangle beneath the hook). I created the double- and single-hook Dubbing Whirls (consult Chapter V) to solve these problems.

Dubbing Block Methods

When using the block, match the spin speed to the material. I use a dubbing hook, formed from stainless-steel wire, for a slow spin and a brass Dubbing Whirl for a fast spin. When forming a dubbing hook make certain that the hook centers on the stem. Long, soft strands, such as CDC or marabou, require a slow spin to prevent them from whipping around and catching on the spinning loop. Short fibers, soft or coarse, work best with a fast-spinning Dubbing Whirl. The following are some specific uses for the spinning block.

Single-Thread Mole Dust

For ultrafine dubbing, attach a single thread to the block. Make a small loop at the end of the thread and hang a Whirl. Wax the thread lightly, and sprinkle finely

The sparse dubbing method: mole dust on Pearsall's Gossamer Primrose silk thread.

diced mole fur along the thread. Spin the single thread tightly while encouraging the diced mole to catch, creating a *finely* dubbed body strand. The spinning thread will gather the mole, resulting in a dubbed strand with a diameter equal to the width of the routered thread groove. Different groove widths create different strand diameters. This method sheaths the thread with mole. Early tyers often used sparse dubbing to reveal the thread color. This is done by spinning the waxed thread briskly between the thumb and forefinger while touching the chopped dubbing to the whirling thread. When wet, the short dubbing blurs the thread to create a translucent body.

CDC Body and Hackle

The dubbing block easily creates CDC body and hackle for dry or emerger patterns. In fact, this type of CDC hackle floats a dry fly better than a traditional dry hackle. Though CDC hackle may be made with a dubbing loop alone or with a split thread, the block allows adjustment of the CDC barbs once they are trapped in the dubbing loop.

Attach a dubbing loop to the block and hang a dubbing hook in the loop. With high-adhesive wax, "lick" the thread where the hackle will be placed. Take two or three large CDC hackles and stack them, matching their curves. Caress the barbs so that they stand at right angles to the stem. Then attach a bulldog clip to the barbs about ⅛" from the stem. Do the same on the other side, and trim the stems away. You now have two clips fully charged with CDC barbs.

The Marc Petitjean transparent Magic Tool clips are excellent. Mention must be made of other Petitjean tools, especially the spring Loop Clamps and Twister. The spring clamps close part of the dubbing loop so that more barbs, especially different colored barbs, may be added to the loop. The Twister locks and holds the loop for wrapping. These thoughtful tools have other applications.

Lift the thread loop off the block and trap the barb base between the thread strands and release the bulldog clip. Carefully add the other barb base in the same

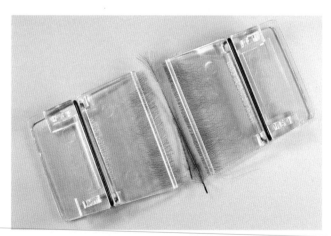

Clips charged with CDC hackle barbs. The stems are cut away.

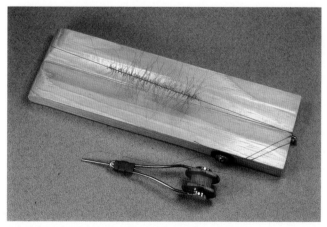

Dubbing loop charged with CDC barbs

manner. Make final adjustments, such as CDC length and density, after you replace the loop on the block. Next, *lift* the CDC strand above the block and slowly spin the dubbing hook to create a tightly spun CDC hackle. Carefully remove and attach the CDC strand to a dubbing card or carrier. I make dubbing cards from stiff plastic sheets, about 2" x 4". The cards have short slits at each end to hold the twisted dubbing strands. You should remember, as Leisenring wrote, "to twist the body again in the right direction as you wrap it about the hook shank. Although leaving them on the card tends to set the waxed threads, they will unwind slightly when removed."

Sparkle and Flash

You can make your own body blends of dubbing and flash with a dubbing block. First, wax the loop thread and carefully arrange the desired dubbing on the under-thread. Then cut a length of narrow, soft flash material (such as Krystal Flash, Holographic Flash, Sparkleflash, Angel Hair, Pearlescent Fly Flash or Hedron Mirage) and distribute it along the dubbed strand. Lock in the flash with the overthread. Then, use a dubbing hook or Whirl (depending on flash length) and tightly spin the dubbed flash strand. Only soft and very narrow flash materials lock well in a dubbing loop.

For a strong flash strand, take a few strands of narrow flash and capture both ends in the bottom and top of the loop. Pull the strands taut. Then, spin tightly and use the strengthened strands as ribbing or body material.

Tools do not the tyer make, but tyers can make the tools. And some tools, like the spinning block, are pleasant to make and use. I suppose that is why New World apes have opposing thumbs and a room full of tying materials.

Dubbing

Dying and blending dubbing was a distinct art of the early tyers. The modern tyer is apt to purchase an approximate dubbing color rather than blend various dubbings for a more appropriate hue and value. An early tyer selected and blended the dubbing palette much like a painter. Some early tying treatises, such as William Blacker's *The Art of Fly-Making, &c, Comprising Angling & Dyeing of Colours* (1843) and Frederic M. Halford's *Floating Flies and How to Dress Them* (1886), offered meticulous instructions for dyeing and blending. Those early tyers, like Halford, who emphasized precise color, were often labeled as "imitationists."

Tyers frequently praised the dubbing "halo"—a fine dubbing haze that revealed the thread color. Early tyers applied just enough dubbing to halo the thread with stubby spikes. To create this halo, *faintly* wax a length of tying thread. Then, run the fingers over the thread to thin the wax coat. Next, spin the thread back and forth between the thumb and forefinger of the left hand, while gently brushing very finely diced dubbing along the whirling thread. The twirling thread gathers and distributes the fine dubbing particles. The color of thread and dubbing subtly meld to produce the proper shade or nuance required. When wet, the sparse, surface fuzz creates dramatic translucency. Many modern tyers *thoroughly* blanket the thread with the dubbing, thereby creating a thick, corded dubbing rope. This latter method completely conceals the thread color, thus limiting subtle color blends and translucency.

Other Body Materials

Preformed bodies have long been a peripheral part of tying. At the turn of the nineteenth century, William Mills & Son sold soft-rubber hellgrammites. Early experiments with cellophane bodies failed: they softened (which was good) and deteriorated (which was bad) in water. The Herter Company sold Fleshex Plastic—a soft, flexible body material for molding nymphs, grasshoppers, spiders, and other such critters. Celluloid floss and acetone or celluloid solvent turned fly bodies into translucent solids. Liquid rubber or latex formed frogs and fish. For most tyers, however, molding flies was akin to model making rather than fly tying.

Leonard West once thought that he had found the perfect body material—the fine, India-rubber core tape in golf balls. In 1921, West called raffia (a rough palm leaf from Madagascar) a "capital material" as a quill-body substitute. Over seventy-five years later, I watched elderly tyers in the French Jura wrap delicate mayflies with it. We gain more materials than we lose in tying history.

The Hackle

> A good cock's hackle is bright, active, sharp, and full of sparkle when held to the light.
>
> —G. E. M. Skues, *The Way of a Trout with a Fly* (1935)

Nothing in tying is more attractive than a sharp and sparkling dry hackle. However, nothing challenges the tyer more. How does a hackle really work? How should you select a hackle? How can you firmly mount a hackle? In addition, how should you wrap a hackle so that its rigid barbs support a pattern? All tyers must master hackling. Poor hackling cannot hide. When I was young, my mother would often tell me—when a flaw or blemish was not important—that no one would notice it on a galloping horse. No hackle, however, should look like it was "ridden hard and put up wet." Here are some thoughts and strategies for effective hackling.

The dry hackle imitates the legs (in function), the wings (in color) and, sometimes, the venation (in design). Colonel E. W. Harding, in *The Flyfisher & the Trout's Point of View* (1931), demonstrated that surface-feeding trout search the area in front of the optical "window" for drifting flies. When the flies float beyond the window, their feet make minuscule dimples in the surface film. Later, the fly drifts onto the window where it is recognized. As Colonel Joscelyn Lane noted, in *Fly-Fisher's Pie* (1956), "Like the hunter, he first sees the footprints and later the quarry." The hackle tips, pressed into the surface film, might just be such a spoor of recognition.

A dry hackle allows a pattern to drop lightly upon the water (like the wings) and (like the insect legs) supports a pattern on the water surface. Although functioning much like insect legs, the hackle barbs seldom match the number and color of the natural. In *The Way of a Trout with a Fly*, Skues pointed out that "A good deal of cheap scorn has been wasted upon the excessive number of legs given by a fly dresser to the artificial fly to ensure flotation, particularly to Sedges. I would ask, how often is it that the hackles of flies are taken for legs?" According to Skues, profuse legs may merely create "buzz," the flutter effect of the wings. Traditionally the hackle serves as a visual match to the dominant color of the insect's wings. Hackle, according to the merge and mingle theory, may imitate wing venation as well as wing color. For example, to imitate the bold, black venation of a drake wing, spiral a black hackle through the paler shoulder hackle or merely add a black face hackle.

Roger Woolley, in *Modern Trout Fly Dressing* (1932), advocated matching, if possible, a two-color hackle to both the wings and the legs. "For a single hackle dry fly, then, remember that the colour of the hackle used should be as near as possible the colour of the wings of the fly imitated or if you can get a two-colour hackle that is pretty well the colour of both the wings and the legs, so much the better." Curiously enough, if the pattern had wings, Woolley then matched the hackle color to the insect's legs. Woolley also mentioned a certain John Hendersen, whose "hackle-fibre wing" method is "the only effective method of efficiently imitating the glassy transparency of the spinner's wings" that gives "sufficient buoyancy to float the fly." For a spent spinner, wrap a traditional shoulder hackle. Evenly divide and stroke the barbs into spent-spinner wings: that is, flat wings that "stand out stiffly on each side of the hook." To complete, figure-eight the wing base with several thread wraps. Upright or dun wings may also be made. Stroke the barbs into an upright position and post "well up to the roots of the fibres, and the wing will be fashioned of the hackle fibres in the divided form of a split double wing." Two hackle turns are all that is necessary for "a light and airy" spinner or dun dry-fly wing. The Hendersen's wing filters "shafts of light" through barbs for a realistic and modern wing method.

The Buzz Theory

Barred or variegated hackle appears to "flutter" on the water, suggesting the appearance of an insect attempting to fly. The multicolored grizzly and Cree are the most common hackles used to suggest this fluttering buzz. Skues, in *The Way of a Trout with a Fly*, noted that "The effect of fluttering and the effect of a bush of hackles may not look so dissimilar to the trout." He believed that Palmers were often taken for struggling sedges rather than the caterpillars they are supposed to imitate.

The Merge and Mingle Theory

The *callibaetis* dun wing—gray with dark blotches—may be suggested with two hackles. After tying in a gray wing, a gray hackle and then a black hackle are added to indicate the dark blotches on the *callibaetis* dun wing. In a similar manner, the Goddard Mayfly used golden calf tail wing and a black hackle. The trout's view from below mixes the black lines of the hackle barbs with the antique gold of the wing to suggest the dark venation and saffron blotches of the *Danica* mayfly wing. Furthermore, a hackle spinner wing, merely a sparse hackle trimmed top and bottom, may suggest the longitudinal veins of an otherwise transparent wing. The light filtering through the glassy barbs suggest the wing color while the vacancies hint at the transparency between the wing veins.

Merge and mingle wrap with facing hackle

The Float-Line Theory

Consider for a moment how the hackle floats a pattern. In theory, a pattern is tied so that only the tail and hackle tips support the pattern. Perhaps Ray Bergman's *Trout* (1962) presents the first testimony of the float line. His illustrations depict the stance of a light-wire dry fly on a hard surface and light-wire dry fly on the water. When on the water, the hook spear just brushes the water surface. Bergman then compared light-wire patterns and heavy-wire patterns and their particular floats. "Comparing the appearance of a light-wire-hook fly to a heavy-wire-hook fly on the water shows the following. The first alights softly in ratio to the thickness of the hackle and the tail, because the hackles offset the weight of the hook sufficiently to prevent a fast and unnatural drop. Also, when it reaches the water it floats well, with the hackle and tail both doing their job as intended. On the other hand, a heavy-wire fly, unless it is considerably overhackled, will drop like a piece of lead, hitting the water so forcefully that often the tail submerges. This brings the hook under the surface and puts the entire fly out of balance as far as it was originally supposed to float. This does not mean that a fly floating this way will not catch some fish, because it will, but certainly it does not imitate a natural as well as the light-wire-hook fly." He found that "flies on which the hook is somewhat concealed when floating" become "more consistently effective, cov-

The theoretical float line

The actual float-line of a fly pattern. Although the pattern floats, part of the tail, body, and hackle sink. The bend and spear are completely submerged. Note the body and hook conspicuously reflected in the surface "mirror." The fan wings create the white smear above.

ering all conditions." Bergman hid the hook by keeping it above the surface. In the traditional float line, the hook bend and spear, which should not quite touch the water, act as a pendulum to cock the pattern. Some hook designs require proportion adjustment, especially the length of tail and hackle, to achieve the theoretical float.

In reality, however, the pattern does not prance on its hackle tips. After a moment of drift, the pattern nestles down in the surface with the tail, hook point, and underhackle submerged. If the barbs are sufficiently waterproofed, then the buoyancy added by the tail and hackle barbs (as illustrated in the fly photograph) will support most of the pattern on the surface. Long barbs may even flex, supporting the pattern with a greater surface contact. To augment floatation, increase the barb length rather than the number of hackle wraps. A moderately longer barb increases the surface area more than a few added hackle wraps.

Selecting Dry Hackle

Selecting a quality dry hackle usually includes some of the following elements:

1. **Appropriate barb length:** Though Roger Woolley actually endorsed trimming hackle tips to length, some tyers maintain that a hackle should never be pruned as that allows the barbs to absorb water and sink. In the tying catechism, clipping hackle tips is a mortal sin.

2. **Uniform barb length:** Limited barb taper produces good hackling. A steep taper makes an inferior hackle because the barb length varies too rapidly for symmetrical hackling. A hackle may be deceptive—it may appear small and narrow, but the barbs which can lie parallel to the stem may be long. Barb taper and barb length are independent factors that should be considered. Limited barb taper creates a hackle with more barbs the same length. This means that more barbs support the pattern. When barbs stand at a right angle to the stem (the barb symmetry), their tips should form a straight line, tapering slightly toward the hackle point.

3. **Limited webbing:** Webbing—actually dense barbules occurring at the base and tapering toward the tip—absorbs water. Trimming may eliminate some but not all webbing in a hackle. Always select the longest hackle with limited webbing.

4. **Rectangular stem cross-section:** Stem cross-section may vary significantly from cape to cape. Rectangular stems (flat-sided stems) wrap easily, creating a proper barb posture.

5. **Fine and flexible stem:** A fine stem wraps easily and increases barb density.

6. **Barb density:** Capes and saddles vary in barb count along stem distance. Select for density. A full 80 percent or more of the Whiting Midge Saddles have size 18 hackles or narrower. Most pelts have hackles that range from size 18 to 20 with some 16s and 22s. There are now breeder roosters that produce true 24- to 26-sized saddle hackles. The Whiting Midge Hackles have remarkable barb density. Above size 24, barb-density is about 84 barbs per 25 millimeters (single-sided count). Below size 24, the hackles may have more than 100 barbs per 25 millimeters (single-sided count).

A Comparator barb count

A premium Whiting platinum dry-fly cape hackle (in size 12 and size 16) had 3 barbs per millimeter (single-sided count). In six wraps (three behind and three in front of the wings), this hackle lays down 99 barbs in a total applied stem length of 16.50 mm. Approximately 60 barbs would support and sustain the pattern on the water surface. A Whiting microhackle (with an *extended* barb width of only .80 mm) had 6 barbs per millimeter (single-sided count). This is approximately 152 barbs per inch (single-sided count). This remarkable microhackle would lay down nearly 200 barbs in only six shank wraps (double-sided count). At the cost of increased space, added hackle wraps increase barb count. Though most tyers avoid barb counting, this hidden trait does influence the final fly.

7. **Hackle density of the cape or saddle:** Examine the back of a cape or saddle (the pockmarks of each hackle) to determine total hackle density. Hackle density increases the total feather count.

8. **Color:** In short, some hackle colors are more useful than others. Invest in usefulness. Do not ignore capes with odd patterns or odd coloration.

9. **Glossy sheen of outer, convex hackle surface:** The light-reflecting sheen usually indicates barb stiffness.

10. **Barb stiffness, straightness, and taper:** Barb rigidity floats a pattern.

11. **Hackle narrowness.** Even narrow hackles can have different barb lengths. The hackle sides should be parallel when the barbs are at right angles to the stem. A steep taper, in contrast to a uniformly narrow taper, usually indicates varying barb lengths.

12. **Hackle range:** A quality cape should offer an adequate range of hackle sizes. A quality saddle is far more restrictive. Many modern, genetic capes lack quality hackles for larger patterns, especially in size 10 and larger.

Preparing the Hackle

There are various ways to prepare a hackle. Hackles may be prepared, mounted, and wrapped as they are. They may be caressed so that the side barbs are at right angles to the stem. Both sides may be caressed together at a right angle or a hackle side may be stripped off. For a "thin hackle," Francis Francis, in *A Book on Angling* (1876), recommended stripping off one side of the hackle. He cautioned that you must strip off the proper side, otherwise "the hackle will not roll on" properly. I often use the "thinned hackle" for sparse, wet patterns, and some dry patterns. This creates a sparse, but neat pattern. Two stripped hackles increase barb density.

Sizing the Hackle

One of the basic tying skills is sizing the hackle. Proper sizing eliminates heavy webbing, reduces stem thickness and removes the long base barbs. The following illustrates proper hackle preparation. Note that the stripped stem also minimizes the webbing without deleting the better barbs.

Folding the Hackle

Folding or doubling the hackle, a method primarily used for palmer or shoulder hackles in salmon tying, may also be used for trout tying. Francis Francis advocated "folding the hackle" prior to mounting and wrapping. With hackle pliers clipped to the tip of the hackle, place a finger through the ring of the hackle pliers and with thumb and forefinger grip the stem. Now,

> bend the hackle back until you take hold of it between the finger and thumb, the bright or upper face of the hackle lying towards the knuckles, moisten the finger and thumb of the right hand, and taking the two sides of the hackle between them, press them together, gently drawing them back towards the butt of the feather at the same times. Continue this process the whole length of the hackle until the fibres remain in an angular position with respect to the quill and each other instead of flat as previously. In this manner the hackle can be laid on very neatly, and the fibres will point all one way with great regularity—albeit the legs of a natural fly by no means do so; and in this respect our neatness rather overdoes nature.

The trimmed and stripped hackle. Note the minor webbing on the tip hackle (left) and the major webbing on the waste hackle.

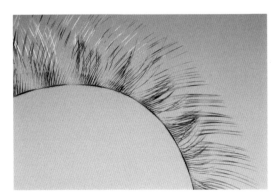

The folded or doubled hackle

When folding trout hackle, the dull side or concave side is often uppermost. This folds the barbs back according to their natural propensity, producing a sharper fold. There may be, however, little or no difference when folding trout hackles. The long-barbed salmon hackles might make a difference. Pryce-Tannatt advocated folding the hackle with the bright side of the feather uppermost. Hale demanded that the dull underside be uppermost. Kelson also doubled the hackle with dull side uppermost and "the bright side being downward."

The Cropped Hackle

Hackles may be cropped or trimmed for specific effects. A palmer hackle may have all the barbs trimmed on one side. This produces sparse hackling. Sir Gerald Burrard, in *Fly-Tying: Principles & Practice* (1945), advocated further cuts to create a delicate barb veil. After cropping all the barbs on one side of the feather, he intermittently trims the barbs on the other side as well. When wrapped, the sparse and sporadic barbs thinly encapsulate the body. I trim the barbs with a razor blade broken to proper width. With floatant, a trimmed side (the stubble side) is more buoyant than a stripped side.

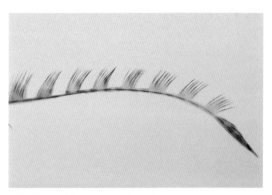

The Burrard intermittent hackle

If the barbs are cropped on both sides (leaving only a fringe of stumpy barbs), then, when wrapped as body, the hackle creates a rough stubble. *Undressed*, the stubble body eventually absorbs water. Spinners wrapped in this manner float low in the water, waterlogged like the naturals. Dense hackle may be trimmed to create profile or silhouette patterns, such as caddis or spinners. The Hackle Caddis is merely a densely wrapped palmer, trimmed to caddis shape. Use a badger or dark-center hackle to suggest a body.

The Reversed Hackle

W. A. Hunter, in *Fisherman's Knots & Wrinkles* (1928), reversed the hackle during wrapping. "If you wish to make a very elegant fly, then turn the hackle over in changing from the back to the front of the wings. The legs will then stand out both ways, those behind sloping backwards and those in front, sloping forward." Hunter, however, offered no details for reversing the hackle. Here is my method.

First, mount the hackle dull side (concave side) facing aft. Wrap the hackle to the base of the wings. Now, at the reversal, attach hackle pliers to the stem near the shank. With the hackle pliers, twist the stem sharply (on its own axis) until the hackle sides reverse. After reversing, the dull side will face forward. Then, continue to wrap until the reversal holds. Once the reversal holds, reattach the pliers farther down the stem and continue wrapping to the head. This maneuver works best with hackles that have pronounced concave or "cupped" barbs.

Barb Flare

If barbs emerge from a twisted stem, they will be erratic. Leaving some "freebore" or space (by detaching a few barbs beyond the thread mount) before the stem is aligned will eliminate those surly barbs. This will avoid the necessity of making the second hackle wrap behind the first to catch and gather any barbs pointing aft.

Number of Hackle Wraps

I usually place the same number of wraps in front of the wing as there are behind the wing. This makes the wings grow out of the middle of the hackle. That appeals to me. "Antique" tying directions often recommended minimal hackle wraps, such as three hackle wraps behind the wing and two in front. Roger Woolley believed that "four turns of good, stiff hackle is all that is needed to give a reasonably good floating fly." On chalk streams and spring creeks four or five may work. Other waters may require more than twice that number of turns. Hackle density should match the waters we fish. Humpies may have double hackles that fill up half the hook shank for exceptional floatation. The singular advantage of lavish hackling is that the pattern floats better. But there the advantage ends. Excessive hackling floats a pattern higher than the low-floating naturals. Abundant hackling may destroy, in fact, the illusion of a delicate and slender insect. Finally, excessive, stiff barbs may actually work, under some conditions, as a guard and therefore decrease effective hooking. Nevertheless, in some of my own steep, heavy Western waters only dense hackling floats a pattern. It is a matter of degree—use enough wraps to float the pattern, but not so many wraps that you destroy the imitative quality of the pattern. A floating, feather brush pile does not look like a delicate *callibaetis*.

The Palmer Hackle

A palmer hackle spirals forward with open wraps along the hook shank. When wrapping a dry palmer hackle, slightly rotate the stem on its axis while angling it forward. This forces the barbs forward, creating the attractive forward-cupped barbs. It will help to wrap the palmer over a soft, thickly dubbed body. Some hackles absolutely refuse to be treated in this manner; the barbs splay randomly. Mount a palmer hackle by the tip so that the longer barbs are placed forward.

The Inlaid Hackle

Inlaying hackle takes advantage of the two available dry hackles: the cape and the saddle. The inlaid hackle uses both hackles to advantage: the longer barbs of the cape hackle extend beyond the shorter saddle barbs. The short barbs increase buoyancy without obscuring the pattern's delicate profile. For an inlaid hackle, select a saddle hackle with barbs less than half as long as those of the cape hackle. Mount both hackles, placing the saddle hackle next to the hook shank. Then, wrap the cape hackle forward, secure and trim the excess. Clip the underbarbs of the cape hackle. Leave the side barbs as outriggers. Finally, wrap the short-barbed saddle hackle through the cape hackle creating a dense support hackle. Secure and trim excess. Excellent spinner patterns may be created by pruning or clipping both the underbarbs and overbarbs before wrapping the saddle hackle. Remember to use short-barbed saddle hackles for inlaying. The Double-Hackle Dun and Double-Hackle Spinner previously described are examples of inlaid hackles.

The Bent Hackle

Datus Proper, in *What the Trout Said* (1982), described the mechanics of the bent-hackle design. "A large, soft hackle—such as dyed French Partridge—is wound on shiny-side-forward, supported by a small, stiff, cock's hackle out of sight behind the main hackle. The function of the stiff hackle is purely mechanical: it strengthens the middle of the soft hackle, while the soft tips bend backwards around the point of the hook. The fly floats on the bend of the soft hackle fibers. Nothing at all penetrates the surface film: something difficult to achieve with any other pattern." This design favors large drake and caddis patterns. According to Proper, "The bent-hackle fly is another ancient wet-fly design gone dry." Due to the large, *soft* hackle, adequate floatation is problematical. Apply a penetrating floatant for increased buoyancy. French partridge and mallard breast feathers usually create the soft hackle. For adequate support, the soft barbs should extend beyond the hook. A palmered, stiff cock hackle (especially one that "denses" behind the soft hackle) creates the best support. Proper also added that "Light-weight is important: if a tail or body are used at all, they should be sparse."

Proper noted that the *Plumeau*, a Bent-Hackle Green Drake, appears in Jean-Paul Pequegnot's *French Fishing Flies* (1987). My own experience with the French bent hackles occurred years ago on the chalk-waters of the L'Iton in Normandy. The L'Iton was a strange stream where large fish were easy and small fish, difficult. According to Pequegnot, the *Plumeau* or "Feather Duster" lacks the troublesome casting spin inherent in many winged drake patterns. Pequegnot's *Assasine*, another Green Drake pattern, shares bent-hackle blood. His tying method reveals the mechanics:

> The partridge hackle, significantly longer than the body hackle, should be wound first with the concave (dull) side facing forward in such a manner that, once tied in, it points a little toward the front and resists bending backward with use. The

stiff, cock hackle is then wound, with a few turns, rather tightly up against the partridge hackle to provide support. The remaining turns are then spaced out along the body to give a ringed appearance. The finishing knot is made at the rear, on the bend of the hook.

The stiff, supporting cock hackle may be either a palmer or a shoulder wrap. Though the partridge barbs cup forward, the long, soft hackle that "resists bending backwards" does support the pattern with a similar bent-hackle stance. The singular problem, detected by Pequegnot, is securing and winding the fine, fragile partridge hackle on small patterns. Both chukor and French partridge contour feathers create excellent bent hackles.

The Bent-Hackle Fly

The Glanrhôs Wing

For lightly dressed patterns, the traditional Glanrhôs method creates a delicate, willowy wing. Roger Woolley, in *Modern Trout Fly Dressing* (1932), described the single-wing method. "The wing is formed of the tip of the hackle used for legs, so is somewhat limited in its application to those flies that have wings and legs of something the same colour." After completing the tail and body, select one dry hackle for wing and legs. Stroke the barbs down, leaving the flat tip as wing. Mount the hackle tip at wing position. Now, wind on the hackle (legs) by taking wraps fore and aft of the single hackle-tip wing. Finish with forward hackle wraps and whip-finish at the head.

The Double Glanrhôs Wing

The traditional Glanrhôs method, however, may be improved. A preferable method creates two wings and a hackle that naturally wraps from rear to front. For a double Glanrhôs wing, select two hackles with wide, rounded tips. The length of the hackle-tip wing should equal the shank length of the hook. Immediately beneath each wing length stroke down the barbs and remove several barbs, creating a space equal to that required by the rear hackle. Mount the two hackle-tip wings (convex to convex) at the wing position. The hackle tips should point to the

The double Glanrhôs wing-mount

The Glanrhôs Double-Wing Mount, sans body and tail. If desired, use a wing burner to create a wide, shaped wing tip.

right, extending over the hook eye. Now, wrap the thread rearward over the hackle stems to the hindmost hackle position. Then wrap the thread forward, passing in front of the wings. To erect the wings, place two or three solid wraps against the forward wing base. Next, spiral the thread forward to the head position.

Finally, wrap the double hackles forward as legs. Because the hackle stems extend aft, the hackle wraps spiral forward, from rear to front, in the traditional manner. The hackle wraps end at the head. I often strip the underbarbs from *both hackles* to create an attractive shoulder hackle. For the Glanrhôs method, select hackles with long barbs near the tip to create supporting shoulder hackles. The single- and double-wing methods produce durable wings and hackles.

The Finger Cone

When whip-finishing, sometimes wayward barbs gather beneath the head wraps. One method that clears the forward barbs before whip-finishing is the three-finger cone. Attach the whip-finisher to the thread and hold it in the right hand. Drape the bobbin over the left ring finger and small finger. Next, form a cone with the tips of the left thumb, index finger, and middle finger. Place the fingertips over the head of the pattern and pull back the barbs with the three-finger cone. The pattern may now be whip-finished without trapping a bundle of barbs beneath the head wraps.

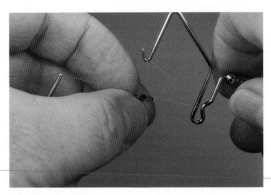

The finger cone.

The Troublesome Underbarbs

When wrapping a hackle, the underbarbs are often caught and spiked forward in a tangle. It is easy for a tyer to place the hackle stem correctly on top by angling the hackle down and back while wrapping. This rearward angle, however, cannot be continued beneath the hook shank effectively. Inevitably, some underbarbs will be caught and forced askew. When winding hackle, increased hackle twist (rotating the hackle stem on its own axis) prevents most problems. Finally, remember to stroke back the previous underbarbs before each hackle wrap beneath the shank.

The Tilted Hackle

In 1933, Paul Young wrote what Paul Schullery later regarded as "a useful little book," *Making and Using the Fly and Leader.* Young advocated tilting the hackle wraps so that the top barbs slant aft while the bottom barbs slant forward. "This method of winding causes the hackle on underside of fly to reach well forward, thus offering the fly much greater support on the water. Another advantage is that the wind resistance caused by casting will not so easily cause the hackles to lay back underneath the hook, thus losing floating qualities."

Tilted hackle wraps

The tilted tactic may trap excessive underbarbs, creating a bramble beneath the hook. This method requires additional care to avoid snaring these underbarbs. Young never mentioned that correct and continuous hackle angulation is better achieved if the tying thread is removed before wrapping the hackle. The dangling thread disrupts smooth, controlled wraps. Furthermore, a larger hook or body diameter enhances the tilt. Young also ignores the additional benefit that the tilted top barbs imitate more precisely the aft-slanted wing of the dun.

Shift Wrap

Other variations of tilted wraps include the shift wrap and the wing wrap. For a shift wrap, lay three or four conventional hackle wraps in. Then follow these wraps with diagonal wraps over them. The conventional wraps serve as a post that secures the slanted wraps. The shift wraps, vertical and diagonal, produce widely splayed barbs.

Wing Wrap

The wing wrap, best done with a rotating vise and a single saddle hackle, creates both the wing and parachute. Mount a tapered, cape hackle by the base for softer, longer wings and a shorter, stiffer parachute. First, make three to four conventional hackle wraps tightly together. Excessive wraps make the wing fuller and parachuting more difficult. After completing the wraps, overlap the hackle stem with one complete thread turn tightly against the hackle base. Then, spiral the thread forward. Turn the pattern upside down in the vise. Place a small drop of penetrating Flexament cement on the hackle base and stroke all hackle barbs down.

Once the barbs are gathered, rotate the pattern upright and complete the tail and body. Sparse dubbing beneath the hackle will also serve to gather and erect the barbs. Next, wrap the remainder of the hackle as a parachute. When completed, tie off the stem and trim excess. A single hackle (and single hackle color) creates both wing and supporting hackle.

The wing-wrap fly: mounted hackle with gathered wing barbs. Note the dubbing beneath the wings.

Completed hackle-wing fly

Wrapping Doubles and Triples

Two hackles may be mounted and wound at the same time. However, it is difficult to maintain equal tension when wrapping three separate hackles. In this case, mount all three hackles together, wrap two and tie off. Then, firmly wrap the third hackle through the barbs of the previous two. Some tyers believe that a stronger and more meticulous hackling happens when both hackles are mounted and each hackle wrapped separately. When thus done, the first hackle is often wrapped leaving a stem space for the second hackle.

Single versus Double

Should a tyer use a single hackle or two hackles for a pattern? For the same barb density, a single hackle often incorporates a greater length of hackle. Greater hackle length often results in a greater taper and, consequently, varying barb lengths. In short, a single hackle, which uses a longer hackle length, usually has a greater range of barb lengths. The singular advantage to a double hackle is that barb length has improved uniformity.

Hackle Wings

There are several effective ways to make hackle wings. A choice method appears in Colonel E. W. Harding's *The Flyfisher & the Trout's Point of View* (1931), subtitled *New Light on Flyfishing Theory & Practice.* This innovative and creative book, though rare, should be read by all fly tyers. Colonel Harding recommended this method for tying the egg-laying or "upright-winged spinner." "Its wings are far more transparent than those of the dun, and in this instance the plain hackled fly is almost certainly a better representation than a fly winged with fibres of wing feather." The method is simple. "If the fly dresser wishes to represent the shape of the wings more accurately than by a single hackle, he can use either single wings or two hackles. In using two hackles, the first is wound and adjusted so as to simulate wings, the under fibres being cut away and not more than three turns made of the second hackle." To make the hackle-wing profile more defined and distinct, I crop only those barbs directly below the shank and then caress all barbs vertically before wrapping the second hackle.

Front view of the Harding hackle wings. A red and honey hackle illustrates the effect.

Hackle Pliers

I prefer smooth-jawed hackle pliers, not the deeply striated jaws that cut delicate hackles, and an older technique that increases grip while decreasing hackle breakage. G. E. M. Skues, in *Silk, Fur and Feather* (1950), advocated melting wax on the jaws of hackle pliers. "I find it an improvement on the common type of hackle pliers to melt a little harness-maker's wax between the jaws, and then to scrape off what exudes, not too closely." Jaw wax reduces the tendency to break tender hackles (the wax covers the metal edge) while it increases the grip on the hackle. Jaw wax must be renewed from time to time. Any moderately hard, medium, or low-tack wax serves as hackle-pliers wax.

Mounting the Hackle

Nothing is more frustrating than having a hackle pull out while wrapping. Usually a long stem allows sufficient wraps to secure a hackle. Some tyers, however, prefer to lock-wrap the stem with special methods. Two methods are sometimes used: the L-lock and kink lock. The kink lock, illustrated on page 77, is used with

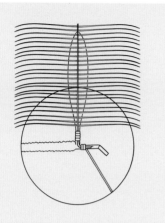

The L-lock for parachute

synthetic tail fibers. Paul Young championed the L-lock mount in 1933. "A hackle, attached in this manner, may be broken off before it will pull out and is the only proper attachment for durable flies. Besides its security, a great advantage is derived from the fact that the hackle starts right, with its first turn around the hook shank." After making three tight overwraps with the hackle stem, the stem is turned at a right angle to the shank and tight wraps are forced against it. The excess stem is closely trimmed. The stem base, which turns at a right angle to the hook shank (the L), prevents withdrawal.

Another mounting method locks a kink in the stem. First, overwrap the stem with two tight wraps. Pull the stem away and wrap twice around the shank. Then, fold the stem down and lock with two or three overwraps.

Wrapping the Hackle

There are many ways to wrap a hackle. Some experienced European tyers mount the hackle without advancing the tying thread. After the hackle is wrapped in touching turns, the tying thread passes *over* the hackle to the head where it secures the hackle and whips the head. Skues pointed out that "Not a fibre need be tied down if the silk is held taut and not wound too rapidly." Do not attempt to weave the thread between the barbs. Merely slowly spiral the thread forward *ignoring* all barbs, allowing the barbs to snap back if caught. This method places the thread wraps over the hackle stem for strength. Most tyers, however, do not like thread exposed at the base of the hackle.

Do you mount the dull side forward or dull side to the rear? The dull side is the concave side, the side against the bird's body. Hackling with the dull side toward the head pushes or cups the barbs forward for a wider, stable stance upon the water. Although hackling in this manner is more common among Americans than some Europeans, it was advocated by Roger Woolley of England. While the forward barbs contradict the rearward slope of a dun's wing, it does improve the imprint on the water. No matter. Like many tyers I wrap "dull forward" for drys and "dull aft" for wets. It should be admitted that the minor barb curvature of small, quality hackles probably has no effect on barb stance. Some hackles may be mounted and wrapped either way.

The advantage of mounting the hackle by the tip is that the longer barbs will appear at the front, supporting the pattern better. The advantage of mounting the hackle by the base is that the thicker part of the hackle is covered by the hackle wraps and the finer tip produces a smaller, neater head. However, a base mount may place the longer barbs unnaturally at the rear of the hackle. Much depends upon the quality and taper of the hackle.

The Standard Hackle Mount

Remove most of the webbing. The stripped mounting stem also eliminates some webbing. After trimming and preparing the hackle, mount it on the near side below the wing. Here it will be seen and will not disturb the wing position. To decrease the bulk tied down, flatten the base of the hackle stem with flat-nosed pliers before mounting it. Position the hackle so that the tip points aft and the dull or concave side faces you. Then, secure the hackle stem with a lock mount or three thread wraps behind the wings. Advance the thread in front of the wings and secure the hackle stem with two more wraps. Trim stem excess. Next, turn the hackle vertically with the dull side forward, facing the hook eye. A free-bore (about two millimeters of barbless stem) at the turning point prevents skewed barbs. Now, wrap the hackle behind and in front of the wings with touching turns, equal wraps, and proper barb alignment. While wrapping, gently fold back the previous barb wraps to prevent capturing any barbs. After sufficient wraps, tie off the hackle tip. Major J. H. Hale noted, in *How to Tie Salmon Flies* (1919), that securing the hackle tip beneath the shank often results in a neater tie. Actually, if the tip is mounted on the near side as advised, then the tie-off point would be on the far side. For consistency, some tyers mount *all* materials on top and tie off or "dismount" all materials beneath the shank. Once the hackle is secured and the excess trimmed, carefully wrap a tapered head over the tie-off point.

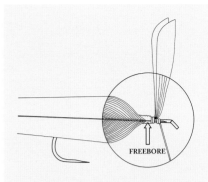

The standard hackle mount: Note the free-bore and thread wraps fore and aft of the wings.

A rooster parades his hackle for display; the glassy, spiky barbs announce his virility. This specialized, stiff barbed feather is one of the small splendors of tying. Knowing how to prepare, mount, and wrap a hackle reveals that splendor. The modern tyer is blessed with the best hackles in tying history. We have an advantage that Halford, Skues, Francis, and Woolley never had. Some modern saddle hackles can tie over a dozen size 20 drys. What would Halford have wrapped if he had a modern bright, active, sharp, and sparkling hackle?

The CDC Hackle: Split-Thread Method

The split-thread method, like many modern methods, has an historic antecedent. W. H. Lawrie, in *All-Fur Flies and How to Dress Them* (1967), quoted an extract from the holograph notes of G. E. M. Skues on "Captain Marryat's Method":

> Take a piece of fine sewing silk and tie a knot at one end. Stick a pin between the strands into your table. About three inches from the pin untwist the silk so that the strands stand wide open—enough to admit your placing a small quantity of fur-fibres or mohair between the strands of silk. Having done so, twist the silk and allow the fur-fibres or mohair to spin like a wire brush, pulling out the superfluous fibres as you twist. One turn close under the wings picked out and trimmed is all sufficient.

Unlike a coarse, stiff hackle stem, a single thread creates a remarkably fine and flexible wrapping "stem."

Modern, multistrand tying thread can be split to create a dubbing loop *within* a single thread. A tyer merely inserts dubbing or hackle barbs in the resulting slit. He then spins the thread or bobbin to create a delicate, dubbing halo around the thread. The simplest way to open thread is to counterspin the thread and, while the thread slowly spins, draw the index finger and thumbnail along the thread to flatten it. Then, pass the point of a fine needle through the flat thread where it

Split-thread CDC hackle

attaches to the hook shank or, easier yet, where the flat thread passes over the fingernail. Slowly draw the needle down to open the slit while using the fingers to keep it open. If sparsely dubbed, this method produces a delicate dubbing haze with the thread color showing through. Because of the single thread and sparse dubbing, this is an excellent method for CDC hackles and micropatterns. If necessary, use a standard spinning hook to keep the slit open.

Spinning a standard bobbin is an inefficient method for spinning a thread. Because the thread is not firmly attached to the bobbin, excessive spins are required. The thread must be spun within the bobbin barrel and down to the spool itself. A special Spin-Bob solves this problem. Another tool, the Splitter, has a needle at one end and a spreader at the other end. Both tools, based on my designs, were constructed by Frank Matarelli. The Splitter (1) splits the thread and (2) manages the loop. The Spin-Bob (3) spins the loop. Although the Spin-Bob is complex, a fine brass or stainless-steel rod can create a Splitter. Both the Spin-Bob and Splitter are demonstrated in Chapter III.

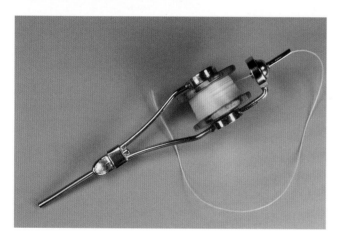

The Spin-Bob

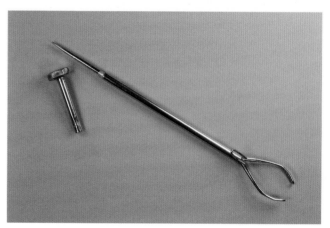

The Splitter

The Parachute Hackle

Leaves twirled down from the branches in the mild autumn light. My Parachute Adams matched their slow descent and drift. It floated long and flush in the surface until a trout took and left a ring in exchange. October always hatches size 18 parachutes. The Adams was small, subtle and, due to the design, seductive. A parachute pattern has a hackle that radiates horizontally (usually) from a vertical stem, such as a wing base, supporting the pattern on the water surface. According to Paul Schullery's *American Fly Fishing* (1987), parachute patterns date back (at least) to the late 1920s.

In 1950, J. Edson Leonard called the parachute pattern "a radical among dry flies." Leonard listed the attributes of the "radical" radials: (1) Parachutes provide maximum surface area with minimal barbs. All the barbs lend support; therefore, few turns are required. (2) Parachutes float the pattern flat on the surface rather than above it, thus eliminating the arching monofilament—that reflecting alarm—near the pattern. (3) Parachutes imitate the "straddle-legged" appearance of natural insects. (4) The horizontal hackle settles the hook softly upon the surface "as delicately as a lazy snowflake." Truly the horizontal hackle retards descent and the splayed barbs increase floatation. The splayed, horizontal barbs may also imitate the *surface imprint* of an insect better than the dense and random barbs of traditional, vertical hackling.

There are several other aspects of the horizontal hackle. Parachute barbs may be shorter than conventional barb length ($^3/_4$ shank length). William Blades, in *Fishing Flies and Fly Tying* (1951), noted that heavy hooks require long and dense parachute barbs. When wrapping parachutes, Blades also strokes the barbs down so they are at right angles to the stem. This allows each barb complete exposure. I often strip one side of the hackle for a neat pattern; merely increase the number of wraps for adequate buoyancy.

Parachutes create a unique light-pattern and imprint upon the surface, perhaps more suggestive of natural insects. Stance and imprint upon the water and the resulting light-pattern produce certain signals that provoke rises. The imprint of parachutes and CDC hackle creates light sparkles that are usually more effective than conventional hackle. Conventional hackling, which punctures the surface film, restricts the barbs to a comparatively small area beneath the wings. In contrast, parachute barbs radiate on the surface. A parachute design cocks the pattern well and permits full view of the wings.

Curiously enough, C. F. Walker, in *Fly-Tying as an Art* (1957), believed that the parachute hackle, with the front or forward barb-arc trimmed (the semicircle barbs cut away) can *only* imitate spent spinners. Walker found no advantage in the parachute. Nevertheless, in the '50s, the parachute became popular. T. R. Henn, in *Practical Fly-Tying* (1950), observed that the "hackle setting [of the parachute pattern] shows up the full values of the body colour; and many fisherman consider this to be the more important component of the fly."

Not all tyers have been enamored of the parachute. Frank Elder, in *The Book of the Hackle* (1979), proclaimed that the parachute and other variations are—according to their inventors—a step forward in the evolution of the dry fly. "They are, of course, nothing of the sort, all that they are attempting to do is to produce an alternative to the proper dry-fly. The dun sits on the surface of the water, so the imitation must do the same." He added that "A parachute fly . . . is not a representation of a newly hatched dun. It is simply a production which is easily seen and will float for a long period before becoming waterlogged. The fact that it will catch fish and indeed at certain times may be more effective than a really good dry-fly is not the point." Elder acknowledged, however, that the parachute may be taken by trout for an emerging or trapped dun. At such times, he then conceded that a parachute may be used. "But," he concluded, "We should clearly realize that we are representing a dun in a special condition, we are not representing a dun as it sails down the stream waiting for the wings to dry." Thus, the undignified parachute emerger, according to Elder, loses to "the proper dry fly." Such attitudes are not prevalent today.

A parachute pattern is usually less durable than a traditional tie. Furthermore, the parachute presents a tying problem: the hackle tip must be secured beneath a tangle of barbs. Some of the following methods appear exacting and difficult. Practice and patience, however, solve most problems.

The Barlow-Gallows Method

It would be remiss to leave out the original stem-loop method. Besides, I love the tale of the method. Years ago, Bob Barlow, an English engineer at the Woomera research station in Australia, stepped into the Veniard Fly Shop in England. The collaboration of John Veniard and Bob Barlow created the gallows tool, a simple wire scaffold with a hanging hook. John Veniard, the doyen of English tyers, described the meeting and the Barlow method in *Fly-Tying Development and Progress* (1972). The concept is simple: a light spring tension holds a stripped and looped hackle stem. The hackle then wraps around its own stem and locks to create a knotted parachute hackle.

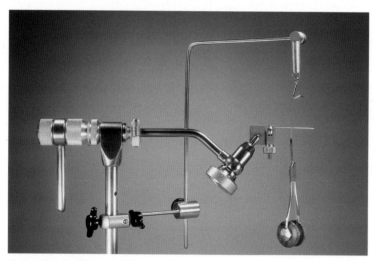

A parachute gallows: needle method

The Self-Parachutes

If the parachute remains in position on the hook, then mount the hackle firmly. However, the Barlow method also permits creating parachute *disks* that may be mounted in *any position* on a hook. The mounting thread does not form the parachute: the stem knot does. To create a *removable* parachute, mount the hackle (with few wraps) on a needle. *When working with needles, use protective eyewear.* Form the stem-loop and continue as explained. After tying the hackle in a knot, merely cut the bottom threads with a razor blade and remove the "self-parachute."

Place a drop of cyanoacrylate gel in the hackle hub and press the parachute between glass sheets for several hours. These flat parachute disks (looking like circular saw blades) may then be sewn on a hook with tying thread, like buttons, in any desired position. Here are the steps.

The Self-Parachutes

 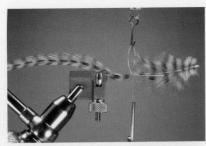 

1. Strip the hackle base of barbs and fluff. For grip, I leave a small webbing tuft at the extreme base. Mount the hackle concave side down with two or three firm wraps. For detachment, mount the parachute on a needle. Alternately, the parachute can be mounted directly to the hook.

2. Loop the stem as illustrated. Use no more than four wraps, held by bobbin weight, to secure the loop. This is important because the stem must be able to slide under these wraps during the knotting process. Connect the tension hook to the stem-loop.

3. Next, wrap the hackle at the base of the loop several times while the loop is held in tension. After sufficient hackle turns, use fine-tipped tweezers or hackle pliers to draw the hackle tip *through* the stem-loop.

4. Remove the tension hook from the loop and gently hold the hackle tip. Then, pull the stem base to knot the hackle. When it's knotted, trim the stem and hackle tip, leaving about 1 millimeter of excess ends for security. For complete security, place a drop of cyanoacrylate *gel* in the hackle hub. Here, the hackle is shown with the stem attached.

5. A parachute disk

John Veniard's *Fly-Tying Development and Progress* (1972) illustrates how the tips of two hackles, wrapped and knotted in this manner, create wings and how the long, base stems form a foundation for an extended body. Practice may be required to achieve proper wing length.

The Parachute Emerger (the Barlow Suspender Method)

This generic pattern uses the Barlow, or stem-loop, method to tie emerger and "suspender" patterns. Match the hatch for size and color. A dark thorax and a pale-yellow abdomen serve well for various emergers and drifting pupa. Note that the parachute is mounted in the final position. This method is simpler and faster than it appears. Position the hook 45° down during tying.

The Parachute Emerger (the Barlow Suspender Method)

Barlow Suspender Pupa

1. Mount, with a dubbed thread, the stripped stem hackle, concave side down. Place dubbing over the wraps.

2. Create a stem-loop and secure with three dubbed-thread wraps. Once formed, it is difficult to place dubbing beneath the parachute hub.

3. Wrap the hackle around the base of the loop and pull the hackle tip through the loop.

4. After sufficient wraps, pass the hackle tip through the stem-loop. Then, while holding the hackle tip, gently pull the hackle stem (merely pull the "cord" of the parachute) to knot the hackle. After knotting the hackle, trim the hackle tip. Then trim and secure the stem end along the hook shank. Add tails if required, dub the thorax and the abdomen. Finally, whip-finish the head.

The Indicator (the Barlow Indicator Method)

It is possible to add an indicator or spinner wing prior to "closing" the parachute. After the hackle tip passes through the stem loop, secure the hackle tip with hackle pliers. Place a small amount of waterproof, long-strand dubbing in the stem loop. Close the knot to trap the dubbing. Remove the hackle pliers and trim excess. Mold the dubbing strands into an indicator "flame" on top of the pattern.

To make a spinner indicator, merely insert waterproof yarn in the loop. Close the loop and trim excess. In addition, the closed stem parallels the shank, thus making an excellent lock for spinner wings. Add a cement dot to the center stem if desired.

The Posted Parachute

Unlike the Barlow method mentioned above, most parachute methods require a supporting post. Feather fibers, animal hairs, hackle stems, yarns, and wires often make parachute posts. Even hook design has incorporated the post. A parachute hook, known as the Gyro, came from William A. Brush, a Detroit automotive engineer. On April 16, 1931, Brush applied for a patent of a special loop-eyed hook for tying parachute patterns. The purpose was to position the pattern on the surface to "closely correspond to the position that a live fly would have on the water." Brush's rather comprehensive patent (#1,973,139 granted September 11, 1934) illustrates three models: (1) a return eye-loop to form the hackle extension, (2) a shank-loop hackle extension, and (3) an attached separate hackle extension.

Parachute hooks were also produced in England (patent #379343) under the name Ride-Rite. In an advertisement, Hardy Brothers of Alnwick observed that "the spread of the hackle lies in the same plane as the hook shank and. . . is better arranged to support the fly in the correct position on the water." Gerald Burrard, in *Fly-Tying: Principles & Practice* (1945), noted that Alexander Martin, a "tackleist" of Glasgow, produced parachute patterns with "a small carrier of stout gut or fine wire which sticks out vertically from the middle of the shank of the hook. The result is that the plane of the hackle lies on top of the surface of the water, and the whole effect of the hackle is to ensure the hook floating in a horizontal position." Parachute hooks usually have that single fatal flaw: weight. The extra shank-wire of the mounting post makes most parachute hooks a tad heavy. Though the parachute hook did not become ubiquitous, the parachute design did.

Parachute proportions and density vary among tyers. The water usually determines the hackling. To imitate insect legs, hackling may be short and sparse. To float over fast or broken water, the hackling may be thick and long. Unlike the standard dry fly, few hackle wraps are required for parachutes. The traditional fly pokes its barbs into the surface: the parachute lays its barbs gently along the surface. For this reason, parachute hackling can be short and sparse. For increased buoyancy, barb length may be the standard ¾ shank length or longer. Datus Proper, in *What the Trout Said* (1982), advocated mounting the parachute thoracic style (hackle mounted at midshank or slightly forward) for better balance.

To offer the trout contrast and sheen, Proper wrapped the hackle shiny side down. Floatation may be improved, however, by mounting the hackle concave or dull side down. For hackles with prominent concavity, this pushes the barbs down for support.

The Parachute Poly Pupa

The parachute pupa is simple and effective. The polypropylene yarn, with a specific gravity slightly lighter than water, forms the parachute post and wing case.

The Parachute Poly Pupa

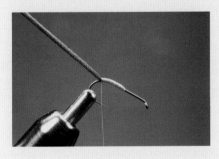

1. Mount a length of poly yarn as illustrated and attach the yarn to a tension hook. Mount the hackle securely and dub the thorax.

2. Then wrap the hackle several times around the base of the yarn. Capture the hackle tip with thread and secure.

3. Pass the poly yarn down between the barbs to form a swollen thorax and secure. Add the abdominal dubbing and whip-finish

Mounting and Wrapping the Standard Parachute

Parachute hackle may be mounted and wrapped in various ways. This method, which I consider one of the best, solves many problems. The classic challenge with parachutes is the finishing wraps. The hackle tip, which must be secured, is usually hidden beneath a logjam of splayed barbs. This method produces a rather neat finish, devoid of ornery barbs.

Mounting and Wrapping the Standard Parachute

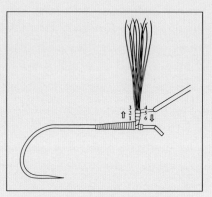

1. First, carefully prepare the hackle. Caress the hackle so that barbs stand out at right angles to the stem. Strip the barbs from the stem base to the proper barb length. In some cases it may be appropriate to remove the inside barbs from one side of the prepared hackle. In any case, clip hackle pliers to the hackle tip and strip both sides of the smaller, top barbs by pulling them toward the base, opposite the growth direction. Strip all barbs not the proper length.

2. Post the wing for parachute placement. After mounting the wings, spiral three flat wraps up, followed by three flat wraps down on the wing base. Put wrap four over wrap three, five over two, and six over one.

3. Next attach the hackle vertically along the post with firm wraps. The post may be held in tension with a gallows clip. Note the illustrated angular L-shape stem lock, the uniform barbs, and the stripped stem.

4. With touching wraps, spiral the hackle down over the post wraps. When the hackle stem arrives at the hook shank, pull the stripped stem down. Push the front parachute barbs back and capture the naked stem with a few firm wraps.

5. If desired, dub the fore-shank. Whip-finish to complete. The stem sans barbs, allows a small, neat finish for any type of parachute post.

The Single Post

By attaching a small wire post, any hook becomes a parachute hook. Use .020" wire (or finer) available in hobby stores. To decrease the added weight, keep wire length short. For safety, wear protective eyewear when shaping and cutting wire. Bend

wire before trimming to length. After mounting the post, add a drop of cyanoacrylate to the wraps. Mount the tail and body after connecting the post. It may be easier to mount, wrap, and secure the hackle before dubbing the front. Pliable post
wires may be crimped down, usually by bending it back, after the pattern is tied.
Although the process approaches "fussy," it allows some unusual mount positions.

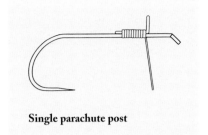

Single parachute post

The Expanded Parachute

For increased floatation, expand a parachute hackle from two posts. This technique works well for terrestrials such as ants and spiders. Dub the post mount
before wrapping the hackle. After hackling, fold down the soft-wire posts. Place
a drop of cyanoacrylate gel at each turning "post." Though typically untidy, the
radial and lateral barbs create excellent buoyancy.

Expanded parachute pattern

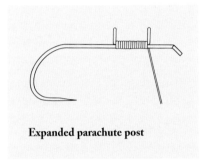

Expanded parachute post

The Stem Post

This method wraps the hackle around its stem. First mount tail and body. Then,
strip the hackle base and mount as illustrated.

Keep the mounting point small. While maintaining tension upon the stem
(with fingers or gallows), wrap the hackle around the stem post. After sufficient
hackle wraps, pass the stripped stem between the barbs and secure. I often cover
the stem base with dubbing.

The stem mount

The stem parachute pattern

Parachuting has never been so simple. These methods take advantage of long, quality hackles. The parachute design is functional and realistic. The advantages of the design have encouraged tyers to explore various ways of "wrapping horizontal." In difficult waters, small parachutes may land more fish than any other fly design and they often work where tradition fails. Nevertheless, the quest for the best parachute method is incomplete. We continue to explore the possibilities of these radical radials.

The Head and Thread

Traditionally, tying thread appears only at the head. Of course, some patterns may use tying thread as body or underbody. In other patterns, the thread color may flicker through the dubbing. In general, tying thread hides deep within the pattern. Early tyers sometimes matched thread color to a distinctive or vivid eye color of the mayfly. The modern tyer often emphasizes the specific head shape:

1. The standard, hook-eye length, tapered head
2. The small ball head of the salmon fly
3. The hidden head with three or four tucked whips
4. The large, shaped head designed for eye mounting
5. The long, thin head for beaked baitfish

Though most tyers admire and wrap a small head, others tyers have advocated the opposite. In *Fly-Fishing and Worm Fishing for Salmon, Trout and Grayling* (1876), H. Cholmondeley-Pennell encouraged tyers to exaggerate the head:

> With regard to the heads of flies, these can, on the above principle of tying, be made almost microscopic without any sacrifice of strength; but I advise the angler, not withstanding, to dress them large. The heads of Trout-flies are usually made much too small—much smaller, that is, than they are in nature, and smaller therefore than is desirable; because it should be the aim of the fly-tyer rather to exaggerate than to diminish in the artificial imitation all the prominent features of the natural insect, so that on a quick glimpse the resemblance may be unmistakable.

Though the distinctly colored eyes of a natural may be imitated with thread, I find no distinct advantage of an exaggerated head. A tippet tied to the hook eye suggests enough bulk for most insect heads.

All heads should be firm and neat. The direction of the whip-finish is important. It matters whether you whip-finish left to right or from right to left. Though the direction of the underwraps of the whip-finish make little difference, the finishing overwraps (for a right-handed tyer) should be from *left to right* (the reading direction) toward the hook eye. Notice that, when wrapped toward the eye, the overwraps finally end where the thread tucks under. Thus, whipping from left to right produces a smooth, tight knot with parallel wraps. The head taper should not be so severe that the thread wraps slide toward the hook eye. When pulled taut, the whip-knot butts against the natural taper of the head.

If done from right to left, there will be an exposed, diagonal thread crossing over the head wraps (note illustration). This whip direction permits slack in the exposed, diagonal stand. The right to left thread travels away from where the thread tucks beneath the overwraps.

Thread hugs and holds the fragments that make a Royal Coachman or an Adams. Without thread, most flies could not stand on their tails and barbs. Thread deserves thought. When selecting a tying thread, consider the various features: material, size, surface, texture, finish, twist, stretch, strength, sizing, wax, and color. Certain techniques, such as hair spinning, may require a strong thread. However, strength alone is not the primary consideration. Color, stretch, texture, or twist may be just as important for a particular pattern.

Most tying threads are either nylon or polyester. Silk is still the choice for traditional soft-hackle patterns. Dacron is a DuPont trademark for a polyester fiber made from dimethyl terephthalate and ethylene glycol. The strength of Dacron approaches nylon but, like other polyesters, it differs significantly in elasticity. Nylon stretches up to 30 percent before breaking; the maximum elongation of Dacron is approximately 10 percent. Depending upon denier and twist, silk expands about 15 percent of its length before rupture.

Silk

Silk, though often now replaced with other fibers, is a traditional and valuable asset to the modern tyer. Under magnification, a silk strand looks like a smooth, glass rod. Because silk does not grow, there are no surface scales: the silk worm extrudes silk as a viscous protein. The scaleless surface produces silk's translucent, lustrous sheen. Silk is both a tying thread and a body material.

Fly tyers have used silk tying threads longer than any other thread. Pearsall of England, established in 1795, has bejeweled the tying table with their silks for over two hundred years. Early tying literature specifically names these silks. The original colors and color codes include White (1), Primrose Yellow (3), Lemon Yellow (5), Amber (6), Gold (6A), Purple (8), Black (9), Grey (9A), Scarlet (11A), Cardinal (12), Olive Green (16), Brown (17), Hot Orange (19), Light Olive (20), Classic Chestnut (33), Royal Hunt (35), and Claret (191). This organzine silk—manufactured from Chinese bombyx raw fibers—is made by twisting a single strand and then counterspinning two or more strands together, creating about ten mild twists per inch. The organzine raw silk strands are about 20/22 denier—a measure of thread size discussed in detail on the following page. After processing (which significantly alters the denier), the eight-strand organzine Gossamer is stouter than the individual silk strands, with a total denier of 126. Unlike shorter, *spun* silk fibers, Gossamer, a *reeled* silk, has two tying attributes—negligible fuzziness and twist. In *Floating Flies and How to Dress Them* (1886), Frederic Halford praised Pearsall's Gossamer silks by name. "For tying-silks, when making small

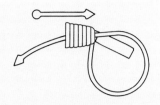

The proper direction for finishing whips. When the final thread wraps travel from *left to right*, the thread tucks beneath the head. As the tag-end draws left, the resulting knot butts against the head taper.

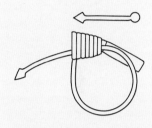

When the final wraps travel from *right to left*, an exposed cross-thread appears over the head wraps. Note that the thread tucks beneath the head *opposite* to where the thread wraps finish.

flies, nothing I have yet seen can compare for quality with Messrs. Pearsall's reels of gossamer silk made for the purpose, and the same silk doubled and slightly twisted for larger patterns." However, by 1910 (*The Modern Development of the Dry Fly*) Halford rejected silk as a body material:

> Silk, which in olden times was used for the bodies of many standard patterns, is quite out of date. Immersion in water effects a startling change in the shades of colour of silk bodies, invariably darkening them, and in many cases quite changing the colour. Thus, for example, white floss silk when wetted becomes a slate grey, many of the yellows assume an olive tint, and all the olive silks darken so much that the very palest shades of olive silk procurable are, when soaked, dark enough for the darkest of olives in the natural insect.

Silk is often criticized because it darkens when wet. However, unlike some materials, silk has a consistent and predictable color shift. Tyers use silk for what it will become, not what it is. Few body materials match the subtle sheen, transparent iridescence, and history of silk. Pearsall's silks, the material of choice, are still used extensively for historic imitations, soft-hackle flies, classic salmon patterns, and traditional wets.

Thread sizing is chaotic. The "aught" rating, such as 3/0 or 6/0, is remarkably capricious in the fly-fishing industry. What one manufacturer calls 3/0 may be another's 5/0. The Gudebrod Company claims that the aught scale originally came from silk sizing, ranging from 00 through 10/0. Tying thread was marketed using the standard correlated sizes of braided silk medical sutures. Gudebrod still uses that standard of measurement.

When comparing thread sizes, think in terms of denier, a manufacturing standard for sizing thread. Denier is simply the gram weight of 9,000 meters of a thread. A 180-denier thread weighs 180 grams per 9,000 meters. An 80-denier thread is finer than a 180-denier thread. Though the denier designation indicates weight (mass) rather than diameter, diameter is usually relative to weight. Thus, the smaller the denier, the finer the thread. One manufacturer's 100-denier thread is another's 100-denier thread. Denier is more explanatory than aught ratings. A tyer, however, cannot accurately calculate the denier of a thread. Fortunately, more companies have determined that the denier rating should appear on their tying-thread spools.

Tyers usually select thread according to hook size and tying method—a strong, flat thread for spinning deer hair, a fine thread for tying Trico spinners, silk for soft-hackle patterns. Many tyers use the heavier threads, such as 3/0 (an "aught" rating), for size twelve and larger.

Which is best, a heavier thread wound around the shank ten times or a finer thread wound twenty times? It makes little difference whether I take ten wraps with a five-strand thread or five wraps with a ten-strand thread. But with a finer thread, my tying seems smoother and more efficient; wrapping a fine thread takes more time but gives more control.

A smooth thread doesn't push or "chase" materials around the hook shank. A "pushy," textured thread, on the other hand, grips and grabs better. Most nylons are usually slicker than polyesters. Some nylons, such as unwaxed Monocord, may require additional skills in controlling materials. Without adequate continuous tying tension, materials may slip and slide under a slick thread. Some hairs, especially slick hairs, can slip through overwraps. A supplemental embedded wrap *within* the hairs usually solves this problem. To some degree, thread texture itself can act like wax, and a rough thread surface helps hold and bond material. To increase the texture and hold of a slick nylon, merely twist it. Though surface texture can be built into threads, at present, most flat, multistrand nylon threads are slicker than polyesters.

Thread twist is commonly the so-called "Z-twist." That is, on a vertical thread, the middle stroke of the Z indicates the direction of the twist. Most thread may be untwisted or flattened by spinning it as the drawing indicates.

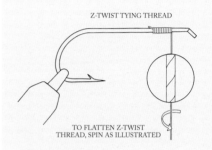

TO FLATTEN Z-TWIST
THREAD, SPIN AS ILLUSTRATED

The Z-Twist

The opposite twist is an "S-twist." Unlike most modern tying threads, which are Z-twisted, Pearsall's Gossamer has the S-twist. To determine twist direction, merely examine the thread under magnification. Some threads may have a very mild twist.

If you need extra width and grip, counterspin or flatten your thread. The first mention of counterspinning, I believe, appears in the first edition of *The Scientific Angler*, by David Foster (1882): "The tying silk should now be untwisted, so as to take all turn out of it, preparatory to wrapping on." Foster also offered the classic rationale: "The utility of the untwisting process will be conspicuously apparent in the making of fine-bodied artificials, as the substance of it is reduced by more than one-third." Fine, flat thread produces fine, delicate flies. Apparently twist does not significantly increase the strength of a thread as much as it distributes the strain more effectively. Some threads are available in a variety of forms, including flat, mild twist, and heavy twist (corded). Flat threads have a tendency to spread at awkward times. This attribute, however, is requisite for the split-thread method. Wrapping any thread, whether flat or twisted, imparts a clockwise twist (when viewed from above) to the thread. This is why dubbing "cords" along the hook shank. This clockwise twist may diminish or augment the thread's original twist.

A flat thread does not cut into the material as deeply as a tightly spun thread. Use flat thread for mounting fine hairs or quill wings, or when making smooth bodies. Tightly spun thread bulks quickly. Use it whenever bulk is required, such as "beading" in front of wings to erect them.

Flat Thread:

1. Hair spinning
2. Mounting quill wings
3. Creating smooth underbodies and bodies
4. Soft mounting tails to minimize flare
5. Creating a smooth head
6. Posting hair wings (base wraps round the wings to consolidate hairs)

Twisted Thread:

1. Beading to erect wings
2. Creating bulk
3. Applying dubbing
4. Positioning outrigger or divided tails

According to Karl Schmuecker of Wapsi Fly, nylon and polyester threads have nearly identical breaking strengths for the same denier. He also points out that nylon, unlike identical-denier polyester, has significantly more stretch. Jean-Guy Côté of Uni-Products claims that polyester has about 20 percent less stretch than nylon and about 10 percent more strength. Schmuecker's research indicates that most tyers prefer the strength and elasticity combination of nylon threads. A fly tied with stretched nylon is under constant pressure. Polyester threads have more limited stretch. Schmuecker believes that nylon usually tells you when it will break. When the stretch stops, the thread pops. In contrast, polyester doesn't declare its demise. It just snaps. Silk is even more subtle—the fibers silently slide apart under the stress. Some special threads, like Kevlar and GSP (gel-spun poly-ethylene) have radical strength with very little stretch. GSP is finer than Kevlar and like Kevlar can be used for hair spinning and saltwater patterns. Both Kevlar and GSP threads require tension when cutting with a sharp, sliding blade. In any case, use the elasticity of your thread to your advantage by continuously stressing the thread during tying. I usually apply about a pound of thread pressure when tying, although some threads and techniques may require as much as 1½ pounds or more. Thread selection and tension relate to hook size, materials, and method. Thread strength alone, however, does not make a thread. No matter what their breaking strengths, most threads can tie most flies if you work within the breaking strength. Age and storage conditions significantly alter the breaking strength of threads: keep threads away from sunlight and heat.

A simple burn test can determine thread material. Use the odorless butane lighter, never a match. Each fiber reveals distinct traits when exposed to a flame. Here are burn tests for some common tying threads:

Acrylic: Acrylic shrinks or melts at an approaching flame and ignites quickly. It burns rapidly with smoke and a bright, sputtering flame. When withdrawn from the flame, it continues to burn, melt, and drip with an acrid odor that results in an asymmetrical, hard, black bead.

Kevlar: Kevlar ignites at approaching flame. It burns rapidly with bright orange-red flame and wispy black smoke. When withdrawn from flame, it extinguishes quickly. Residue is a fine, soft, black feathery filament. Kevlar is a slick and extremely strong thread that cuts only under tension.

Nylon: Nylon melts and shrinks from an approaching flame. Once in the flame, it burns slowly, smells like celery, and produces smoke. Once withdrawn, it tends to self-extinguish. The burnt residue is a hard, shiny brown, or gray bead.

Polyester: Polyester melts and shrinks from approaching flame. In the flame, it burns slowly and melts with a sweet smell. When withdrawn, it melts and drips, producing a hard, shiny black or brown bead.

Polypropylene (Olefin): Polypropylene melts and shrinks from an approaching flame. In the flame it burns with a candle-wax odor and melts. When withdrawn, it continues to burn and produces a tough tan bead.

Rayon: Rayon scorches or chars and ignites from an approaching flame. It smells like burning paper. When withdrawn from the flame, it continues to burn rapidly with a red afterglow. The residue is a gray to charcoal, feathery and wispy ash.

Silk: Silk curls away from approaching flame. In the flame, it burns slowly, sputters and smells like singed hair. When withdrawn from the flame, it may burn slowly or self-extinguish. It creates easily crushed shiny, round black beads.

To produce a lasting fly, early tyers waxed the silk and cemented the heads. Modern synthetics are remarkably durable; a tight whip-finish is all you need. Cement is more cosmetic than functional and, in fact, may add unnecessary weight to small drys. A thin wax coat reduces fraying and improves control over some materials and methods. A waxed thread captures a fine dusting of mole better than a slick synthetic. A heavily waxed thread may hinder flattening, jam the bobbin tube, and prevent cement penetration. On unwaxed thread, add a fine, high-tack smear when necessary. Many threads already have a bonding agent that stiffens and consolidates the fibers.

Early tyers usually selected thread colors based on the insect body color, the insect eye color, the color shift when wet or when melded with a particular dubbing. Polyester tying threads are available in more colors than nylon. Some nylon colors are rather garish. Usually, I prefer the more subtle colors of polyesters for trout flies. Like some tyers, I favor the stronger, brilliant nylons for saltwater and large freshwater flies.

The more I tie trout flies, the more I use just one thread color—white. With permanent markers, I can create colors that are not commercially available. Moreover, if desired, I can change the thread color several times on a single fly. Even small understandings about tying thread make a better fly. Thread and thread-work constitute the essential definition of artificial "flyness." Thread is the common denominator of fly tying. Without thread, a fly is merely a pile of floss, steel, and feather. With thread, there is a pattern.

The Synthetics

Since the publication of *The Treatyse of Fysshynge Wyth an Angle* (1496), the first detailed English commentary on fly fishing, there has been an ongoing quest for tying materials. The *Treatyse* lists the essential materials of the time: duck feather, peacock herl, and "cocke hakyll"—all still used today.

A mere two hundred years later, tying materials were remarkably more numerous and diverse. By 1700 the tyer, according to James Chetham's *Vade Mecum*, had "plentifully furnished" his "large Magazine Bag or Budget" with more than fifty materials, including such oddities as hog's down, colt hairs, camlet (various combinations of wool, silk, Angora goat, and later of cotton and linen), marten cheek fur, fieldfare (a thrush), throstle (another thrush), cop or crown of plover, and water coot.

There were, of course, no synthetics in the *Treatyse* or *Vade Mecum*, and many natural materials they listed were the staples of tying for the next three hundred years. This does not mean that tyers avoided experimenting with new materials. In fact, they debated the virtues of marten cheek fur, hog's wool, pike scale wings, eel skin bodies and Madagascar raffia. *Natural* insects, obviously, were best imitated with *natural* materials. Even Frederic Halford, the doyen of the dry fly, explored the dimensions of tying in 1886. He wrapped mayfly bodies with the "wheaten straw" or maize that covered Mexican cigarettes and used India rubber for extended mayfly bodies. His curiosity would surely have led him to synthetics had they been available.

Tyers wrapped new materials as soon as they were discovered or developed. Discovery and development exploded beyond imagination in the twentieth century, when scientists took simple, chemical molecules (monomers) and combined or synthesized them into larger molecules (polymers). Most synthetic fibers are relatively strong, lightweight, man-made liquid polymers. In 1938, DuPont led the development of nylon, the first synthetic fiber thought superior to a natural fiber. Before 1940, a few tyers wrapped fly bodies with cellophane and gum-rubber crepe. Since World War II, however, synthetics have surely become an important part of fly tying—the past sixty years have seen greater change in tying materials than the previous six hundred years. Attitudes have also changed.

There are perhaps three different attitudes toward tying with synthetics. The minimalist approach incorporates a *sparing* use of the fake stuff. Like most tyers, I may use some synthetics—a dash of Antron to spark dubbing or a shimmering slip of Z-lon—but only when it will produce an effect I cannot get from nature. Many tyers fall into the minimalist category.

The utilitarian approach, however, is perhaps more rational: it recognizes that natural and synthetic fibers have different attributes. This approach favors choosing materials based solely upon their individual properties. For example, a grizzly hackle might imitate the supple, barred body of baitfish, but a synthetic might best suggest the scale and flash.

Finally, the unabridged approach favors using *only* synthetics for some types of patterns. The unabridged tyer believes that synthetics are equal or superior to natural materials. Certainly, a traditionalist might argue that the exclusive use of synthetics produces a lure rather than a fly and is more akin to model building than fly tying. That argument is antique. Everything depends on how we define a fly. If a fly is anything "wound or tied to a hook" then this generic definition permits purely synthetic patterns. One such synthetic imitation, the peacock Tracer, appears later in the text. If pattern's purpose is to catch fish, then synthetics prove their worth, especially for warm- and saltwater species.

However, this is far more involved than fishing itself. Usually I admire a natural fly more than a synthetic fly. Natural materials usually require more tying skill than synthetics. For one thing, natural materials are less uniform than synthetics. As angling historian John Betts notes, "With synthetics, you don't have to worry if the rabbit slept on his left or right side." You may never know what challenges arise with natural materials until you begin tying. You must select a natural material carefully to determine its craft potential—what it can or cannot do. Furthermore, natural colors are usually more muted and subtle. Simply put, natural materials may give more challenge and, consequently, more pleasure. Still, while I appreciate the tradition and performance of natural materials, I recognize that synthetics are now part of tying history. They enrich our patterns with greater possibilities.

Selecting which synthetic to use may be the greatest problem of all. A tyer may not even know what is available, since there are a remarkable number of synthetics on the market. Manufacturers and distributors who use different names for the same product compound this difficulty. Seldom are synthetics manufactured exclusively for the fly tyer: they usually come from other industries and applications, such as tapes, fibers, cords, and specialized fabrics. In fact, a local fly shop may sell a number of products available at fabric and craft stores.

Synthetics offer some inherent problems. Terms like "nylon," "Antron," and "Mylar" are generic and fundamentally meaningless in themselves. The labels placed on synthetics (and commonly used) may be proprietary trademarks or marketing ploys. The term "nylon," for instance, describes a whole range of materials with a variety of properties. Rather than look for a particular product name, look for a product that has the characteristics you desire. Some synthetics are virtually useless unless you know the application or tying techniques. Fortunately, a few products come complete with tying directions as more manufacturers recognize the need to educate the tyer. Another problem with man-made materials is market longevity. Some will be available for a short time before newer and "better" products replace them. Polypropylene and Antron have become, if we may use the term, "traditional." Nevertheless, newer products challenge them. If a tyer appreciates a particular product, then it may be best to acquire a generous cache against a future famine.

To some extent, synthetics replace natural materials no longer available. Prohibitions on polar bear hair and seal fur increased the need for a translucent and reflective fiber. Both polar bear hair and seal fur have translucent fibers with shallow scales that scatter and disperse light. Poul Jorgensen's Seal-Ex, a synthetic seal fur, was one of the first accepted tying synthetics. For some tyers, Seal-Ex was better than the natural fur. A synthetic could actually make dubbing easier while increasing sparkle.

Synthetics have been more readily accepted by tyers for saltwater and warmwater patterns. Such patterns are less constrained by tradition. Even a traditionalist has to admit that few natural materials imitate, as well as synthetics, the scale flash of baitfish or the air bubbles and trailing shucks of emerging insects. Those who totally denounce synthetics needlessly restrict themselves.

Tying with Synthetics

Most standard tying techniques work well with synthetics. Some synthetics, such as the ultrafine dubbings, are much easier to use than their natural counterparts. There are, however, two inherent problems.

Due to the slick, uniform surface of man-made fibers, added attention may be necessary when mounting fine, synthetic strands. Often the strand ends are over-wrapped, folded back, and then overwrapped again to lock them in place. Also, a tyer should use a thread with some stretch and catch to "bite" into the material.

Also, tyers often use more material than required; only a few strands of Crystal Hair are required for flash and flame. Too much makes a fly gaudy and clumsy. Synthetics add electricity to patterns, but a tyer should regulate the voltage. Some patterns require a full charge; others, only a twinkle. Depending upon its denier and volume, synthetic dubbing can either increase or decrease its dubbing ease when blended with natural fibers. Clear Antron, for example, should not comprise more than 20 percent of the blend because it can weaken color and reduce dubbing quality.

The Characteristics of Synthetics

The reflection, translucence, and iridescence of synthetics are, usually, superior to natural materials in their ability to shatter and scatter light. Iridescence is one of the more complex qualities; it is the prismatic quality caused by differential refraction. Twisted and crinkled strands merely offer reflective, angled surfaces. Light bubbles seem to cling to curled strands.

1. **Absorption:** All natural fibers contain 10 percent or more of water. Some natural fibers, such as wool, can absorb up to 30 percent of their weight in moisture. In general, synthetic fibers have little or no absorbency. At 95 percent humidity, nylon has 6.5 percent moisture content; acrylics have 2.5 percent moisture content while polyesters have a mere 2 percent. Fibers with such low absorption usually have static cling. Several modern synthetic dubbings are waterproofed for even greater floatation. Float foams, however, may lose buoyancy when tightly compressed with thread.

2. **Texture and Shape:** Synthetics have a wide texture range. They may be rough and stiff or soft and supple. Although a smooth surface and uniform shape characterize synthetic fibers, manufacturers can "build" various shape and textures into them. The material, the processing, the diameter, the crinkle, and the cross-section all determine shape and texture.

3. **Color:** In general, synthetics have a wider and brighter color range than natural materials. Synthetic colors can also be iridescent, fluorescent, phosphorescent, and (so-called) holographic.

4. **Density:** The density of some synthetics increases water entry and sink. Some synthetics, such as polypropylene, are lighter than water. Fibers are compared by measuring the specific gravity based on the density of water at 39° Fahrenheit. The fibers with low specific gravity are lighter than those

with a high number. Polyethylene and polypropylene (an olefin) fibers are lighter than water and, consequently, are excellent for dry-fly patterns. The specific gravity (sg) of water is 1.0. Polypropylene has a specific gravity of .91 to .92. Polyester ranges from 1.32 to 1.38. Acrylic is 1.7 and nylon, 1.14.

5. **Durability:** Most synthetics are superior to natural products in their resistance to chemicals, insects, saltwater, sunlight, heat, humidity, mildew, and general deterioration. Furthermore, some synthetics are remarkably strong: a typical nylon tying thread rates a high 7 grams breaking strength per denier, compared to silk tying thread, at 5 grams per denier.

6. **Dubbing Ease:** Synthetics may be easy or difficult to dub. Denier, cohesiveness, fiber length, crinkle, twist, texture, shape, and stiffness all affect dubbing. Ultrafine dubbing may be a mere 1.2 denier, which is remarkably fine when you consider that 7 denier nylon is nearly transparent. Most polypropylene dubbings range from 2.8 to 3 denier.

I admit that I am curiously ambivalent about synthetics. I greatly resent them and yet admire what they do: I am probably not alone in this. No matter, synthetics are now standard. The shine and quality of synthetics can surpass some natural materials that it replaces. My first encounter came many years ago when I began using nylon thread. Oddly enough, I never considered it a synthetic. I was just solving a tying problem; silk was too thick and too fragile. A more perverse problem, though, was wrapping metallic tinsel. The sharp edges cut thread and fingers. Tinsel refused to lie quietly, and it tarnished with astonishing speed. I then tried the new Mylar tinsel. It was bright and clean, with silver on one side and gold on the other. It neither kinked nor dulled. Furthermore, the elasticity produced a tight, smooth body. Clearly, a tyer could not wish for more. As synthetics grew, so did my opinion of them.

Tying can be as simple as wrapping woolly buggers or as complex as weaving gnats. It accommodates all interests and all skill levels. Like many tyers, I enjoy past methods. Few, if any, tyers will wrap William Blacker's charming and challenging winged larvae. Early materials may no longer be available, but this, for a modern tyer, is no limitation. The range of modern materials and methods would stagger early tyers. Yet, the past offers something more than material. It offers creative imagination. Modern tyers should substitute available materials and modify these methods for their own delight. A thoughtful and creative tyer limits neither knowledge nor skill. Tying is perpetual discovery. Tying history, if properly read, is remarkably rich and modern.

No matter how limited your tying, there is a method or pattern to match it. And no matter how brilliant your tying, there is always a method or pattern to challenge it. Most tyers broaden their skills. Good tyers are seldom entirely satisfied with their creations. They enjoy the challenge as well as the pleasure and the history of tying. Do not think that tying is only about methods and materials, insects and fish. Good tying is functional, but the love of form and precision of workmanship go far beyond anything that practical necessity requires. As Dr. Thomas Whiting once declared, "Fishing is fishing, but tying is an art." Good tying is mostly about the tyer.

CHAPTER III

PERSONAL PATTERNS

THE FOLLOWING "PERSONAL" PATTERNS INCORPORATE VARIOUS antique and modern methods. Some patterns are variations on historic themes; others are entirely mine. Even the included traditional patterns often have a personal touch in design or method. For a few patterns, there are new methods and tools, such as the Spin-Bob, the Splitter, and the Curling Cross. Many have history and enchanting tales. To me, these intriguing wraps explore new methods or solve old problems. Some also reveal the theories or assumptions behind the wraps. Some patterns include imitative elements, such as eyes and antennae. Such detail reveals imitative possibilities, not functional requirements. Merely omit any element deemed superfluous. Only curious, creative, or complex tying methods are illustrated. The text should clarify all other procedures. In any case, all patterns are "expansive" and encourage exploration.

The CDC Crane Fly

Curiously enough, crane fly imitations appear early in tying history; the earliest fly patterns were often those that duplicated the large naturals used as bait, such as mayfly drakes, grasshoppers, and crane flies. The term Daddy-long-legs (1814, *OED*) or Harry-long-legs was a term used for both the harvestman (genus *Phalangida*) and crane fly (family Tipulidae). The Harry-long-legs was the crane fly in the older tying texts, and not the harvestman. Charles Cotton's August Harry-long-legs had "the body of bear's dun, and blue wool mixt, and a brown hackle feather over all." Perhaps this pattern might be used either for a harvestman or a crane fly. An identical pattern appears in James Chetham's *The Angler's*

Vade Mecum (1700). For reasons unknown, Charles Bowlker rejected crane fly imitations, but both George C. Bainbridge (*The Fly-Fisher's Guide*, first printed in 1816) and Henry Wade (*Halcyon; or Rod Fishing with Fly, Minnow and Worm*, 1861) list patterns.

In *The Natural Trout Fly and Its Imitation* (1921), Leonard West recommended that crane fly patterns should have a few turns of *stiff* (italics mine) cock hackle at the thorax to support the wings and increase buoyancy. The wings are "speckled cock" hackle points and the legs, knotted pheasant-tail barbs. The heavy but realistic body is fawn-colored raffia ribbed with fine gold wire.

The crane fly, a *Tipulid*, has extremely long legs and body, ranging from ½–2". Many larvae are terrestrial, living in damp soil, while others are semi-aquatic, burrowing along streams and marshes. Some are truly aquatic, living as larvae under streambed gravel or silt. During and after a spate, heavy waters often flush them from their lairs and send them adrift in the current. Adults have a slender body, narrow wings, and long trailing legs. Though the adults tend toward brown, gray, tan, cream, and ginger, a dusty orange or a soft "salmon-color" attracts well. There are often small dark patches or splotches along the body.

Tying the CDC Crane

The CDC Crane Fly

Hook:	Short-shank, wide-gap dry-fly hook, size 12 or 10
Thread:	6/0 medium tan
Body:	Salmon, tan or cream, and dark brown or black polypropylene, furled and mounted
Legs:	Pheasant tail barbs (4 to 6) bundled and, to aid mounting, knotted at the base
Wings:	Two long, narrow, dun CDC feathers
Hackle:	CDC barb collar

1. To imitate the body blotches, furl two strands of polypropylene yarn together. First, one fine strand of black (or dark brown) should be tightly twisted before both are furled together. Slightly spin the paler strand to consolidate the fibers. The darker strand is fine and spun tightly to create fine blotches along the furled body. Notice the hand position prior to the *double* furling.

Hand position for furling: The right hand twists each strand and then combines them for double furling.

After twisting both strands, combine the strands (light and dark) and tightly spin them together. Pull on the center of the united strand, furling and forming the blotched body. To furl the strand, I merely hook the middle of the strand on the hook eye, and then slide it off. After furling, mount the body on the hook shank.

2. The legs are pheasant tail barbs. T. J. Hanna, I believe, popularized knotting pheasant tail barbs to make joints in legs. Such legs are attractive, but fiddly and time consuming. The following method makes legs much faster: Select six long barbs and, for expediency, knot them together at the base with a single overhand knot. Mount the base knot at the thorax position on the shank. This creates a trailing leg cluster much like the natural crane fly.

3. Firmly "delta mount" two narrow CDC feathers for wings. If desired, place a drop of cyanoacrylate glue gel (superglue) on the crossed stems. Other wing combinations might include stacked black and white CDC feathers. A top black feather may suggest the prominent wing venation.

4. Make a dubbing loop, insert CDC barbs and spin firmly. When mounting the CDC collar, wrap between the wings to divide them and finish with wraps in front of the wings. To complete the fly, whip-finish the head. The CDC collar enlarges the thorax and increases floatation.

The CDC Crane is simple, soft, and suggestive. It is especially effective for difficult fish in slow, clear water. This pattern is different enough to seduce when standard ties fail. Furthermore, the CDC Crane is an excellent bass pattern when twitched on the surface. Sometimes, soft deception seduces better than hard truth.

The CDC Particular

Beginning in 1887 and for forty-five years thereafter, William James Lunn was the river keeper of the Houghton Club waters on England's River Test. Three generations of Lunns—William, Alfred, and Mick—keepered those waters until Mick's retirement in 1992. J. W. Hills praised William Lunn's natural talents, including his effective fly patterns, in *River Keeper* (1934). The world-famous Lunn's Particular, an imitation of the ubiquitous olive spinner, is still presented to shy trout. "Therein lies its excellence: it kills well when fish are taking olives, and is marvelously good when they are shy or are taking spinners. It succeeds whether sunk or floating. If I had to be limited to one fly, I should choose it." Lunn created several other popular patterns, including the Houghton Ruby, the Sherry Spinner, and the Hackled Caperer, but it is his Particular—a simple, sparse tie—that seems to take impossible trout.

According to John Waller Hills, William James Lunn was fishing with Gilbey—the Gilbey of London Gin fame—on Park Stream, the 26th of April 1917. Fishing was poor. Gilbey eventually complained to Lunn, "The trout are too particular today." Lunn gave him a new pattern that immediately caught three fish. "Why, what's this fly?" Gilbey queried.

"It's a Lunn's Particular," was the reply.

Evidently, according to Harold Hinsdill Smedley, the term "particular" was English slang for "particular favorite," a reference to one's accustomed or favorite drink. So, as Smedley concludes, "Lunn was really making a little joke when he told Gilbey, a liquor distiller, that this fly was his particular." It has been the particular of particular trout ever since.

Lunn did not add a soft touch to his Particular; he probably considered the pattern delicate enough for most fishing conditions. He was, however, well aware of the value of soft patterns—patterns dominated by soft feathers and fibers. He used soft partridge hackle on several patterns, such as the Little Red Partridge. Hills described Lunn's appreciation of the singular benefit of softness. The Little Red Partridge

> has one immense advantage: being small and composed of a soft feather, it is easy to suck in. Lunn considers this very important. Trout, especially as the season gets on and they become fat and lazy, hardly open their mouths when taking a fly, either real or unreal. They draw in a thread of water, the fly with it, expelling the water through their gills and retaining the fly. Once, watching a trout being fished for on a hot day in slow water, Lunn saw it attempt to suck in the angler's artificial, but failed to get it into its mouth, as the fly did not pass its hardly opened lips.

Lunn encouraged the angler to change to the Little Red Partridge, which the trout took. Hills found that "far too little attention is paid to the softness of fibre and general collapsibility of a fly." He concluded that a soft feather is superior to the traditional stiff dry hackles and that "this difference exists even with the smallest 000 [approximately size 18] patterns."

Dressed on a small, offset Limerick hook, the original Particular used Pearsall's shade 13 Gossamer tying silk—the crimson worn by the Houghton Ruby pattern. Four barbs from a Rhode Island hackle made the tail. A stripped, undyed Rhode Island hackle stem created the segmented body, and two medium-blue cock hackle points, tied spent, formed spinner wings. Another medium Rhode Island cock hackle completed the fly. A feature of the pattern was the stripped and wound hackle-stem body. This wound stem appears to seduce trout when dubbing does not. According to Mick Lunn, in *A Particular Lunn* (1990), William positioned the wings across the hook shank and secured the trimmed stalks. He then separated the wings with figure eights, adjusted the wing length by pulling the stems, then folded the stems back and wrapped them as the body. This created a pattern that kept its wings.

The slender body with contrasting segments seemed to seduce the most selective trout. Such bodies appear in several effective patterns, including the Red Quill. The crimson thread probably drew attention to an otherwise muted fly.

Although the traditional tie cannot be improved, the Particular may be adapted for softer takes. Like many tyers, I have a perverse need to modify patterns for *particular* conditions (pun intended). By subtracting the stiff hackle and adding soft wings the fly gains "the softness of fibre and general collapsibility." The result is a simple, soft pattern for slow or slack water.

The imprint of all insects produces a telltale spoor. The CDC Particular has a more realistic imprint and profile in clear water than the original Particular. Furthermore, the fluffy CDC wing barbs trap bubbles, creating "the star burst of light" that Brian Clarke and John Goddard identify as the "first trigger" to a rise. The sparkles of a spinner wing may also initiate such a trout trigger.

The starburst "spoor" of a *callibaetis* dun created by the feet. Note also the abdominal imprint in the surface.

An adult stonefly reveals bright dimples as well as mirror reflections.

The CDC Particular (A Soft Variant)

1. For the tail, stack and mount Rhode Island cock hackle barbs or, for a variant, coq de Leon hackle barbs. Also various dyed stems can imitate a variety of spinners.

2. Mount and wrap stripped hackle-stem body.

3. Use wing burner to shape CDC wings. A drop of cyanoacrylate glue positions the wings together prior to mounting. Mount the wings securely with figure-eight wraps.

4. Split the thread and insert CDC barbs; then spin thread firmly.

5. Figure-eight CDC barbs to build thorax and create "hackle." Wrap fore and aft of the wings for adequate floatation. Finally, whip-finish and trim excess.

The Corixa

Many years ago when trout were large and summer days were very long, I scooped up a corixa, a water boatman, in my hand to examine it. As I closely admired its glistening wing case and long oar legs, it startled me with an abrupt flight. Stunned, I stared as it flew away and dove into the water. I had never seen a corixa on the wing before. They filled the shallows of the lake, resting at the surface and then diving down among the weeds. Underwater, their bodies shimmered in a silver sheath. Here was an insect as curious as its tying history.

It was not until Charles Edward Walker, in *Old Flies in New Dresses* (1898), that the corixa received proper "tying" attention. Walker dedicated a complete chapter to his pattern. The success of the pattern, however, did not silence the criticism that the artificial corixa was "a lure which should not be allowed on waters" devoted to flies only. Walker considered such criticism an attack upon his ethics as well as his tying. To defend both his pattern and reputation, he listed the various reasons why the corixa was a legitimate fly: (1) Corixae live in the water and are eaten by trout. (2) They possess wings and sometimes fly considerable distances. (3) The efficacy of the pattern depends upon imitating the movement of the insect. Walker even added that some noted anglers used a similar short, jerky retrieve with the popular sunken, downstream alder pattern. Thus ". . . if the lure in question is the imitation of an insect which can and does fly, made of ordinary materials used in fly-making upon one hook, this lure has a perfect right to be called a *legitimate trout-fly*." Though it was not a true *dry* fly, it was a fly. Walker concluded that his corixa imitation had met, both in his hands and in those of others, "with greater success than any other form of wet fly."

Walker's Corixa

Walker's corixa had a body of pale-yellow Berlin wool mixed with hare's mask dubbing, ribbed with silver tinsel. The wing case was two woodcock quill sections, stacked and laid flat over the body. A pair of paddle legs, made from a quill feather of a starling wing, maintained their spring even when soaked for long periods. To make these legs, Walker stripped the barbs from one side of the feather and "nearly so on the other, leaving however a few short stumps at the end to represent the paddle shape of the legs." Walker mounted the legs with the stem butt to the rear, and then bent the legs out at right angles to the body. He believed that the flexible paddle legs were critical to any corixa imitation. "I have seen the hind legs of the corixae when the insects have been suspended motionless in mid-water, standing out at right angles on each side of the body." Walker cast the pattern, allowed it to sink and then retrieved it in short jerks that flexed the legs. "Thus the *movement* of the legs of the natural insect when swimming is accurately imitated." Walker noted that the pattern was often taken during the dive as well as during the retrieve. His early imitation is still one of the best. In 1921, Leonard West, in *The Natural Trout Fly and Its Imitation*, gave another corixa in which he emphasized the wide head of the insect with brown wool eyes. The rest of the pattern, however, was far more conventional: merely a silver tinsel body, game-hen legs and a bustard wing case. In *Nymphs* (1973), Ernest Schwiebert offered a pattern with a hare-mask body and mottled brown turkey wing case. Fine oval tinsel suggested the air bubble while two pheasant tail barbs imitated the swimming legs.

The Insect

Though Walker's pattern appeared in June of 1897, anglers recognized the insect as a preferred food for fish as early as 1888. With well over one hundred species, they constitute the largest group of water bugs and are a principal fish food in late summer, fall, and winter. The corixa, the water boatman (family Corixidae), is often confused with the similar backswimmer (family Notonectidae). As the name implies, backswimmers swim dorsal-side down. Unlike the corixa, the highly predaceous backswimmer can inflict a stinging bite. Both insects occupy shallow water and have a jerky, sculling motion. Though there are some differences, both have oval bodies and whitish abdomens. The abdomens of some corixae are pale tan, brown, yellow, or white. They have four wings, tightly folded. The hind wings resemble the leathery wing case of beetles. Backswimmers often rest at the surface with the body at an angle, head down and swimmer legs extended. The wing case of the backswimmer is sometimes paler than a corixa case. Both are active in the shallows, rising and diving to replenish their oxygen. Fine hydrofuge hairs hold an air bubble in place along the abdomen. When submerged, corixae cling to plants, often for some time. Mating and migration may be the cause for most flights. They splat into the water like hail drops. Though I have not been privy to their music, the curious corixae even sing to each other. Due to the similarities of the boatman and backswimmer, a single pattern usually suffices.

The Elements of Imitation

Walker created the simple body shape, the conspicuous paddle legs and, with tinsel, the body bubble. The oval body, the elongated legs, and the bright air bubble are essential elements of imitation. Modern patterns usually incorporate glass or metal beads, silver tinsels, bright dubbings, and synthetic or feather wing cases. The pattern requires little weight: often a 1X or 2X heavy hook is sufficient. Because these are shallow running bugs, a floating line or sink-tip helps. Here are two effective corixa patterns: one for shallow running and one for deep running.

Tying the Corixa

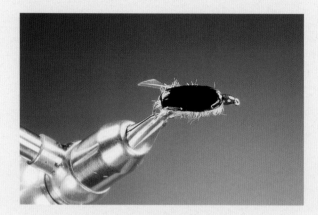

Hook:	Daiichi 1560, Mustad AC3906B, and Tiemco 3761BL, sizes 16 to 12
Thread:	Bright white and dark brown or black. For an alternate method, darken white thread with a permanent marker when required. Bright dubbing usually dulls with a dark thread. White thread will preserve the flash of bright beads and dubbing.
Dubbing:	Master Bright Pearl dubbing
Wing Case:	Black or dark brown Swiss Straw
Swimmer Legs:	A prepared quill feather. An excellent small feather is found on the jungle cock cape.
Air Bubble:	Spirit River glass bead, pearl, size large for a #12 hook.

1. Mount the hook securely in the vise and lay down a thread base. After the underbody is complete, whip and remove the white thread. Later, mount a dark thread for securing the wing case (i.e., the front of the wing case) and whipping the head. Alternately, a black permanent marker can change the colors when required.

The Corixa wing case, paddle legs, and partial underbody dubbing

2. Fold the Swiss Straw, typically 5 centimeters wide, several times to create approximately a 6 mm wide strip. Folding increases the wing-case bulk. Once folded, mount the Swiss Straw with mild tension. For a smooth, tight wing case, *wet* the Swiss Straw immediately *after* mounting. Swiss Straw accepts permanent markers and conforms better to the body than feather panels.

3. Next, add a small pod of Master Bright dubbing to the rear half.

4. The finest leg feathers come from the jungle cock cape. Select the small tapered feather with a pale center, not the "eyed" jungle cock feather. Other rapid-taper feathers, such as hen hackles, may be used. Next, prepare the swimmer legs as illustrated. This will create a small paddle tip at the end. With razor blade or scissors, trim off the barbs on one side, leaving short barb stubble along the stem to create some width for the leg. On the other side, pull off all barbs except those at the very tip. These barbs become the hairy paddle. Extended leg length should be approximately ³/₄-body length. Now make an opposing duplicate leg for the other side. For increased durability (though decreased flexibility), coat each leg with a fast-drying nail polish.

5. With figure-eight wraps, mount the legs on the shank immediately in front of the dubbing. For a weighted pattern, add a *small* pod of rear dubbing. Mount the legs, prepared as before. Then slip on a pearl bead in front of the legs and add the forward dubbing. Note that a single bead makes a shallow running bug. For even greater sink, add two or more glass or silver metal beads. The Spirit River glass bead—pearl, size large— fits a size 12 hook. The bead, glass or silver brass or tungsten, should slip over the hook eye and firmly fit on the thread foundation. Glass beads have more flash and less weight than metal beads. For depth control, tie the pattern with one, two, or more beads. Remember, however, that most corixae inhabit marginal waters less than 3 feet deep. After mounting the bead or beads, continue tying by adding the forward dubbing.

6. Add dubbing in front of the legs and whip-off the white thread. Now mount the dark thread. The dubbing should fill the wing case and create an oval body.

7. Fold the damp wing case forward and overlap the thread three times. Trim the excess and whip-finish the head. Build an adequate dark head.

8. Finally, add a coat or two of clear fingernail polish to the wing case. Let dry.

The beaded Corixa

A clutch of Corixa

A final observation: Writers have emphasized the flicking legs of the pattern when retrieving. During a rapid twitch, the legs do flex back. However, when they spring forward they encounter the density of water. The forward flex is not truly imitative of the quick, pulsing paddle of the insect. In fact, flex is only apparent if the pattern legs are long and supple. In corixa patterns, perhaps form is more important than function. In any case, these corixae are simple, attractive patterns that can prove effective during slack summer hatches or winter ice. Trout know them well and so should the tyer.

The Extended-Body Drakes

The extended fly body—one that projects above or beyond the hook shank— has been around for more than a century. Early tyers called extended bodies either *detached* (when mounted immediately behind the wings) or *semidetached* (when mounted at midshank or beyond).

In the 1880s Frederic Halford, that father of the floating fly, used shoemaker's bristles for the foundation of detached bodies. He often used horsehair, with India rubber, maize, or "wheaten straw" as a covering. The folded bristle straddled the shank with limbs mounted close behind the wing. Halford noted that most tyers make the body too long. The illustrations in his *Floating Flies and How to Dress Them* (1886) place the body length just beyond hook length, with the body mounted well forward. Halford's patterns included the Detached Badger, Olive, Iron Blue, Red Spinner, Jenny Spinner, and Spent Gnat. The sheer number of them, and the space allotted to them, not to mention their intricate tying, suggests that Halford considered them valuable.

H. G. McClelland, the gifted author of *The Trout Fly Dresser's Cabinet of Devices* (1898), used a needle as a temporary support for tying an extended body. A slotted cork wedge held the tying materials—India rubber and tail fibers—in place. After wrapping the body, McClelland removed the wedge and slid the body off the needle.

Roger Woolley questioned the efficacy of the extended body in 1932: "Detached bodies are not in any great demand. When well made and properly proportioned they look very neat and natural, but in practice they kill not better, if as well, as bodies tied on the shank of the hook." Despite this, in *Modern Trout Fly Dressing* (1932), Woolley included tying directions for both detached and semidetached bodies. His body used bristle or gut and oiled silk cloth. A wool underbody covered three cock-pheasant tail fibers and a transparent slip of oiled silk sheathed the "soft, juicy-looking body."

Woolley believed that flies formed on foundations of bristles or gut were unnaturally stiff. He noted that "many anglers object to them on account of this stiffness." McClelland, however, had already brought some perspective to the debate. He believed that we can have no final argument against the extended stiff body until we can "dispense with a hook of tempered steel as an essential portion of our fly."

There are special hooks, such as Partridge's K10 Yorkshire Fly Body Hooks (a 1991 improved design first patented by Peter Mackenzie-Philps in 1973), with a wire extension for the body. Tying on such hooks requires two steps. The hook mounts in the vise with the vertical eye facing left (for a right-handed tyer). After mounting the tail and extended body, the hook reverses, eye facing right, for completion. The Yorkshire hook, with nearly double the weight of an ordinary hook, finds few tyers today. The body extension, however, does permit rapid tying and the design hides the hook point in the hackle.

My own cursory experience suggests that extended bodies are most effective when imitating larger flies, such as mayfly drakes. The extended-body Green Drake, a standard Western wrap, is merely rolled deer or elk hair laced with thread. However, I find its abrupt, ragged butt unattractive.

Extended bodies are tied in a variety of other ways: with stretch yarns, nylons, wires, and needles. Some techniques are decidedly convoluted. Here, however, are two methods that deserve a try: Ernest Schwiebert's wire body and my own sleeve body.

Schwiebert's Wire Body

William F. Blades, a remarkable tyer who greatly influenced American pattern designs, wrote *Fishing Flies and Fly Tying* (1951). Blades tied extended bodies

Schwiebert's Wire Body

1. Once the wire is taut, mount the tying thread, tail fibers, and ribbing. Thinly coat the body length of wire with Dave's Flexament and let dry.

2. Mount the dubbed dorsal strand: either a length of dubbed thread or long-fibered dubbing twisted into a taper and mounted with the thin tip at the tail.

3. Apply dubbing to thread, dub forward and secure. This forms the underbelly.

4. Fold the dorsal strand forward along the top of body, and secure with a few thread wraps at the front (wrapping thread on the wire rather than the body itself). Spiral the ribbing forward, capturing the dorsal strip, and secure at the front with thread.

5. Finally, half-hitch and trim excess. A touch of Flexament fore and aft on the body locks the ends. To remove the completed body, reduce the wire tension and closely trim the wire at the tail, taking care not to cut a tail fiber. Leave about ¼" of wire at the front for seating. To attach the body on a hook shank, merely overwrap the seating wire, fold it back and secure it with more wraps. Then dress the fly conventionally with the hackle hiding the hook.

on a length of heavy nylon. Ernest Schwiebert, one of America's most knowledgeable angling writers, learned to tie from Blades. Schwiebert, however, creates bodies on a taut span of fine wire, about .005" in diameter, held between two vises. To minimize wire deflection, he keeps the span short (about six inches); he ties several bodies on a single wire. Like Blades, Schwiebert does not use a thread bobbin, and this method is best done without one. It is faster and simpler to use a length of thread and, when required, heavy English hackle pliers for weight.

For larger flies, Schwiebert may use several dubbed threads to create various body patterns. For example, two dubbed threads (lateral or dorsal) may extend any distance along the sides or the top. He may also add a facing hackle—a few front wraps of a different hackle—for contrast. Although this body does take some skill and time, Schwiebert rejects the tying methods that create stiff, "quick and dirty patterns."

The Extended Sleeve Body

If Schwiebert's extended body recalls the nylon core method of William Blades, my own technique favors that of H. G. McClelland. We both use a fine, stiff needle as a removable truss. My body base, however, is a polypropylene sheath or sleeve that encases the needle. After tying on the tail and body, I withdraw the poly sleeve, which flexes and floats, from the needle. This quick method permits the use of bobbins and whip-finishers. ***Special Note:*** *Remember to wear adequate eye protection when tying on an exposed needle.*

The Extended Sleeve Body

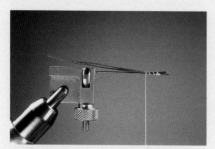

1. Firmly mount a needle (size 5–15) in your vise, with the point to the right (right-handed tying). The needle should be adequately long, stiff, and fine with minimal flex. Avoid a thick-diameter needle that produces slack in the completed body. The compact HMH tube fly tool firmly holds needles and clamps into any vice. For easy removal of the completed body, securely mount thread on the *tapered* needle point.

2. Next, select and mount, on top, two or three pheasant tail barbs for tails. Add several wraps to align tails along needle.

3. After mounting the belly (ventral) strand on the needle point, mount the back (dorsal) strand. The back strand, the darker strand, covers the tail base. Select polypropylene yarns, approximately three times the body length, for the back and belly strands. Few fibers are required for a delicate body. The proper yarn diameter for a #12 hook is *less* than a single strand of three-ply polypropylene yarn. A fold of yarn or dubbing mounted beneath the needle can create an egg sack extending slightly beyond the belly strand.

4. After mounting, flatten the strands so that they encircle the needle. The poly strand should sheathe the needle with a thin shroud. Do not build a bulky sleeve.

5. Tightly spiral the thread back to the end of the underbody and whip-finish the butt. After whip-finishing, spiral the thread forward on the underbody for the first body segment.

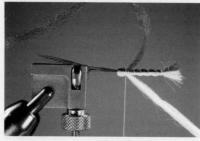

6. Fold both the overbody strands forward along the needle. Exit the thread between the back and belly strands. Firmly wrap one or two times in place for the first body segment or suture.

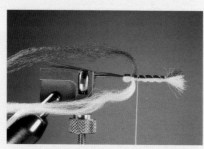

7. Then spiral the thread forward on the *underbody* for the next body segment. For parallel body sutures, advance the thread on the *underbody* before over-wrapping both body strands. For a rapid pattern, merely spiral the thread forward to secure the overbody.

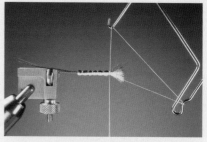

8. Complete all body segments.

9. At the needle point, whip-finish and trim excess yarn. For durability, add a drop of cement.

10. Firmly hold the entire body between your fingers and swiftly slide the body off the needle. Mount the body on a hook shank, at midshank or shoulder, to complete the particular pattern.

11. Although more elaborate patterns may be tied, a functional fly requires only a shoulder hackle and, if preferred, a facing hackle.

12. A burnt-wing, extended-body pattern

Though extended bodies appear primarily on mayfly drakes, other flies—such as damsel nymphs and adults—might benefit from these methods. These bodies are soft, supple, realistic, and attractive. For hook-shy fish, an extended body creates a larger fly on a smaller hook. Depending upon body mount position, the hackle may mask and conceal the hook point. Most influential angling writers have presented patterns and tying directions for extended bodies, though often warily. Yet clearly, some extended bodies are effective and elegant. They have a delicate charm and, with appropriate methods, are pleasant to wrap. Sometimes even taciturn trout admire them.

The Folded-Wing Wets

They say the Scots like at least two things naked: their whiskey and their flies. The soft-hackle winged wets in the Tweed, Clyde, and Tummel styles are frugal, sparse, and enchanting. If I were a novice tyer, I would begin with these flies: there are many subtle lessons from the North Country traditions. There is charm in taking a simple pattern and tying it well. For more experienced tyers, there is the challenge of minimalism and stark simplicity. The Scottish wets require only a pinch of materials, but a stack of skill in dubbing, hackling, winging, and proportions. Though writing about the sparse Usk style, Skues, in *The Way of a Trout with a Fly*, really defined the Northern patterns: "Here the theory appears to be that the artificial fly is a sketch. Note the slight shred of wing, the slim body, the slight but active hackle." He described the skeletal flies dressed for the tumbling Yorkshire streams. The wet fur body is "remarkably transparent and lets through, while it darkens and accentuates, the olive colouring of the waxed silk with which the fly is tied, and the tumbled hackle from the waterhen (moorhen) suggests the tumbled, dilapidated state" of a fly caught by the current.

These patterns imitate a variety of insects—emerging mayflies, drowned duns and swamped spinners as well as nymphs and larvae. They are readily submersible and swim well in the tumbling waters of fast-flowing streams; anglers generally cast them *upstream*, seldom allowing the patterns to pass below them. In *Scottish Trout Flies* (1966), W. H. Lawrie noted that the "Deliberate restraint in the use of materials, the short, slender bodies, sparse hackle, spare wings, and a preference for the sober hues of nature, all accord with the national tradition in respect to frugality and modesty." With considerable craft and a modicum of materials, the Scottish winged wets achieve the impression of delicate naturals.

Lawrie also discussed the unique variable body lengths of the Tweed, Clyde, and Tummel styles. The body length determines the required sink rate. The Tweed has a body that ends somewhere between barb and hook point; the Clyde body stops at midshank; and the Tummel body hugs the hackle, consuming only the first third of the shank.

Lawrie explained the rationale behind the abbreviated body and naked shank. "The implication is that Clyde fishermen required that their trout flies be more instantly submersible than those designed for fishing the larger Tweed; while the old Tummel fishermen went to extreme lengths to ensure that flies would sink immediately. In other words, the ranker the hook shank the better it would sink the fly; and the matter of degree to which the hook itself should act as a sinker is regulated by the character of a particular river. . . ."

When hook becomes *sinker*, the portion of naked shank defines the submergibility and explains the variation in wet-fly design. Since these traditional wets— or teams of wets—are fished upstream in fast water, the drifts are short. Rapid and frequent false casting dries a fuller wet fly, delaying the sink. The naked shank, however, absorbs no water and sinks a sparse pattern quickly.

Hooks

Select your upstream wetfly hooks carefully, paying particular attention to symmetry and weight. Those with standard-length perfect or round bends in 1X and 2X heavy wire are typical. W. C. Stewart, in his *Practical Angler* (1857), noted his preference for Bartleet's round-bend hooks; modern tyers often select Partridge's L2A (medium weight), L3A (light weight), and L4A (feather weight). Partridge's G3A, although designated a standard wire, is a medium-weight wet-fly hook. You can even use Partridge's J1A, with its bold wire and Limerick bend. Tiemco's 3769 (2X heavy), 9300 (1X heavy), and 101 (1X fine) make attractive upstream wets, as do Daiichi's 1530 and 1550, and Mustad's 3906, 3906B (1X long), and AC80000BR.

Herein drifts a contradiction. Conspicuous, heavy hooks sink quickly. Flies on inconspicuous, lightweight hooks—more suitable for selective trout—may not sink readily enough. Scottish tyers developed their original upstream wets for fast water that allowed the trout only scant scrutiny of the fly. In such waters, perhaps thick, bare shanks made no difference.

There has always been controversy concerning the proper method of tying the Clyde, Tweed, and Tummel styles. There may be as many methods as there are tyers. The following tying directions are for the two most abbreviated body types: the Clyde and the Tummel.

Like spiders or soft-hackle patterns, Scottish winged wets use Pearsall's Gossamer silk tying thread rather than floss for the body. For a slender body, wrap once out and once back. For an ultrathin body, divide the thread strands or counterspin to flatten the thread before wrapping.

E. M. Tod, in *Wet-Fly Fishing* (1914), demanded, "The wings of a fly should never be longer than the hook." Tails are seldom necessary in winged wets; if you add them, they should match the design—sparse and somewhat long.

Use just a haze of dubbing; it should halo the shank and allow the thread to show through a sparse, fine mist of fur. This melds the thread and dubbing colors into a final subtle blend. Typical traditional dubbings include mole, water rat and hare. Single, folded wings are often from starling and duck quills.

The "umbrella" hackle should be sparse—only one or two turns. The hackle barbs should only extend to the end of the Tweed body (to the end of the shank for Clydes and Tummels). According to Oliver Edwards, the tips of the mounted hackle should fall somewhere between the hook point and barb or at the end of the shank. Although most early writers recommended that the hackle be soft, some tyers mounted stiff, active hackles on their wets.

There are several ways to mount the hackle. Some tyers use W. C. Stewart's spider directions. First, attach the hackle by the bottom stem and trim the excess. Then, "take the thread and lay it along the centre of the inside of the feather, and with the forefinger and thumb of your right hand twirl them round together till the feather is rolled round the thread; and in this state wrap it round the hook, taking care that a sufficient number of the fibres stick out to represent the legs; to effect this it will sometimes be necessary to raise the fibres with a needle during the operation." Such a mount splays the barbs erratically. You can achieve a more symmetrical mount by stripping one side of the hackle and mounting the other side to "cup" over the body. I tie the feather in by the tip to create a smaller mounting point. This method uses only the smaller stem diameters. To give extra kick to the soft hackle, several tight thread wraps behind the hackle will spread the barbs. Pass the thread through the barbs before whip-finishing.

The Folded Wing

The folded wing adds grace and charm to the upstream wet, and contrasts with the customary divided wings (matching panels from opposite wing feathers), or rolled wings (a barb bundle from a body feather). You can mount the folded wing slanting back (downstream wet), erect (upstream wet), or forward (upstream wet). Roger Woolley, in *Modern Trout Fly Dressing* (1932), pointed out that the down-wing wet is "the down-stream fisherman's fly, and is so tied to prevent, as far as is possible, the fly causing a ripple on the surface of the water when held against the stream." The up-wing and forward-wing wets evidently imitate foundering duns gone awash, "tumbling hither and thither by the action of rough, swirling streams." For a forward wing, one can mount the wing first, cover the wing base with the body and then add the hackle *behind* the wing. Thread wraps in front of the wing erect it. There are, of course, alternate tying methods. According to Ted Niemeyer, the late Charles De Feo believed that the forward wing quivered seductively during the drift. De Feo called such patterns "vibrators."

H. G. McClelland, in *How to Tie Flies for Trout* (1939, ninth edition), described making the single folded wing for wet flies. First, from a mallard primary feather, clip out a section twice the width of the finished wing. A common error is to make the wings too broad. With a thumb and forefinger on each end, gently rock and caress the feather back and forth, aligning the natural tips. Carefully stroke together any barbs that threaten to separate. Finally, fold the feather lengthwise in the middle to produce a slender, tapered wing. Mount the wing immediately behind the head space on top of the shank.

Prior to mounting the wing, some past tyers coated it with lacquer to form the delicate tip. A better method is to apply cement *after* you have mounted the wing and it has attained its natural curve. Apply only a thin cement coat, and only to the trailing edge of the folded wing. This imperceptibly solidifies the barb tips, and preserves the wing arc.

In *Practical Fly-Tying* (1950) T. R. Henn described shaping the folded wing. First, a tyer tears off a quill panel. He then folds the quill to expose either the light or dark side (choice of two shades). "The shred of quill which will come away with the tearing will serve to keep the fibre together, until the stump is finally cut off as waste." Actually, the "shred of quill" seldom keeps the barbs together. Finally, Henn said a tyer should "ease the wing into shape by stroking it with his fingers; and will nip off the fibres at the end of the wing so as to obtain a fair rounded surface. Never cut the ends of a wing: nipping with the nails of the thumb and forefinger gives a slightly translucent edge, whereas cutting with the scissors gives a hard, opaque one." Rather than nip the end with the thumbnail and forefinger, I may scrape it firmly. This makes it soft, translucent, and easy to shape. However, if tied properly, no tweaking should be necessary.

In *The Vade-Mecum of Fly-Fishing for Trout* (1841), G. P. R. Pulman recommended the tyer align the barb tips while the quill is still attached to the stem. The tyer merely strokes the barbs at a right angle to the stem to even the tips. I find, however, that I have fewer detached barbs if I cut the panel off and then rock and caress the panel to align the tips. But you should try both methods.

Greenwell's Glory, Clyde Style

John Reid, in *Clyde Style Flies* (date unknown), describes tying the Greenwell's Glory, Clyde style.

Greenwell's Glory, Clyde Style

1. Apply brown wax to a pale yellow thread. This turns the tying thread a pale, dingy olive. Mount the thread behind the hook eye, and then mount a short length of fine gold wire at midshank. Counterspin the silk thread to flatten, and then wrap a smooth body to midshank.

2. With evenly spaced turns, wind the wire over the silk toward the eye of the hook and tie off.

3. Wrap the thread forward between the turns of gold wire. Secure at the wing position with a half-hitch.

4. Mount a single, folded wing. After securing the wing with several wraps, pass a few wraps behind the wing to lift it into a "mild" dun position.

5. After a few hackle wraps fore and aft of the wing, whip-finish and cement the head. Strive for a short, sparse hackle.

The Black Gnat, Tummel Style with Advanced Wing

The wing on this particular fly slopes forward over the hook eye.

The Black Gnat, Tummel Style with Advanced Wing

1. Mount the black thread. Then attach the folded wing, with tips over the hook eye, directly on top of the shank, immediately aft of the eye.

2. Then wrap the thread back one-third the length of the shank. Attach peacock herl and wrap (cup forward) to hackle position. Note: Some tyers wrap the herl body *before* mounting the wings. The wing-first method creates a neater pattern.

3. Mount the hackle and trim excess. Erect the wing to the desired position by placing hackle wraps behind the wing. (Some tyers wrap the hackle behind *and* in front of the wing.)

4. Whip-finish and cement the head.

The winged wets are graceful and ethereal, tied with few materials and few wraps. These simple and modest upstream Scots make the tyer concentrate on his skill more than his material. W. C. Stewart believed that every possible advantage lies with the lightly dressed fly. Its artificial nature is not as easily detected and the unencumbered point hooks freely. For the tyer as well as for the trout, there may be beauty in a scantily dressed Scot.

The Hawthorn

The Hawthorn fly (*Bibio marci*) wears basic black. This insect appears in southern England during warm weather about the end of April or the beginning of May. The species designation (*marci*) indicates its emergence on St. Mark's Day, April 25. Often found near hawthorn trees, the insect is a staple on English chalk streams. This modest insect (approximately 12 mm long) has a slender, fuzzy body with a humped thorax. On the wing, it trails long, graceful legs. The smaller female has blackish or pale gray wings, while the larger male has pale blue, white, or transparent wings with a dark leading edge.

Cotton offered an early "Thorn Fly" with a black lamb's wool body, black silk ribbing, and light gray mallard wings. *The Angler's Sure Guide* (1706) lists the "Haw-thorn flie": "The Body very small, of an absolute Black, mixed with eight or ten Hairs of Isabella-Mohair; the Wings, of the Wing of a Throstle; best in clear Weather and Water." Oddly enough, the pattern is listed for March, not April.

John Jackson's *The Practical Fly-Fisher* (1854) listed it later for June. Perhaps the Hawthorn calibrates with climate shifts. In any case, Alfred Ronalds popularized the "Hawthorn fly," calling it a first cousin to the smaller Black Gnat (*Biblio johannis* and others). He used a black ostrich herl for the body, a black cock hackle or a feather from a pewit's topknot, and a feather from a "sea swallow" (apparently any of the various terns) for wings. Ronalds also noted that the insect is called the "Black Caterpillar." Such a name may have been inspired by the natural's fine, fuzzy body. Richard and Charles Bowlker, in *The Art of Angling* (1839), identified it as the "Black Caterpillar" that "is to be fished with after hot sunshine mornings." The Bowlker "caterpillar" had an ostrich body, wings from the jay and "a fine black cock's hackle over the body." John Jackson, in *The Practical Fly-Fisher* (first edition 1854), merely increased the size of his Black Midge: black silk or black ostrich herl body, black hackle, and starling quill wings. Charles Walker, in *Old Flies in New Dresses* (1898) used black Berlin wool body, ribbed with silver tinsel, a black hackle and "the transparent part of the quill feather of starling" for the wing.

My Hawthorn has an extended, black polypropylene, furled-yarn body. Consult the crane fly recipe for furling directions. Use long CDC barbs for better buoyancy and the illusion of legs. The furry appearance of CDC barbs imitates the fuzzy natural well. The tying paradigm should be delicate and sparse.

The CDC Hawthorn

Hook:	Standard dry fly, TMC 100BL or similar, size 12 to 16
Thread:	6/0, black or gray
Body:	Furled black propylene yarn (or furled black goose CDC barbs)
Wing:	Cream, gray, or white CDC hackle, shaped with wing burner
Hackle:	Black mole fur or black CDC barbs create both the distinctive thoracic hump and the hackle
Legs:	Two black pheasant tail barbs, tied long

The CDC Hawthorn

The Humpy

Several years ago, I was asked the perennial question, "If you could fish only one fly, what would it be?" At the time, I answered with conviction, "the Humpy." But, because the Humpy was not a hatch, my answer only gathered frowns and censure. Obviously, I was an angler with much to learn. If asked today, the answer might be the female Adams or a parachute female Adams. There is, of course, no true answer to this question. In one way, however, the Humpy is the answer because the Humpy is legion. It is more method than pattern.

In the West, the Humpy and its variations can constitute over 30 percent of the total patterns sold by a shop in a single season. A Western angler who has not cast a Humpy is usually an angler without experience. I thought then as I think now that the inquisitor did not realize the creative possibilities of the Humpy. There are, of course, the standard variations such as Double Humpy and Royal Humpy. Even the traditional Humpy appears with various tails, hairs, under-bellies, and hackles. This buoyant, "insectile" pattern works well in fast and still waters. And with minor variations on the Humpy's body-wing lap, a horde of delicate and practical patterns hatch.

The Humpy comes from several people and several protopatterns. However, in the discussion of origins, the argument usually leads back to a tyer from San Francisco. The late Jack Horner, a member of the Golden Gate Angling and Casting Club, tied the Horner's Deer Fly, which had a folded deer-hair body ribbed with thread and a natural hair-tip wing. As a master of deer hair, Horner had also created a popular deer-hair shrimp pattern about 1938. According to Jack Dennis, the term "Humpy," descriptive of its distinctly arched or humped body, may have originated near Jackson Hole, Wyoming. Dan Bailey of Montana popularized the name "Goofus," a term sometimes given to a Humpy with mixed brown and grizzly hackles. True, the Humpy is effective because it imitates anything that the trout wants it to imitate, especially caddis and terrestrials.

The following variations use the Humpy's "body-wing lap method" with materials other than the traditional deer hair. Despite the name, these patterns are almost humpless. They have, instead, a delicate, easily tied two-tone body. These variations may be effective imitations of mayflies, caddis, and terrestrials. Here then are some variations on the Humpy hatch.

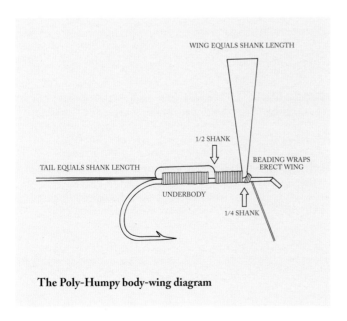

The Poly-Humpy body-wing diagram

When tying any Humpy, proportions—especially wing and body length—are the key. If proportions are wrong, the pattern is gauche. Even a small error in proportions significantly distorts the pattern. However, these four patterns eliminate most proportion problems and create a slender, subtle fly. Select a Humpy hook carefully. A Humpy hook must have adequate shank and gap space for body and hackle. Avoid short-shank hooks. For simplicity, use the tying thread to create the underbody for small patterns.

The body-wing material must account for underbody, overbody, and wing length. Using long, soft fibers (poly yarn, CDC barbs, wood-duck barbs, and pheasant tail barbs) makes all these patterns simple. Bulky body-wing materials, such as the traditional deer hair, require more length due to the wider body and wider bends. These new body-wing materials require less length. If the tail and wing equals shank length, then the body-wing materials will be slightly more than twice the shank length. The total body-wing length is about $2\frac{1}{4}$ shank lengths. A body-wing length of slightly twice shank length (including the hook eye) usually is adequate. Body-wing length may be measured directly on the tailed hook and easily adjusted for the proper proportions.

The Shucking Poly Humpy

Hook: Daiichi 1222, 1220; Tiemco 100, 102, 5210; Mustad 94840
Thread: 6/0 Unithread, pale yellow
Shuck: Cream, yellow, or white polypropylene yarn
Body: Polypropylene yarn
Hackle: Quality dry hackle to match the hatch

1. Polypropylene yarn makes an excellent shuck; it is buoyant and available in a variety of colors. The durable poly shuck readily expels water during the cast. Here are two quick, simple methods for making a poly shuck. Tie an overhand knot in a few fibers of white or pale yellow poly yarn. This creates a "capsule" shuck. Seal the end of the poly shuck by flame or gel.

   Flame method: Trim the excess poly yarn and melt the knot tip with a butane lighter or match. Melt only the extreme end of the knot, not the entire knot.

   Gel method: Apply a small drop of cyanoacrylate gel glue to the knot. When completely dry, cut the knot in the middle to create two shucks, one on each side of the severed knot.

2. Mount the shuck at the tail position. Shuck length should equal body length.

3. Precise mounting of the poly yarn is critical for proper proportions. Take a length of poly yarn, about three inches long, and mount the tip at midshank or slightly short of midshank. Three-ply poly yarn may be thinned for the smaller flies. Two-ply or a ply-and-a-half may also be used for smaller flies. Overwrap the mounted butt smoothly with tying thread to create the underbody color.

4. Fold the yarn forward and overwrap so that the yarn extends to the forward ¼ shank point.

5. Select and mount a hackle. For a clean head, strip the hackle tip first so that when whipping off, the thread captures only the hackle stem. This avoids a close trimming of any trapped hackle barbs. Wrap the hackle as many times behind the wing as in front. Note that the hackle fills the front half of the shank. Tie off hackle.

6. For a standard shank-length wing, trim the wing equal to the rear extremity of the hook. Extend the poly wing to the rear of the hook and trim to length. Because the wing extends from the wing mount point to the rear of the bend, the wing will equal the shank length when trimmed. Take care not to cut the shuck or tail.

The CDC Humpy

Hook:	Daiichi 1220 or 1222 (size 18 or 16); Tiemco 100 or 102
Thread:	6/0 Unithread, pale yellow
Tail:	Stiff feather barbs
Optional Shuck:	Furled CDC barbs or nipple plume. For the emerger, furl a few strands of long CDC goose barbs or mount a small nipple plume (also known as a CDC tuft) for a trailing shuck. The nipple plume may be tied in at the base bud, or by gathering and mounting the open ends to create a shuck "capsule."
Body-Wing:	CDC feathers (duck). Alternately, bundled CDC goose barbs may be used. Strip off long goose CDC barbs, trim the butt for alignment and mount at midshank.
Hackle:	Standard dry hackle or, for excellent floatation and realism, mount a CDC barb hackle (dubbing-loop method)

1. For a standard dry tail, stack and mount a bundle of stiff hackle barbs.

2. For the body-wing, select and overlap two CDC feathers with fine stems and long, fluffy barbs. Trim the butts and mount them at midshank. Overwrap with tying thread to create the underbody color. Although CDC wings may be trimmed to length, it is best to proportion the body-wing.

3. Fold the overbody forward and whip down.

4. Add CDC barbs to a dubbing loop, trim barb base to length and spin, creating a faux hackle. A dry hackle may also be used.

5. Mount and wrap the CDC "hackle" in equal turns behind and in front of the wing. Whip off. If the wing requires trimming to proper length, extend the wing back and trim the length equal to the rear of the bend. However, try to mount and proportion the body-wing to avoid trimming the wing tips.

The Woody Humpy

Mounted and folded in the same manner as other variant body-wings, the lemon brown flank feather of the wood duck provides a delicately mottled body and wing. Since the days of the Quill Gordon, the wood-duck flank feather has furnished some of the most attractive fly wings possible.

The Woody Humpy

Hook:	Daiichi 1220 or 1222; Tiemco 100BL, various sizes
Thread:	6/0 Unithread, pale yellow
Tail:	Stiff hackle barbs
Body-Wing:	Bundled wood-duck barbs
Hackle:	Dry hackle

The PT Humpy

Pheasant tail barbs make a durable and attractive body-wing. Merely cut a small barb bundle off the stem. Finger-stack to align the tips. Trim to the appropriate length. Mount and fold in the traditional manner.

All these Humpy variants are heirs of the body-wing lap method. With creative, lateral thinking, various materials (polypropylene yarn, CDC feathers,

The PT Humpy

Hook:	Daiichi 1220 or 1222; Tiemco 100BL, various sizes
Thread:	6/0 Unithread, pale yellow
Tail:	Stiff hackle barbs
Body-Wing:	Bundled pheasant tail barbs
Hackle:	Dry hackle

Synthetic Humpy

A synthetic Humpy with polypropylene hackle.

1. **Lay out and tape down (on tissue paper) the ends of polypropylene yarn strands.**

2. **Sew down the middle and trim to proper barb length.**

wood-duck flank feathers, and pheasant tail barbs) create delicate and effective Humpies. Moreover, these patterns are simple. From sizes 12 to 20, my Humpy variants have taken cutthroat in Montana, marble trout in Slovenia, wild browns in England, Finland, and South Africa. Perhaps there is a new perennial question: Which insect does a variant Humpy not match?

The Husk Body

The husk method creates a sack body—a soft, glowing body enclosed in a wispy shuck or husk. It has innumerable applications for ant, beetle, grasshopper, caddis pupa, emerger, and spider imitations. The method also allows for tailed imitations. The husk or outer sheath may be any yarn or long-strand dubbing. For many patterns, I use a fine and crinkly dubbing, such as Master Bright, for the inner body. The husk or outer sheath may be any yarn, such as polypropylene or Antron. Long-strand dubbing also may serve as a husk. For the bulky inner body of the Spant pattern (a spider-ant imitation), I use a coarse, crinkly dubbing such as Master Bright for airy bulk and a wispy poly husk. Caddis emergers use a bright, fluorescent white Antron husk. A long-strand dubbing husk and fine body dubbing, such as Nature's Spirit Finest Dubbing, create micropatterns.

Unlike a traditional hook body, the husk body rides directly above the hook shank. When mounted at midshank, the hook point hides among the hackle or legs. If color-matched, the hook melds into the hackle barbs. The hook point, rather than traditionally trailing the body, becomes part of the pattern, and the *naked* hook encourages penetration. Furthermore, the husk body—rather than stiff and straight—is softly curved. The inner body glows within the filmy shroud. Sometimes a unique or odd tie, such as a husk body, takes trout when tradition fails.

The Single and Double Husk Body (Antron or Polypropylene Husk)

1. Mount a slender, stiff needle in the vise. *Special Note: Remember to wear adequate eye protection when tying on an exposed needle.*

Comb the strands to separate them.

2. Select polypropylene or Antron yarn about three times the required body length. Match the yarn mass to the pattern size. For example, a size 12 hook requires approximately 2 ply of a 3-ply poly yarn.

   Because the strands entwine, comb the husk prior to mounting. This widens the husk and allows it to encircle the needle. The husk *foundation* should completely encircle the needle; however, the husk, when folded forward, need *not* completely encircle the body. Interesting effects are possible if the husk covers just the sides or the back of the body.

3. Firmly mount the yarn at the needle point and then spiral the thread back to the rear of the body space. Remember that the yarn foundation should completely encircle the needle. Whip-finish at the rear of the body.

4. Dub a full, wispy body and position the thread at the body front.

5. Next, fold the husk forward to encircle or sheathe the dubbed body. Pass the tying thread through the husk, overwrap and whip-finish for a *single husk body*. With a quick tug, remove the body from the needle.

6. After dubbing the required bodies, fold the husk forward, capture the husk strands and whip-finish. Finally, with a quick tug, remove the bodies from the needle. For a secure finish, add a drop of cement or cyanoacrylate to the final whip wraps. Once dry, the forward "lip" (which ultimately forms the head) may be trimmed short.

The Single and Double Husk Body (Antron or Polypropylene Husk)

If required, several body segments of varying sizes, shapes, and length may be dubbed and enclosed in this manner. Interesting effects result from contrasting dubbing and husk colors. Other long-strand fibers, such as the dubbing itself, may be used as the husk. Strand length should be about three times body length. Any dubbing long enough may serve as a husk. Master Bright dubbing, for example, is as long as 8". Even Nature's Spirit fine natural dubbing has strands about 6" long. Small insect bodies, even to a size 20 or smaller, may be made with fine dubbing. Brief finger stacking aligns most fibers prior to mounting. Again, make certain that the husk completely, though sparingly, encircles the needle. The body should show through the filmy husk.

The body or bodies may now be mounted in any manner, detached or extended, on a hook shank. Add other requirements such as legs, hackle, wings, and antennae to complete the pattern. Here are several single- and double-body husk patterns.

The Caddis Pupa (Single Husk Body)

This realistic caddis pupa—replete with antennae, legs, and wing pads—may be weighted with glass or metal beads hidden within the husk. Though this pattern has antennae and emergent wings, simpler and more practical patterns may omit these. The bright Antron husk sheathes the inner body with a silver sheen, much like the natural. A wing burner creates the wing buds from speckled hen patch feathers. "Drape mount" the wings to slant back beneath the body.

The Caddis Pupa (Single Husk Body)

Hook: Daiichi 1560 Nymph hook; Tiemco 3761, size 14 and 12.

Thread: Dark brown, size 3/0

Bead: Glass or metal, optional

Husk: Antron yarn, fluorescent white

Body: Master Bright rusty orange dubbing

Thorax: Antron, dark brown

Wing Buds: Speckled or patterned hen patch feathers

Legs: Two or four pheasant tail barb tips

Antennae: Two pheasant tail barbs

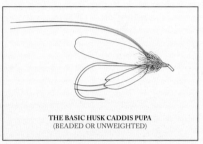

THE BASIC HUSK CADDIS PUPA
(BEADED OR UNWEIGHTED)

3. After folding the husk forward, whip-finish. Dismount the husk body with a quick tug.

5. Complete with dubbing and whip-finish the head. Brush thoracic dubbing aft with a dubbing teaser.

1. First, make a single husk body, approximately shank length. Mount Antron yarn on needle and spiral thread back and whip-finish the butt.

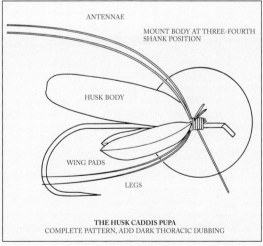

ANTENNAE

MOUNT BODY AT THREE-FOURTH SHANK POSITION

HUSK BODY

WING PADS

LEGS

THE HUSK CADDIS PUPA
COMPLETE PATTERN, ADD DARK THORACIC DUBBING

2. Dub body. Note: To mount an optional bead, add butt-dubbing, whip-finish, and remove the tying thread. Slide bead over the needle and husk base. Add the front dubbing and then fold the husk forward to trap the bead. Remount the thread and continue the pattern.

4. Mount the body at three-fourth hook-shank position. Add a pinch of thoracic dubbing prior to mounting the legs and wings. A soft hackle may also imitate legs and wings. Add more dubbing before mounting the antennae. If desired, add small eyes.

The Husk Ant (Double Husk Body)

Alfred Ronalds (1836) gave an ant dressing—peacock herl tied with red-brown silk, starling wing, and red hackle. G. P. R. Pulman (1841), though he cared little for the lowly ant, still felt obligated to give a dressing "for the sake of a good variety": copper-colored peacock herl, red hackle, dark red silk, and jay wing. Though Pulman claimed that he was "indifferent" to ants, he did insist, curiously enough, that the wings had to lie flat along the body like the natural.

Michael Theakston (1853), writing with more reverence and respect for the humble ant, recommended peacock-herl body, amber thread, reddish-brown mohair legs, and snipe or starling wings. In these wet dressings, peacock herl was the staple. Although iridescent, it hardly matches the lustrous ebony or amber and apparent hardness of the actual insect body. F. M. Halford, *The Dry-Fly Man's Handbook* (1913), while bestowing only an abrupt and brief paragraph on the ant, did list it as one of the six insect families exploited by the dry-fly angler. Halford's red ant was tied with a honey dun hackle, a copper-colored peacock herl, and orange tying silk with or without starling wings. Halford noted that it was "one of the best patterns" during hot weather and "one which is too often neglected by dry-fly fishermen." G. E. M. Skues, that sage of the sunken fly, offered a red ant made from chestnut-colored pig's wool in *Silk, Fur and Feather* (1950). He also advocated a blob of thread and varnish for smaller, wet patterns.

J. W. Dunne's *Sunshine and the Dry Fly* (1924) presented perhaps the most ingenious ant pattern devised. Dressed with a synthetic "cellulite silk" on a white-painted hook, the pattern had hackle-point wings and a honey dun hackle. When soaked in colorless paraffin, the hook shank disappeared and the body darkened to a deep, ruddy, translucent chestnut. The radiant beauty of the ant confirmed his theory of "translucent tying": "The ball-like abdomen of the brown ant is fairly transparent, so that it constitutes really a sort of spherical lens, in some part of which you will nearly always see a beautiful gleam of red, transmitted light." Dunne, who wanted to capture that gleam of transmitted light, went on to say the pattern is not often needed. But when needed, it is truly needed.

Vincent Marinaro, in *A Modern Dry-Fly Code* (1950), observed that only the red ant glows "as though lighted by some inner fire," while the black ant is "absolutely opaque." Marinaro's red ant incorporated transparent horsehair or nylon dyed golden brown to realize some transparency. No matter, even translucent insects, such as fragile spinners, fail to glow if lighting conditions are not suitable.

The Husk Ant (or Spant—spider and ant) pattern has a double husk body and a slender waist. Note that the single husk body is merely half of a double husk body. The generic Husk Ant is extremely buggy, especially when tied with a dark body and speckled legs. The husk creates both the abdomen and the thorax of the insect.

The Husk Ant (Double Husk Body)

The Husk Ant

Hook: Daiichi 1100 or 1180; Tiemco 100 or 5210 or similar dry fly hook, size 18 to 12

Thread: Dark brown, size 3/0

Husk: Polypropylene yarn, tan, cinnamon, brown, dark brown, or black

Body/Thorax: Master Bright dubbing, lustrous black, rusty orange, or other colors

Hackle: Speckled hen hackle with contrasting marks

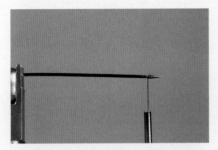

1. Firmly mount needle in vice and attach thread to point. Comb yarn to spread, straighten, and fluff. Poly yarn wrapped on cards invariably has kinks.

2. Mount the yarn at the needle point and then spiral the thread back to the rear of the body space. Whip-finish at the butt.

3. Dub a full, wispy body and position thread at body front.

4. Next, fold the husk forward to encircle or sheathe the body, overwrap and whip-finish to create a *single husk body*. For a *double husk body*, do not remove the body from the needle. Instead, pass the tying thread through the husk strands and continue to overwrap the yarn to create a short, slender mid-section, the willowy "waist" of many insects. To add another body section (such as a smaller thorax), merely push the yarn husk back, advance the thread and then dub another body segment. Finally, fold the husk forward, capture the husk and whip-finish. The thorax should be about ½ the diameter of the abdomen. Body segments may vary in size, shape, and length.

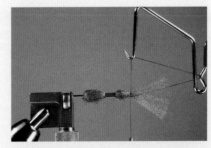

5. With a quick tug, remove the double body from the needle. For a secure whip, after removing the body, add a drop of cement or cyanoacrylate to the final whip wraps. Once dry, trim the "lip" (which ultimately forms the head) short.

   Once completed, mount the husk body in any position, detached or semi-detached, on the hook shank. Add other requirements such as legs, hackle, and wings to complete the pattern

The Husk Ant (Double Husk Body) (cont)

6. For an ant pattern, mount the double-husk body at midshank. Mount the body assembly with three or four thread wraps immediately behind the thorax (the first body segment). Position the forward "lip" directly above the head space.

7. Select a dappled hen hackle and remove the barbs from one side (the inner side when mounted). Attach hackle by the tip and secure firmly at the body mount point.

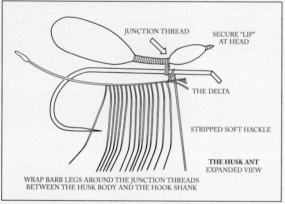

JUNCTION THREAD   SECURE "LIP" AT HEAD

THE DELTA

STRIPPED SOFT HACKLE

THE HUSK ANT EXPANDED VIEW

WRAP BARB LEGS AROUND THE JUNCTION THREADS BETWEEN THE HUSK BODY AND THE HOOK SHANK

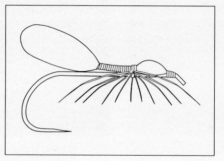

The Husk Ant

8. Wrap the soft hackle, parachute style, once or twice around the thread junction that secures the double body to the hook shank. Pass the stem under the thorax in front and secure with several thread wraps. Trim excess stem. Capture the front "lip" of the thorax and wrap down for a head. Whip-finish the head and bend the leg barbs for realism.

The husk body comes from thinking beyond the fly box, from playing with materials and methods. Such small solutions can make substantial differences in tying. The husk is simple, attractive and, in appropriate colors, possesses a seductive glow.

The Nirihuao Hopper

Terrestrials—ants, grasshoppers, beetles, bees, and countless other creatures born on land—have a lengthy lineage in fly tying. They are, in fact, some of the earliest recorded artificials. *The Treatyse of Fysshynge Wyth an Angle* (1496) includes a "waspe flye" with "the body of blacke wull & lappid abowte wt yelow threde: the winges of the bosarde." This "waspe," however, is still enigmatic;

W. H. Lawrie believed that it may have been, in fact, a crane fly rather than a wasp. In the 1676 edition of *The Compleat Angler*, Charles Cotton wrote about the Ant Fly and the Palmer-Worm. The Palmer, which imitated a caterpillar, would eventually evolve into our Wooly Worm and Woolly Bugger, patterns that imitate a variety of creatures, including stonefly, dragonfly, leech, and perhaps even a drowned hopper. Joe Brooks, in *Fly Fishing* (1958), delineated the value of all

The Nirihuao Hopper

Hook:	Tiemco 200R or similar in appropriate sizes
Thread:	Pale yellow to imitate the distinctive abdominal sutures
Body:	Cream or dyed gold, pale yellow, orange deer hair to match the hatch
Underwing:	Orange, red, or yellow CDC barbs
Overwing:	Scotch wing
Legs:	Burnt or razor-cut grizzly hackles
Hackle:	Cree, dyed grizzly, or CDC faux-hackle

1. Mount deer strands and wrap underbody. For great durability, coat underbody with Dave's Flexament prior to folding overbody forward.

2. Fold body hairs forward, forming a plump abdomen. Pass tying thread through body hairs and spiral forward. If desired, create *parallel* sutures by advancing thread on the underbody. Consult the sleeve body for the parallel wrapping directions.

3. The completed body segments.

4. Mount the orange CDC barbs. For increased bulk, add sparse deer hair.

5. Firmly mount the Scotch hopper wing and burnt, matching legs. Consult Scotch-Wing Caddis entry (page 177) for wing-making. Apply a drop of Dave's Flexament to knee and tibia. If desired, color the femur purple with a permanent marker for realism.

6. Finally, mount and wrap the hackle. For greater attraction, wrap the hackle area with orange or yellow thread and space the hackle wraps to reveal the contrasting undercolor.

terrestrials. "There is something about a terrestrial that appeals mightily to trout, be it the juicy crispness of the grasshopper, the tart taste of the ant, or the pepper speck on the tongue of the tiny jassid."

The Nirihuao (*nee-ree-wow*) Hopper, named after the graceful Chilean meadow stream and its hopper hordes, is an excellent compromise between attractor and imitator. The underwing imitates the radiant yellow, red, or orange hindwings of many short-horned grasshoppers. The bright hindwing may be an escape mechanism. The abrupt color flash can startle a predator and, when the predator searches for that color on the ground, the "flash" hides beneath the forewings. A hopper with a trace of bright hindwing, when seen from below the surface, may also attract trout.

The juicy, crisp Nirihuao Hopper is an engaging pattern. Opportunistic trout favor such morsels especially during the warm and windy days of late summer. Many terrestrial patterns are pleasurable ties. Moreover, as the past proclaims, the "compleat" angler always has a few "land-borns."

The Quill Gordon (Catskill Style)

The Quill Gordon: Catskill Style

The first time I saw a Catskill pattern, I thought—in my ignorance—that it was a tying mistake. It seemed sparse and poorly proportioned. It looked like a fly trying to wear a hook one size too large. Yet, although I have never fished a Catskill stream, I am, like all American tyers, part of the current Catskill tradition. The Catskill style is a frugal Yankee, clean and practical, born in America.

Catskill is a *style*, not a pattern. The Quill Gordon, the Hendrickson, the Gray Fox Variant, and the Cahill are all patterns that grew out of the Catskill style. According to Harry Darbee, in *Catskill Flytier* (1977), the Catskill tradition was founded by "the hallowed four"—Theodore Gordon, Herman Christian, Roy Steenrod, and Edward Hewitt. This uniquely American style, born about 1865, reached maturity about 1915. Many anglers and tyers contributed to it, and we are fortunate that it survived.

Although Herman Christian fished regularly with Gordon, Darbee asserted that Gordon never showed him "a thing about flytying." Christian had to learn by taking Gordon's patterns apart. "It is interesting to note that Herman Christian, who didn't see Gordon tie, didn't show others how either, and that Roy Steenrod, to whom Gordon taught nearly everything he knew, was perhaps the best-known flytying instructor in the Catskills." Darbee then concluded that "Roy Steenrod was perhaps more responsible than anyone else for passing on the distinctive features of the Catskill style." Harry Darbee described a typical Catskill pattern.

> Its characteristics: a good-sized hook, typically size 12 Model Perfect, a notably lean spare body, usually of spun fur or stripped quill of peacock herl; a divided wing of lemon-colored, mottled barbules of a wood-duck flank feather; and a few sparse turns of an incredibly stiff, clean, glassy cock's hackle, mostly either blue dun or ginger. The wings and hackle are set back from the eye of the hook, leaving an unusually long, clean 'neck' at the expense of a slightly shortened body. This puts the sustaining hackle so close to the point of balance that the fly rides over broken, turbulent waters like a coast guard lifeboat, so nearly balanced that often the tail of hackle whisks (originally, a little curlicue of several wood-duck barbules) doesn't touch the water at all.

In *American Fly Fishing*, Paul Schullery believed that Theodore Gordon is granted too much credit as the headmaster of the Catskill School of fly tying. Schullery asserts that "the Catskill style . . . which grew from Gordon's work, must be his main claim to a contribution." Yet about half the characteristics of the Catskill style, Schullery noted, were not favored by Gordon: "He did not prefer to divide the wing. He did not often leave a bare 'neck' on the fly, and he was sometimes inclined to slant his rolled wood-duck wings back over the body . . . ." Schullery added that Theodore Gordon's "important start was taken and refined substantially by such later masters as [Rube] Cross, the Dettes [Winnie and Walter], the Darbees [Elsie and Harry], and [Art] Flick." No matter; as Larry Duckwall notes, we prefer to keep our icons.

Exactly what the distinctive features of this graceful American style were and who created them is still a controversy. Roy Steenrod was perhaps responsible for passing on the distinctive features of the Catskill style. Darbee inventoried those various features:

1. A light, generous hook, typically a size 12, perfect bend. According to Ted Niemeyer, the original hook was the Allcock 04991, #14 or #12. Other model perfect hooks create a heavy, runty appearance; the fine return on the tapered eye makes the Allcock 04991 look delicate. Although Larry Duckwall calls the Mustad 94845 barbless #12 the present "hook of choice," the Allcock had finer wire and a shank two eye lengths longer. When the Allcock was no longer available, Darbee wrote that the Mustad 94840 was "our standard dry fly hook."

2. A few sparse wraps of stiff, glassy hackle (often blue dun or ginger), with shank-length barbs, wrapped equally behind and before the wings.
3. Wings set a third of the shank length behind the eye.
4. A distinct, bare "neck" (about one eye length from the hook eye) in front of a modest head of just a few wraps. Paul Schullery noted that "the bare neck appears only intermittently" on modern commercial patterns. Originally, the bare neck allowed space for the gut knot. A gut knot, such as a standard figure-eight jam knot, would occupy the head space.

   In Niemeyer's collection, there is a Hewitt pattern with a simple half-hitch gut knot, with the gut threaded through the hook eye and the half-hitch then tied around the shank. The large diameter and stiffness of silk gut at times made it difficult to tie a clinch or turle knot and, unlike slippery nylon, wet gut tightens upon itself for a good hold. The long neck may have allowed space for the gut connection, and then survived long after the demise of gut.

   The wings and hackle are set back from the eye of the hook, leaving, "a clean neck at the expense of a slightly shortened body." The hackle moves closer to the balance point of the pattern. Minimal thread wraps form a modest head. Traditionally, the head was sparsely wrapped. Elsie Darbee once said that anything beyond two head wraps is superfluous.
5. A sparse tail often slightly longer than the shank.
6. A particularly slender and sparse body. Usually spun fur or stripped peacock herl. A short, slender, tapered body that begins on the shank above the rear of the barb and the hook point.
7. A divided wing usually made from the mottled barbs of wood-duck flank feather. Wings are often slightly longer than shank length and sometimes moderately canted forward, mounted one-quarter to one-third shank length behind the eye. Catskill patterns may be tied in traditional dry-fly proportions, i.e., tail and wing may equal shank length.

Several years ago, I asked both Larry Duckwall and Ted Niemeyer—each directly influenced by the Catskill tradition—about the Quill Gordon. As you read their comments, remember that there is more than one correct way to wrap a Catskill, and not all traditional Catskill flies were elegant creatures. And Niemeyer says that with today's hackle and thread we can produce delicate flies unmatched by the older Catskill tyers.

The Catskill Wing

Living in the middle of the Eastern wood-duck flyway, the early tyers used the abundant "woodie" breast feathers for wings. With flat 6/0 or 8/0 thread, Niemeyer wraps a wing foundation a third of the way down the shank from the hook eye. He strips the hazy base fibers from a large, well-marked wood-duck flank feather and selects two wing slips from one side of the feather. Then he matches and places one slip atop the other, for one wing. He selects and matches two other slips from the other side for the second wing. There are two wing curvatures: the mounted wings should curve away from each other and their tips should curve forward. The wing sections, flat rather than rolled, should be parallel where they are tied in and in the same plane as the hook shank. Duckwall, who demonstrates the strength of wood duck by pulling on a clump of it until the hook bends, believes that trout may key on these Catskill wings.

After the wings are mounted, three wraps of thread jam in front of the tie-in point to erect the wings and figure-eight wraps divide them. Each wing is then "posted" with a couple of wraps around the base to gather the barbs. Duckwall makes a series of increasingly deeper cuts into the wing base, and then butts the end of the tail against the base. This gives the body a smooth foundation, and the tapered wing base provides a "ramp" for the wrapped quill, producing an evenly tapered body.

The Catskill Tail

Usually the long, straight, stiff hackle barbs from the side feathers of a dry neck produce tail barbs. However the best barbs, according to Elsie Darbee, come from the shoulder "spade" feather—actually a wing covert feather—from an old cock. Niemeyer has some Darbee shoulder spades; they are indeed long, stiff, and straight. Elsie took two turns of thread *under* the tail to lift and spread the barbs. This greater surface area improves floatation.

Niemeyer lays six to eight tail fibers crosswise to the shank for the first thread wrap; the second wrap then aligns them along the top of the shank. If they start out aligned, the first few wraps just twirl them to the far side of the shank. Niemeyer notes that Rube Cross often mounted his tails with soft webbing showing at the base; when greased they perhaps floated better than hard, stiff barbs. Cross, adds Larry Duckwall, was a huge man with hands like canoe paddles, but he created the most exquisitely delicate flies.

The Catskill Body

Niemeyer selects a herl, the "quill" of the Quill Gordon, by fanning the back of a peacock eye and looking for a hard, *whitish* herl with a prominent black edge. There are several ways to strip the "flue" off the herl, but it's often done with a wax bath: after slowly melting paraffin in a double boiler, dip the feather. Due to the extremely low flash point of wax, use the low heat setting—and *extreme caution*. Cool the waxed eye with cold water, and then strip the flue with a fingernail. The result is a pliant, waterproof, glossy herl.

Duckwall mounts the herl so that its dark edge faces the hook bend. Niemeyer lays the herl, together with a fine gold wire, at the wing base and along the hook shank, wrapping the thread back to above the hook point and then forward again. He then wraps the herl forward over itself for a smooth, slender body. Then he counterwraps (toward the tyer rather than away) the gold wire forward, spaced at twice the width of the herl; this laps the herl securely and also prevents the wire from slipping between the herl wraps. Finally, thin, penetrating cement saturates the body.

The Catskill Hackle

Niemeyer selects a hackle with barbs about a sixteenth of an inch shorter than the wings. He strips the webbing and trims the stem of a blue dun hackle, leaving some stem stubble to catch the thread; after the head is whipped, he can trim any errant barbs. Niemeyer whips the head with two wraps only—Elsie Darbee again told him that anything beyond two wraps was superfluous. He then takes his thumbnail and pushes the head against the wing base to ensure a naked neck. A drop of cement secures the head.

Duckwall, who ties in two hackles, strips the hackle quill base for mounting, then wraps thread over the quill stem a few millimeters from the barbs. This allows the stem to form a dam that kicks the barbs forward. The singular advantage to wrapping two hackles, rather than one, is that there are more barbs of the desired length. Half the normal wraps may be used with a double hackle, thereby using less hackle length while obtaining more uniform barb length.

After mounting both hackles, Duckwall wraps the front hackle first, leaving a "quill space" for the second. He will tie one hackle off beneath the head and the other on top, creating the small, symmetrical head typical of the Catskill style.

Duckwall once asked Harry Darbee who tied the best Catskill. His first reply was, "Whoever has the guts." Then Harry thought a moment and added that he did not know, but did know who the nicest tyer was. Elsie, his wife, was in the room, and Duckwall expected him to name her. He replied, "Art Flick." Niemeyer, in contrast, believes the best Catskill patterns came from the vise of Walt Dette in the '40s. No matter. We may never know the origin, nor who perfected it, but the Catskill style will remain a thoughtful and graceful wrap in American tying.

The Sack Spider

Terrestrial as well as aquatic spiders sometimes fall prey to trout. However, not all spiders are spiders. W. C. Stewart's short and slender "spider" patterns imitate various nymphs, larvae, and emergers rather than actual spiders. His spider, also known as a soft-hackle fly, takes its name from the arachnid-like legs (the long, radiating barbs) rather than the object of imitation. Trout, however, do take real spiders.

Actual spiders ballooning through the air on silk strands may fall upon water. Some spiders, such as the semiaquatic fishing spider (genus *Dolomedes*), the small wolf spider (genus *Pirata*) and a few of the longjawed spiders (family Tetragnathidae), live in or near water and hunt small insects and fish. True aquatic spiders live part of their lives underwater. Many spiders may be 50 mm long or greater. Their body consists of two primary segments: the cephalothorax and abdomen. Many spiders are predaceous and some scamper upon the water surface. Longjawed spiders weave orb nets on overhanging plants for capturing insects. Fishing spiders and small wolf spiders do not weave nets; they rely instead upon capturing prey trapped in the water surface. Fishing spiders even dive beneath the surface for several minutes, apparently breathing air trapped in a plastron. Terrestrial spiders whose webs hang in riparian vegetation may also fall upon the water. True water spiders are unique. Joscelyn Lane, in *Fly-Fisher's Pie* (1956) described their habits:

> This spider frequents slow-moving and still waters, and spins a silk nest of about the size and shape of an acorn, open at the lower end, which it moors to some convenient clump of weeds. In this cell the female lays about a hundred eggs. As it is unable to breathe under water, it uses its nest not only as a dwelling place but as an air storage tank, and so is obliged to obtain its supplies of air by making a series of visits to the surface. After attaching itself by a silk thread to its home, it swims to the surface, usually on its back, and there, thrusting its abdomen through the film, snatches a bubble of air, which it holds against its body by crossing its legs. It then descends, carrying the silver globule with it, and, inserting its abdomen into the opening in the nest, releases the bubble. Bubble after bubble has to be collected in this way, entailing sometimes over a dozen trips before the cell is full. As one can well imagine, these journeys are not infrequently interrupted by a hungry fish. Directly the cell is fully air-conditioned the spider enters it, head downwards, to rest, and thereafter uses it as a lair from which it makes occasional sallies in search of prey—not always with impunity.

Even if trout are not taking spiders, often a novel pattern like a spider or beetle will take trout. Small, wet-spider patterns may be tied much like Skues' wet ant—with thread and colored cement. The Sack Spider, however, requires a small nylon tube or "sack" and a float ball. Spiders come in diverse colors, shapes, and sizes. Permanent markers provide various body colors and designs.

There were days when I believed that *authentic* tying was only about mayflies and caddis. Yet, even a glance at the literature reveals that anglers have tied and tossed terrestrials for over five hundred years. They tie and toss them for a simple reason: trout take them. One warm English summer, while I was fishing the River Kennet, hordes of ladybugs blanketed everything. After increasing their population by one small artificial, I tossed it near two cruising trout. Sure enough, one swung over for a take.

Remember that trout selectivity is not confined to aquatic insects. Matching the hatch with terrestrials can be as difficult as matching duns and spinners. Lee Wulff, in *Lee Wulff on Flies* (1985), described terrestrial selectivity: "A profusion of terrestrials coming down the stream can sometimes be even more confusing than a difficult hatch. There may be some insects hatching out and trout rising furiously but

The Sack Spider (Single Ball)

The Sack Spider

Hook: Daiichi 1190, size 14 and 12 or any short-shanked hook
Thread: 6/0, to match the dominant color
Body: Small, closed-cell foam ball and a swatch of white or cream net nylon. Sheer, elastic women's nylon stocking material is excellent. Small packaging balls, used to protect items during shipment, range from 4.5 mm to 6.5 mm diameters. Various fly-tying foams may be used if cut into balls and inserted into the nylon tube. The elasticity of the nylon forms a rounded, realistic body.
Legs: Soft hen hackle or pheasant tail barbs. Stiff barbs produce the best legs. If available, emu feathers are realistic. Remove the wiry barbs from one side. Wrap sparsely and, when mounted, bend the barbs for realism.

1. First, to create a tube or sack, fold the nylon. Adjust the sewing machine settings to create a very short, straight stitch. Sew, with slight tension on the fabric, parallel to the folded edge. For a tight tube, make the tube width approximately the diameter of the balls. For sewing, ultrasheer material may require an underlay of tissue paper. After sewing, merely tear away the tissue. Sewing may also be done by hand.

2. After sewing the tube, trim the excess fabric two or three millimeters from the seam. With a stiff wire, turn the tube inside out to conceal the selvage edge.

3. To load the tube with balls, I stretch the nylon tube over a plastic straw. Insert foam balls into the straw and push them down into the nylon tube. Continue to feed balls through the straw as it slowly withdraws. A single tube may contain several dozen balls.

4. Place the charged tube above the hook and secure a single ball with forward thread wraps. After mounting the abdominal ball ⅓ shank length from the eye, trim excess and wrap the narrow, extended thorax (cephalothorax) common to many spiders. Notice that thread and the abdomen-ball mounting tag creates the cephalothorax.

5. Attach a soft hackle at the ball mount. Next, wind the hackle one or two times around the ball mount to create radiating legs. Tie off the hackle stem on the hook shank and continue to wind the tying thread down the shank. The shank wraps can imitate various belly colors or markings.

6. Capture the rear tube tag (which becomes the spinnerets) and secure with a whip-finish at the bend. Trim excess.

   Complete the pattern with a dubbed cephalothorax (the head-body segment) in front of the body. The cephalothorax may be distinctive on some arachnids. Although most spiders are predominately black, gray, or brown, gaudy blotches and baroque patterns adorn others. Test the permanent marker on a foam ball prior to marking. Some permanent markers may melt the ball. The tube method accommodates a menagerie of other terrestrials. Once a nylon tube is "charged" with balls, the tyer may create various terrestrial patterns. The nylon sack (after enveloping one or two float balls) may be single or double mounted for different terrestrial profiles, including ants and beetles.

refusing to take any of the hatching aquatic insects." Instead, the trout are intent on tiny drifting beetles trapped in the scum or flying ants adrift like spent spinners. Truly, the juicy, crisp grasshopper, the tart ant, and the peppery jassid all add spice to the trout's table and, more importantly, to our tying bench. Terrestrials, however, are more than a late-season condiment.

The Scotch-Wing Caddis

There have been several methods for creating realistic and durable wings. Various reinforcements, such as glues and nylon backing, have been used to strengthen and shape wings. The Scotch method, quickly born of common materials, is perhaps the simplest of all. Tape backs the feather, creating a moderately rigid wing that may be trimmed to shape. Tapes require no drying time, and they allow the use of feathers. It would be good to use a waterproof tape; however, few commercial tapes are truly waterproof. Most tapes are, nonetheless, highly water resistant, and water resistance is all that is required in a functional fly pattern. After all, no practical imitation needs to last forever. If I can catch one good fish on a fly, it has served well.

Like many tyers, I have experimented with the tape wing through the years and I have yet to find the perfect backing tape. 3M's Waterproof Kevlar tape (#838) unfortunately is white, heavy (3.4 mil thick), and available only in long commercial rolls. Scotch's Satin tape (#600), in ¾" width, is appropriate for most applications and wing sizes. I sometimes use the 3M Scotch Tear-by-Hand Packaging Tape. It is tough, thin, and glossy. I do prefer a matte tape for a more natural surface. And, though it shears crosswise, casting creates negligible rips. After hard use, there will be minor delaminating. But, by then, the fly has served its purpose. A backing tape must, within reason, withstand the rigors of casting and drowning.

I also use Scotch Magic Tape, an invisible, matte tape. Magic Tape has the added feature that you can write on it with pen, pencil, or marker to create additional coloration or markings. Although many tapes work, some are clearly better than others. Though all criteria seldom appear in a single tape, try to select one with the most desirable characteristics:

1. Waterproof or extremely water-resistant
2. Lightweight
3. Thin membrane
4. Single high-tack, sticky surface
5. Nonreflective, dull, or matte finish
6. Shear and shred resistant

I use tape for adult caddis and small grasshopper wings, as well as dragonfly, damsel, and stonefly nymph wings. Inordinately large tape wings, which can be heavy, are less serviceable on dry patterns.

Wing shapes include caddis and grasshopper wings as well as damselfly, dragon-fly, and stonefly nymph wing cases. The tape adds strength and shape to each wing. Furthermore, the sheer simplicity is attractive.

Making the Scotch Wing

1. To make a Scotch wing, take a length of tape, sticky side up, and tape it (at each end) to a smooth surface.

2. Select the proper feathers, especially the wide, soft, mottled contour or body feathers from grouse and hens. Most wide, soft feathers with a fine stem will work. Trim the base fluff and gently caress the feather to align the barbs.

3. Touch the feather tip to the tape and then gently pull the feather, aligning the barbs nearly parallel to the stem, while pressing the feather onto the tape. Avoid tangled or overlapped barbs.

4. After mounting all the feathers required, trim the tape close to the feather border.

5. Create symmetrical wings by folding the feather along the stem before cutting. For example, fold the feather along the stem and then trim to shape, leaving a small mounting tab. The base tab should be wide enough so that the wing lies flat. Pruning the dubbing or hackle on top of the body may encourage this.

Tying the Scotch-Wing Caddis

The Scotch-Wing Caddis

The Splitter

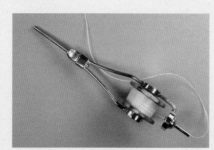

The Spin-Bob

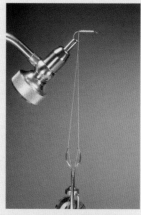

The needle point divides the thread and the hook keeps the loop open.

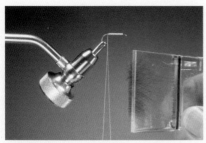

1. Use a split-thread loop for a delicate CDC body and hackle. I designed the Splitter to divide the thread and maintain the loop, and the Spin-Bob to spin the thread rapidly. Frank Matarelli, the master toolmaker, kindly crafted my designs in steel.

2. Adjust barbs for a sparse, fine CDC hackle. Long barbs increase floatation. Hackle length creates both the palmer and the shoulder hackle.

3. Twirl the Spin-Bob and then wrap an open palmer to reveal the contrasting belly thread.

4. Prepare and mount an appropriately shaped and colored Scotch wing

5. Capture the wing and wrap CDC palmer as shoulder hackle.

6. Add pheasant tail or coq de Leon barb antennae (if desired), and whip-finish the head.

The fuzzy CDC appearance of this caddis corresponds to the order name, *Trichoptera* (Greek *tricho* = hair, *ptera* = wing), the "hair-winged" insect. The imitative elements for the adult caddis usually include size, color, wing shape and, occasionally, antennae length. The tent wings hide the hook bend and, consequently, create a pattern for hook-shy trout.

The Shrimp

In *Minor Tactics of the Chalk Stream* (1910), G. E. M. Skues offered an attitude and an early shrimp pattern. "I was at one time greatly interested in an

A well-wrought Shrimp

attempt to imitate the fresh-water shrimp, and I tied a variety of patterns, including several with backs of quill of some small bird dyed greenish-olive, and ribbed firmly while wet and impressionable with silk or gold wire; but somehow I never used or attempted to use any one of them." Skues had "felt qualms" when he caught fish on an artificial alderfly larva and was "conscience-stricken" when he had "mad success" with a caddis larva pattern. He was not certain as to the sporting propriety of imitating these insect stages. It seems that he also had some misgivings about the modest shrimp. He never did cast his shrimp fly; instead, he gave it to a colleague who promptly lost it to a large fish. That should have told him something.

The freshwater shrimp fly is curiously young. Early shrimp patterns were tied for salmon, but it would be some time before the trout variety was developed and accepted. It has been claimed that the Shell Fly in the *Treatyse* is a shrimp imitation. Though now generally considered a caddis, the green wool body, peacock herl rib and bustard wing might suggest a shrimp. The name, perhaps, suggests shrimp carapace or caddis case.

Eric Taverner, as early as 1933, thought that traditional wet flies (such as the Partridge and Orange) and nymphs (the ubiquitous Gold-Ribbed Hare's Ear, for instance) might imitate freshwater shrimp. Traditional slip-wing wets may be shrimp surrogates. Perhaps their arched gray wings suggest the carapace or shellback. Even the familiar Zug Bug might proxy for shrimp. William Blades, in *Fishing Flies and Fly Tying* (1951), offered a shrimp pattern. Tied on a straightshank hook, it is made with goose or swan fibers coated with cement.

Gil Nyerges created his Nyerges Nymph to imitate the shrimp in the shallow alkaline lakes of the Northwest. The Nyerges Nymph has a chenille body and trimmed palmer hackle. George Herter, who had potent opinions about most things, was never satisfied with his personal shrimp patterns. Although Herter made shrimp imitations for "a great many years," he "never felt that they were really what they ought to be." They were "difficult to imitate because of their unusual actions." Evidently, Herter found the erratic, flicking darts of the shrimp impossible to imitate by design alone.

The Natural

A few tyers, like J. Edson Leonard in *Flies* (1960), make a distinction between the shrimp (*Gammarus*) and the smaller scuds (*Hyalella*). In tying and trouting, however, there is no notable difference. Shrimp are laterally flattened and have a distinct shellback or carapace. Although competent swimmers, most spend their time among plants or on the bottom. General shrimp patterns may also imitate the stalk-eye and cylindrical fairy shrimp (*Anostraca*) as well as the horizontally-flattened, aquatic sowbugs (*Asellidae*).

The unusual shape and structure of the shrimp has sired some curious imitations. International fly-fishing competitions affirm the effectiveness of modern mid-European shrimp flies. These, including the woven Polish nymphs, are usually heavily weighted on curved hooks, often with several colors in a single fly for a sense of life.

The *Prestranica*

Indeed, some of the strangest and most innovative shrimp flies come from Europe. Neil Patterson's Red-Spot Shrimp, a popular English pattern, has a touch of fluorescent red wool to represent developing eggs. Ljubo Pinter, a Slovene, ties a *Gammarus* pattern, the *Prestranica*, made with dormouse fur and an eel skin carapace.

Ivo Kajnik, another Slovene, creates remarkably realistic hand-painted flies. Hans Nischkauer, of Austria, uses catfish skin treated with picric acid to form the shellback. And T. Preskawiec, of France, has his *Gamma* pattern made with a gray palmer hackle and two colored pike scales.

Despite these strange ties, shrimp patterns are extremely simple—a weighted hook, a dubbed underbody, and a carapace, synthetic or natural, ribbed with wire. Though many patterns call for a round or circular-bend hook, swimming shrimp are usually elongated. If desired, it is possible to *suggest* a body curve, rather than to tie on one. All hooks may be tied slightly down the bend to suggest a curved body while preserving a wide gap.

Another factor may recommend the straight shank: some circular or rounded hooks may be reluctant hookers. Recently, while fishing a spring creek, I met heavy rises. My Adams tempted nothing on the surface. So I tossed a round-hook shrimp pattern that was immediately taken by an athletic trout. After a twist and turn, he was off. The problem may be more the angler than the hook, but I have always been wary of circular steel.

Gary Borger, in *Naturals*, notes, "During swimming the thoracic legs are pointed to the rear and the body is held straight. For this reason, scud patterns should not be tied humpbacked, but with a straight body." Some shrimp even swim on their sides; thus there is no need to provide a "keel" with weight. Weight, however, is often required to quickly sink the fly to the trout. I often use Skues' preferred bend, the Limerick. Shrimp hooks include the Partridge J1A (Limerick Wet Fly Hook) and the K12ST (caddis hook); the Tiemco 2302 (nymph hook) and the 2457 (round bend); the Daiichi 1530 (round hook), the 1150 (heavy), and the 1480 (Limerick fine-wire). Most medium-wire, straight-shank hooks work well. An adequate gap is necessary, as much of the tie is beneath the hook shank.

The Czech Shrimp, tied by Jan Šiman of the Czech Republic, is an effective pattern. It achieves maximum realism with minimal tying. A spun-wire dubbing brush or a dubbing loop usually forms the body. A fine, black netting, seen through a transparent carapace strip, creates the etched dorsal plates of the shrimp. The netting, an ultrafine mesh tulle, is available at most fabric stores. Black is basic, but white tulle is easily colored with permanent marking pens. Select a net color that contrasts with the body dubbing, and use a dubbing loop to flare the fibers. Also mix and vary the dubbing colors along the dubbing loop. A pinch of red or amber at midpoint, suggesting the viscera or an egg sack, adds a spark to the imitation. The spiky dubbing, which emulates the body and bushy swim-legs, should be long enough to touch the hook point. Dubbing expressly for shrimp and aquatic sowbug patterns is available. Various synthetic sheets make excellent carapaces. These transparent sheets, with matte and gloss sides, have appropriate stretch for shrimp backs. Ribbing is often done with fine gold wire or clear monofilament. The following pattern, a mild variation of the Czech Shrimp, is tied with fine tulle netting.

Twenty years after his first shrimp search, Skues found his fly. In the 1931 *Field Magazine*, Skues wrote about an acceptable freshwater shrimp pattern. He dubbed pale orange and olive seal fur on a #16 down-eye Limerick hook, wrapping down into the bend to suggest the shrimp's curve. He then palmered on a pale red hackle, added fine gold-wire ribbing, and trimmed the barbs off the back. Skues' shrimp had an adequate gap, a suggested curve, a dappled body, and trimmed hackle. With triumphant epilogue Skues' shrimp, no longer a fugitive from his fly-tying, took two good fish, both heavy with natural shrimp.

The Net Shrimp (Variant)

Thread:	6/0 Unithread, color matching dominant dubbing color
Hook:	Partridge J1A or K12ST; Tiemco 2302 or 2457; Daiichi 1530, 1150, or 1480
Underbody:	Wapsi Sow-Scud in various colors
Shellback or Carapace:	Fine, black mesh tulle-net strip, and Wapsi's Thin Skin, color print matching the natural. The tulle netting suggests the body plates of the shrimp.
Rib:	Fine gold wire or clear monofilament

1. Mount the hook (and weight if required). For weight, mount two or three wire strands on top of the shank. These increase sink while preserving the hook gap.

2. Mount the wire rib, the synthetic carapace and net strip. When folded over—after dubbing—the carapace should be wide enough to pull down the dubbing fibers beneath the shank. Shrimp patterns look best when the fibers flare and fold beneath the body.

3. Select a multicolored dubbing, such as amber, olive, brown, and gray. Mount the short, spiky dubbing at right angles to the dubbing loop.

4. Spin the loop tightly. Hold the dubbed loop firmly and then comb out the dubbing with a Velcro hook patch to extend and align the fibers before wrapping the dubbing along the shank. The Velcro hook patch, merely a two-inch strip of *hook* Velcro, aligns the fibers prior to wrapping.

5. When wrapping the dubbing on the shank, pull the fibers back to avoid trapping them in subsequent wraps. The dubbing should extend far enough to screen the hook point.

6. Fold the net strip forward and secure at the head. Then fold forward the carapace strip and secure at the head.

7. Spiral the ribbing forward and tie off at the head. Whip-finish. Darken the head and carapace, if desired, with a permanent marker.

The Shucking Midge

Reverse patterns—flies tied back to front—are old. Datus Proper, in *What the Trout Said* (1982), noted that Alexander MacKintosh described a back to front wet fly as early as 1806. In 1886, Wakeman Holberton patented his Flutter, a reverse wet fly. Supposedly, the tilted, transposed wings flexed and "fluttered" during the retrieve. Holberton's pattern was once described as "unquestionably the greatest and most radical improvement in fishing tackle." Holberton claimed, although quite erroneously, that reversed wings offered less casting resistance. Known as the "Scarlet Ibis" in the angling press, he was secretary of the Neversink Club in 1884.

H. G. McClelland's *The Trout Fly Dresser's Cabinet of Devices* (1898) illustrates a reverse down-wing dry fly and offers detailed tying directions for a reverse up-wing dry. He believed that his reverse pattern, which concealed the hook and allowed for a more natural downstream drift, was close to "mechanical perfection" with "its centre of gravity almost beneath its wings." Eric Tavener pointed out that, "This idea, however, did not bear fruit, largely because anglers have not experienced the need of so dressing the dry fly and because the fish have taken neither exception nor umbrage at patterns that sail down 'stern' foremost."

Though reverse patterns have never been popular, they do have some unique attributes. Among their *advantages* are the following:

1. They do have a tendency to float better. The hackle supports the heaviest part of the hook: the bend and projecting spear.
2. The hackle barbs obscure or screen the bend and spear, perhaps creating a more realistic design.
3. The screened point produces an almost weedless hook.
4. The reverse fly rides higher in the water than traditional ties. Datus Proper noted that the design is "the only fly of normal size and shape in which the hook usually stays out of the water."

There are also some *disadvantages*:

1. Wrapping the hackle at a tight bend is somewhat more awkward than the traditional shoulder wrap.
2. Excessive hackle stiffness and excessive bulk may prevent trout takes.
3. The reverse design may not appeal to the modern angler's sense of aesthetics.

One pattern, the Shucking Midge, seems to have more virtues than vices. It mimics the moment of eclosion (adult emergence), the most vulnerable time for insects—and the most attractive for trout. It is especially suitable for the emerging "bloodworm," the crimson species of *Chironomini*. During emergence, the insect's tracheal system contains enough air to enable the pupa to ascend to the surface aided by a few wiggles. Once it arrives, the pupa stretches out along the surface and pumps blood into its thorax to split the pupal case. As the insect emerges from the shuck or pupal case, the thorax and wings are orange-red. The thorax, pumped full of blood to split the case, then inflates the wings with blood to expand them. Once the insect is free from the case, muscular contractions return the blood to the abdomen. The wings gray as the blood drains.

The Shucking Midge takes advantage of the unique and seductive red emergence phase. Some angler's call this the "pink hatch." This fly has proven especially effective on selective, spring-creek trout.

Tie this emerger with limited wraps and minimal bulk. A small, silver hook might be more obscure under certain conditions. Chameleon-like, a silver hook may mirror watery reflections and bubbles, thereby hiding even more. The visibility of the hook will depend, of course, upon the direction and condition of the light. Col. E. W. Harding, in *The Flyfisher & the Trout's Point of View* (1931), recognized the possibilities of a reflective hook under various light conditions. He further declared that light condition, light direction, and hook color determine hook visibility:

> When the light falls directly on the parts of the hook that the trout sees, a polished bronze hook, even when only just through the surface, and so duplicated by reflection, is not usually very conspicuous. Its rounded edges reflect their surroundings and merge into them, leaving only a threadlike core, which tones in colour with the surrounding water. In these conditions of light a highly polished nickel-plated hook, especially if the bend is showing, reflects the direct light and shows up at times rather more clearly than the bronzed hook.
>
> On the other hand, when light is shining from a direction behind the hook, the bronze is more conspicuous than the nickel-plated hook. With the light behind them and sunk a little below the surface, both sorts of hooks are inconspicuous. The threadlike core of the bronzed hook takes up an olive tone slightly darker than the rest of the water, while the nickel-plated hook seems to reflect its surroundings completely. When the sun is straight ahead and low down, it is very difficult to see the nickel-plated hook at all. This is exactly in accordance with the theory of the subject. In diffused light it [the silver or nickel-plated hook] should be nearly a perfect mirror and reflect its surroundings completely. When facing a direct light, it should reflect it and so flash. It does, and therefore it shows up.

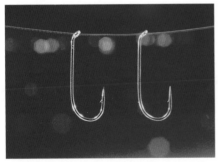

Direct lateral lighting: submerged Daiichi crystal (a bright silver finish) and bronze hooks, size 12. The crystal hook (left) reflects the blue surroundings with highlights. Note also the bright edge flare of the silver hook. The bronze hook (right) has a duller edge. The dark "thread-line" centers of both hooks appear nearly equal.

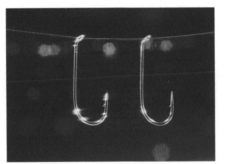

Front lighting: front lighting ignites the crystal silver hook. Again, the crystal silver surface reflects the blue ambient light.

Distant hooks are, of course, much less visible than those shown in the photographs. In direct light, bronzed hooks were less visible. Though it is interesting to consider the value of hook color, it is difficult to determine the importance of Colonel Harding's directives. Few anglers want to change hook color based on light direction and conditions. Furthermore, a bronze hook, the standard in conservation, may disintegrate faster than a silver-finish hook when lost to a fish. Nevertheless, the maximum deception of a silver hook becomes the skeleton for the following pattern.

The crimson polypropylene creates the budding body. The hackle forms the legs, and the mole fur suggests the body still trapped within the shuck. The sparkling Antron fore-shank is the empty shuck, looking much like a capsule of silvery mercury.

The Shucking Midge

Hook: Daiichi 1222, size 16, 18, or 20 with "crystal" (silver) finish or similar silver hook.

Thread: Unithread, bright white, 8/0 or finer.

Budding Body: Crimson polypropylene yarn, furled and mounted. Long, blood-red goose CDC barbs may be substituted for poly yarn. The budding body may be mounted in such a manner as to droop and cloak the hook bend.

Hackle: Dark brown, Cree, grizzly, or silver badger. Barb tips should cloak hook point.

Body: Black or dark gray mole fur.

Shuck: Ultrafine, fluorescent white Antron dubbing wrapped on a bare, silver hook shank.

1. After mounting the hook, wrap a thread base on the rear ⅓ of the shank. Use a permanent marker to darken the thread for the budding body, hackle, and mole fur: use bright, white thread for the shuck. No thread should cover the front half of the hook shank. Next, tightly twist a slender strand of poly yarn (or long CDC barbs) between your fingers, then carefully fold it in the middle so that it furls together, forming an emerging body. Spot-mount the budding body over the hook bend at the tail position. Note the naked fore-shank in the photograph above.

2. Mount and sparsely wrap a dark brown grizzly hackle. The hackle barbs should be just long enough to shroud the hook spear. For greater deception, the barbs should match the color of the hook; use dark brown for bronze hooks and grizzly or silver badger for silver hooks. The dark center of the silver badger may imitate the body still enclosed within the shuck. Omit the mole fur body described below if you use a silver badger. Use only a few hackle wraps to cloak the point. I sometimes use appropriately colored CDC barbs in a split-thread loop as hackle. This creates a "downy" fly for spring creeks. Remember, the barbs should cloak and extend slightly beyond the hook spear. After hackling, blacken a short length of thread for the mole fur body.

3. For a delicate, smooth wax coat, use a wax wand (a flat, brass applicator). It is difficult applying a smooth, even coat of wax directly from a wax tube. Spin the thread back and forth as you gently touch the finely chopped mole fur to the waxed thread. Touch finely diced mole fur to the spinning waxed thread and wrap. This fuzzes the thread with mole fur, and, when wrapped, imitates the dark, midge body still within the shuck. Wrap only a diminutive mole fur body.

4. Again, apply a smooth smear of wax to the thread, and spin the thread back and forth to pick up the finely diced (about 2 millimeters cuts of ultrafine 3 denier) Antron fuzz. Complete the fly with a "shuck" of dubbed Antron down the shank and whip-finish.

5. Applied in this manner, the Antron creates a sparkling, transparent sheen along the hook. The bright, shiny shank maintains the reflective integrity and preserves the dazzle of the finely diced Antron.

Perhaps the Shucking Midge is an effective pattern because of the touch of crimson, the dark body, and the crystalline shuck. Perhaps it is effective because it is backward. The late C. F. Walker believed that every beginner eventually creates a reverse fly design. He also believed that the beginner will inevitably discard it. There are some flies, however—like the Shucking Midge—that thrive on backward tying and perhaps some forward thinking.

The Tracer

Our biplane, a slow but faithful Antonov, droned over a dense green canopy that spread to all horizons. The Amazon watershed is immense, approximately the size of the continental United States. Moreover, the river itself flows 4,000 miles and holds over 2,000 fish species and more water than the Mississippi, the Nile, and the Yangtze combined. Though our flight to camp took about three hours, it seemed like decades back in time. The Antonov bucked wind as we turned to final approach and then slowed to a walk as we touched down on a dusty, jungle strip. The powerful radial engine roared a welcome before "switches off." It is remarkable that the Portuguese penetrated this hot, dense green in 1669, about the same time that American Puritans flourished in New England. Even after several trips to the Amazon, I still seem to enter a 1920s adventure novel—a novel about a beautiful and prehistoric land.

The heat and high humidity of the Amazon challenged both casting and tying. Pushing a large baitfish fly through the heavy air was exhausting. Sometimes, however, the exhaustion was rewarded with a ravenous strike that sliced through the water.

Clearly, I needed a large, light fly that would cast and swim well. This, of course, is a basic tying conundrum when creating bulky baitfish patterns for large, aggressive gamefish. I admire Bob Popovics' Spread Fly, on which epoxy creates a wide, flat

The flooded jungle: Tucanare Territory

body of Superhair. The Spread Fly, though, has a single dimension; I wanted width as well as height. I wanted a pattern that was castable, yet one that created disturbance during the retrieve. I also like Big Fly Fiber for tying large flies. I wanted, however, that same wispiness for all synthetic strands, including the Holographic and Mirage Flashabous. In short, I wanted intense flash in a large, castable pattern.

Though the concept was simple, the solution was not. I tried to curl various strand materials with heating curlers and clothes irons. Nothing really worked. When my wife, Sandra, saw me using her best clothes iron on tying material, she offered me a simple solution—use boiling water. First, I had to make a tool that would form the curl before it was heated. After several prototypes, I designed a Curling Cross that created the "frizzled" strands I sought. And when the bright strands became a fly, it cast like a burning bullet, a tracer. And so it was christened.

The Tracer method produces a boundless variety of large fresh- and saltwater patterns. With the proper tools and materials, it can also create small trout patterns. Curled synthetics offer an illusion of bulk while creating a smooth, slick fly that collapses during the cast to achieve minimal wind resistance. Frizzled synthetics create "empty," airy patterns that have size, form, and flash. Even a full, fine-strand body can capture water, making the fly difficult to pick up and cast. Curled bodies, however, need few strands for bulk and, when aerialized, quickly expel excess water. Depending upon the strand density, even large 4/0 and 5/0 flies cast easily.

The Predator and the Prey

I wanted to imitate brightly-colored, generic baitfish. Many large gamefish, such as the so-called "peacock bass"—the Tucanare (*Cichla temensis*) and the "butterfly peacock" (*Cichla ocellaris*)—specialize in eating various, large, brightly-colored bait-fish of a pound or more. The peacock bass, not a true bass, is an aggressive cichlid—a pursuit predator that continues the chase and attack if unsuccessful at first. All peacocks wear an ocellated black spot ringed with cream at the base of the caudal fin. The tail spot suggests the vivid "eye" of the peacock tail feather, hence their popular name. They can attain weights of 25 pounds or more, though most adults are 20 pounds or less. Their explosive strikes—like a grenade throwing water shrapnel from a violent crater—are legendary.

A male Tucanare

I wanted an imitation that was about five to six inches long and about one inch in diameter at the head. Some prey fish, in fact, are nearly transparent, much like the wispy Tracer pattern itself. My fly needed a number of characteristics.

The Wide Eye

Eyes add color and contrast, and perhaps betray the alarmed look of a frightened and fleeing baitfish. I often use Spirit River's 3-D Molded Eye inserts, in gold or red, in the appropriate Real Eye or Deep Sea Eyes. For ultralight patterns, I can avoid excess weight by using only the 3-D Molded Eye inserts or prismatic tape eyes. The large tape eyes have the added benefit of trapping the fibers for a secure hold.

One can make a light bait head with EZ body tubing. The curled body strands completely fill the tubing. Prismatic tape eyes can then be added. To make the EZ-body head, mount the tubing over the hook eye, then fold it back to invert itself, creating a head.

The Flash Back

What sequence should I follow in mounting materials? First of all, I wanted some highly reflective materials on top to create a "flash back." In the thick Amazonian waters, the sun penetrates the rivers and streams to ignite the backs of baitfish. This bright back is then reflected in the surface mirror (the surface underside), broadcasting the presence of baitfish to predators. A bright, shimmering topping might be an enticement to hungry fish. There were several appropriate flash materials for the topping, such as standard Flashabou or Holographic Flashabou. However, I liked the bright, iridescent color-shift in Hedron's opal Flashabou Mirage. These highly reflective strands prove attractive.

The Painted Heart

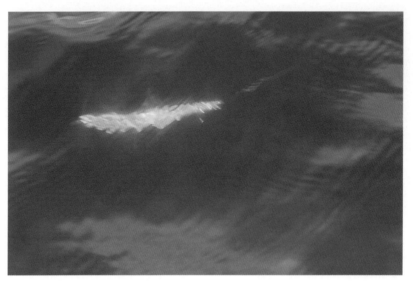

The flash of a submerged Tracer

Many Amazonian baitfish are brightly colored. They often flush colors when pursued by predators. I wanted that vivid panic in the eye and body of the fly. I also wanted the colors—such as bright red, orange, or yellow—to give a sense of life and flash, to make contrast with the bright body and dark water. The new Mirage Flashabou is excellent for this kaleidoscopic shimmering blush; the iridescent color shifts in each fiber.

The Bend Wrap

Excessively long patterns may encourage annoying wraps around the hook bend. If properly curled, patterns up to eight inches or more seldom have this problem. Although bend wraps are only a problem with *extremely* long Tracers, some tyers may want a solution. To prevent long tail strands from wrapping around the bend, you can increase the curled length. The swollen, frizzed strands actually prevent bend wrap. In addition, long dangly strands may be controlled with epoxy, silicone, or Softex. Tying "tarpon style," in which the body is mounted at the extreme rear of the hook shank, also minimizes bend wrap. There are, in fact, some "beaked" baitfishes, such as the Characin, that the tarpon-style might imitate.

There are other solutions to the bend-wrap problem. Many years ago, I received a steelhead fly from Frank Matarelli. It had a spun-wire loop that elevated the tail of the fly. This idea suggested another possible solution to prevent tail wrap: the body harness. A harness, made from fine, stiff stainless-steel wire (.0140" in diameter), holds the long body away from the hook bend during the cast and retrieve. A 14-gauge stainless-steel electric guitar string works well when shaped and mounted securely with tying thread and cement.

Mount this harness on the hook before adding any materials. Notice that, for extremely long patterns, the harness loop may project beyond the hook bend. After completing the fly, pull the body through the harness loop with a monofilament noose. Unlike hard and heavy epoxy, a harness adds little weight and allows the material some expansion and movement. Although bent during the strike and struggle, the vibrant waltz of fly and fish, a harness is readily reformed.

However, I have found that when the body is properly curled, bend wraps are not a significant problem. Tracer patterns seven inches or more do not require either epoxy or harness: the curls alone resolve the problem. To eliminate bend wrap, *the curled length should match the shank length*. Moreover, if for any reason the tails are snarled around the bend, the strands are readily freed.

Making Curls

I wanted a 2/0 to 5/0 baitfish pattern that was easily cast, yet pushed water on the retrieve. To achieve a bouffant body and head, I decided to make synthetic ringlets for volume. This technique, which tightly curls a determined length of material, may be used on virtually any synthetic strands. To make a Curling Cross or "frizzle rod," simply bend a single brass rod. Solid brass rods—36" long and .062" diameter—are available from craft, hobby stores, and specialty catalogs. For a standard 8" Curling Cross, use a 19"-long rod. Fold the rod in the middle and slip a 3" heat shrink onto the doubled rod. Bend the curling arms as shown, position the heat shrink and shrink. The heat shrink should expose a $\frac{1}{3}$" crotch for catching the strands. Remember that the smaller the brass rod diameter, the tighter the curls. However, brass rod diameters .055" and smaller make Curling Crosses that bend readily. Fine diameter stainless steel rods make the tightest curls. In any case, for small curls, do not over-wrap previous strand wraps. Once the curls are formed, they must be removed from the Curling Cross and expanded. Though some fine-toothed combs work well, I make a small, needle comb to separate and puff the curled strands.

Tying the Light Tracer (Unweighted)

For a Trout Tracer use very narrow, supple strands to imitate small baitfish. The Light Tracer, however, is especially appropriate for imitating large baitfish. For the standard Light Tracer omit the brass eye and mount all curled body strands forward, immediately behind the hook eye. Head length should equal mounted eye width. I often place a drop of cyanoacrylate on the head wraps, let dry and, with

Making Curls

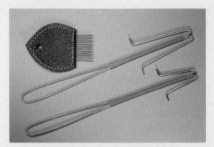

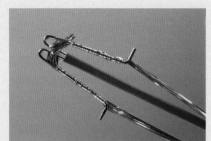

1. Curling Crosses and needle comb

2. To frizzle the fibers, capture the end of a modest fiber bundle with a size 18 nylon cable tie and trim excess cable. The end may also be whipped tightly with thread. Only a few strands are required to make a plump fly: do not be tempted to use superfluous strands. Divide the bundle into two equal sections.

3. Catch the cable tie in the curling crotch. Then tightly spiral one strand around its respective rod arm (about four times or more) as shown. Avoid wrapping over previous wraps. Over-wrapping merely concentrates dense curls. With the same number of turns, *counterwrap* the other arm with the second strand bundle. The second arm should be a mirror image of the first arm. This produces balanced and symmetrical curls.

4. Then, while trapping the trailing strands against the end of the rod handle (to protect the hand), immerse the tightly wound sections in boiling water for about four seconds.

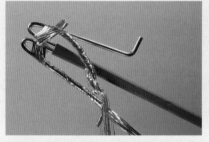

finer strands, the needle-comb folds for denser teeth. Once combed, the strands will puff up to provide bulk for the fly. Due to the open lattice of the curled strands, air easily penetrates the fly and dispels water during casting.

5. Then plunge the heated wraps into cold water and dry with a cloth. You can also pour boiling water over the wrapped strands.

6. Now, carefully take the curled strands off the rod and gently comb and tease them out with long strokes. The comb separates and plumps the strands. For

small pliers, laterally flatten the head. Then, add a full, ball head with Loon Outdoors orange Hard Head polyurethane.

Quick-drying epoxies or polyurethane "epoxies" may be used. When using Loon Outdoors Hard Head, place the pattern immediately in a rotator for partial drying, approximately 20 minutes. Due to polyurethane shrinkage, more Hard Head may be required to avoid any gaps after the eyes are mounted. Wait until the second (or subsequent coats) are partially dry, but tacky. Then firmly press two Spirit River 3-D molded eyes onto the adhesive head and return the pattern to the rotator for complete drying. If the ball head is sufficiently large in the beginning, no gaps appear. I usually leave all Tracers long and trim when required. A short 3/0 or 4/0 Light Tracer is an excellent aruana pattern.

The Tracer

Hook:	Tiemco 600 sp big game hook, any appropriate size.
Thread:	Orange Uni Big Fly (Uni-Products) or Ultra Thread 140 (Wapsi)
Eyes and Inserts:	Spirit River Real Eyes (¼ inch gold) and Spirit River 3-D molded eye inserts (size 3.5, pearl/orange).
Underbelly Strands:	Curled orange Flashabou Mirage (#3067)
Belly Strands:	Curled purple Flashabou Mirage (#3066) or flourescent yellow Flashabou Mirage (#3061)
Topping Strands:	Curled opal Flashabou Mirage (#3005)

1. **After attaching thread to the front third of the shank, mount the Real Eyes with 3-D inserts, adding a drop or two of cyanoacrylate to the wraps.**

2. **Mount the underbelly strands beneath the shank *immediately* behind the eye position.**

3. **Next, mount the side strands (the middle strands) immediately behind the eyes, adding a drop or two of cyanoacrylate to the wraps.**

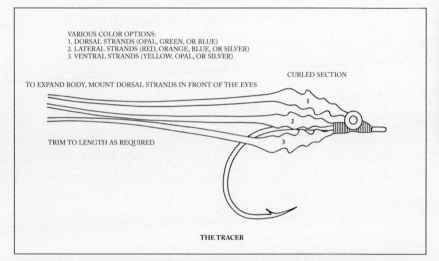

VARIOUS COLOR OPTIONS:
1. DORSAL STRANDS (OPAL, GREEN, OR BLUE)
2. LATERAL STRANDS (RED, ORANGE, BLUE, OR SILVER)
3. VENTRAL STRANDS (YELLOW, OPAL, OR SILVER)

CURLED SECTION

TO EXPAND BODY, MOUNT DORSAL STRANDS IN FRONT OF THE EYES

TRIM TO LENGTH AS REQUIRED

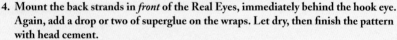

THE TRACER

5. **After mounting all the strands, trim the fly to length. Use Anvil's Taperizer scissors if you wish to thin or taper the body. If left long, the pattern can be trimmed to proper length to match angling conditions.**

4. **Mount the back strands in *front* of the Real Eyes, immediately behind the hook eye. Again, add a drop or two of superglue on the wraps. Let dry, then finish the pattern with head cement.**

The Aruana

The aruana (*Osteoglossum bicirrhosum*) is a leaper, a surface-to-air missile. It has a powerful, smooth serpentine swim and can catapult five or more feet out of water to take insects, small birds, and bats from boughs. Indigenous to the Amazon and the Orinoco watersheds, the aruana (also spelled arawana or arowana) remains unchanged since the Eocene, 50 million years ago. The genus, *Osteoglossum*, refers to its "bony tongue," actually rows of bony teeth in the lower jaw that mesh with those in the upper jaw. It has two olfactory "barbells" or sensors attached to its exaggerated lower lip. Apparently, the barbells are extremely sensitive to vibrations in the water made by insects or fish. In oxygen-starved swamps, the aruana has an accessory respiratory organ on the fourth gill arch for breathing atmospheric air. Large

Tying the Light Tracer (Unweighted)

The Light Tracer

Eyes: For the Light Tracers, Spirit River 3-D molded eye
inserts (size 5.0 or larger, pearl/orange)

Head: Loon Outdoors polyurethane Hard Head (orange),
Loon Outdoors Salt Water Skalze (white pearl)
or similar

Build a small head for the Light Tracer

scales cover the elongated, "scimitar" body while the scaleless head is smooth and shiny. The dorsal, caudal, and anal fins appear fused and continuous around the tail. Pectral fins extend like wings, while the long ventral fin dangles like a pennant.

The remarkable whiplike leaps invariably result in lost fish. Aruana fight like snagged snakes. Many merely open their mouth to release a fly or tail dance with furious and frenetic contortions and convulsions that dislodge the hook. They patrol the surface for insects and prey fish, often cruising in pairs, pods, or shoals. They are a gallant and noble gamefish.

The Aruana

The aruana is cousin to one of the largest (over 400 pounds and 10 feet long), scaly freshwater fishes in the world, the pirarucú (*Arapaima gigas*). Once, a pirarucú took a peacock bass that had taken my Tracer. The pirarucú shredded my terminal tackle. When the food chain is only a link long, everything eats everything. And most of them eat Tracers.

These Tracer techniques, where form follows function, create a variety of patterns. Small Tracers make trout and bass streamers; large Tracers create excellent baitfish for large saltwater and freshwater predators. Moreover, all Tracers make long, clean casts. When cast, the glowing Tracer arcs out and drops, burning brightly until extinguished by dark waters and large fish.

These patterns from Shucking Midge to Tracer are all experiments in tying. Although these patterns are effective, it would be remiss to think that tying stops here. There are better ways yet unknown. Every tyer must create an individual and inimitable process and pattern. We have examined a backwards pattern, an eel-skin carapace, a tube of spiders, a Catskill debate, a needle husk, a hook reflection, a nearly naked hook, and other topics and techniques. In fact, the process—creating new tools, studying the insects, exploring past methods, developing new techniques, and discovering the perfect materials—is far more important than the pattern. The theories and solutions, the thinking process itself, is the greatest pleasure of tying. This pleasure may even exceed the satisfaction of tying flies or catching fish. The power of these patterns is the tales they reveal: the imitative theories, the false solutions, the successful answers, the ingenious tyers, and the historical passages. Their true worth, if they possess any, must lie in their intellectual provenance.

Sunrise on the Agua Boa do Univini, Roraima, Brazil

CHAPTER IV

THE HOOK

𝔜e makynge of your harnays: ye hokis

𝔜e shall understonde that the moost subtyll & hardyste crafte in makynge
of your harnays is for to make your hokis.

—The Treatyse

SOME OF MY BEST "ANGLING" COMES FROM THE PAGES OF antique angling
books. Early angling "harnays" (harness, tackle) fails to match our modern
equipment—our rods shoot long, flat trajectories. Our fly patterns mimic a
moment of the gnat's hatch. The study of antique tackle-craft is fascinating, but
in light of modern tackle, it functions mainly as an intriguing window to the past.
Fly patterns have always been handmade; their evolution and methods can be
instructive today. The modern fly pattern has a direct historical continuum to the
past. The hook, more than line and rod, still evokes its ancestor in manufacture
and design. Time and technology, however, have transformed the line and the rod.
There was a time when anglers handcrafted *all* tackle. It is in these headwaters
that we find our concepts and methods for making hook, line, and rod.

No matter how competent our talent or efficient our tackle, every angler eventually wonders how it was back then. Some of those forgotten skills—such as line,
hook, and rod making—hide within the foxed and faded pages. Perhaps we vali-
date the ancient angler by re-creating his experience. Today, there is no imperative to make or use ancient angling "harnays." Yet, no reason is necessary to
appreciate those quaint and curious pages. The early angler, though limited in
many ways, was creative, skillful, and successful. Here then is a look at early hook,
line, and rod making.

The Treatyse of Fishing Wyth an Angle (1496) presents the first concise English
instructions on hook making, "the moost subtyll & hardyste crafte." Though
described as "the most abstruse and difficult skill," hook making is simple.
Throughout the centuries, the fundamental tools and process have remained
unchanged. Any angler with a modicum of attentiveness and a few simple tools
can make functional hooks. Practice and patience solves most problems. Like fly

tying, hook making is a satisfying craft. Hook making is especially important when duplicating historic hooks or designing new hooks. Many early angling books—such as *The Treatyse, The Angler's Sure Guide, The Gentleman Angler*, and *The Art of Angling* include instructions for hook making. Others, such as Pulman's *Fly Fishing for Trout*, Francis' *A Book on Angling*, O'Gorman's *The Practice of Angling, Particularly as Regards Ireland*, present detailed information on hook design and selection. Hook making was part of the ancient angler's "harnays"— part of his equipment, skill, and knowledge. However, by the 1700s, hook making became less compulsory. *The Gentleman Angler* (first edition, 1726) cautions anglers about hook making, since ". . . they are scarce worth the Pains or Troubles that are taken about them, since the best may be purchased at a cheap Price." The modern angler, nevertheless, can still find pleasure in this ancient art.

The *Treatyse* illustrates the essential tools: *Hamour* (hammer), *Wegge* (wedge), *Fyle, Knyfe, Pynsons* (pinchers or tongs), *Wreste* (wrest or bender), *Clamm* (clamp, and *Anuelde* (anvil). The tools and process are basic. In the *Treatyse*, hook making appears, quickly and concisely, in a single, 172-word passage. The smallest hooks come from small "quarell nedlys" (square-headed needles), the largest from embroidery, tailor, or cobbler needles and nails. To soften, heat the needle red hot in a charcoal fire and cool. Raise the barb with a knife and sharpen the point. Heat the metal again to prevent breaking "in the bendyng." Then bend the needle. When the hook is bent, beat the "hinder ende abrode." File it smooth to prevent fraying your line. Finally, for a tough springiness, give it "an easy redde hete" and suddenly quench in water. Now the hook is hard and strong.

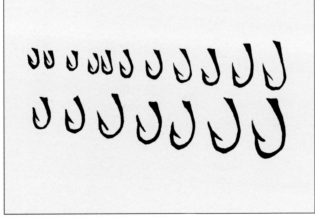

The *Treatyse* hooks

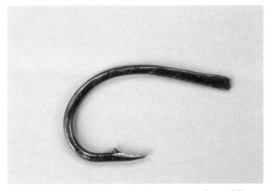

Hook replica based upon the *Treatyse* woodcuts. The original *Treatyse* hook may have been decidedly superior.

These directions accompany the rudimentary woodcuts that illustrate the hooks. According to John Betts, modern angling historian and studio hook maker, the *Treatyse* probably illustrates the hooks from a three-quarter view. If so, then the flattened spade may be at a right angle to the bend plane.

Although the medieval *Très Belles Heures* depicts delicate hooks, the *Treatyse* woodcuts illustrate hooks with heavy wire, short shanks, and "rank" or coarse barbs. Perhaps the limitations of a woodcut account for much of this. Most print methods, apparently, could not match the possible delicacy of a hook. In addition, hook size is problematic. The smallest *Treatyse* hook is about ¼ the length of the largest shown. In *A History of Fly Fishing for Trout*, John Waller Hills concluded: "The hooks, if the plate can be taken as a guide, and it probably can, were not large. Measured across the bend they run from about 2 or 3 to 15 on the modern scale, but they are shorter in the shank and thicker in the wire." This, of course, assumes that the largest is a size 2 and that all the hooks are proportional. Such may not be the case. Hill's determination is based on hook gap, not shank length, and the ratio between length and gap varies among the hooks illustrated. Betts' "three-quarter view" would reduce the hook gap and thus increase the size of the actual hooks. The hook-wire thickness may be printing practice rather than actual hook-wire diameter. Blind hooks were often left long and cut to proper length as required. It is also quite likely that anglers made hooks in unique shapes and sizes, according to personal preference.

Betts also uses the turned-up blind eye advocated by James O'Gorman in the nineteenth century. O'Gorman noted that "The inside and outside part of the shank of the hook should be filed flat, and the end of the shank a little turned up to prevent cutting the link where armed," that is, cutting the line where it attaches at the hook. An ingenious, squared shank kept the pattern from rotating. The turned-up blind eye, as Betts indicates, also keeps the head wraps on the shank and off the snell.

W. Lauson's "augmentation" (*c.* 1620) of *The Secrets of Angling* illustrates both plain and spaded hooks with near "perfect" bends and turned-up spears. His annotation defines the perfect hook design:

> The best form for ready striking and sure holding and strength, is a strait and somewhat long shanke and strait nib'd, with a little compasse, not round in any wise for it neither strikes surely nor readily, but is weak as having too great a compasse: some use to batter the upper end thus to hold the faster: but good thred or silke, good band may make it fast enough, it is botcherly, hinders the biting and sometimes cuts the line.

A spade end on the bend plane certainly would "hinder the biting" and "cut the line." Flattened spade ends, which secured the silk wraps, were either on the bend plane (vertical) or across the bend plane (horizontal). *The Secrets of Angling* illustration suggests that, sometimes, the spade tip was vertical, on the same plane as the bend. The vertical spade reduced the gap and chafed the gut. The woodcuts illustrate rounded or "perfect" bends. Lauson rejected the vertical spade and the round bend (a wide bend?) as "it neither strikes surely nor readily, but is weak as having too great compasse. . . ." According to the *OED*, the term "compass" has several meanings beyond arc or circumference, including "proper proportion"

The Secrets of Angling: the Lauson hook with spade end

The Secrets of Angling: the Lauson Paradigm hook

(1612) and "due limits" (1579). "Arc" is, however, the probable meaning: a wide bend—a wide circumference or "arc"—weakens a hook.

Robert Venables, in *The Experienced Angler* (1662) provided remarkable insight into hook design.

> Let your hooks be long in the shank, and of a compass somewhat inclining to roundness, but the point must stand even and straight, and the bending must be in the shank; for if the shank be straight, the point will hang outward, though when set on it may stand right, yet it will after taking of a few fish, cause the hair at the end of the shank to stand bent, and so, consequently cause the point of the hook to lie or hang too much outward, whereas upon the same ground the bending shank will then cause the point of the hook to hang directly upwards.

John Betts—in his perceptive article "Robert Venables' Experience as an Angler," (*The American Fly Fisher*, Vol. 29, No. 4, 2003)—thoroughly explicated the passage that he regarded as the most sophisticated ever written on hooks. Venables argued for the *bent* shank—line stress on a straight-shank hook positions the point outward: line stress on a bent-shank hook aligns the point with the pull. Only the left pattern on Venables' frontispiece might *vaguely* hint at a bent shank. Another method is to extend the "compass" or arc of the bend so that the point aligns with the line. This appears in Lauson's hook (*c.* 1620) above, approximately four decades before Venables. Lauson apparently took the design from John Dennys who preceded him by six years. Such a hook, Lauson wrote, is "the best form for ready striking, sure holding and strength." *The Secrets of Angling* hook was "incompast round/ Like to the print that Pegasus did make." In the literal sense, a horse-hoof imprint, much like Lauson's hook design, stretches and straightens the arc tips *slightly*. If imaginary lines extend from both arc ends they would, after a short span, intersect. That intersection would determine the proper hook length.

"Long in the shank" is an unknown length. Shank length, nonetheless, is a major contributor to hook strength. A longer shank encourages greater distribution of stress and, consequently, increases the integrity and reliability of a hook. A longer shank usually deforms and flexes to accommodate or absorb some stress. Venables may have selected a longer shank for other advantages: it increases the span allotted to line attachment and facilitates shank bend and point alignment. "The point must stand even and straight" may describe the point or spear as neither dropped nor offset. That is, the spear (from point to bend base) is straight. The shank bend aligns the spear with the end or tip of the shank. Venables' insight is a functional, rather than static, assessment of hook design. It truly is a remarkable passage.

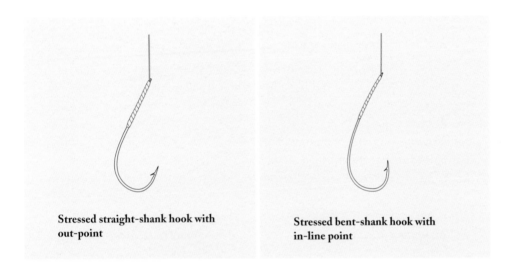

Stressed straight-shank hook with out-point

Stressed bent-shank hook with in-line point

The Angler's Sure Guide (1706), attributed to Robert Howlett, included an unusual hook-making process. Though Westwood and Satchell found the *Sure Guide*, "a somewhat close resemblance" to Chetham's *Vade Mecum*, the latter omits hook making. In the *Sure Guide*, you soften Spanish needles over a "chafer." The chafing-dish held burning fuel that heated anything placed over it. Flatten "the place for the beard" and then file a "beard" and point. A pin bender shapes each hook. After forming and shaping the hooks, you "lap them in the end of a Wire" to temper them.

When toughening a brittle hook:

> Take hold of the very end of the shank, and hold them over a red hot Iron, one by one (but not to touch it) till they be of a fit heat to temper; then put or dip them in Oyl, Butter, or Tallow, and a little Sope well mixed together, which is the tempering of them. But if your Hooks be too soft, stretch or stand bent after tempering, then you must heat them again red hot, and put them so hot into cold Water, which will make them hard and brittle, and then heat them over the hot Iron, and temper them as above-said.

If the hooks, after tempering, are still too brittle, then you did not heat them enough. If they "stretch and stand bent," then you have overheated them. Only "Experience must teach you upon often trial."

Hook-Making Tools

1. Small machinist's anvil: I mount a brass plate to protect the anvil face and barbing blades. A brass screw plate locks down the hook wire for barbing.
2. Barbing hammer: A small, jeweler's chasing hammer ($5\frac{1}{2}$ ounces) works well. Chasing hammers shape and emboss metal.
3. Propane burner: Many small, portable propane stoves—such as Primus, MSR, Optimus, or Coleman—can reach and even exceed the temperatures (over 2,000° Fahrenheit) required for hook making. To maintain an even temperature throughout the hook wire, select a stove with a wide flame. The hook placement within the flame determines the temperature. A built-in Piezo ignition is convenient.
4. Barbing blade: Various blades, such as the Heavy Duty Xacto Razor Blade, and chisels, such as the Stanley #18-606C $\frac{1}{4}$" (6.35 mm) or the Craftsman #42971 WF $\frac{1}{4}$" (6.35 mm), can be used for barbing. The single-edged, Xacto Razor Blade cuts the best barbs—barbs that are remarkably fine and delicate.
5. 4" Disk sander and fine-grit emery disks
6. Hook benders: A hardwood dowel and small brass plate make traditional template benders. A pin bender requires a hardwood dowel and bent wire.
7. Safety glasses
8. Cotton gloves and nonmagnetic (brass) tweezers
9. Aluminum heat chafer or dish: A heavy aluminum plate makes an excellent heat dish.
10. Hook holders: Stainless-steel rods with a tight curlicue at the ends serve as hook holders.
11. Emery paper (400–600 grit) and steel wool pads (4/0 Fine)
12. Pliers, round nose, tapering to $\frac{3}{64}$"
13. Files, fine and small
14. Micrometer for measuring hook-wire diameters

An Overview

There is a natural sequence in hook making: selecting the wire, tapering the shank, pointing, bearding (barbing), bending, sizing, bowing (eyeing), cold forging, hardening (a cherry-red heat), and tempering (a purple heat). Not all steps are required for all hooks. Merely omit the steps not required for your particular hook design.

Wire Selection

Finding quality hook wire is an interesting challenge. My hook wire comes from a variety of sources—especially, requests to hook manufacturers and representatives. Some hook companies may be willing to sell small amounts of hook wire. High-quality hook wire, approximately $3\frac{1}{2}$" to $4\frac{1}{2}$" long (approximately 9 to $11\frac{1}{2}$ cm long), are available in a range of diameters. Each wire makes two hooks. Hook-wire diameter usually determines hook size. These soft wires require no

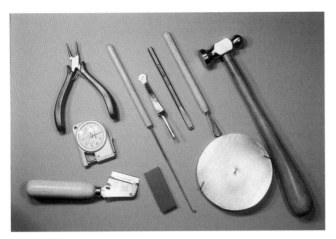

Some of the basic hook-making tools: round-nose pliers, micrometer, blade holder, hook holder, emery pad, tweezers, chisel, heat pan or chafer, and chasing hammer

Hook wires

annealing (the heat treatment that softens or "stress-reduces" the wire) and are easily worked. Select the appropriate diameter for the hook required.

When making or handling hooks, *use safety glasses and cotton gloves.* Cotton gloves prevent body oils upon the wire. Follow all safety directions when using power equipment.

Hook-Wire Diameters

The following wire diameters, based on a wide range of hooks from diverse manufacturers, vary greatly. *Note: Use the dimensions as a rough guide only.* Wire diameters indicated by decimal millimeters and decimal inches.

Hook Size	Millimeters	Inches (Approximate Dimensions)
Size 6	.75 mm to .80 mm	.029" to .031"
Size 8	.65 mm to .75 mm	.025" to .029"
Size 10	.55 mm to .65 mm	.021" to .025"
Size 12	.50 mm to .55 mm	.019" to .021"
Size 14	.45 mm to .50 mm	.017" to .019"
Size 16	.40 mm to .45 mm	.016" to .017"
Size 18	.35 mm to .40 mm	.014" to .016"
Size 20	.30 mm to .35 mm	.012" to .014"
Size 22	.30 mm	.0120"

For heavier nymph and wet fly hooks—2X to 4X heavy wires—add about .05 mm to .08 mm (.002" to .003") to each "dry" wire diameter. For greater strength and barbing ease, *increase* wire diameters. Form eyes on tapered shanks or fine-diameter wires. A studio hook maker can readily adapt different wire diameters for different patterns and angling conditions. To offset a hook point, bend the spear at the hook heel (the base of the spear) rather than at the rear of the shank (the top of the bend) where the hook is weakest under stress.

Tapering

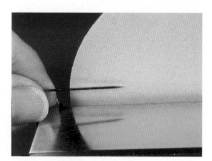

Hand-tapering the shank

Though a smoothly tapered shank permits better eye formation, it is a challenge. To taper heavy hook wire, I merely insert the wire into a close fitting tube (stainless steel or aluminum) and allow the wire to spin when held against a fine, high-speed emery disk. A beveled tube can determine the actual length of the taper. With a block support or steady hand, hold the tube at an exceptionally acute angle against the spinning emery disk. Apply mild pressure so that the appropriate wire length spins against the rotating disk. For a nonbeveled tube, allow fine wire to bend *slightly* while spinning. This prevents a cavity at the base of the taper. The wire, during spinning, may advance or retreat: control the movement by changing the vertical angle. I taper most wires by hand-holding them against a spinning emery disk. To avoid flat spots, slowly rotate the wire *continuously* between the fingers whenever it touches the rotating disk. When completed, carefully finish the taper with ultrafine 600-grit emery paper. I usually taper wires .025" diameter (.64 mm) or greater. Tapering the shank—perhaps the most difficult single process in hook making—requires great care and control.

There are other ways to taper a shank. To create a flat taper, gently press the shank against the emery disk. After tapering, remove any sharp edges with fine emery paper.

Pointing

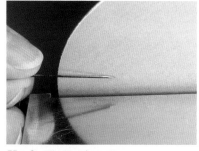

Hand-spinning the point

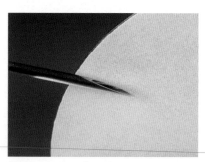

Tube-spinning the point

Fine files alone can shape and sharpen points. With a fine file, flatten the sides to a point and flatten the top, tapering to the undersurface of the wire. Polish with fine-grit sandpaper. Though files can make attractive points, I usually make quick points on a high-speed disk sander, such as a 4" sander/grinder, with 220-grit, or finer, aluminum oxide metal-cutting disks. Ultrafine 400- and 500-grit papers, available from automotive paint stores, produce excellent hook points. A 600-grit wet/dry emery paper polishes the finished point. Like the shank-tapering method, pointing can be done by placing the hook wire inside a beveled brass tube. The bevel controls the point length. The wire protrudes from the bevel and is ground to a sharp point when held against the spinning cutting disk. The spinning hook wire forms a precision cone point. Another pointing method (one that offers the greatest control) is to finger-spin the point on the grinding disk. Once again, prevent flat spots by *continuously* rotating the wire. The hook wire-disk angle determines the length of point. Remember to form the point on the *downward spin* of the grinding disk. This method quickly cuts accurate points. I often file and flatten the sides and top of a cone point, creating a delicate and attractive point. Various points may be fashioned with an ultrafine file and then polished.

Barbing

Many of my finished hooks lack barbs. Barbs, however, do complete some traditional hooks. For barbing, I clamp the wire firmly on the anvil. The hook wire locks beneath a bolt-mounted brass plate. Another brass plate covers the anvil face to protect the barbing blade.

Barbing with a heavy-duty razor blade

Barbing vise with lock plate

For fine microbarbs, select a Heavy Duty Xacto Razor Blade. A razor blade creates a small, delicate minibarb. I clamp the single-edged razor blade in a side-lock holder when barbing. Various utility blades, especially those with handles, may also be used.

A ¼" cold chisel cuts barbs for thicker wires. Unlike a razor blade, the chisel blade angle determines barb angle. Chisel blades should be extremely sharp. To create the barb, place the blade slightly or immediately behind the beginning of the point taper. Begin with a vertical blade and then angle the blade down while tapping to lift the barb. When tapping, avoid rolling or curling the barb forward. Barb angle varies from about 25° to 30° from horizontal. Most attractive is a shallow, short, slender barb. The barb cut should be 20 percent or less of the wire diameter. A microbarb cut may be significantly shallower. Create the barb with *several light taps* from the chasing hammer. If struck too hard, the blade will completely sever the hook wire. After barbing the hook wire, remove it from the anvil; gently polish the barb and point with fine emery paper.

Barbing with a cold chisel

There are, of course, other methods for barbing. W. Lauson's marginalia, in *The Secrets of Angling* by John Dennys, advocates hammering the spear flat (on the same plane as the bend) and then filing a beard and point. In fine wire, the spear would require excessive flattening to create an adequate barb.

The pointed and barbed hook wire

Bending

The hand-held hook bender traps both the barb and the point so that the hook wire may be drawn or pulled into a prescribed shape. Traditional bends—such as perfect, sproat, and Limerick—are rapidly replicated, as well as historical and experimental shapes, such as vertical eyes, sneck, or swan bends. David Foster, in *The Scientific Angler*, regarded bending as the special operation that "decides the *shape*, and consequently, the particular species of hook to be produced." A bender, merely a hardwood handle, brass template, and metal pin, is easily made.

The Wrest and Pin Bender

The wrest, an antique hook-bender illustrated in the *Treatyse*, appears tapered to accommodate various bend diameters. The wrest usually has a groove, slot, or notch that holds the barb or point as the hook wire is "pulled" or drawn to shape. Pulling the hook wire tends to form a Limerick-like bend with a peculiar "elbow" in the middle of the bend. When slowly pulled, the elbow is less apparent. According to John Betts, other bends are nearly impossible to form by pulling. Betts does create some graceful Limericks with a modern plate wrest. The pin bender, another bender, is a simple tool for shaping hooks. W. Lauson's marginalia, in *The Secrets of Angling*, illustrates a pin bender.

The Secrets of Angling: **The Lauson pin bender: "a bender, *viz.* A pin bended, put into the end of a stick, an handful long, thus."**

The pin bender is merely a bent pin mounted in the end of a hand-length stick. The hook point catches on the pin loop. The hook wire "pulls" to shape. The pin loop must be narrow enough to trap the wire. On small hooks, it will also determine the length of the hook spear (from bend to point). Otherwise, the *length of wire* inserted into the loop will determine the spear length. Merely insert more wire into the loop for larger hooks and longer spears. The best pin gap for most hook bends is 1.5 mm (approximately .06") or narrower. Steel or brass wire—"staple bent"—and a hardwood dowel make an excellent pin bender. With a scrap of practice, any studio hook maker can slowly "pull" lovely sproats and Limericks.

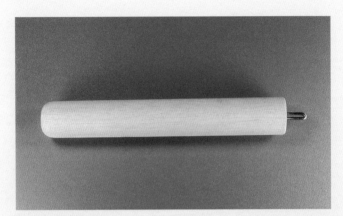

Replica pin bender

1. The length of the wire inserted through the wire loop determines the spear length.

2. Slowly pull the wire and twist the bender to form the bend.

3. Due to its innate spring, the wire will recover slightly. Bend the wire slightly beyond what is required.

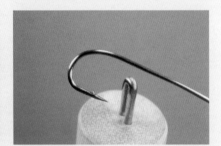

4. The finished bend

The Template Bender

Neither the wrest nor the pin bender consistently replicates a hook shape. Much depends on the force and direction of the pull or twist. Accurate shape duplication is best done with a traditional "template bender." Even during the second half of the nineteenth century, when mechanized hook making flourished, considerable hand-work was required in making hooks. Template hook benders, small hand tools with a pin and metal template, shaped the soft, pointed and barbed hook wires into standard bends. Women and children working at home did piecework for such companies as Sealey, Allcock, and Partridge. I make template hook benders with a small brass plate. Brass bends and shapes more easily than the original steel template. A .025" (approximately .64 mm) thick brass plate forms the bending template. Cut out a strip of brass about 2" long (approximately 50 mm) and about .25" wide (approximately 6.35 mm) wide. Make the brass strip purposely long for holding. A single template accommodates one hook size (based on gap) and *various* hook lengths: the template length—that only forms the bend—may be shorter than the actual hook length. Bevel one end of the template as illustrated. This bevel catches the barb for bending. For entry into the wood dowel, carefully sharpen one long side.

With small, round-nose pliers, carefully pull or bend the brass strip to shape. To prevent scarring the brass template, tape the jaws of the pliers.

Test the shape by bending soft wire over it. Once acceptable, cut the brass strip to length. Due to the natural spring of the hook wire, the template bend or arc must be slightly tighter (i.e., exaggerated) than the actual hook bend desired. The hook wire will spring back slightly to a final shape.

Center the brass template, sharp side down, on the end of the hardwood dowel. Place upon a hard, smooth surface and gently tap the bottom of the dowel, imbedding the brass template approximately $1/8$" deep into the dowel end. Finally, add a small pin to catch the hook point. Catch the hook barb in the bevel to determine the exact placement of the pin. Tap the pin in, leaving a length, approximately template height, exposed to trap the hook point.

The bend strip: note the bevel on the left and bottom edges.

Carefully "pull" the strip to desired hook bend.

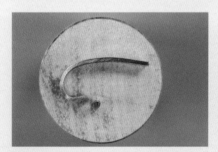

Position the pin to trap the hook point.

Catch the hook point by the barb and pin.

Rotate the hook wire around the template.

The completed hook bend

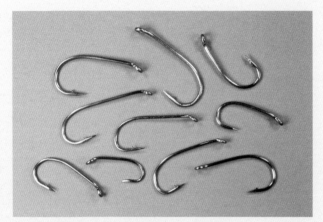

Assorted template benders   **Various replicated hook shapes**

Bowing

After pointing, barbing, and bending, "bow" or eye the hook wire. Although James O'Gorman referred to the hook bend as the "bow," *bowing* usually refers to forming the hook eye. If desired, hooks may be left blind (eyeless). On these, a short snell (made of gut, horsehair, or nylon) attaches the hook to the line. For a blind hook, merely cut the wire to length and continue the sequence. Though exacting, it is possible to make a tight, neat hook eye by hand. According to John Betts, the loop eye, made on a tapered shank, is perhaps the easiest eye to form. Fold the eye loop back, align with the shank and gently raise the eye about 25°. Loop eyes are attractive when done on a tapered fore-shank.

The Bowed Eye

After cutting the shank wire to length and prior to bowing, carefully file and polish the shank tip so that, when eyed, the edges do not cut tippets. I mount, with double-stick tape, 600-grit emery paper on a strip of dense, closed-cell foam for polishing the shank tip. The foam encircles the hook shank and conforms to the hook shape. To make the standard ball eye, use a fine wire or a tapered shank. John Betts suggests filing down the tips of round-nose pliers. I use 4" round-nose channel lock pliers that taper down to $^3/_{64}$". If desired decrease the diameter of *one jaw* with fine emery paper. The smaller jaw, which *must be glass smooth*, forms the inside of the eye. Hook eyes should close completely and center on the hook shank.

Carefully bend the eye to shape. When mounted in a tying vise, the closed end of the eye faces a right-handed tyer. A reverse or counterbend may be required to align the eye center with the hook shank. Completely close the eye with smooth-jawed pliers. To prevent the eye from twisting, file small grooves in the pliers.

With flat-jawed pliers, I turn the eye down about 20°–30°. Traditionally, the inside diameter of the eye equals the outside diameter of the particular hook wire. This may

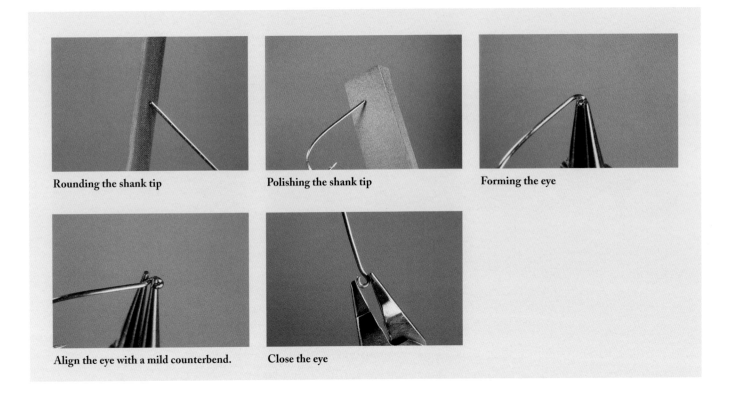

Rounding the shank tip

Polishing the shank tip

Forming the eye

Align the eye with a mild counterbend.

Close the eye

A bowing jig with a *tapered*, stainless-steel pin. A heavy brass and hardwood base holds the pin.

be difficult to achieve in fine wires. My handmade hooks may have an inside eye diameter slightly greater than the wire. This is both graceful and functional.

For small eyes on fine-wire hooks, merely bend the eye around a pin or wire. Remove the pin, and pull the wire to close the eye further if necessary. Snip excess. File and polish the wire end. Open the eye slightly with a needle, align, and close the eye wire with small pliers. Practice makes this a natural act. If desired, a simple jig can form the eye around a pin. I use a *tapered*, stainless-steel pin. The taper allows various eye sizes for different sized hooks. The eye may be opened or closed on the pin as desired. File small grooves in the pliers' jaws to prevent twisting during bowing. To align the eye properly, a slot in the jig can accept the hook bend.

The tapered eye

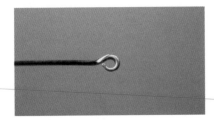

The ball eye

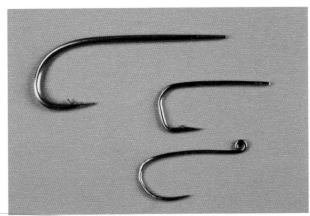

For the flame: a blind, tapered shank hook, a blind sneck and a vertical-eyed swan bend

Tempering the Hook

After forming the hook, clean the wire with 400- and 600-grit emery paper. Wrap the emery paper around a fine-diameter rod to clean bend, barb, and point. Avoid body oils on the hook by using cotton gloves or nonmagnetic tweezers to handle the hook hereafter. After cleaning, the hook enters the flame. With practice and a consistent light source, you can determine steel temperatures with remarkable accuracy. Low-carbon steel (approximately .15 percent to .30 percent carbon) has insufficient carbon for adequate hardening. Test steel wire by holding it against a grinding wheel. The percent of carbon determines the density of bright white sparks produced. High-carbon steel throws *bright, white star sparks*, similar to a shower of fizzy, bursting sparklers. Low carbon yields dull, round, orange sparks or few white sparks.

The Two Heats: Hardening and Drawing the Temper

After forming the hook in soft wire, it first must be hardened (a high heat) and then made springy tough (a second, lower heat). Hooks come from steel wire. Alloying iron with carbon increases the strength and hardness of iron, thus turning iron into steel. The hardness increases if the steel wire glows orangey-red (high heat) and is then quenched—suddenly immersed in a bath of oil or water. Though this hardens the wire, it also makes it extremely brittle and fragile. After firing, remove all gray-oxide scale from the hook with fine emery paper. Careful cleaning and polishing allows accurate determination of colors in the final heating. After polishing the hooks, heat them to purple or dark blue (low heat) to *draw the temper* (for want of a finer phrase) and reduce the brittleness.

In this second heating (the lower heat for purple), allow the heat to travel throughout the wire. When you expose steel wire to heat and air, its surface assumes different colors as the temperature increases. First, there is a grayish straw color. With increasing heat, the straw passes into browns, purples, blues, and finally into the visible cherry reds and beyond. The surface colors come from the thin oxide film that forms over the wire during heating. Drawing the temper is merely heating the wire to the appropriate color, usually to a blue-purple. Observe the wire color carefully to achieve the proper drawing color (temperature). A single hook when heated may show several colors. Some colors may not even appear due to rapid temperature changes. Moreover, these colors are fleeting and ephemeral; be prepared to act quickly. The longer or higher the heat, the softer or more flexible the hook. Between the low and high heats arise various degrees of hardness. Once drawn and cooled, the hook should lose some hardness and becomes springy tough. This process makes functional hooks.

The following temperature color scale shows the "surface" temperatures and the higher "glowing" temperatures of the hook wire. The yellows, browns, purples, and blues are *surface* colors; the reds and oranges are *glowing* colors. Use the scale as a *casual* guide to temperature and color change. Truly, hook making, as in the beginning, is more art than science.

The Temperature Color Code

Fahrenheit	Color
460	straw yellow
470	deep straw yellow
480	dark yellow
490	yellow brown
500	brown yellow
510	spotted red brown
520	brown purple
530	light purple
540	full purple
550	dark purple
560	full blue
570	dark blue
640	light blue
650	blue
752	red, visible in the dark
885	red, visible in twilight
975	red, visible in daylight
1077	red, visible in sunlight
1292	dark red
1472	dull cherry red
1652	cherry red
1832	bright cherry red
2012	orange red

Hardening the Hook (High Heat)

Now, lock the hook in a hook holder and place the complete hook into the flame of a butane propane burner. Avoid any large metal holder or clamp, such as pliers, which may act as a heat sink. I use stainless-steel rods with a fine, tight curlicue to hold the hook in the flame. Hold the hook by the eye, shank or the fore-shank and place it into the flame. Allow the total hook, if possible, to achieve *a cherry red or bright cherry red*. Tune the flame and position the hook to achieve the proper color. For the studio hook maker, the color that appears may be more akin to a soft glowing orange. With my high-carbon wire, the soft orange creates a functional hook. Then, immediately plunge the hook into water (or salt water) to quench and cool. When the hot hook touches the water, it throws off dark scale. Now, with cotton gloves, cautiously handle the very brittle hook. *Carefully* remove all scale with 600-grit emery paper.

Drawing the Temper (Low Heat)

The hook now goes back to the flame. I use a small, circular aluminum heat pan or chafer. Use a *very low* heat to draw the temper. Closely monitor the temperature—*excessive heat can melt aluminum*. Though challenging, the hook should

Hardening the Hook (High Heat)

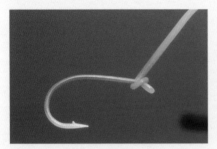

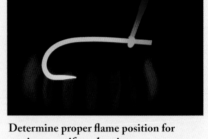

Heat the hook to a "cherry red," approximately 1832˚ Fahrenheit. Under heat, some sections of the hook may be above or below the targeted temperature. The hook shown is 2075˚ (± 100) Fahrenheit at the heel, the base of the bend. Other parts of the hook vary in temperature. Note the higher temperature, indicated by the pale yellow, at the spear and point. Though the heat is somewhat higher than the targeted temperature, it creates a serviceable hook. Temperatures measured by a Leeds & Northrup optical pyrometer.

Color (temperature) changes may appear and fade rapidly. Note the differential temperature colors.

Determine proper flame position for maximum uniform heating.

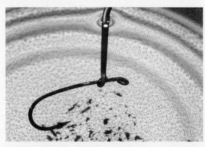

Note the scale flakes at the bottom of the quenching pot.

Carefully remove final scale and polish the hook.

achieve an even color. If eyed, only part of the hook will touch the pan and the heating will be uneven. To achieve even heating, I place the hook eye in a dimple or small pan hole. Merely punch a dimple or drill a small hole in the middle of the heating plate to accommodate the eye. The hook then lies flat upon the pan. Betts offers a clever solution; he spreads a layer of fine sand on the pan. He buries the hook in the sand, exposing some shank for judging color change. When the proper color appears, he dumps all into the quenching bath.

Place the pan and hook over the flame. Depending upon carbon content of the wire, draw the hook to *a dark blue or bluish purple*. Anticipate the color change: blue and purple appear and fade quickly. Be prepared: the various color shifts are subtle and swift. There is no returning to the proper color.

A full or deep purple is usually too brittle and a yellow, too soft. Experiment to determine the best color for your particular wire. Once the color appears, immediately quench and cool the hook. Quenching may be done in cold water, salt water, oil, soap, butter, or in open air. Cold water, which I use, removes maximum scale. Rapid or slow cooling (depending upon the particular hook wire) also affects hook quality. Experiment "upon often trial" is the key. Remember the adage: if you fail to make mistakes, you will probably make nothing. James O'Gorman, in *The Practice of Angling*, offered a perceptive passage on tempering:

. . . and when you find that the hooks assume a blood-red appearance, dip them instantly into a bowl filled with cold water, and when you take them out of the ladle, try with a knife whether it scrapes them; and be careful how you handle them, for, if hard, they are brittle as glass. If they scrape, they are not hard enough, and you must repeat the process until they are. You must next have a flat, even board, on which put some sea sand, or pounded brick bat, [brickbat: a piece of a brick] and rub each hook carefully until it assumes a bright appearance, by doing which you will soon perceive the blue appearance in the temper. You must also have a long-handled square of iron, which should be at the large end about four inches in length, and three in breadth, and about half an inch in thickness: this you are to put into the fire, where it is to remain until sufficiently, but not too hot. This you will be able to judge of, by rubbing a bit of tallow to it, which, if it lights, it is too hot, except for very large hooks. You then put on the iron as many hooks as you can examine at a time, and when they turn to a light blue or sanguine colour, tip them with the tallow, or bit of small candle, and as soon as it dries on the hooks throw them off, and let them cool before you try them. The flat part of the iron should be perfectly smooth.

Drawing the Temper (Low Heat)

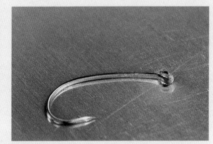

Slowly heat the hook to a dark blue, approximately 540° Fahrenheit. The hook illustrated browned at 540° and quickly blued at 580° Fahrenheit. For temperature monitoring, the wire probe connects the hook to a Fluke digital thermometer.

The blue, as illustrated in this photograph, quickly defeats the brown.

Gently test the hook by looping a line over the bend and pulling. A flexed hook should reveal a tough springiness. The finished hook is naked and ready for use. If desired, add a protective finish. Betts suggests that the hook may be polished, degreased in acetone, and lacquered. If lacquered, he recommends dipping the hooks in thinned Rustoleum™ enamel, drying, and then baking them for 45 minutes in a 350° oven. A simple and effective finish is cold gun bluing. Birchwood Casey Super Blue and Perma Blue, available at most sporting or gun shops, create a deep lustrous finish. Carefully follow all directions on the label. Test the intensity of bluing with scrap wire: excessive bluing can eat carbon steel and quickly damage a hook. For a lustrous bluing, clean the hook with Birchwood Casey cleaner-degreaser or denatured alcohol and rinse with cold water. Use gloves or tweezers to handle the hook. Brighten the hook with fine steel wool or an abrasive cloth. Immerse the hook (tethered to a tough thread) into the bluing for 20 to 30 seconds; then rinse with cold water and dry. Lightly polish the hook with extrafine steel wool. Repeat the process to obtain a darker blue. Though the studio hook maker cannot compete with modern technology, he can create elegant and functional hooks with common tools. The quantity, though perhaps not the quality, will fall short of commercial hook making. The singular advantage, however, is that the amateur can experiment with unique or historic hook designs. There is pleasure in taking fish with your own patterns wrapped on your own hooks. Remember, there are only three ways to make a good hook: experiment, experiment, and experiment "upon often trial." Greater appreciation and respect for all hooks result.

The hook or "angle" does make *anglers* of us all. With the variety and quality of the modern hook, no angler ever needs to make a hook. Only a curious and "compleat" angler may wish to enter into hook making. Personally, I admire the graceful curve as a hook pulls to shape. Moreover, I appreciate the tough springiness of a well-wrought hook as well as the historic theories and designs encountered. But the time and care required for a single fly hook is immense. The studio hook maker is certainly no threat to the major hook companies. Nevertheless, there is no reason why a modern angler cannot enjoy the history, the discovery, and the beauty in a sproat's fiery birth.

CHAPTER V

THE LINE

Ye makynge of your harnys: ye lyne

"To teach the way or manner of how to make a line were time lost, it being so easy and ordinary. . . ."

—Robert Venables, *The Experienced Angler* (1662)

Fly Lines

In the early days, there was no running line and no distinction between the fly line and the leader. The line was whipped directly to the rod tip or attached to a small tip loop. Rods lacked reels. Lines were made from a variety of materials, particularly horsehair, Indian weed, gut, and silk. "East India weed" also formed hook links. Izaak Walton praised Indian grass: "If your grass is coarse, it will fall heavily on the water, and scare away the fish; on which account gut has the advantage. But, after all, if your grass be fine and round, it is the best thing you can use." He concluded that "Indian, or Sea-grass makes excellent Hook links; and though some object to it, as being apt to grow brittle, and to kink in using, with proper management it is the best material for the purpose yet known. . . ." In James Chetham's *The Angler's Vade Mecum* (1700), an advertisement claims that "East India Weed" proves "so strong and fine, of a water colour, that it deceives the Fish much better than Hair or Silk." Although this "Oriental" plant appeared throughout the eighteenth century, it has yet to be identified. Andrew Herd, in *The Fly*, and John Betts believed it may have been jute (*Corchorus ssp.*). Kenneth Mansfield, in *The Art of Angling* (first printed in 1960), presented a dubious account of the weed. According to Mansfield, although "it was thought to be vegetable in origin (hence the words 'grass,' 'weed')" certain "experiments done at Kew in 1864 proved it to be Chinese or Japanese silkworm gut." Exactly what those experiments were is unknown. He concluded that these long, fine strands, about four and one-half feet long, were less reliable than the Spanish gut that eventually replaced it.

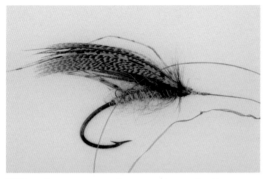

This early pattern may show a rare example of an Indian-grass snell. Similar hooks and patterns, tied by Cornelius Gorman in 1791, appear in J.R. Harris's *An Angler's Entomology*, Plate 31, b. An entry in the *OED* lists Indian grass as "an old name of silkworm gut used by anglers." Early descriptions however, differentiate and actually compare Indian grass with silk gut. This and the illustrated O'Holleran fly, if valid, reveal that Indian grass was a plant fiber. The North American Indian used various hemp substitutes, such as *Apocynum cannabinum* for twine, bags, fishing nets, and lines. PHOTOS COURTESY OF YOSHI AKIYAMA, COLLECTION MANAGER, THE AMERICAN MUSEUM OF FLY FISHING.

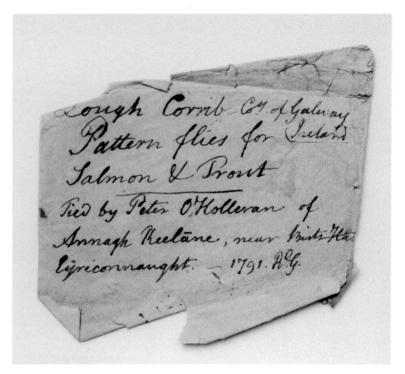

Dry, unprepared Indian weed was extremely brittle. The preparation is something short of charming. Thomas Shirley's *The Angler's Museum* (1790)—evidently relying much upon Richard Brookes' *The Art of Angling, New Improved with Additions and Formed into a Dictionary* (1766)—prepared his "Indian or sea grass."

Take as many as you please of the finest you can get, put them into any vessel, and pour thereon the scummed fat of a pot, wherein fresh (but by no means salt) meat has been boiled. When they have lain three or four hours, take them out one by one, and stripping the grease off with your finger and thumb, stretch each grass as long as it will yield, coil them up in rings, and lay them by. You will then find them become nearly as small, full as round, and much stronger, than the best single hairs you can get.

Keeping them moist was essential.

To preserve them moist, keep them in a piece of bladder well oiled, and before you use them, let them soak about half an hour in water, or in your walk to the river side, put a length of it into your mouth.

There is no mention, fortunately, of the taste.

Robert Howlett suggested that "if you cannot get Indian-Grass, make use of the smallest and roundest Bowel or Lute-strings you can procure: But before you arm your Hooks to Bowel-strings, sear the Point-ends only, on a burning Coal. . . to prevent its slipping from the Hook." Catgut, or bowel-string, was a strong cord usually made from dried and twisted sheep intestines (less often from other animals) and used for musical instruments. The term "catgut," a sixteenth century word, is essentially obscure. A *catling* was catgut, a kitten, or a small lute-string (1606, *OED*). Chetham, in *The Angler's Vade Mecum* (1700), referred to "a young rabbet, Whelp, or Catling" when making a carp paste. In the plural, *catling* referred to any stringed instrument. Catling may derive from *kit*, a term once used for a small violin. In Shakespeare's *Romeo and Juliet* (1597), the fiddler is Simon Catling (Act 4, Scene 5). Though lacking historical evidence, the term *catgut* may derive from *cattle+gut*. "Cattle" was formerly a collective name for any livestock "held as property, or reared to serve as food, or for their milk, skin, wool, *etc.*" (*OED*). When silk "gut" appeared, it was erroneously called, at times, catgut. The confusion is logical: silk gut was similar in form and function. According to John Waller Hills, "silkworm gut is first mentioned by James Saunders in 1724 in the *Compleat Fisherman*." Westwood and Satchell, in the "James Saunders" entry to *Bibliotheca Piscatoria*, quoted a writer in *The Field* (January 2, 1864): "About three months since, Mr. Geo. Bowness, of Bellyard, shewed me an advertisement of his grandfather's, date 1760, announcing that the new article, silk-worm gut, is to be had there. This pretty much fixes the date of its introduction into the tackle trade."

Silk gut is also misnamed; it is not the gut of the silkworm. It is the viscid, embryo silk contained within the glands of a mature silkworm. By slitting open a mature silkworm, the glands are removed and a filament is stretched out to about a half-yard length. Exposed to air, the silk filament dries and hardens. Silk gut is relatively transparent in water and was used for fishing lines and medical sutures. The traditional method of making a silk gut leader was to water-knot various diameters of gut links together to create a taper. Some early angling authorities, such as H. Cholmondeley-Pennell in *Fly Fishing* (1876), deplored drawn gut. Drawn gut—gut drawn through a diamond hole—was "artificially fined" or shaved and not as glossy as natural gut. He believed that natural gut neither frayed nor deteriorated as quickly as drawn gut. Gut and grass are, however, nascent lines, appearing long after the introduction of horsehair.

Gut and horsehair

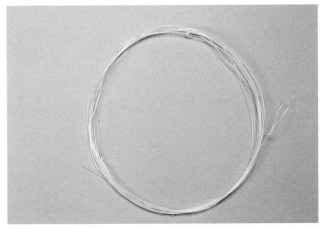

Gut strands of different diameters are water-knotted to form a tapered line

Bastard Lines

In *The Experienced Angler* (1662), Colonel Robert Venables argued against bastard or mixed lines: "Further, I do not like the mixing of silk or thread with hair, but if you please, you may, to make the line strong, make it all of silk, or thread, or hairs, as strong as you please, and the lowest part [near the fly] of the smallest lute or viol strings, which I have proved to be very strong, but will quickly rot in the water, you may however help that in having new and strong ones to change for those that decay; but as to hair, the most usual matter whereof lines are made, I like sorrel, white and grey best: sorrel in muddy and boggy rivers, and both the latter for clear waters." This echoes the sentiment of *The Angler's Museum*: even if the hairs are mixed with silk, "a good angler will always make the lowest part of such lines of the smallest lute and viol strings." Some authors extolled the virtues of bastard lines of mixed materials. J. March, *The Jolly Angler* (1842), advocated "good horse and mohair woven together; this is much lighter, finer and stronger than any other substance used for that purpose; at the end of which, have a loop about half an inch long, to fasten your gut lengthener to, which should be about two yards and a half long. . . ." To prevent trout teeth from snipping fine hairs, horsehair lines often terminated in a length of gut or Indian grass at the fly. Since the beginning, the casting or dapping line itself was horsehair and early line making was ingenious.

Making Horsehair Line

Aelian, in *De Natura Animalium* (written about 200 A.D.), was the first to mention the fly rod and fly line, both about six feet long. For well over 2,000 years, horsehair has formed fly lines. Horsehair lines were common well into the nineteenth century. They appear sporadically even today in isolated, rural areas, such as the Balkans. All-silk lines did not become important until the latter half of the nineteenth century. Horsehair is the most common fly-line material in history. Though I do not advocate replacing the modern fly line with a horsehair line, making and angling with horsehair fly line does tell us much about our angling ancestors. A horsehair fly line has three attractive attributes: stiffness, stretch, and concealment. I usually make dapping lines or short casting lines. State game laws may determine or restrict how such lines are used. Longer lines, such as 20 to 30 feet, may be made according to several methods. Surprisingly, horsehair lines cast well (though the earliest lines were apparently dapped rather than cast) due to their mass and relative rigidity. In *The Practical Fly-Fisher* (1899), John Jackson described the attributes of horsehair: "I prefer hair to gut for Fly-fishing, generally: hair being a hollow tube, swims better, falls straighter and lighter on the water, and from its stiffness the drop flies are not liable to wrap around the foot length or casting line." The following directions for horsehair line making, with minor variations, traveled down through the centuries.

Selecting and Preparing Horsehair

Sir Izaak Walton listed the requirements of good horsehair: ". . . take care, that your hair be round and clear, and free from galls, scabs, or frets; for a well-chosen, even, clear, round hair, of a kind of glass-colour, will prove as strong as three uneven, scabby hairs, that are ill-chosen, full of galls or unevenness." *The Gentleman Angler* includes a brief inventory of terms relating to hair. A *flaw* is a "gouty," rotten part of the hair that breaks easily. A *bawk* is a knot. Hairs that twist well are *well bedded*. A *link* is several hairs twisted together, and a *line* is made of several links connected by water knots. A line is *spliced* when the ends are overlapped and whipped with waxed silk.

The number of hairs varied with the fish sought. Line tapered from twenty or more at the butt down to one to three at the fly. The *Treatyse* presents a more realistic hair count: trout and grayling require nine hairs and large trout, twelve hairs. Thomas Barker, ever the competent and hopeful angler, concluded, "If you can attain to Angle with one hair, you shall have the more rises and kill more fish." More rises perhaps, more netted, doubtful. Angling prowess was a matter of "splitting hairs." Every writer had a hair count. The *Treatyse* advises "one here" for the small "menow." Walton preferred the single hair for roach or dace. Lauson's marginalia, in *Secrets of Angling* by John Dennys (1613), noted that an angler with "a nimble hand, a weak and light rod" needed "but four or five hairs at the most, for the greatest river fish." Apparently, "a nimble hand" and a "weak" or soft rod is the key to landing good fish on four hairs. Charles Cotton, in Part II of *The Compleat Angler*, lowered the hair count with the edict that "he that cannot kill a Trout of twenty inches long with two [hairs], in a river clear of woods and weeds . . . deserves not the name of an *Angler*." I shall never be an angler. Smaller trout have readily broken my three hairs.

Music quality, Siberian horsehair

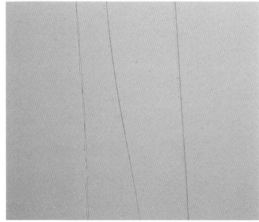

Left to right: horsehair, silk gut, and monofilament lines underwater. The two-ply horsehair line becomes nearly translucent (approximate line diameters).

Bow Hairs

Though relatively expensive, the finest horsehairs are long, musical-instrument quality. I usually select violin or cello bow hairs obtained from bow stringers. The hair count for a single violin or cello bow is about 175–190 hairs, depending upon the hair diameter and the bow. A strung violin bow requires approximately $26\,^3/_4$" (68 cm) length hairs. Raw hanks are approximately 32" long with some waste. Quality, virgin hair hanks from Mongolia or Siberia (Northern hairs) may be as long as 36" or more. Twisting, obviously, will significantly reduce link length. *The Angler's Sure Guide* includes a charming passage on hair selection: "Choose such hairs as are biggest, longest, roundest, and strongest, and the most inward of the Dock of the largest, stoutest and lustiest Stone-horse [an uncastrated or entire horse; a stallion. *OED*], or Gelding, not above five or six Years old, and not under three." According to most writers, the center hairs from a gray or white stallion offer the finest hairs. *The Gentleman Angler* concluded: "A young, vigorous healthy Stone-horse, who is in his Prime, affords the strongest Hair; and the most proper Time for plucking his Tail, (from hence alone Hair for making Lines is to be taken) is when he goes to cover a Mare." Supposedly, a mare, due to its urination posture, could offer only inferior hair. Early writers believed that hair from a mare's tail had diminished quality. The best hairs, they argued, come from the center of a stallion's tail. Evidently, provenance is everything.

Ink bottles empty over the various horsehair dye formulas, formulas often pilfered from previous writers. Copperas, verdigris, walnut leaves, ale, and soot created various greens, yellows, russets, browns, and tawnies. "The most choice and most useful for an Angler," Walton advised, "is the water-colour or glass-coloured hair."

To prepare the horsehair before making a line, wash all hair in warm water with a modicum of mild detergent, such as Woolite®. All hairs should be clean and clear. Trim all hairs to length by eliminating any tender or brittle ends. *The Gentleman Angler* advised the angler (as does nearly every early writer) to "Turn the Top of one Hair to the Tail of the other, which will cause every Part to be equally strong." Align half the tips over half the butts to ensure uniform strength.

Hair quality and strength vary greatly. Tests on single hairs range from .79 pounds to 1.36 pounds. The lowest breaking strength was about half the maximum breaking strength. The *average* breaking strength of a single hair was about one pound. Curiously enough, three, furled strands tested out at about 3.60 pounds. Six tightly furled strands, however, only tested to 4.62 pounds. Line failure, sudden and spontaneous, was apparently a serious problem. However, thick horsehair line, unless slapped down on the water, frightened few fish. If dapped, the thick line would be in the air, not the water. White or translucent horsehair nearly "evaporates" in water. It lacks, perhaps, some of the frightening flash of nylon. Once hydrated both horsehair and gut sink quicker, though not deeper, than standard nylon. There are several early methods—including the *Treatyse* jig, Walton's engine, hand plaiting, and Williamson's quill—for making horsehair line.

The *Treatyse* Jig

The *Treatyse of Fysshynge Wyth an Angle* offers directions for making horse-hair lines. The following excerpts are from *An Older Form of the Treatyse of Fysshynge Wyth an Angle* (*c.* 1450) published by Thomas Satchell in 1883. Except for minor differences, the *Older Form* and *The Book of St. Albans* text are essentially identical in the excerpted text. Though the detailed directions and jig illustration offer some ambiguity, the general process of hair line construction is understandable.

The Treatyse Jig

Treatyse jig replica: this working model has a single-cleft holder slotted through a narrow wood slat. A three-cleft holder, on the opposite end, slides along the slat, adjusting to the changing length of the hair strands.

The *Treatyse* jig

Fyrste loke that ye haue an instrument lyke vnto this figure portrayed folowynge. . . . And for to knowe to make your Instrument: loo here it is in figure. And it shall be made of tree sauynge [except, with the exception of, but, *OED*] the bolt [metal pin with a head, used for holding things fast together, *OED*] vnderneath: whiche shall be of yren.

The function of the "yren" bolt is obscure. In the *Treatyse* illustration, the bolt appears to adjust or secure the placement of the 'three-cleft' holder. In late medieval times, metal was important. It was used strategically when other materials would not do. It is difficult to understand why this bolt is necessary: there is only minor tension on the plate and friction alone may position it.

The Treatyse Jig (cont)

Three-strand end knotted together and secured in the single-cleft holder.

Thenne take your heer & kytte [cut] of the smalle ende an hondfull large or more, for it is nyther stronge nor yet sure. Thenne torne the toppe to the taylle eueryche [every one, each, *Satchell*] ylyke moche. And depart it in thre parties. Thenne knytte euery part at the one ende by himself.

Trim off a "hondfull large" of the fine and tender hair tips. A "hondfull large," rather than the amount held in the hand, may be a linear measurement, perhaps similar to the method of measuring the height of horses. The "hand" was originally equal to three inches, now four inches. In any case, the removal of three to four inches would eliminate any broken, soiled, or damaged hair tips. Then, to equalize stress, take about half of the hairs and swap ends, "top to tail." Divide the hairs into three equal strands (single or multiple hairs) and knot each strand at the end. The *Treatyse* offers no information on the number of hairs per strand or the possible tapering of strands by adding or subtracting hairs.

Position the three-cleft holder three inches shorter or more than the untwisted strands.

And at the other ende knytte [knot or tie] all thre togyder: and put the same ende in that other ende of your instrument that hath but one clyft.

At the opposite end, tie all three strands together. Slide the three-cleft holder to about three inches shorter than the strand lengths. A wedge apparently secures the hair holder. John McDonald's *The Origins of Angling* (1963)—offering a new translation, facsimiles, and advanced scholarship—reads: "And fix the other end tight with the wedge the width of four fingers from the end of your hair." The "other ende" apparently refers to the instrument. Though word-muddled, the general action is clear: At one end, knot the hair together and fasten that end in the single-slit holder. Divide the other end into three strands and separately knot each strand. Then fasten each strand in one of the slits of the three-cleft holder. The strands will extend beyond the holder. Now, remove each strand, one by one, from the three-cleft holder and tightly twist it. As each strand twists, it will shorten to fit the three-cleft holder. After tightly twisting each strand, return it to its three-cleft holder slot. Firmly secure each strand in its slot to prevent unwinding.

After tightly twisting each strand, secure it in one of the clefts. Note the longer, as yet untwisted strands.

And sett that other ende faste with the wegge foure fingers in alle shorter than your heer.

Slide the three-cleft holder about three inches shorter than the strand length and secure with a wedge ("wegge").

Thenne twine euery warpe [warp, a lengthwise strand] one waye & ylyke moche: and fasten theym in thre clystes [probably an error for clyftes, clifts, *Satchell*] ylyke streyghte.

Then tightly twist each strand a single direction and secure it in one of the three clefts. As each strand twists, it will shorten to fit the three-cleft holder.

Take thenne out that other ende and twine it that waye that it woll desire ynough. Thenne streyne it a lytyll: and knytte it for undoynge: and that is good.

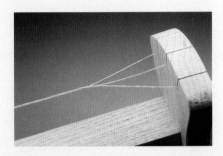

When you remove the single-cleft end, the three strands furl tightly together toward the three-cleft holder, forming a link.

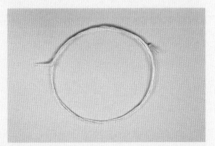

Finally, remove the knotted hair from the single-cleft end and allow the three strands to furl or twist together. Then, stress it slightly and knot the *three-cleft end* to prevent unfurling.

A twisted horsehair snood with end knots

When ye haue as many of the lynkys and ye suppose wol suffyse for the length of a lyne: thenne must ye knytte theym togyder with a water knotte or elles a duchys knotte. And whan your knotte is knytte: kytte of the voyde [the void; the waste, *OED*] shorte endes a strawe brede for the knotte. Thus shall ye make your lynes fayre & fine: and also right sure for ony manere fysshe.

When sufficient snoods are made, knot them together with a water knot or a Duchess knot. Trim the waste ends of each knot closely, just the width of a straw. Thus you will make fair and fine lines for any manner of fish.

And by cause that ye sholde knowe bothe the water knotte & also the duchys knotte: loo theym here in figure cast vnto the lyknesse of the draughte.

No illustrations of the knots appear in the text. The Duchess knot is apparently unknown. Clifford W. Ashley, in *The Ashley Book of Knots*, noted that many original angling knots, surprisingly, were never recorded. The water knot, however, comes down faithfully through angling literature. Ashley also noted that the water knot, though secure and strong, may snag due to the exit angle of the trimmed ends.

A horsehair fly line

Walton's Engine

For furling lines, Walton advocated a twisting engine: "I would recommend an engine lately invented, which is now to be had at almost any Fishing-tackle shop in London: it consists of a large horizontal wheel and three very small ones, inclosed [*sic*] in a brass box about a quarter of an inch thick, and two inches in diameter; the axis of each of the small wheels is continued through the

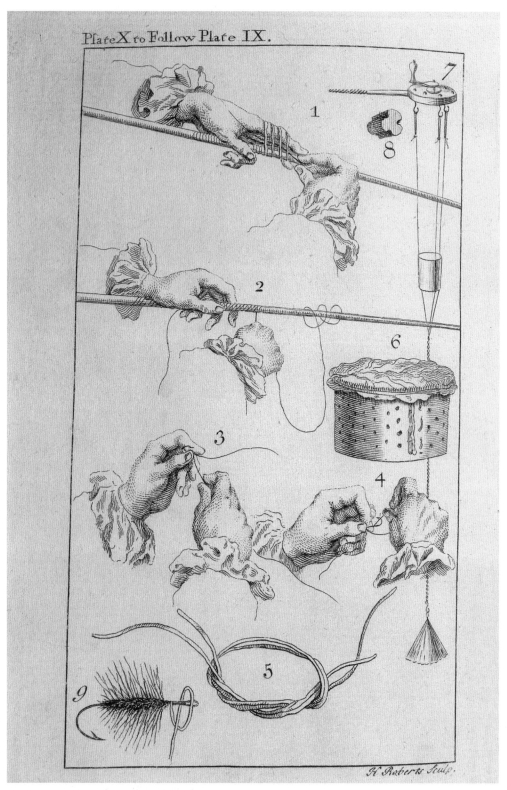

The Compleat Angler (second Hawkins edition): Walton's engine (*figure 7*), cork separator (*figure 8*), and water knot (*figure 5*). Note the placement of the cork and the lead cone attached to the bottom of the links.

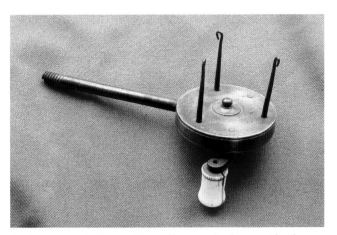

Antique engine in the Ian Hay Collection: the three post hooks spin the same direction when furling horsehair links.

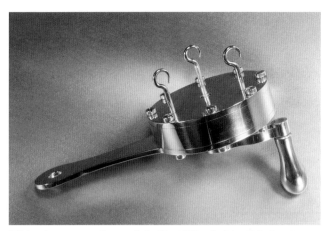

Walton's engine replica made by David Vogel of Anvil Industries.

under-side of the box, and is formed into a hook; by means of a strong screw it may be fixed to any post or partition, and is set in motion by a small winch in the centre of the box."

The engine produces three, twisted horsehair strands that furl into a snood or link. To prevent the engine hooks from breaking the horsehair, a short length of wool yarn or twine attaches the hair to the hook. Yarn cushions the shock: hair cannot tolerate a tweak or sudden twist. Cranking the handle spins each strand in the same direction. When removed from the engine, the three strands twist or furl together to form a snood section. Once a snood is complete, both ends must be knotted or whipped to prevent unraveling. Each snood is made with a decreasing number of hairs that, when tied together, make a tapered horsehair fly line. Though based on Walton's *The Compleat Angler*, Thomas Best, in *The Art of Angling*, condensed the process, albeit in rambling prose.

> To twist the links with this engine, take as many hairs as you intend each shall consist of, and dividing them into three parts, tie each parcel to a bit of fine twine, about six inches long, doubled and put through the hooks which impend from the machine: then take a piece of lead of a conical figure two inches long, and two in diameter at the base, with a hook at the point; tie your three parcels of hair into one knot, and to this by the hook hang the weight. Or, take a common bottle cork, and into the sides, at equal distances, cut three grooves; and placing it so as to receive each division of hairs begin to twist. You will then find the links twist with great evenness at the lead; and as it grows tighter shift the cork a little upwards, and when the whole is sufficiently twisted, take out the cork, and tie the links into a knot, and so proceed till you have twisted links sufficient for your line, observing to lessen the number of hairs in each link, in such proportion that the line may be taper.

The twisting engine was popular well into the nineteenth century. As John Bickerdyke noted in *The Book of the All-Round Angler* (*c.* 1899), "The twisting engine is a useful little appliance for twisting gut and hair into snoods. . . ." Though Bickerdyke mentioned gut, only the *fine*, silk gut near the fly was twisted. This gut tippet connected the fly to the horsehair line.

When completed, the total fly line, according to Walton, "must be 'very stong' and should be about eighteen or twenty [horse] hairs at the top, and so diminishing insensibly [imperceptibly] to the hook." Water knots commonly connected the snoods. My snood spinner or replica engine—made from three geared rotary hooks—slowly spins each strand to form a snood.

Engine replica mounted to furling stand.

Dubbing whirl, cork separator, and brass furling tabs

Making Horsehair Line

In this illustration, the horse-hair strands are mounted with tape to brass spin tabs and connected to furling hooks.

1. **Begin at the butt. Select quality horsehairs for three, multihair strands. Wash and dry the hairs. Place half the tips over half the butts. Each strand may have 6 to 8 hairs, creating a butt section of 18 to 24 hairs.**

2. **Whip one end together firmly.**

3. **Divide the opposite end into three equal strands and tape each end onto a spin tab. The spin tabs—which replace Walton's lengths of yarn—minimize hair breakage during spinning. Alternately, a loop of twine or cord may be used.**

In this illustration, we see how the cork separator divides the strands at the cone whirl.

4. **Connect each spin tab to an engine hook.**

5. **Hang a weight (such as a single-hook Dubbing Whirl) on the single end and suspend the strands. Near the lower weight, insert the separator cork (the slotted plug) within the strands. Traditionally, the strands hang, as illustrated, beneath the engine. Horizontal spinning is possible, though awkward, requiring three hands: one to hold the link end, one to slide the cork separator and one to twist the engine.**

6. Maintain proper tension on the strands during spinning. As the strands twist, they will shorten. The tighter twists will appear at the anchor, the whirl. While spinning, control the twist density by slowly sliding the cork toward the engine.

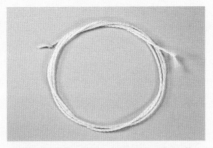

8. After spinning the strands, gather all three ends and hold them. Gather and dismount the spin tabs from the engine and allow the link to relax. Remove the cone Whirl. Then, remove each spin tab from its strand and whip the three strand ends together to form a snood, as shown.

10. Connect the snoods with water knots and whip the tag ends down for a smooth knot. Continue to add snoods (with diminishing hairs) until the line is complete. An alternate, but tenuous method connects the snoods with a thread whip about 1" from each end. After whipping, apply varnish or lacquer for a strong, smooth connection.

9. Detail of the furled snood

11. Furled horsehair fly line

7. Continue to "spin and slide" until the strands are completely furled together.

The Knotless, Tapered, Plaited Fly Line

A continuous taper comes from plaiting or braiding strands together. The result is a fly line void of knots. In *The Alphabet of Angling* (1849), James Rennie praised the knotless, plaited lines. "But the best lines for artificial fly-angling are those wove, and are all in one piece...." There are "no knots to prevent them from running glibly through the rings of the rod." Technically, unlike weaving, plaiting or braiding does not have a set of warp or filling yarns that interlace at right angles. Plaiting is the simplest, and perhaps slowest, method for making strong, knotless fly lines. Though plaited lines cast well, some anglers reject these flat, ribbon lines. Furthermore, the hair tags (the embedded hair tips that escape) often become exposed and impede smooth running. Such tags must be trimmed periodically. The following directions produce the basic three-ply, plaited fly line.

Plaiting Line

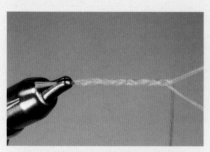

1. Begin at the butt. Select hairs for three strands. Each strand may have six to eight hairs, creating a butt section of eighteen to twenty-four hairs. Wash, dry, and reverse the ends of half the hairs. Tightly whip-finish one end. Unlike a whip-finish, a knot consumes an excessive hair length. If desired, *lightly* wax each link to consolidate the hairs.

2. Clamp the knotted end in a vise for weaving. Keep one link full length. Trim another link by one-third and the final link by two-thirds. This allows a staggering connection that produces a smoothly tapered line. To create staggered connections down the line, trim only the first butt strands in this manner: all subsequent strands have full-length hairs.

3. Next, firmly plait or braid the links together. The simplest plait is the common hair braid (the three-strand, English sennit). This is the familiar "pigtail" or hanging braid. For those needful readers, braiding directions

follow. To create a *somewhat* rounder line, plait two strands of equal diameter with a third, smaller-diameter strand. Secure the whipped end in a fly vise.

Hold two strands in the right hand and one in the left hand. Bring the outer right strand down across its partner strand and lay it parallel to and below the single left strand. Now, the outer right strand has a new partner. *For a tight plait, pull each strand out at a right angle as you braid down the line.*

Then bring the outer left strand down across its partner strand and lay it parallel to and below the single right strand. The outer left strand now has a new partner. Repeat alternately until near the end of a strand.

4. When within about 1½" of the end of a strand, embed the new strand and continue plaiting. To lock in a new strand, first whip-finish the end of the strand to consolidate the hairs. Create a bulky whip-finish that catches in the braid. With each added strand, decrease the number of hairs to create the desired taper. Subtract one or two hairs from each strand for a gentle taper; subtract more hairs for a steeper taper.

After trapping the new strand, continue to plait the strands. After plaiting past the new strand several inches, trim the protruding hairs (the tag ends) of both strands for a smooth line. Continue to add strands until the line reaches the desired length.

5. When approaching the tippet end, complete the plait. Trim to make even and then fold over the end, creating a small loop. Whip to secure the loop. This allows attaching looped-links with flies. Most looped-links will be furled or plaited with three or more hairs per strand. Robert Venables advised the angler to form loops at each end of a line. "Leave a bought, or bout [a loop], at both ends of the line, the one to put it to, and take it from your rod, the other to hang your lowest link upon, to which your hook is fastened, and so that you may change your hook as often as you please."

The Williamson Quill Twister

Captain T. Williamson, in *The Complete Angler's Vade Mecum* (1808), offered another method for twisting horsehair fly lines. "Having knotted the hairs together, take a quill, and after cutting away both the feather end, and the soft part which was in the skin of the goose, plug up one end with a piece of cork, having in its sides three or four very small nicks or grooves; so that each hair may pass through the quill, and by the side of the cork with some resistance."

In the text, a rudimentary drawing shows the quill (figure 3a), hair strands, and knot.

My "quill" is a fine brass tube, .28" to .38" in diameter. Such tubing is readily available from most specialized hardware or hobby stores. Rather than cork (or balsa wood), a better "cork" (or plug) is made from dense, closed-cell foam. The dense foam creates the consistent and smooth friction required.

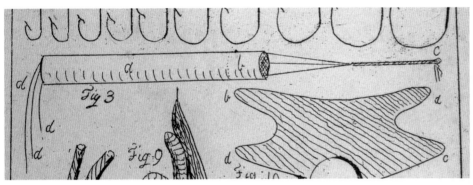

Williamson Quill: text, figure 3

Williamson Quill Twister

For the quill and cork, I use a ⁵⁄₁₆" diameter brass tube and ³⁄₈" diameter popper foam. Cut a 4" length from the brass tube and smoothly polish both ends to prevent cutting the hairs. To cut your own foam corks, take a rejected tube section and sharpen the inside edge to create a foam plug cutter. Depending upon the compression of the foam, a slightly larger diameter tube may be required. Push the plug cutter into the foam and rotate to create a plug about 1" long. Remove the plug. Taper one end of the plug for insertion into the brass quill.

With a razor blade, make three—or more, depending upon the number of strands required—equally spaced, shallow, longitudinal slits along the plug side. Then, select three or more strands. For a thick line, lay several strands in each groove. For example, there may be nine hairs tied together with three hairs in each groove. Reverse (tip to butt) half the hairs to create a strong line. Align the hairs and tie an overhand knot in one end. Trim the knotted hairs to equal length.

Next, pass the knot through the brass quill and insert the strands into the "cork" grooves. If twisting more than one hair in a groove, tie the strand together before inserting the hairs through the tube. Once all the tied ends exit, whip them together. Divide the hair equally so that each strand (single or multiple hairs) rides within a cork groove.

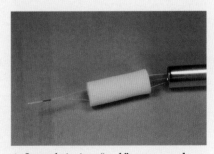

1. Insert hairs into "cork" grooves and through brass quill.

To twist hairs, insert the loaded "cork" into the quill. The hairs, when drawn through the quill, should moderately resist. If the hairs are too tight, they will break; if too loose, they will not twist. Proper tension is everything.

Williamson Quill Twister (cont)

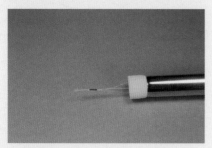

2. Insert the loaded "cork" into the brass quill

To furl the hairs, Williamson then twists the knot. "The knot, which will thus be on the outside, beyond the cork, should be turned between the finger and the thumb; by which means the hairs, coming like so many rays from the edges of the cork will begin to twist in the most regular even manner, and will gradually be drawn through."

Twist or roll the knot one direction only. *Do not allow the knot to untwist during the process.* The long, untwisted strands should drape on the table. Never allow the hairs to untwist. Take care that the long, loose strands entering the rear of the tube do not whip together and tangle. As the exiting hairs twist together, *slowly* pull the hairs out of the quill, creating the twisted link. You will feel a slight lessening of tension when the end nears. Then merely grip the ends and knot all strands together. Transparent tubes, such as those made of clear plastic, would allow seeing the hair ends immediately before they exit.

3. Roll the knot between the thumb and forefinger while slowly pulling hairs through the brass quill

When twisted and pulled, the hairs should feed slowly through the quill. Prevent the hairs from exiting freely. If they do, all the twist is undone. Williamson cautioned: "The person twisting the hairs should be careful to observe when the further ends of the hairs are about to come through the grooves, which he may easily perceive, and should then grasp what he has twisted close to the cork; then draw out the residue, tie the ends as in the first instance: but in order to keep the twists correct, he should as he proceeds, pass the line round his hand, so as to coil it up in a small ring."

4. A quill link

Allow the link to relax and partially uncurl. Though the link will not be as tight as though done by a twisting engine, if done carefully, the quill method is efficient. Create several links in this manner and tie together with a water knot or surgeon's knot. If desired, whip the knot and hair tags down with silk thread for a smooth connection.

The Quill-Roll Method

The traditional twisted-knot method makes manipulation of the quill and hair strands awkward. For a tighter twist, I *rotate the quill* rather than the knotted hairs. Quill rotation imparts a taut, *axial* twist in each hair. In this method, hold the knot in the left hand and *roll the quill* with the right hand.

Each quill rotation (regardless of quill diameter) produces a single axial rotation in each hair or strand. To increase the number of rotations per roll, use a small-diameter quill. If the diameter is too small, however, the tail strands may interlock and fail to feed into the quill. A .30" to .40" diameter brass tube seems to work best: it creates adequate rotation with minimal tangle. Remember to keep

The Quill-Roll Method

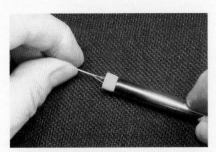

1. Rolling the quill

Roll the quill along the pad and then slide it back for another roll. Prevent any counterroll during the roll and slide. Slowly pull the strands from the quill as they twist together. Prior to exiting the quill, the strands will decrease tension. Never allow the strand ends to exit the quill freely. When tension lessens, grip the strand ends, remove them from the quill and secure with an overhand knot. Decrease the hairs per link to produce the desired line taper. Finally, connect all links (snoods) to form the fly line.

Sometimes long, dangly hairs whip, tangle, and halt when pulled through the quill. Alleviate tangled hairs by inserting three plastic or brass tubes (approximately 2.5 mm inside diameter) into the rear of the standard brass quill. Insert a foam plug to hold and position them. These tubes hold and separate the three strands, thus eliminating any "wild hairs."

2. Brass quill with auxiliary tubes for long hair

the strands taut and prevent any counterrotation during the rolling and return. A rubber pad creates the necessary friction for rolling.

The Tapered, Furled Leader

Furled leaders—knotless and tapered—have characteristics that make them superior, in some ways, to both monofilament and braided leaders. They recall the original twisted horsehair fly lines created centuries ago. The antique running lines were knotless, tapered horsehair. Knotted lines, such as those previously illustrated, were often made by the angler. The tapered, furled line and leader, made from various threads, is a nearly forgotten art, recently remembered. My first encounter with furled leaders, years ago in Spain, was a startling revelation. The soft, supple lines cast remarkably well. Furling, though an early art, continues into the present to create effective and functional *lines* and *leaders*. Furling requires few tools, and most tools (the T-bar, anchor hook, and auxiliary hooks) are readily made from heavy wire. The advantages of a furled line or leader are enough to encourage their use:

1. Drag reduction. The soft and supple lines promote a natural drift.
2. Natural turnover. Even for short distances, the weight encourages full extension on the forward cast.
3. Cracks and crannies. The natural density of a naked, furled line produces a slow sink and natural drift for nymphs. The twisted interstices of a furled line trap "sink" or floatant for diverse drifts.
4. Limited shine. Unlike monofilament lines, most threads have negligible casting flash.

5. Tight loops. The extreme suppleness achieves tight casting loops even at close range.

6. Elasticity. Depending upon material and twist, a furled line may stretch 15 percent or more of the total length. This elasticity absorbs the shock, strike, and the struggle.

7. Variable design. Part of the pleasure of furling is exploring new designs. The dressing, the thread, and the twist determine whether a line sinks or floats. Embedded wire or sink paste accelerate the sink. Lines may be designed in numerous ways that redefine their function.

The disadvantages are few:

1. Snarls and tangles. If you do not take care, the remarkable suppleness of a furled line increases snarls and tangles. Extract tangles by gently pulling the end of the twisted fold. Afterwards, a sharp tug will straighten and relax the line.

2. Dressing and redressing. Furled leader may require dressing or periodic redressing.

3. Confused casting. Furled leaders require smooth, controlled casting: sharp snap casts often create macramé.

Making furled leaders is straightforward. After acquiring some proficiency, it is easy to make complete leaders in about ten minutes. Furthermore, with practice and the proper tools, you can design furled leaders for a variety of angling situations—leaders that parachute softly on spring creeks or leaders that push wind-jamming patterns. It is also satisfying to design leaders for your own requirements. It is possible, in fact, to create complete fly lines.

Although my wire forms (the T-bar, the anchor hook, and the auxiliary hooks) are made from stainless-steel wire, such forms can be made from any rigid wire, bent to the proper shape. The illustrated practical and portable T-bar and anchor hook conveniently clamp into a fly-tying vise for making furled leaders. A more specialized T-bar mounts in a fly-tying base.

Other furling tools are readily fashioned from common materials. For example, you can string furled leaders on a pattern board, about 4" wide and 10' to 12' long. Holes, drilled every 2" or 3" apart along the runner tracks, allow the insertion of wood or metal pylon pegs, creating various leader designs. For convenience, a mid-

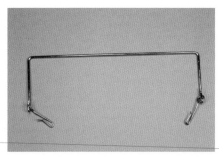

A basic T-bar or "singletree" with auxiliary hooks

Pattern board and movable pylon

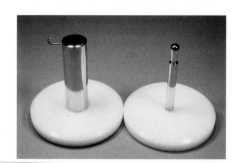

Positionable anchor hook and pylon

dle hinge permits compact storage. The pattern board allows precise duplication of leader designs. T-bar and anchor holes can be added to the board.

Another method is to make movable, individual pylons. Simply pound a nail through a small block of wood. Grind and polish the nail points so that the thread attaches and detaches without damage. Polished brass posts and Delran bases create attractive pylons. Position the movable pylons anywhere desired.

The Required Tools

The furling tools: a Dremel Minimite, an adjustable-tension bobbin (a special truncated bobbin by Merco Products), extension bars for spun and shortened runners, auxiliary hooks, single-hook Dubbing Whirls, and vise T-bar with hooks]

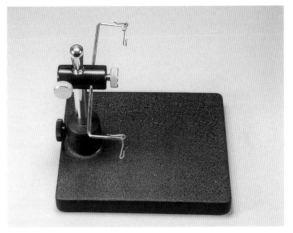

A T-bar mounted in fly-tying vise base. A T-bar may also lock horizontally in the jaws of a tying vise.

1. **The Dremel Minimite, model 750-02 and Dremel Lithium-Ion Cordless, model 800:** Other rotary tools may work, but the cordless Dremels (models 750-02 and 800) are compact and easily handled. On the low speed setting, the Minimite is approximately 6,500 rpm. Though more bulky, the cordless Dremel 800 has a low speed of approximately 5,000 rpm. The lower the speed, the better the control when forming leaders. Both will require a small hook for spinning the runners.

2. **The Wire T-bar:** The T-bar, resembling a miniature singletree or whiffletree, holds the butt ends of the runners and allows each end to be spun. When the butt ends are spun and united, the runners furl together, creating a single, knotless, tapered leader. For increased stability, clamp a T-bar into a tying vise.

3. **The Anchor Hook:** The anchor hook holds the lapped tippet end of the leader.

4. **The Single Hook Whirls:** Any small, single-hook spinner, such as a single-hook Dubbing Whirl, will work.

5. **The Thread:** Various threads form furled leaders, including silk, Dacron, Nylon, Kevlar, and other synthetics. Multistrand, low-denier (150 or less) synthetics, such as Vectran HS or Ultra Threads Cerise, create very strong and delicate leaders. Though a bulk purchase may be required, Web sites will locate many appropriate threads. Multistrand, low-denier fibers necessitate

careful stringing and furling. For improved presentation, some light, fine threads (such as silk) may require extra thread loops in the butt or midsections. When furled, the multiple thread laps form a strong line. For precise and finely tapered leaders, use fine thread and multiple pylons. Try a six- or eight-pylon leader. Multiple pylons produce a delicate taper while the extrafine thread creates a soft, supple leader. For dry-fly, saturate the leader with a nontack grease or liquid floatant. Different threads, different thread diameters and different pylon distances create leaders for every angling condition. The most delicate leaders are made from ultrafine silk thread. Colors can blend with the sky or brighten for visibility.

6. **The Bobbin:** A small, adjustable-tension bobbin works best. Short or truncated bobbins pass readily between the threads. Make certain that the bobbin contains sufficient thread for a single layout. Even an eight and one-half foot leader requires over ninety feet of thread.

7. **The Pylons:** The pylons or posts may be as simple as a polished nail. The best pylons are those with a shoulder that holds the thread. When stringing the layout, pylons hold the thread loops until another thread loop captures it. The distance between pylons and the number of loops determines the basic leader design.

8. **Auxiliary Hooks:** Auxiliary hooks mounted to the T-bar allow quick and convenient manipulation of the runners. They facilitate attaching and detaching the Dremel and Dubbing Whirls.

The Four-Pylon Leader

This four-pylon leader design has a two-ply differential between each of the five sections. The butt is fourteen-ply; midsections are twelve-ply, ten-ply, and eight-ply. The leader ends with a six-ply tippet section. The following directions for a nine-foot layout will produce an eight and one-half foot furled leader. With a two-foot tippet attached, the total leader length is approximately ten and one-half feet. The number of pylons, the staggered distance between pylons, the number of loops and the type of thread determine the taper and character of the completed leader.

Furled-Leader Layout

First, select an appropriate thread. For practice, your first furled leader may be made with a heavy thread or 3/0 tying thread. Though it will produce a thick leader, you will quickly learn how to string (lay out), spin, and furl leaders. Finer threads, either silk or synthetics, may be used once the procedure is understood and the skill acquired. Of course, leaders may be made from various other lines and threads. Many newer, synthetic threads are extremely strong and cut only under tension. Monofilament leaders can be made from 5X tippet material.

Begin by staggering four pylons (*two pylons in each runner*), the appropriate distance as illustrated.

The Furled-Leader

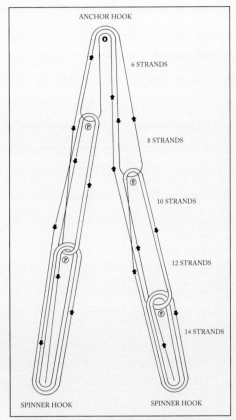

ANCHOR HOOK

6 STRANDS

8 STRANDS

10 STRANDS

12 STRANDS

14 STRANDS

SPINNER HOOK   SPINNER HOOK

1. Expanded, four-pylon furling diagram. Pylons form the letter V. To create different lengths and tapers, alter the spacing and number of pylons. Begin stringing the layout at the right spinner hook. This schematic illustrates a line/ leader tapering from fourteen to six strands.

Then, double the end of the thread and tie a single, overhand knot in the loop (the bight) to create a locking, two-inch loop. Attach the thread loop to the auxiliary hook and trim excess closely.

2. Attach the butt loop to an auxiliary hook connected to the T-bar
   Note: If you wish to attach a braided line loop to the leader, merely tie the thread directly to the auxiliary hook.

Then, "string" the four-pylon leader as illustrated, and secure the thread to another auxiliary hook. Attach this hook to the opposite T-bar hook. To create a strong leader, add a single strand of an ultrastrong synthetic, such as Kevlar. First, with an auxiliary hook, attach the synthetic strand to a T-bar hook. Lay the thread out along the pylon path. Loop the strand over the anchor hook and back to the opposite T-bar hook, again with an auxiliary hook. When the runners spin and furl, the superstrong synthetic imbeds within the other strands. In actual layout, the thread connects to auxiliary hooks and is taut. Note that only one thread captures the pylon. Connecting threads only capture other threads, not pylons.

3. Pass the bobbin through the thread loop

4. Capture the thread only (not the pylon) with the connecting thread

Stringing (the thread layout) the leader is best done when the thread feeds smoothly from an adjustable-tension bobbin. A small bobbin also makes it easier to pass the thread through the pylon loops as required.
   When the returning thread captures loops at the pylon, make certain that the thread captures all the thread loops held by the pylon and not the pylon itself. If the pylon itself is

captured (especially if captured both directions by the loops), then the space occupied by the pylon will produce slack in the leader.

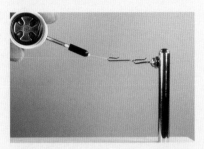

5. Threads lap on the auxiliary anchor hook

The formula for the four-pylon, as depicted in the diagram, is three full loops around the butt pylon and two full loops around the tip pylon of *each* runner. The thread will lap the auxiliary hook attached to the anchor hook three times, thus creating a six-ply "tippet" end.
   After stringing the leader according to the diagram, tie off the thread on the opposing T-bar. Keep the leader connected to the anchor hooks and T-bar. When later joined, the two T-bar butt *loops* combine to form a single loop on the finished leader. Remember to attach each butt loop to an *auxiliary hook* connected to the T-bar: the auxiliary hook spins the runner. After the leader is spun and popped off the pylons, it will retain its shape due to the interlocking loops. Now, prior to spinning each runner, place tension on the runners to eliminate any excess slack in the loops.

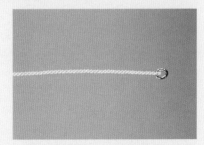

6. Silver ring on six-ply silk line

Sometimes I add a small silver ring, popularized by the late Edgar

The Furled-Leader (cont)

Pitzenbauer of Bavaria, to the tippet end of the leader at this time. The ring does not influence the cast, and it allows quick tippet changes. Years ago, I met Edgar in Slovenia on the Unica. For more than a decade, I returned to Slovenia and Edgar. He was the best grayling angler I have ever met. The Unica grayling are large and selective: they do not fall to trout tricks. Edgar always returned with new ideas. He wore his angling tools on a small chest plate long before the modern packs. He designed a light pullover with waterproof sleeves for landing fish in deep water. He modified his waders by attaching arm-length, waterproof pockets on the outside for his tackle. And he fished for grayling with a rod-length leader of fifteen-pound Amnesia monofilament with a small silver ring at the end. The weight of the Amnesia allowed him to cast, when required, just the leader and tippet. The Amnesia threads through the line tip and then nail-knots around the line: this connection readily slides through the guides when extending line. Merely by changing tippets, this leader system works all season.

Prior to spinning, the ring may be slipped over the butt of one runner and slid to the far tippet-end near the anchor. Then, hook the ring, held by the leader, to the auxiliary hook at the anchor and continue to make the leader. The ring creates a permanent loop for tippet attachment. Otherwise, I merely attach tippets to the loop created by the leader point.

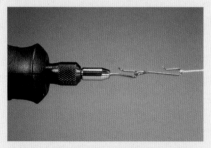

7. Dremel attached to auxiliary hook on runner

Mount a small hook in the Dremel and select low speed (approximately 6,500 rpm). A small hook may be made with a heavy wire. When forming the hook, make certain that the stem centers on the

hook bend. This averts wobble when spinning. To accommodate the adjustable chuck in the Dremel, it may be necessary to wrap strong tape on the stem of the hook. Otherwise, use a microchuck to securely hold the hook.

8. Spinning the runner

Use only "low speed" when spinning. The low speed increases accurate calculation of revolutions and minimizes runner "whip." Even at the low speed, each runner should be spun only a few seconds. At 5,000 revolutions per minute, 5 seconds equal approximately 416 rpm. Time the duration of spin to duplicate the same degree of twist in each runner. At 6,500 rpm, 5 seconds equal approximately 540 rpm. Remember to keep both runners taut and secure while spinning. The key to a perfect leader is to maintain constant, but not excessive, tension while spinning and forming each runner. Tension prevents the leader, especially the fine tip section, from coiling upon itself prior to final furling.

To spin a runner, disconnect one runner and its auxiliary hook from the T-bar. Now, connect the Dremel hook to the auxiliary hook attached to the butt of the runner.

The nine-foot, four-pylon, 3/0 thread leader will require about 20 seconds of spin at 5,000 rpm or 18.5 seconds at 6,500 rpm for each runner. This gives each runner about 2,000 twists. Using a sweep second hand, time the revolutions accurately for each spin. Spin the runner twenty seconds. Note that each runner must be separately spun at the butt and that the Dremel must be attached and detached for each spinning. The duration of spin will determine the degree of twist imparted to each runner. For example, a typical thread leader—depending upon

the length, the diameter, and the material—may require from fifteen seconds (approximately 1,248 revolutions) to twenty-five seconds (approximately 2,080 revolutions) or more for each runner. Make further spin and time adjustments as necessary. Trial spinning may be necessary to determine the proper degree of twist for a given leader length, thread laps, thread diameter, and material. Experiment to determine the appropriate degree of spin. Usually, twisted threads should be spun the same direction as the intrinsic thread twist. Loosely twisted threads can be spun any direction as long as both runners are spun the same direction. As the Dremel is hand-held when furling, the shortening or shrinking runner is easily accommodated. Remember to keep the auxiliary hooks attached to the leader.

After spinning the first runner, reattach the runner to the T-bar. Because the runner is now shorter, an extension bar must connect the butt to the T-bar. Then, detach the second runner and spin the second runner in the same manner as the first runner. After spinning each runner the appropriate time, match and unite both butts. It is imperative to use constant and appropriate tension when overlapping and aligning the butt loops. Firmly pull the united butts to align all strands.

9. Attach single-hook Whirls to each end of the leader and allow leader to spin.

Next, while maintaining the tension and the tight twist of the leader, remove it from the T-bar hook and attach a single-hook Whirl to the auxiliary hook connected to the butt. After dismounting the butts, secure with an overhand knot. Then, remove the tippet end of the leader, keeping its auxiliary hook attached. Hang another Dubbing Whirl to the tippet-end auxiliary hook. We now have Whirls connected at each end of the leader (the butt and tippet end). *Hold the leader so that the dangling Whirls slowly spin, furling and forming the leader.* To allow complete furling, move the hands during furling as the runners twist together. To encourage tight furling and to avert tangles, keep the spinning Whirls separated while moving your hands along the leader.

After the Whirls stop counter-spinning, remove them. Keep the auxiliary hooks attached to the leader so that you can find the end loops. *Finally, gently shake the leader allowing it to relax completely.* Create a small butt loop, whip closed, and varnish. Trim excess, including the terminal butt knot. Other butt loops are possible, such as attaching a braided line-loop to the butt.

10. Basic butt loop

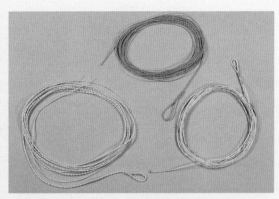

11. Furled leaders with loops. Note the leader with the silver tippet ring.

The relaxed leader (or line) can be used immediately. If desired, dip the leader loops in flexible, waterproof cement to keep them open. Frank Matarelli, toolmaker and master furler, whips a length of the leader immediately in front of the butt loop to prevent the looped strands from separating. I prefer to fold the butt back to form a self-loop or to mount a braided line-loop to the butt. A whipped section secures the butt loop in place.

Furling a few leaders summons some ancient shadows. We hear the far, faint music of milkmaids. Then we meet Walton and Cotton over frothy pints of dark ale. Walton, of course, begs us to join them. Cotton opens his "leathern case" to share his flies and leaders. He selects a finely furled horsehair line and, with a droll smile, turns to us and proclaims (as he did in print) that if you cannot take a twenty-inch trout with only two hairs next to the hook, you don't deserve the name *Angler*. Walton slyly winks.

CHAPTER VI

THE LOOP-ROD
Ye makynge of your harnays:
ye rodde

And how ye shall make your rodde craftly here I shall teche you.

— The Treatyse

IN SEPTEMBER 1897, G. E. M. SKUES AND A FRIEND SPENT sixteen days in Bosnia. They found fly fishers with eight to nine foot, one-piece fly rods and lines "composed of hairs from the tails of their pony stallions tapered from the rod tip to the point fly (which was on three hairs) and with two droppers. The flies were hackled from soft feathers from under the wings of geese, owls, and eagles—very flexible, and they were tied on hooks forged locally (sometimes from French nails from packing cases) and running about the same as No. 9 Limerick. With these flies fished down stream I have seen the natives yank a three-quarter pound grayling from the water and catch it in the left hand." Skues did not mention the line length, but did record that the rods lacked reels and running lines. The line attached directly to the tip or to a loop, hence the term *loop-rod*. A tip loop, usually of horsehair, allows line replacement. For greater safety, the line could pass though the loop and attach to a stronger, lower rod section.

Skues was not clear whether the method was wet, dry, or damp. However, with the buoyancy of horsehair, it probably had the versatility of all three. The local method—soft-hackles downstream—was traditional and, according to Skues, "it might have come down with little variation from that described by [Aelianus]. . . ." Nearly all early illustrations—Egyptian, Greek, and Roman—depict relatively short rods. Artistic limitations alone did not shrink all rod illustrations. Aelian's rod, mentioned about 200 A.D., was six feet long with a matching length of horsehair line. The short Aelian rod and fixed line suggest dapping, where the angler conceals himself while touching or dancing the pattern on the water surface. Various insects oviposit by "dapping" their eggs on the water surface. A short rod with fixed line significantly restricts the angling area. William Radcliffe noted, "There is no example of a running line in ancient literature or art. . . ." He dated the fixed line "down to some date between 1496 and 1651."

The *Treatyse of Fysshynge Wyth an Angle* (1496) presents a detailed account of rod making. It included the appropriate time of year—between Michaelmas (September 29) and Candlemas (February 2)—for collecting materials. Timber felled in the cooler, wetter months slowly exhaled its moisture content: that felled in the warmer, dry months dried too quickly, creating cracks and warp. The *Treatyse* rod had a butt section of hazel, willow, or aspen and a tip section of blackthorn, crabtree, medlar (*Mespilus germanica*), or juniper. The stock, a fathom and a half long and as thick as your arm, was hazel, willow, or "aspe" (poplar). A fathom (the length of two arms outstretched or six feet) and a half made the staff nine feet long. The curing process included soaking the staff in hot water, setting it straight, and baking it in an oven. After cooling, the rod maker tied the staff with "a cockshoot cord" (a cord that hangs a net across a "cockshoot" to capture woodcocks as they shoot past) to a straight timber and dried it for a month. Then the rod maker pushed white-hot plumber's wire through the center pith, followed by an equally hot bird spit down the center to enlarge the hollow. Other, larger spits increased the taper and diameter of the hollow. After cooling for two days, the builder untied the stock and seasoned it in house-roof smoke until completely dry, then soaked, straightened, and dried the top sections with the staff. Once spliced together, the entire tip section fit inside the tapered, hollowed staff. Storing the top in the hollowed stock not only protected the slender, spliced top but also concealed its purpose. The finished rod, according to the *Treatyse*, "will be 'lyghtє & nymbull' [light & nimble] to fish with at your 'luſtє' [pleasure, "lust"] and 'so perfєt & fєtє' [perfect & neat] that you may walk therewith: and there shall no man know where about you go." Even in 1496, it was best to hide your favorite fishing spot. John Waller Hills, like R. B. Marston before him, praised the *Treatyse* rod: "the rod, which in the picture looks like an ungainly pole, is really light and flexible: a hollow butt, a springy middle joint of hazel, and a light yet tough top make up something which would throw a fly uncommonly well." Neither Hills nor Marston appear to have constructed or angled with a *Treatyse* rod.

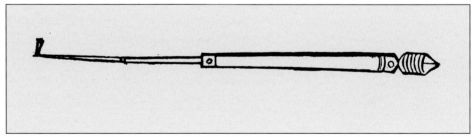

The *Treatyse* rod

When fishing, the hazel wood midsection sockets into the top of the butt section. A tapered splice wrapped with hemp connected the top sections together. For strength, both ends of the butt had "ferrules," more like bands or hoops of iron or latten (a sheet of bronze, brass or brasslike alloy). With the middle and top sections, the rod was at least fourteen feet long and, consequently, hand heavy.

Perhaps the most obscure section on the *Treatyse* rod was the final line assembly. "Than arme yowr crop [rod top] at þe ovir ende down to the frete [binding, tie] with a lyn of vi herys & double the lyne & frete hyt fast yn þe top with a nose [noose] to fasten an your lyne. . . ." With a cord of six hairs, strengthen your top at the upper end as far down as the binding (top splice?). Then double the cord and tie a noose at the top to connect the fishing line. The line may attach to a loop at the "binding" (spliced joint?) between the tip and midsection. Alternatively, the line may merely anchor to a loop mounted at the midsection of the tip. It then strings through the top loop (hence loop-rod) on the blackthorn tip. In case of top fracture or failure, the horsehair line remains anchored below the tip. Though it seems logical, it is uncertain if the line secures *below* the tip-section splice. There would be greater security if the line anchors on the *lower* rod section. If the tip or splice then broke, an angler could still hold and land the fish.

The *Treatyse* "angler woodcut" reveals some information. The rod portrayed is much shorter than described. The line, carrying a "float plumbe" or "lede plumbe," appears wrapped five times around the tip section and secured at midtop. As today, "The float plumbe shall be so heuy þat the leest plucke of ony fysshe maye

The *Treatyse* angler

pull downe in to þe water." The manner in which the line anchors on the rod precludes any letting or taking of line when fighting or landing a fish. A tip noose does not appear in the angler woodcut.

The Evolution

Modern fly fishing evolved, not from rods and casting lines, but from running lines, guides, and reels. *The Gentleman Angler* (c. 1736) advised the young angler to carry "*Reels* for his *Silk Lines*, a *Pouch* or Book for his Hair Lines, which ought to be rolled up in a circular Form." *The Gentleman Angler* also recorded the placement and function of rings (guides):

> It will be very convenient to have Rings, or Eyes, (as fome call them) made of fine Wire, and placed fo artificially upon your Rod, from one End to the other, that when you lay your Eye to one, you may fee through all the reft; and your Rod being thus furnifh'd, you will eafily learn from thence how to put Rings to all your other Rods. Through thefe Rings your Line muft run, which will be kept in a due Pofture, and you will find great Benefit thereby. You must alfo have a Winch or Wheel, affixed to your Rod, about a Foot above the end, that you may give Liberty to the Fifh, which, if large, will be apt to run a great way before it may be proper to check him, or before he will voluntarily return.

Evidently, an angler could cast the heavy, knotted horsehair line and then fight the fish with the (knotless?) running silk line. This description of guides is accurate and early. In general, running lines were more common for trolling and salmon fishing. Long loop-rods could also defeat feisty fish. In the seventeenth century, two-handed, fixed-line rods would be remarkably long, 14–18 feet or more.

A sketchy reel illustration appears in *Barker's Delight or The Art of Angling* (1651). For salmon, Barker used "a little wire ring at the upper end of the top for the line to run through, that you may take up or loose the line at your pleasure; you must have your winder within two foot of the bottom . . ." Furthermore, he

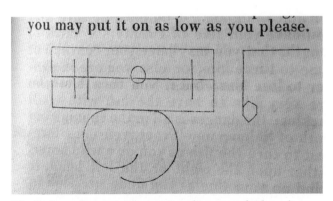

The Barker reel *appears* to be a spring-clip mounted side-reel with a two-piece closed case and detachable handle. The handle apparently has a knob, nut, or bend-stop of some sort. The illustration is one of angling's classic conundrums.

recovered line: "wind up your line as you find occasion in the guiding of the fish to the shore." The Barker reel illustration is an exasperating conundrum—the construction and operation still debated.

In 1662, Robert Venables used stout shoemaker's thread for a running line, a tip-ring, and reel when trolling for pike. Like other early anglers, he used a slender rod and a fixed, horsehair line for trout. The loop-rod lacked the advantages of reel and running line. Howlett first mentioned rod rings in 1706. Reels—first mentioned by Barker for trolling (1651) and Walton for salmon (1655)—were not used in trout fishing until later. Knotted horsehair line does not slide through rings or run from reels. Even knotless horsehair lines can kink and catch in the rings. However, Francis Francis, in the nineteenth century, extolled the virtues of hair and silk mixed for the running line. "Some anglers prefer plaited dressed silk, but I do not like such lines for single-handed rods; they want lightness and elasticity." Though the reel emerges in the seventeenth century, trout "harnays" would include the loop-rod through the next century and beyond. It took time for the modern reel to hatch. And by then the rod was already centuries old.

put my hookes and lines in.
    I use a rod of two parts, to joyne in the midst when I come to the river, with two pins, and a little hempe waxed, thus the pins joyne it, the hempe fastens it firmely.

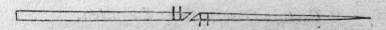

    A whale-bone made round no bigger than a wheat-straw at the top, yields well, and strikes well.
    Let your rod be without knots; they are dangerous for breaking, and boughts are troublesome.

The Secrets of Angling **spliced rod**

According to John Waller Hills, William Lauson first mentioned the spliced rod in 1620. Lauson recorded, in an emendation to John Dennys' *The Secrets of Angling*, that "I use a rod of two parts, to joyne in the midst when I come to the river, with two pins, and a little hempe waxed, thus the pins joyne it, the hempe fastens it firmly." A woodcut depicts a two-piece rod with two pins near each splice. When wrapped, the pins apparently kept the sections together. The short, abruptly tapered splices depicted are absurd: they lack adequate overlap and strength.

For centuries after the *Treatyse*, the fly rod was solid wood with the horsehair fly line either attached or looped directly to the tip or anchored at midtip. A line loop, either at the tip or at midsection, allows line changes. Some rods were merely willow reeds or shoots cut from the bank. A short rod severely limits the "swim" or range of the fly. One major development was the increased rod length. Eventually, river size would determine rod length.

David Webster with loop-rod

David Webster, in *The Angler and the Loop-Rod* (1885), described his spliced, two-handed fly rod.

A two-handed spliced rod, measuring from 13 feet 6 inches to 13 feet 8 inches. It consists of three pieces. The butt is made of ash, the middle piece of hickory, and the top of lancewood. When greater lightness is desired, lime tree may be used for the butt:

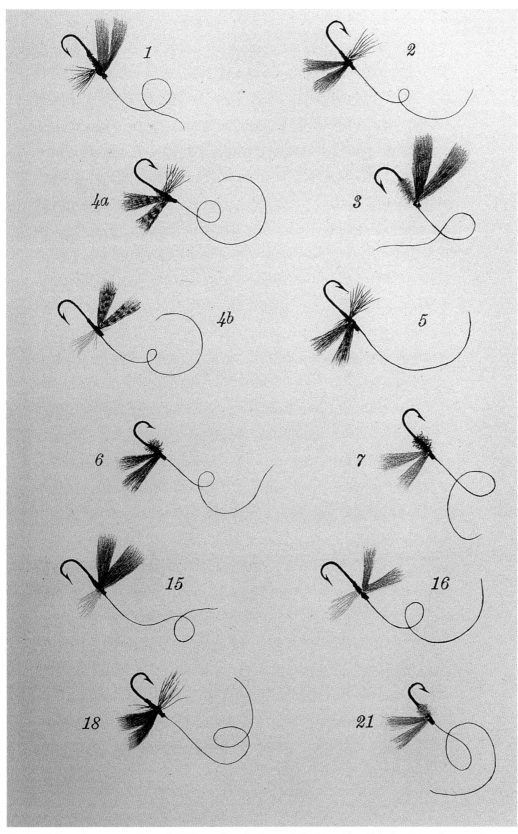

David Webster fly patterns. Though Webster thought that soft-hackle spiders fished well in sultry weather when winged insects were absent, he preferred winged patterns. The soft dressing of spiders deteriorates swiftly and, after a few fish, "there is very little left of the spider to conceal the hook."

what the rod gains, however, is lost in durability. Attached to the extremity of the top piece is a strong loop of twisted horsehair that anchors the casting line. The horsehair loop at the tip characterizes the loop-rod. The horsehair casting line is about 18 to 20 feet long, tapering from 45 or 36 hairs at the butt to 6 or 5 hairs at the gut. A knotted silk-gut line (the ancestor of the leader and tippet) extended another 16 or 17 feet, thus creating a total line length (from line loop to tail fly) of 34 or 37 feet.

Clearly, this length exceeded any dapping line. A veritable hatch of nine flies, on 2-inch looped droppers, attached to the long gut "tippet." Webster was a commercial angler who made a modest living with such tackle.

Webster cautioned that the middle rod section—often the shorter section—should be somewhat stiff. "A spliced rod of this kind is much lighter than the ordinary brass-jointed rod, and casts a much better line." The Webster double-handed loop-rod, a palpable anachronism during this time of reels and rod rings, had length and lightness. This lightness, however, was relative. By modern standards, these were heavy rods.

Frontispiece from *The Secrets of Angling* (circa 1620 edition) by J. D. (John Dennys), Esquire. Though the line appears directly attached to the rod, the woodcut may have omitted rod-loop detail. Note that the foreground rod has a modest tip flex. The background angler has an odd line butt (probably an engraving fault) and a curious catch. The lines read: "well fayre the plesure that bringes such treasure" and "hold hooke and line then all is mine."

For broad rivers with abundant, large fish, Webster attached "the loop line to the end of the line wound off the reel." For ordinary angling, however, he preferred the loop-line and reel-less rod. Unlike a lighter, reel-line, the sheer weight of a thick horsehair loop-line penetrates a breeze and covers 40 or 50 feet of water. Wind and weather, naturally, always limit the angler. Curiously enough, there are claims that a certain Dr. Livingstone ghostwrote Webster's *The Angler and the Loop-Rod*. No matter who the literary midwife, Webster's late-nineteenth-century work is a belated glance at the eighteenth-century angler.

The Loop-Rod Line

Most early "casting lines," until the seventeenth century, attached, either tied or looped, directly to the rod. The rod loop certainly had one advantage; a line could quickly be replaced with a different line for changing conditions. These were the days before trout anglers used a reel and running line. The horsehair casting line (loosely comparable to the thirty-foot head of a modern fly line) lacked a running line and a reserve backing line. Despite the modern British reference to a leader as a "cast," the longer and heavier horsehair casting line did not become the leader. Modern fly fishing arose when knotless casting lines ran through rod rings from a *wheel* or *winch* (reel).

The Historic Loop-Rod

Many fly rods were a "stock" or "staff" bored out by burning to accept a midsection with a spliced tip section. Quality rods usually had a supple, tapered tip of whalebone (sometimes no larger than a "wheat-straw") and strong loop of horse-hair. Thomas Shirley, in *The Angler's Museum* (first edition 1784 and later, undated editions), gave a succinct account of making a "dedicated" fly rod:

> To make a very neat fly-rod, you must proceed in the following manner. Get a yellow whole deal board [a yellow-pine board], which is free from knots. Cut off about seven feet from the best end, and saw it into square breadths. Let a joiner plane off the angles, and make it perfectly round, a little tapering: this will serve for a stock. Then piece it to a fine straight hazel, of about six feet long, and then a delicate piece of fine-grained yew, plained [*sic*] round like an arrow, and tapering, with whalebone, as before, of about two feet in length. There is no absolutely fixing the length of a fly-rod, but one of fourteen feet is as long as can well be managed. To colour the stock, dip a feather in aqua fortis [nitric acid], and chafe it into the deal, which will then become of a cinnamon colour.

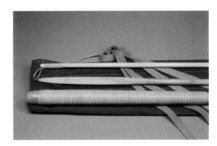

Modern, three-piece bag rod. Note the long, leather handle wrap.

A strong loop of horsehair attaches to the whalebone tip. According to Shirley, some rods form walking sticks and others—those composed of many sections that store in a bag—are "bag-rods," most appropriate for travel. To connect the rod sections, he waxed each splice and firmly whipped it with waxed thread. He also

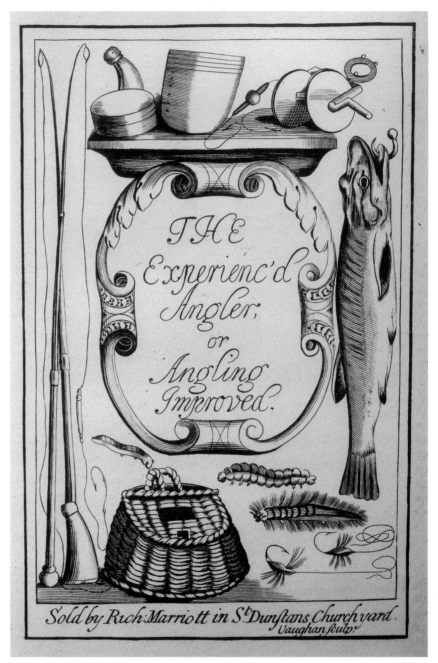

Three-section loop-rods in *The Experienced Angler*, **Robert Venables**

declared that an angler is a novice until "he can throw fifteen yards nearly" of horsehair line.

Robert Venable's seventeenth-century work showed a three-sectioned loop-rod. The butt "stock" had a ball base and heavy socket joints or ferrules. "A powder or bait horn," according to Andrew Herd, concealed the butt of one rod. A similar horn sat on the shelf above. The Venable reel, on the shelf to the right, is a remarkable, "modern" contrast to Barker's sketchy and perplexing reel woodcut on page 244.

The background angler, in the frontispiece of Robert Howlett's *Angler's Sure Guide* (1706), has a loop-rod with the line passing through the tip-loop down toward his hand. A pin or loop may have connected the line to the lower rod. However, this would allow only limited line tension when landing a fish. A knotted line could not be retrieved and a knotted, anchored line could only be extended. Merely holding the end of a line is both awkward and dangerous: a single slip would loose both line and fish.

Frontispiece from *Anglers Sure Guide* by Robert Howlett (1706)

The Rod Wood

For centuries, various woods made fly rods. Indeed, it seems that few woods, native or foreign, have escaped the angler's eye. In addition to those woods previously mentioned, rod makers experimented with white deal or fir board, snakewood, reed, basswood, hornbeam, barberry, cedar, osage orange (*Toxylon*), bethabara, greenheart (*Nectandra* and others), purpleheart (*Peltogyne*), lemonwood (*Pittosporum*), Calcutta cane (*Dendrocalamus*), and the mainstay Tonkin bamboo (*Arundaria amabilis*, "the lovely reed"). Various woods and materials combined to create the quality rod. In the late seventeenth century, James Chetham's "neateſt" and "curious Rod, if artificially work'd" had a seven to eight foot white deal or "fir-board" butt tapered and rounded by the local arrow maker with a six or seven foot hazel midsection (in two or three pieces), a two-foot yew top and a five- or six-inch whalebone tip. Thaddeus Norris, as late as 1864, preferred a white-ash butt section, ironwood midsection, and four-strip bamboo tip. Hazel, yew, ash, and slender whalebone tips were all fashionable. Greenheart was still a premier rod wood well into the early twentieth century. Many exotic woods, made available through colonial expansion, became popular. James Ogden made rods from "blue mahoe" (indigenous West Indies tree, *Paritium elatum*). For an invaluable discussion of rod woods, consult Volume II of Ernest Schwiebert's *Trout* (1978).

In *River Angling for Salmon and Trout* (first edition, 1840), John Younger praised rods made from a single wood. "If a rod is made up of various kinds of wood or even different trees of the same kind, you can never have the same equal degree of fine elasticity; whereas, by making the whole rod out of the same short piece, you not only improve the spring, but also find the best precaution against its twisting. . . ." The Younger red hickory trout rod, from 14 to 16 feet, had glued and tied joints as well as rings. Length was important: "We cannot command much water with a rod of less than fifteen or sixteen feet." Whether or not Younger's pronouncements are correct, a single-wood rod has matching grain density and consistent resiliency.

Younger glued rod sections together and then planed them to a continuous taper. "If the planing could be so managed, the perfection of the rod would consist in having it to taper properly the whole length, from butt to top, and the wood being of the same piece and growth, the *spring* must be equal and correct throughout." He then cut the seasoned red hickory rod into two, three, or four sections and connected the sections with brass ferrules. Silk wraps and varnish on the glued joints completed the rod. Although this is not a loop-rod (as it had guides), this method of gluing and planing produces delicate loop-rods. I might add that each new rod I make is lighter and more delicate than the last one. The Younger method allows continual testing during planing to achieve the preferred flex.

Making a Basic Spliced Loop-Rod

The following directions make a two-, three-, or four-section, spliced loop-rod. I offer no more rationale for making an antique rod than for tying a Fan-Wing

Coachman: it is merely a pleasant learning process. Making and fishing a loop-rod define, though modestly, what it was to be an angler. If for no other reason, I came to appreciate more fully the challenge of ancient angling and the remarkable efficiency of modern tackle. Power equipment—such as band saws, orbital and belt sanders—quickly create a rod. Hand tools, however, are more intimate; they let you feel the wood. The slower and more thoughtful hand process illustrated here is a simple craft. A wooden block plane seems to announce the nuances of grain better than an all-metal plane. Sometimes, I wax the plane base for a smooth, slicing glide. It is inevitable that modern materials and methods would replace the old tools and handcraft, but the construction of the loop-rod is merely a matter of planing a wood blank. Straight-grain ash blanks create an attractive and functional single-wood loop-rod.

First, square the ash blanks to remove excess; and then with a concave spoke-shave or block plane, shave and taper to the desired flex.

Though moderately heavy, white ash (*Fraxinus americana*) is close-grained and resilient. Traditionally used for tool handles and oars, it splits with precision and has supreme strength and elasticity. As noted previously, white ash has a long history as a fly-rod wood. Thin blanks make excellent loop-rods. White ash baseball-bat blanks (3" × 3" × 36") or longer ash blanks (50" or more) are often available at hardwood stores. Select wood blanks that have a dense, straight grain: *straight grain is more important than a straight rod*. Although the taper slices through grain, some grain should run from end to end of each rod section. With band saw, rough-cut the blank lengths about ¼" thicker than required. The number of rod blanks planed determines the number of splices and total rod length. Use plane and spokeshave to strip down each rod blank to proper dimensions. Preferred rod action determines the dimensions. A spokeshave can always make a rod softer, never stiffer. Frequently test the flex to achieve the preferred performance. I plane the rod to near final diameter before cutting the splices. Final sanding should create round, smooth rod sections. For the *final* sanding, ultrafine sandpaper taped to a *foam* block conforms to the rod shape better than a flatbed sander.

From square to round

Block plane, spokeshave and ash rod

Whenever possible, plane with the grain to avoid blade stutter. Exceptionally sharp and properly adjusted blades quickly reduce the wood to long, rough-rounded blanks and bushels of woody ringlets. The following dimensions create a two-piece, eight-foot (excluding the splice) ash loop-rod. For a lighter and more flexible rod, merely make more shavings. However, test the flex periodically: shavings cannot be returned to the rod. Although their "swim" or angling area is greater, rods longer than 10 feet become laboriously heavy. Adjust rod dimensions, both length and diameters, for desired rod performance. Diameter and grain density will determine the final rod flex. The rod illustrated here has the following approximate diameters. This is quite arbitrary, as I always seek the greatest flex and lightness possible with each new rod made. Through choice, a minimal use of power tools creates only the initial wood blanks and the splices.

1. Rod tip diameter: 5 mm (approximately .197")
2. Rod middle diameter (excluding the swelled splice): 10 mm (approximately .39")
3. Rod butt diameter: 20 mm at the butt (approximately .80")

Rosewood plane with wedge-set, ¹¹/₁₆" concave blade

The Splice

For adequate splice face contact, slightly swell or enlarge each splice section. Make the tapered splice long, about 6"–8". O'Gorman, in *The Practice of Angling* (1845) described the tapered splice: ". . . and let your splice in the two-pieced rod, where you tie top and butt together, be a good long lap, not a short splice, or sharp in the points . . . for everything that comes into contact with the points of sharp splices, is sure to injure them." These tapered "splices" are merely matching bevels; slanted or angled cuts that, when overlapped and wrapped, create a straight rod. The bevels adjust easily for a straight rod. The wrapped splice is yet alive and well. Lovely tapered splices appear on my nine foot, modern bamboo rod from J. S. Sharpe of Aberdeen, Scotland. As the poet Keats noted, "a thing of beauty . . . will never pass into nothingness."

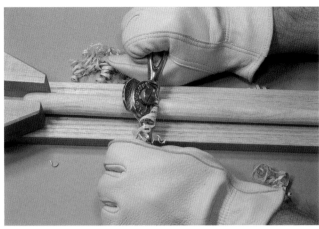

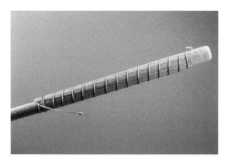

A swelled, slant splice with protective
hardwood guard

Rod locked in screw clamp for spokeshaving

Hardy's lock-fast splice

O'Gorman also recommended the splice guard. "There should always be a bit of wood adapted to open splices of all kinds, to fit them; and when you are going anywhere, tie them fast on the different splices; it is little trouble and a great preservative." The guard protects the delicate splice tip.

There are some curious splice designs. E. M. Tod, in *Wet-Fly Fishing* (1914), praised a unique splice. "The Messrs. Hardy Brothers sell a patented joint named the *lock-fast*, which I myself have used, and can speak of as a thoroughly serviceable invention. It does not, I think, add to the appearance of a rod, but is, notwithstanding, simple and effective, and is one of the best joints I have ever fished with." This splice must be precisely shaped and matched. Though this "lap lock" would prevent separation, it may be overly prone to break at the inner-angle of the "step."

A long, narrow splice flexes and functions like a continuous piece. Both tapered splice surfaces must be remarkably flat and smooth. A mildly swelled splice section can increase contact and strength. A swollen splice, widest in the center, may also prevent separation: when pulled apart, the splice wraps jam against the swell. Though W. C. Stewart wrote in a time of brass joints, rod guides, and reels, he praised the tied slip splice. "A tied rod is not nearly so liable to break as one with brass joints. . . . A tied rod also bends most equally throughout; and no angler will deny that it is the most agreeable to use." He went on to tell how tying should be done. "When the tie system is adopted, the splices should be well waxed, as also the thread with which they are tied, otherwise they will be constantly slipping." In contrast, Ogden, in *Ogden on Fly Tying* (third edition, 1887), noted,

> The splices should be made a little stouter than the other parts, by leaving a little more wood in them. On no account put wax on the splices. The wrapping for these should be four or five strands of hemp, well waxed, not twisted, but kept as flat as possible, as it will hold the splices much firmer when flat than when twisted, and is better than string or whipcord. In wrapping the splices together, commence at the top of the splice, and start with two or three easy wraps; then holding the hemp tight in the right finger and thumb, close to the splice, and twisting the lower joint with the left hand, it is done at once. I usually put my wraps about a quarter of an inch apart, but that is of no consequence so long as it is firm.

Waxing the sliced face may work well for rods that are assembled for a season. However, like Ogden, I use adhesive wax only for the whipping cord, and never the splice face. An unvarnished, natural splice face holds well. A waxed splice face, in fact, might promote separation during warm weather. Anglers debated, often fervently, the worth of waxing the splice face. In any case, mount the thread with a taut whip and finish with a tightly tucked whip.

Modern hemp cord may have sizing that creates a slick surface, unfit for rod wrapping. Soak the hemp in hot water and detergent to remove the sizing. Webster wrapped loop-rod splices with well-rosined and doubled shoemaker's thread. A strong "wrap" is a supple strip of leather (such as deer hide), approximately $\frac{1}{4}"$ to $\frac{3}{8}"$ wide and 50" long. A wide strap enhances hold. The elasticity of leather provides a commanding embrace. Applied with adequate tension, the leather firmly hugs and holds the splices together. Apparently, early anglers used sheep or colt leather for bindings.

The traditional waxed-hemp splice

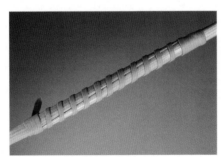

An open-wrapped leather splice

A closed-wrapped leather splice provides maximum strength

O'Gorman favored leather cord or strapping: "The best tier for the splices of large sized two-piece rods is common sheepskin leather; and so it is for all two-piece rods—the string nicely proportioned to the size of the rod. This observation applies equally to the upper splice of screw and socket-rods; if this description of skin cannot be procured, try to get some nice foal-skin from your saddler, which may answer the purpose. In this instance, and in many others, you will find that 'there is nothing like leather.'"

Leather strips from the back of the animal have less elasticity and would require tight, rigid wraps. Some elasticity is preferred: it actually sustains the grip. All straps or cords hold best when wrapped over bare wood. For this reason, leave the entire splice space unfinished. Severe wetting can loosen most wraps, including leather. When fishing, avoid rod separation by periodically checking all splice wraps.

Carefully cut the tapered "slip splices" with a fine-toothed saw. To do this, firmly tape a wood block to the rod: mount the block so that the wood grain aligns (parallel) with the saw blade. This prevents the rod from rolling during cutting and assures that the cut is flat and parallel to the grain lines. Although it can be done with saw and block plane, I use power equipment—a long, fine-grit belt sander or disk sander—for greater accuracy when adjusting the length, the smoothness, and angle of the splice. For a straight rod, alter and adjust the splice angle as required.

Finally, polish the splice on ultrafine (400-grit or finer) sandpaper taped to a flat metal plate. Obviously, each overlapping splice will significantly shorten the rod and must be considered. When the splices are connected, the rod should bend as a single piece, an improvement over the early brass tube ferrules.

Complete the rod with several light coats of preferred clear finish. For a traditional finish, use spar varnish or lacquer. Ash is a rather "bright" wood. To avoid rod flash and frightened fish, some early rods were painted black or brown. Modern finishes, such as Varathane Exterior Crystal Clear Wood Finish or Plasti-kote Classic Lacquer may also be used. Lightly sand each coat (220-grit or finer) and remove sanding dust before the final finish. Do not coat the splice space or "mating" flats with a finish. When thoroughly dry, firmly whip a horsehair loop (18 to 24 strands) on the rod tip.

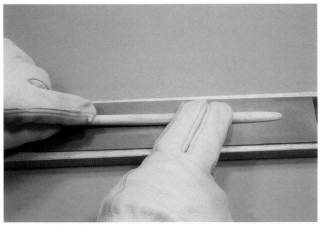

Polishing the splice with 600-grit emery

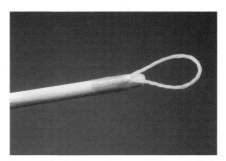

A varnished silk wrap secures the horsehair loop

John Betts, antique rod and hook maker, wraps the splices by stepping on the cord and pulling up as he rotates the rod sections down toward his feet. This delivers maximum pressure on the wraps. I often attach the leather strip to something and lean away as I wrap. A "finger wrap" alone, if firmly completed, can achieve adequate pressure. A tucked whip-finish, like a guide wrap, secures the final wraps. Like Ogden's rod, the rod is "handled with leather"—the long grip is merely a spiraled leather strip. In *The Compleat Angler* (Hawkins edition, 1766), Plate X, figures 1 and 2, illustrates repairing a *broken* rod top. These directions are much the same for connecting and wrapping any spliced-rod section.

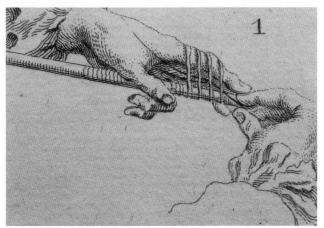

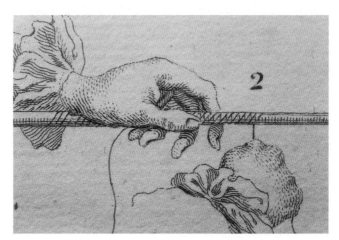

Wrapping the splice. *The Compleat Angler*: plate x, figure 1   **Completing the splice.** *The Compleat Angler*: plate x, figure 2

After cutting long slopes on each broken section, match the ends neatly,

"then fpread fome wax very thin on each flope, and, with waxed thread or filk, according as the fize of the broken part requires, bind them very neatly together: to faften off, lay the fore-finger of your left hand over the binding, and with your right, make four turns of the threads over it; then pafs the end of your thread between the under-fide of your finger and the rod, and draw your finger away; laftly, with the fore-finger and thumb of your right hand, take hold of the firft of the turns, and gathering as much as you can, bind on till the three remaining turns are wound off, and then take hold of the end, which had before put through, and draw clofe."

Thus, waxed splices and whip-wraps reconnect the broken rod sections. It is virtually impossible to pull a rod apart when firmly wrapped with wide leather strips.

A Six-Strip Tip

Adventurous anglers may wish a unique loop-rod tip. This will require more time and care than a standard, solid-wood tip. A few early rod makers actually constructed wood rods from four tapered wood strips glued together. *Fly-Rods and Fly-Tackle* (1885), by Henry P. Wells, described the construction of a four-strip wood rod, and warned that "if in craving after lightness, as is now the fashion, you are niggardly in material, your rod will be slow and withy, and lack that nervous promptness of action." Perry D. Frazer, in *Amateur Rodmaking* (1939), discussed how early rod makers glued four bamboo strips together with the enamel side within. The convex enamel surface made it difficult to produce tight seams. Later, rod makers placed the enamel on the outside. Wooden, multistrip rod sections, however, have several attributes. A glued tip can be strong, stiff, and slender. For a softer rod tip, select the four-strip construction, generally the better action for a loop-rod. Additionally, the cutting, gluing, and wrapping of the four-strip is less complex. Other than the strip number and grain orientation, the constructions of the four-strip and six-strip rod sections are similar. The following directions are for the more complex, six-strip rod tip. A complete, multisectioned loop-rod can be made in the same manner.

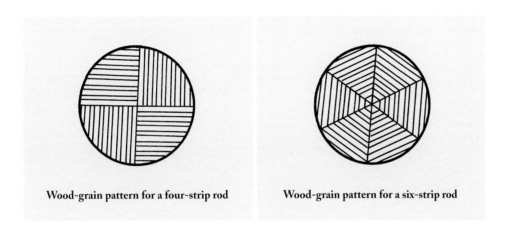

Wood-grain pattern for a four-strip rod   Wood-grain pattern for a six-strip rod

Although historically unprecedented, it is possible to make a six-strip ash tip. By the time rods were six-strip construction, bamboo, not ash, was the chosen material. Delicate rod tips to ⅛" diameter are possible. John Betts, who builds six-strip wooden fly rods, router cuts six pie-shape strips with 60° angles. These triangular strips may be marked and cut from a single ash blank. According to Betts, it is best to arrange the rod-section grain lines so that they reveal, in cross-section, concentric circles, much like the natural growth rings of a tree. For a slightly softer tip, I ignore the grain lines. Although the routered strips scramble the wood grain, the resulting glue seams, acting like grain lines, create extraordinary strength and stiffness. Tips made in this manner are extremely stiff, though remarkably strong and fine.

Once cut, firmly tape the sections together to form the tip. Wrap the sections in three places with heavy masking tape. Make certain the sections do not twist or skew when wrapped together. For gluing, cut the masking tape bands down one side to lay it open. The tape will continue to hold all sections together when opened.

Using latex gloves and a soft brush, coat the inside of all strips with waterproof Titebond III Ultimate Wood Glue (Franklin International). Although other glues may be used, this nontoxic glue has bond strength, extended assembly time, and water cleanup. Thin Titebond III with less than 5 percent water: add only a *few drops* as water significantly decreases the final bond strength.

After gluing and closing the strips, spiral-wrap the section with a strong cord about every quarter inch. At the end, reverse the wrap to create opposing pressure. For a tight wrap, I attach the cord to a post and lean away as I wrap. This creates maximum wrap pressure and squeezes out any excess glue. Immediately after wrapping, wipe the section with a wet cloth to remove excess glue. Hang and let dry for 24 hours.

After drying, remove the cord and clean the section with a rasp. Mark the center at both ends, and keep the center in the middle when planing. Plane and finish the rod section as desired. Wood lacks the bamboo "enamel," the fibrovascular bundles concentrated on the periphery of the culm (the bamboo stalk). This enamel bundle powers a bamboo rod. Bamboo, actually a grass, must taper with the enamel on the outside. Not so with a wood-strip rod: you taper the section *after* gluing up. Once planed, the glue lines are virtually invisible.

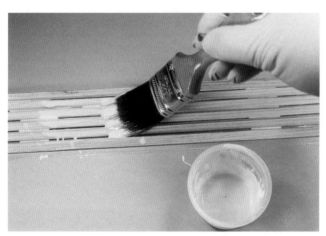

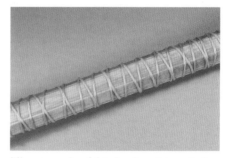

The wrapped and dried rod section ready for cleaning. Note the reverse wrap that creates equal pressure. All crevices and cracks will disappear with planing.

Gluing a six-strip tip section. Note the tape backing that holds the strips. Carefully coat all interior surfaces with glue.

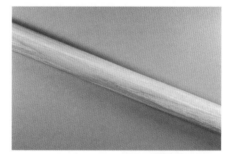

Six-piece rod section with preliminary planing.

The Aerial Sweep Cast

The wood loop-rod and horsehair line cannot generally tolerate sharp, quick casts. Abrupt casts stress and rip hair. Make all casts slowly and smoothly. If not slowly thrown, a stiff, heavy horsehair line can slap water. Webster's "horse-shoe curve" cast is not an anchored switch or roll cast. Unlike a modern rod with powerful, flat trajectory, loop-rods made slow, sweeping arcs. David Webster described this smooth "sweep" cast.

> Having made his first cast over the water mainly to get his line out in front of him, the young angler must now raise the point of his rod a little to bring the line round in a curve sufficiently near him, and so much under command as will enable him to lift it gently from the water and to make the next cast. This movement is effected by raising the rod gradually towards the perpendicular, and causing the point of it to describe something of a horse-shoe curve, when line will be brought gently round in a corresponding sweep overhead, and derive, from this motion and its own weight, sufficient momentum to urge it forward to its full length. The point of the rod should not be carried much behind the body, and the line should not be sent out to its full length behind, but brought round in a curve, following the motion of the rod until fairly on the forward movement, when a slightly quickened action is imparted, and the rod is brought nearly to the horizontal. The line is thus gradually straightened in its forward course until it measures its full length over the stream—first touching the water near the middle point of the hair-line, when the droppers will fall gently, and almost simultaneously, with the tail fly.

This sweep cast does not rely on the fly or leader "anchoring" or touching the water prior to the forward stroke. Webster's aerial "sweep" swings back and lifts the line off the water. The line creates the "horse-shoe curve" *before* full rear extension. Then, the rod immediately and smoothly thrusts the line forward. The rod tip has *continuous* contact with and pressure on the line throughout the cast. The unrolling line should "sweep overhead" rather than carve the near-vertical arc of a traditional roll cast. The forward stroke should "ease" halfway, rather than abruptly halt, to dissipate the line energy. Aim the line about three-feet or more above the water surface. This aerial sweep cast (perhaps the best label) is most appropriate for a fixed length of line. "The motion imparted to the loop-line," wrote Webster, "is continuous, but it is gentle . . . there is no pause and no doubling back." Furthermore, the rod sweep, when done without touchdown, does not disturb the water as much as an anchored roll cast. The lack of water disturbance makes this—the aerial sweep cast—an important loop-rod cast. Roll casts that rip the surface with a limited line length do not encourage trout rises. Remember too that Webster throws nine dropper flies on a single line. Without soft, smooth sweep casts, horsehair lines tangle and snarl.

A fine, long horsehair line floats a fly longer, but when saturated, the line will pull the fly under. With handmade hooks, most patterns become emergers on an "intermediate" horsehair line. The loop-rod makes short and soft downstream drifts. Without the give and take of line, side pulls and a soft rod must master fish. An adequate bend is required in a loop-rod. A long, light, and slender rod casts farther, absorbs the struggle, and decreases hand fatigue. According to Venables, "the slender rod saveth the line; but my opinion is, that the equal bending of the rod chiefly, next to the skill of the Angler, saveth the line, and the slenderness I conceive principally serveth to make the fly-rod long and light, easy to be managed with one hand, and casteth the fly far, which are to me the considerations chiefly to be regarded in a fly-rod. . . ."

Large fish, often devoid of spirited struggle and rapid runs, may be easier to land than smaller, athletic fish. A loop-rod and fixed line severely limits the methods for landing fish. The tackle encourages bank fishing. The angler needs to retreat or move to maintain tension on the fish. Keeping a fish upstream of the angler to fight the current and rod appears in the *Tegernsee Fishing Advice* (*c*. 1500), edited and translated by Richard C. Hoffmann. ". . . and you stay entirely below, [and] so let it pull and lead about freely, and where you can get a calm place, lead it in there so that you may haul it" and lead it "willingly into [the] dip-net." The upstream fish also holds the hook better. Some antique illustrations suggest that fish are either pulled to bank, "hand-lined," or netted when they are close. Sometimes, a long-handled net or "gillie" is imperative.

Any angler who believes that a reel is only for *line storage* should attempt to land fish with a loop-rod. It requires remarkable skill to fight a strong fish and maintain tension on a fixed line length. The advent of the reel and running line, which granted varying line lengths, was a momentous advance in fly fishing. So too the early barbed hook. With a fixed, limp line, keeping contact with a fish on a barbless hook is another worthy challenge. Once a fish is hooked, the value of the barb becomes apparent. The barbed hook is a near necessity for countering slack line. A barb is merely a reverse point that prevents removal. When fishing from a stationary position, such as a boat, I lost nearly every fish that took. Boat fishing may require remarkable contortions and hand-lining. Although the angler limits the "fly swim" in bank fishing, he can retreat to keep the line taut. Otherwise, it becomes touch and release only.

The Tale of the Harnays

My early experiments connected the horsehair line, handmade hooks, and antique patterns to a standard fly line and rod. Although I lost a few, I could land fish. Nevertheless, there was something missing. What I required was a complete antique harnays—a pattern wrapped on a handmade hook, a tapered and knotted horsehair line, and a lithe, light loop-rod. This is the tale of that *harnays*. In time, I was ready. With my son Michael as gillie, we canoed a small, Northwest lake. On a previous trip, we had lost good fish on slack line and barbless hooks. Now I had barbed hooks and a supple loop-rod. After two hours of dapping and casting however, no fish took. Another empty day. Just as I raised the rod for a fly change, a trout took. I lifted and pulled the rod sideways as the fish ripped along the surface. I stood up (in a broad, stable canoe) and swept the rod behind me to pull the trout home. My arm was not long enough. When slack started, I grabbed the line and tried to keep the trout close. Pulling the trout to net, I slid into the bottom of the canoe. My "tender" execrations rang across the lake. So much for the quiet, gentle sport of

The angler and the modern loop-rod on River Itchen waters, England.

angling. How Michael netted the trout, I do not remember. I had landed a double-digit trout on nine hairs, a nine-foot loop-rod and a handmade hook. Sometimes luck beats skill. Truly, I was more surprised than the fish. Even with such a large trout, I do not think it would have amazed our angling ancestors.

In 1921, John Waller Hills, in *A History of Fly Fishing for Trout*, gave us our only conclusion. "And then I believe that there must be others also like myself, whom the history of the sport attracts, who are fascinated by the devices of other days, and who are never weary of going back to the old writers, of reading them again, of getting at their real meaning and of seeing where they have anticipated us and where we have improved on them."

Trout taken with modern loop-rod, horsehair line, and handmade hook.

CODA

Those silent waters weave for him
A fluctuant mutable world and dim

Where wavering masses bulge and gape
Mysterious, and shape to shape

Dies momently through whorl and hollow
And form and line and solid follow

Solid and line and form to dream
Fantastic down the eternal stream

—"The Fish," Rupert Brooke (excerpt)

IN 1915, J. J. MOTTRAM, THE ENGLISH ANGLING AUTHOR, wrote about fly fishing in the year 2014. His prophecy of a brave new angling world was quaint and curious. In it, insects are artificially raised and then planted prior to the angler's arrival. Analysis of the nymph's coelomic fluids determine the specific hatch time. The "artificial" flies—very expensive at 14 shillings a brace—are "candied" natural insects. Each stocked trout is known by name and habits. Rods are willowy; reels have only the slightest drags. To protect this fine tackle, all waterweeds are pruned to six inches. The hookless fly is glued to the gut about a foot from a small treble hook. With the help from an assistant, the angler drifts rather than casts the fly over a fish. Where the fish will rise is known; only the drift and distance must be calculated. When the trout takes the fly, the angler "homes" the hook and thus draws it to the fish's mouth. No angler is allowed to keep a trout unless he has previously caught and tagged the trout three times.

Whether Mottram considered his brave new world a heaven or hell is not clear. His vision is now only a few years away. Well, we have gone beyond gut and greenheart, beyond loop-rods and horsehair lines. And the modern angler would, I hope, reject candied insects. After all, we still take pleasure in wrapping flies with the same materials that Mottram used a century ago, although our technology offers infinite choices. We practice catch and release. We have light and powerful rods; our fly patterns and theories cover creatures both great and small.

Today "our waters" spread over the world. The Zambezi, the Spekboom, the Agua Boa, the Itchen, the Sava Bohinjka, and the Stillaguamish are only a handful of hours away. Our waters, however, are not without problems. The etymology of *rival* reveals the conflict. The term comes from the Latin *rivus*, meaning "brook" or "stream." From this came the adjective, *rivalis* for "one who shares a stretch of water with another." In time, the term came to mean "competitor," not one who *shares* but one who *competes* for water. Although we are all rivals, we must protect and preserve our waters so that they do not become part of the past.

Mottram knew that change would take place, but he never divined the range of that change. Nevertheless, I would like to think that as an angler he knew the ever-expanding value of nature. Neither nature nor fish are here for us: we are truly their keepers. Furthermore, we are the keepers of our past.

This book, to be truly comprehensive, requires a lifetime of research. There is, however, a time when a book must leave the author, even though the author never leaves the book. We met our early anglers along the bank—only brief encounters with a nod and a few words. We would have learned so much more if we had stayed longer. But life is too impatient. Although the book ends, it is not complete. So much more needs to be done and, with further research, even redone. This is only a beginning.

I do not dare guess how fly fishing or fly tying will change in another century. I only know that as we pass into this new world, we must take with us an enduring regard for nature and the past. The old writers and the old books trap some of the past. Nevertheless, the past fades, and nature is fragile and fugitive. I hope there will always be places with wild fish and wild insects. Like nature itself, fly fishing can only survive if we cherish the weeds and the wilderness.

—Darrel Martin
Tacoma, Washington
August 2005

BIBLIOGRAPHY

The following bibliography contains first and subsequent editions. Revised or augmented later editions often contain information not available in earlier editions. For example, the second 1766 Hawkins edition of *The Compleat Angler* by Izaak Walton contains the copious annotations of Sir John Hawkins' first edition of 1760, and *The Secrets of Angling*, first printed in 1613, is "augmented with many approved experiments" by W. Lauson in several later editions. *An Older Form of the Treatyse of Fysshynge Wyth an Angle* (*c.* 1450), printed in 1883, includes the preface and glossary of Thomas Satchell. The notations of Hawkins, Lauson, and Satchell offer critical information not available in all editions.

Adams, J. R. *Aelian on Fly Fishing*. Berkeley, California: Poole Press, 1979.

Aelian [Aelianus, Claudius]. *On the Characteristics of Animals [De Natura Animalium]*, translated by A. F. Scholfield, Volume III, Books XII-XVII. Cambridge: Harvard University Press, 1959.

Aldam, W. H. *A Quaint Treatise on Flees, and the Art of Artyfichiall Flee Making*. London, 1876.

Ashley, Clifford W. *The Ashley Book of Knots*. New York: Doubleday, undated and corrected reprint of 1944 edition.

Bainbridge, George C. *The Fly-Fisher's Guide to Aquatic Flies and Their Imitation*. London: A & C Black Ltd., 1936.

Bark, Conrad Voss. *A History of Flyfishing*. Ludlow: Merlin Unwin Books, 1992.

Barker, Thomas. *Barker's Delight or The Art of Angling*. London: Printed by J. G. for Richard Marriot, second edition much enlarged, 1820.

Barnes [Berners], Dame Juliana (attributed author), *An Older Form of the Treatyse of Fysshynge Wyth an Angle*, printed from the Alfred Denison manuscript. Preface and glossary by Thomas Satchell. London: W. Satchell & Company, 1883.

Bergman, Ray. *Trout*. New York: Knopf, 1938.

Bernard, J. *Fly-Dressing*. London: Herbert Jenkins Ltd., 1932.

Berners, Dame Juliana (attributed author), *The Book of Saint Albans*. Includes facsimile reprint of *The Treatyse of Fysshynge Wyth an Angle* (1496). New York: Abercrombie & Fitch, 1966.

Best, Thomas. *The Art of Angling*. London: Printed by T. C. Hansard of Fleet Street, eleventh edition, 1822.

Betts, John. "Robert Venables' Experience as an Angler." *The American Fly Fisher*. Volume 29, Number 4, Fall 2003.

Bickerdyke, John. *The Book of the All-Round Angler*. London: Bazaar Exchange & Mart Office, seventh revised edition, *c.* 1899.

Blacker, William. *The Art of Fly-Making, &c, Comprising Angling & Dyeing of Colours*. London: George Nichols, Earl's Court, second edition, 1855.

Blades, William F. *Fishing Flies and Fly Tying*. Harrisburg, Pennsylvania: The Stackpole Company, revised and enlarged edition, 1962.

Bowlker, Charles. *The Art of Angling*. Ludlow: Richard Jones, 1839.

Brookes, Richard. *The Art of Angling: New Improved*. London, publisher unlisted, 1766.

Burgess, J. T. *Angling and How to Angle*. London: Frederick Warne & Company, revised by R. B. Marston, 1895.

Burrard, Sir Gerald. *Fly-Tying: Principles & Practice*. London: Herbert Jenkins, Ltd., second edition, 1945.

Caucci, Al and Bob Nastasi. *Hatches II*. New York: Lyons & Burford, revised edition, 1986.

Chetham, James. *The Angler's Vade Mecum*. London: William Battersby, third edition, 1700.

Cholmondeley-Pennell, H. *Fly-Fishing and Worm Fishing for Salmon, Trout and Grayling*. London: Longmans, Green and Company, second edition, 1886.

Cutcliffe, H. C. *The Art of Trout Fishing on Rapid Streams*. London: Sampson Low, Marston, Searle & Rivington, 1883.

Darbee, Harry with Austin Mac Francis. *Catskill Flytier*. New York: J. B. Lippincott Company, 1977.

Davy, Sir Humphry. *Salmonia*. London: John Murray, Albemarle Street, fifth edition, 1869.

de Bergara, Juan. *El Manuscrito de Astorga*. Denmark: Gullanders Bogtrykkeri a-s, Skjern. Translated by Preben Torp Jacobsen, "Flyleaves" Søndermarksvej, 116 Hvilsom DK 9500, Hobro, Denmark, modern reprint, 1984.

Dennys, John (J. D). *The Secrets of Angling: Augmented with Many Approved Experiments by W. Lawson*. Reprint of John Harrison, 1652 edition. London: Reprinted for Robert Triphook, 1811.

Diez, Jesus Pariente. *La Pesca de la Trucha en Los Rios Leoneses*. Argentina: Editorial Nebrija, S. A., 1979.

Dunne, J. W. *Sunshine and the Dry Fly*. London: A & C Black, Ltd., 1924.

Elder, Frank. *The Book of the Hackle*. Edinburgh: R & R Clark, 1979.

The Essential G. E. M. Skues. Kenneth Robson, editor. New York: Lyons Press, 1998.

Fitzgibbon, Edward (Ephemera). *The Book of the Salmon*. London: Longman, Brown, Green & Longmans, 1850.

Fitzgibbon, Edward (Ephemera). *A Handbook of Angling*. London: Longman, Brown, Green & Longmans, 1848.

Flavell, Linda and Roger. *Dictionary of Word Origins*. Reading, Berkshire: Cox & Wyman. Great Britain, 2004.

Foster, David. *The Scientific Angler*. London: Bemrose & Sons, Ltd., compiled by his sons, sixth English edition, undated.

Francis, Francis. *A Book on Angling*. London: Longmans, Green and Company, revised and much enlarged, second edition, 1867.

Frazer, Perry D. *Amateur Rodmaking*. New York: The Macmillan Company, 1939.

Garrow-Green, G. *Trout Fishing in Brooks*. London: George Routledge & Sons, Ltd., *c.* 1920.

———. *The Gentleman Angler*. London: Printed for C. Hitch, at the Red Lion, third edition with large additions, undated, *c.* 1736.

Goddard, John. *The Super Flies of Still Water*. London: Ernest Benn, Ltd., 1977.

Goddard, John, and Brian Clarke. *The Trout and the Fly*. London: Ernest Benn, Limited, 1980; New York: Nick Lyons Books, 1981.

Hale, J. H. *How to Tie Salmon Flies*. London: Fishing Gazette, third edition, 1930.

Halford, Frederic M. *The Dry-Fly Man's Handbook*. London: George Routledge & Sons, Ltd., 1913.

Halford, Frederic M. *Modern Development of the Dry Fly*. Boston: Houghton, Mifflin & Company, American edition, 1923.

Halford, Frederic M. *Floating Flies and How to Dress Them*. London: Sampson Low, Marston, Searle and Rivington, 1886.

Hanna, Thomas J. *Fly-Fishing in Ireland*. London: H. F. & G. Witherby, 1933.

Harding, E. W. *The Flyfisher & the Trout's Point of View*. London: Seeley Service & Company, Ltd., 1931.

Harris, J. R. *An Angler's Entomology*. New York: A. S. Barnes & Company, 1939.

Hawksworth, David. *British Poultry Standards*. London: Butterworth Scientific, 1982.

Henn, T. R. *Practical Fly-Tying*. London: Adam & Charles Black, 1950.

Herd, Andrew. *The Fly*. Ellesmere, Shropshire: The Medlar Press Limited, 2001.

Herter, George Leonard. *Professional Fly Tying, Spinning and Tackle Making: Manual and Manufacturers' Guide*. Waseca, Minnesota: Herter's Inc., nineteenth edition, 1971.

Hewitt, Edward Ringwood. *Telling on the Trout*. New York: Charles Scribner's Sons, 1926.

Hills, John Waller. *A History of Fly Fishing for Trout*. London: A & C Black, 1921.

Hills, John Waller. *A Summer on the Test*. London: Geoffrey Bles, 1946.

Hills, John Waller. *River Keeper: The Life of William James Lunn*. London: Geoffrey Bles, 1934.

Hoffmann, Richard C. *Fishers' Craft & Lettered Art: Tracts on Fishing from the End of the Middle Ages*. Toronto: University of Toronto Press, 1997.

Hofland, T. C. *The British Angler's Manual*. London: H. G. Bohn, York Street, Covent Garden, revised and enlarged by Jesse, E., 1848.

Howlett, Robert. *The Angler's Sure Guide or Angling Improved*. London: F. H. for G. Convers at the Ring and T. Ballard at the Rising Sun, in Little-Britain, 1706.

Hunter, W. A. *Fisherman's Knots & Wrinkles*. London: A & C Black, Ltd., second edition, 1928.

Jackson, John. *The Practical Fly-Fisher*. London: Gibbings & Company, fourth edition, 1899.

Jackson, W. S. *Notes of a Fly Fisher: An Attempt at a Grammar of the Art*. London: The Fishing Gazette, Ltd., 1933.

Jennings, Preston J. *A Book of Trout Flies*. New York: Derrydale Press, 1935.

Johnson, Frederick Gardner. "Senses and Taxes in Trout" in *Trout*, Judith Stolz and Judith Schell, editors. Harrisburg, Pennsylvania: Stackpole Books, 1991.

Johnson, Gunnar and Anders Forsling. *Izaak Waltons & Charles Cottons Flugor*. Strålin & Persson AB, Falun, 1992.

Jorgensen, Paul. *Salmon Flies*. Harrisburg, Pennsylvania: Stackpole Books, 1978.

Kelson, George. *The Salmon Fly: How to Dress It and Use It*. London, 1895.

Koch, Ed. *Fishing the Midge*. New York: Freshet Press, Inc., 1972.

La Branche, George M. L. *The Dry Fly and Fast Water*. New York: Charles Scribner's Sons, 1922.

Lane, Joscelyn. *Fly-Fisher's Pie*. London: Herbert Jenkins, Ltd., 1956.

Lawrie, W. H. *All-Fur Flies & How to Dress Them*. London: Pelham Books, Ltd., 1967.

Lawrie, W. H. *A Reference Book of English Trout Flies*. London: Pelham Books, Ltd., 1967.

Lawrie, W. H. *Scottish Trout Flies: An Analysis and Compendium*. London: Frederick Muller, Ltd., 1966.

Leisenring, James E. and Vernon S. Hidy. *The Art of Tying the Wet Fly & Fishing the Flymph*. New York: Crown Publishers, Inc., 1971.

Leiser, Eric. *The Book of Fly Patterns*. New York: Alfred A. Knopf, 1987.

Leonard, J. Edson. *Flies*. New York: A. S. Barnes, 1960.

Lunn, Mick and Clive Graham Ranger. *A Particular Lunn*. London: Adam & Charles Black, 1990.

Malone, E. J. *Irish Trout and Salmon Flies*. Gerrards Cross: Colin Smythe Ltd., 1984.

Mansfield, Kenneth, editor. *The Art of Angling*. Three volumes. London: Caxton Publishing Company Limited, 1960.

Marbury, Mary Orvis. *Favorite Flies and Their Histories*. Boston: Houghton Mifflin, second edition, 1892.

March, J. *The Jolly Angler*. London: J. March. Fourth edition, *c.* 1842.

Marinaro, Vincent. *In the Ring of the Rise*. New York: Crown Publishers, Inc., 1976.

Maunsell, G. W. *The Fisherman's Vade Mecum*. London: Adam & Charles Black, third edition, 1952.

McClane, A. J., editor. *McClane's Standard Fishing Encyclopedia*. New York: Holt, Rhinehart and Winston, 1965.

McClelland, H. G. *How to Tie Flies for Trout*. London: Fishing Gazette, Ltd., 1939.

McClelland, H. G. *The Trout Fly Dresser's Cabinet of Devices*. London: The Fishing Gazette, Ltd., seventh edition, 1931.

McCreight, Tim. *The Complete Metalsmith*. Worcester, Massachusetts: Davis Publications, Inc., 1991.

McDonald, John. *The Origins of Angling*. New York: Doubleday & Company, 1963.

Merwin, John, editor. *Stillwater Trout*. New York: Nick Lyons Books, 1980.

Mottram, J. C. *Fly-Fishing: Some New Arts and Mysteries*. London: The Field & Queen (Horace Cox), Ltd., first edition, 1915.

Mosely, Martin E. *The Dry-Fly Fisherman's Entomology*. London: George Routledge & Sons, Ltd., 1932.

Murray, James and Henry Bradley, W. A. Craigie, C. T. Onions, R. W. Burchfield (editors), and J. A. Simpson and E. S. C. Weiner. *The Oxford English Dictionary*. Oxford: Clarendon Press, second edition, 2000.

Niven, Richard. *The British Angler's Lexicon*. London: Sampson Low, Marston & Company, 1892.

Nonnos, Panopolitanus. *Dionysiaca*. Translated by W. H. D. Rouse, Cambridge, Massachusetts: Harvard University Press, Volume III, 1963.

Norris, Thaddeus. *The American Angler's Book*. Philadelphia: Porter & Coates. Memorial edition, 1865.

Ogden, James. *Ogden on Fly Tying*. London: Sampson Low, Marston, Searle & Rivington, third edition, 1887.

O'Gorman, James. *The Practice of Angling, Particularly as Regards Ireland*. Reprint of the first 1845 edition, in two volumes. The Fly Fisher's Classic Library Edition. Bath, England: Bath Press Limited, 1993.

Pain, Ernest C. *Fifty Years on the Test*. London: Phillip Allan, 1934.

Partridge, Eric. *Origins: A Short Etymological Dictionary of Modern English*. New York: Greenwich House, 1983.

Pequegnot, Jean-Paul. *French Fishing Flies*. New York: Nick Lyons Books, 1987.

Pritt, T. E. *North-Country Flies*. London: Sampson Low, Marston, Searle & Rivington, second edition, 1886.

Proper, Datus. *What the Trout Said*. New York: Alfred A. Knopf, Inc., 1982.

Pryce-Tannatt, T. E. *How to Dress Salmon Flies*. London: Adam and Charles Black, first edition, 1914.

Pulman, G. P. R. *The Vade Mecum of Fly-Fishing for Trout*. London: Longman, Brown, Green and Longmans, third edition, 1851.

Radcliffe, William. *Fishing from the Earliest Times*. Chicago: Ares Publishing Inc., unchanged reprint of the London, 1921 edition, 1974.

Reid, John. *Clyde Style Flies and Their Dressings*. London: David & Charles, 1971.

Rennie, James. *Alphabet of Angling*. London: Henry G. Bohn, York Street, Covent Garden, third edition, 1849.

Rhead, Louis. *American Trout Stream Insects*. New York: Frederick A. Stokes Co., 1916.

Ronalds, Alfred. *The Fly-Fisher's Entomology*. London: Longman, Brown, Green and Longmans, third edition, 1844.

Rosborough, E. H. "Polly." *Tying and Fishing the Fuzzy Nymph*. Manchester, Vermont: The Orvis Company Inc., 1969.

Sandeman, Fraser. *By Hook and By Crook*. London: Henry Sotheran & Company, second edition, 1894.

Schwiebert, Ernest. *Nymphs*. New York: Winchester Press, 1973.

Schwiebert, Ernest. *Trout*. New York: E. P. Dutton, two volumes, 1978.

Schullery, Paul. *American Fly Fishing: A History*. New York: Nick Lyons Books, 1987.

Sheringham, H. T. *Elements of Angling*. London: Horace Cox, 1908.

Shipley, Joseph T. *Dictionary of Early English*. New Jersey: Littlefield, Adams & Company, 1968.

Shirley, Thomas. *The Angler's Museum*. London: John Fielding, third edition, *c.* 1790.

Skues, G. E. M. *Minor Tactics of the Chalk Stream*. London: Adam and Charles Black, 1910.

Skues, G. E. M. *Side-Lines, Side-Lights and Reflections*. Philadelphia: J. B. Lippincott Company, first American edition, undated.

Skues, G. E. M. *Silk, Fur and Feather: The Trout-Fly Dresser's Year*. Beckenham, Kent: The Fishing Gazette, Ltd., 1950.

Skues, G. E. M. *The Way of a Trout with a Fly*. London: A & C Black, Ltd., third edition, 1935.

Smedley, Harold Hinsdill. *Fly Patterns and Their Origins*. Muskegon, Michigan: Westshore Publications, revised and enlarged fourth edition, 1950.

Stewart, W. C. *The Practical Angler*. London: A & C Black, Ltd., introduction and note by W. Earl Hodgson, 1919.

Stoddart, Thomas Tod. *The Angler's Companion to the Rivers and Lochs of Scotland*. Edinburgh: William Blackwood and Sons, second edition, 1853.

Stratmann, Francis Henry. *A Middle-English Dictionary*. London: Oxford University Press, based on first edition of 1891, 1967.

Sturgis, William B. *Fly-Tying*. New York: Charles Scribner's Sons, 1940.

Sturgis, William B. and Eric Taverner. *New Lines for Fly-Fishers*. London: Seeley, Service & Company, Ltd., 1946.

Swisher, Doug and Carl Richards. *Emergers*. New York: Lyons & Burford, 1991.

Swisher, Doug and Carl Richards. *Selective Trout*. New York: Crown Publishers, Inc. 1971.

Talleur, Dick. *The Versatile Fly Tyer*. New York: Lyons & Burford, 1990.

Taylor, Samuel. *Angling in All Its Branches*. London: Longman & Rees, 1800.

Taverner, Eric. *Fly-Tying For Salmon*. London: Seeley Service & Company, Ltd., 1942.

Taverner, Eric. *Fly-Tying For Trout*. London: Seeley Service & Company, Ltd., 1939.

Taverner, Eric. *Trout Fishing from all Angles*. London: Seeley, Service & Company, Ltd., 1933.

Theakson, Michael. *British Angling Flies*. England: Ripon, 1883.

Tod, E. M. *Wet-Fly Fishing: Treated Methodically*. London: Sampson, Low, Marston & Company, Ltd., third edition, 1914.

Venables, Col. Robert. *The Experienced Angler*. London: T. Gosden. Reprint of Richard Marriot's 1662 edition, 1827.

Veniard, John. *Fly Dresser's Guide*. Illustrated by Donald Downs. London: A & C Black, 1952.

Veniard, John. *Fly-Tying Development and Progress*. London: Adam & Charles Black, 1972.

Wade, Henry. *Halcyon; or Rod Fishing with Fly, Minnow and Worm*. London, 1861.

Walker, C. F. *Fly-Tying as an Art*. London: Herbert Jenkins, Ltd., 1957.

Walker, Charles Edward. *Old Flies in New Dresses*. London: Lawrence and Bullen, Ltd., 1898.

Walton, Izaak and Cotton, Charles. *The Compleat Angler*. London: John Hawkins of Twickenham, second Hawkins edition, 1766.

Webster, David. *The Angler and the Loop-Rod*. Edinburgh and London: William Blackwood and Sons, 1885.

Wells, Henry P. *Fly-Rods and Fly-Tackle*. New York: Harper & Brothers, Franklin Square, 1885.

West, Leonard. *The Natural Trout Fly and Its Imitation*. Liverpool: William Potter, 1921.

Westwood, T. and T. Satchell. *Bibliotheca Piscatoria*. London: Peyton & Company, reprint of 1883 text with 1901 supplement by R. B. Marston, 1966.

Willers, W. B. *Trout Biology*. Madison, Wisconsin: The University of Wisconsin Press, Ltd., 1981.

Williams, A. Courtney. *A Dictionary of Trout Flies*. London: Adam & Charles Black, Ltd., fifth edition, 1982.

Williamson, Captain T. *The Complete Angler's Vade Mecum*. London: B. McMillam, first edition, 1808.

Woolley, Roger. *Modern Trout Fly Dressing*. London: Fishing Gazette, 1932.

Wulff, Lee. *Lee Wulff on Flies*. Harrisburg, Pennsylvania: Stackpole Books, 1985.

Wulff, Lee. "The Wulff Fly Patterns." *Roundtable*, January/February, 1979.

Young, Paul H. *Making and Using the Fly and Leader*. Detroit: Paul Young, second edition, 1935.

Younger, John. *River Angling for Salmon and Trout*. Kelso: J. & J. H. Rutherford. Edinburgh: William Blackwood & Sons, 1864

INDEX

NOTE: Bold number indicates principal entry.